U.S. MARINES IN VIETNAM

THE LANDING AND THE BUILDUP

1965

by

Jack Shulimson
and
Major Charles M. Johnson, USMC

HISTORY AND MUSEUMS DIVISION

HEADQUARTERS, U.S. MARINE CORPS

WASHINGTON, D.C.

1978

Library of Congress Card No. 78-600120

PCN 190 003075 00

For sale by the Superintendent of Documents, U.S. Government Printing Office
Washington, D.C. 20402 (Paper Cover)

Stock Number 008–055–00129–3

Foreword

This is the second volume in a series of nine chronological histories being prepared by the Marine Corps History and Museums Division to cover the entire span of Marine Corps involvement in the Vietnam War. This volume details the Marine activities during 1965, the year the war escalated and major American combat units were committed to the conflict. The narrative traces the landing of the nearly 5,000-man 9th Marine Expeditionary Brigade and its transformation into the III Marine Amphibious Force, which by the end of the year contained over 38,000 Marines.

During this period, the Marines established three enclaves in South Vietnam's northern-most corps area, I Corps, and their mission expanded from defense of the Da Nang Airbase to a balanced strategy involving base defense, offensive operations, and pacification. This volume continues to treat the activities of Marine advisors to the South Vietnamese armed forces but in less detail than its predecessor volume, *U. S. Marines in Vietnam, 1954-1964; The Advisory and Combat Assistance Era.*

The co-author, Mr. Jack Shulimson, is the senior civilian historian on the Vietnam project. He has been with the division since 1964 and has worked on Vietnam studies since 1965. Mr. Shulimson has a MA in history from the University of Michigan and is a PhD candidate in American Studies at the University of Maryland.

Major (now Lieutenant Colonel) Charles M. Johnson was with the History and Museums Division from September 1972 until September 1973. He has a BA in history from the University of Minnesota and was commissioned in the Marine Corps upon graduation in 1959. Lieutenant Colonel Johnson served two tours in Vietnam, first as Commanding Officer, Battery L, 4th Battalion, 11th Marines from May 1966 until May 1967 and then from December 1970 until August 1971 as public information officer in the Public Information Office, U. S. Military Assistance Command, Vietnam in Saigon. He is now Commanding Officer, Headquarters and Service Battalion, 1st Force Service Support Group at Camp Pendleton, California.

E. H. SIMMONS
Brigadier General, U. S. Marine Corps (Ret.)
Director of Marine Corps History and Museums

Reviewed and Approved:
15 June 1978

Preface

U. S. Marines in Vietnam, 1965 is largely based on previously classified studies prepared by the History and Museums Division in the 1960s and early 1970s. These are: Lieutenant Colonel John J. Cahill and Jack Shulimson, ''History of U. S. Marine Corps Operations in Vietnam, January-June 1965''; Jack Shulimson, ''U. S. Marine Corps Operations in the Republic of Vietnam, July-December 1965''; and Jack Shulimson, ''U. S. Marines in Vietnam, Introduction,'' and ''U. S. Marines in Vietnam, May-December 1965,'' Parts 1 and 2 of a then projected eight-part, single-volume history, entitled ''Marines in Vietnam, 1954-May 1968.''

In 1972, Major Johnson was given the task of combining these four separate histories into one coherent narrative. Upon Major Johnson's departure from the division the following year, Mr. Shulimson continued with the revision, incorporating new research material as it became available. In addition to the four studies listed above, the authors have consulted the official records of the U. S. Marine Corps, records of other Services when appropriate, the Oral History Collection of the History and Museums Division, comment files of the History and Museum Division, and pertinent published primary and secondary works. Although none of the information in this history is classified, some of the documentation on which it is based still has a classified designation. Comment drafts of the manuscript were reviewed by over 110 persons, most of whom were directly associated with the events and many of their remarks have been incorporated into the narrative. A list of all those asked to comment is included in the appendices. All ranks used in the body of the text are those ranks held by the individual in 1965.

The production of this volume has been a cooperative effort on the part of several members of the History and Museums Division. The manuscript was prepared under the editoral direction of Mr. Henry I. Shaw, Jr., Chief Historian of the History and Museums Division. Lieutenant Colonel Lane Rogers completed the final editing and also wrote the reconnaissance section of Chapter 11. Mr. Benis M. Frank prepared the index. Mr. Paul D. Johnston, head of the Publications Production Section, skillfully shepherded the manuscript through the various production stages. Special thanks go to Mrs. Mary Lewis, who helped type the first comment draft, and Miss Catherine A. Stoll, Corporal Denise F. Alexander, and Lance Corporal Paul W. Gibson of the Production Section, who worked unstintingly on both comment editions and the final version. Staff Sergeant Jerry L. Jakes was responsible for preparing all maps, charts, and cover layouts. Unless otherwise credited, photographs are from official Marine Corps files. The authors, of course, assume sole responsibility for the content of the text, including opinions expressed and any errors in fact.

Charles M. Johnson

Jack Shulimson

Table of Contents

Maps

Introduction

In 1965, the Marines were the first of the U. S. Armed Services to deploy large ground combat units to South Vietnam. By the end of the year, more than 38,000 Marines made up the III Marine Amphibious Force (III MAF) under the command of Major General Lewis W. Walt. III MAF was part of the United States Military Assistance Command, Vietnam (USMACV), commanded by General William C. Westmoreland. General Westmoreland in turn was responsible to Admiral Ulysses S. Grant Sharp, Commander in Chief, Pacific (CinCPac) in Hawaii, and through Sharp to the Joint Chiefs of Staff (JCS) in Washington. The American command's mission in Vietnam was to assist the Republic of Vietnam (RVN) in its war against the Communist insurgents, the Viet Cong, who were being provided with leadership, reinforcements, and supplies from the north by the Democratic Republic of Vietnam (DRVN).

Since July 1954, when the Geneva Accords ended the Communist Viet Minh war against the French in what was then called Indochina, Vietnam remained divided along the 17th Parallel with a Communist government in the north and an anti-Communist regime in the south. Throughout the following decade, Vietnamese Communists conducted a sub-rosa political war, which after 1960 became an active guerrilla war to overthrow the southern government. Long before 1965, the United States had been involved in this embattled nation.

A U. S. Military Assistance Advisory Group (MAAG) existed in Vietnam as early as 1950 and continued to function after the signing of the Geneva Accords. At the end of 1954 the United States agreed to support the South Vietnamese Armed Forces in conjunction with the French. After the last French military advisors departed Vietnam in 1957, the entire advisory effort came under American auspices.

In the first year of his administration, 1961, President John F. Kennedy sent a high-level mission, headed by former U.S. Army Chief of Staff General Maxwell D. Taylor, to determine what the United States could do to prevent a Communist takeover in South Vietnam. Acting on General Taylor's recommendations, President Kennedy directed the implementation of a series of military and political measures to strengthen the South Vietnamese regime. These actions included the provision of substantial amounts of military equipment, as well as sending U.S. military advisors and support units to Vietnam.

With the growing U.S. commitment in South Vietnam as a result of the Communist insurgency, on 8 February 1962 the United States established the United States Military Assistance Command, Vietnam under Army General Paul D. Harkins. By the end of the year, more than 12,000 U.S. military personnel, including technicians, advisors, pilots, and supply and administrative personnel, were in Vietnam. Among this number were 18 Marine advisors to the South Vietnamese Marine Corps and a Marine helicopter task group, code named SHUFLY, consisting of a helicopter squadron and support elements.

Despite this infusion of American assistance, an open dispute between the South Vietnamese government and the Buddhist hierarchy tore apart the delicate fabric of the South Vietnamese political structure. Faced with increasingly violent and dramatic Buddhist demonstrations against his rule, Ngo Dinh Diem, the controversial President of the RVN, attempted to crush the Buddhist movement in August 1963 by arresting its leaders. The crisis eventually resulted in a successful military coup against Diem's government in November and his death.

Following the coup, there was a drastic realignment of the South Vietnamese civil and military apparatus. More than 31 high-ranking military officers were dismissed for having actively supported the Diem regime. On 6 January 1964, the provisional government appointed a three-man military junta consisting of Major General Duong Van "Big" Minh,* as Chief of Staff, Major General Tran Van

---

*Ironically General Minh was to be the last President of South Vietnam. He ordered the surrender of South Vietnam to the Communist forces on 30 April 1975, two days after assuming the Presidency when the South Vietnamese cause was already lost.

Don, and Major General Le Van Kim, to run the government and the armed forces. Twenty-three days later, a new personality, Major General Nguyen Khanh, assumed the leadership from the junta. He became the chairman of the Revolutionary Military Council while General Minh remained as the nominal chief of state. In August, Khanh, having encountered Buddhist opposition, promised liberalization of his regime. On 26 September, the Vietnamese Revolutionary Council elected Phan Khac Suu as Chief of State, and the former mayor of Saigon, Tran Van Huong, as Premier. Real power, however, continued to lie with the military, which on 20 December dissolved the Civilian High National Council, although Suu and Huong remained in their respective positions.

With this political instability and growing enemy strength, the U.S. increased its military support to the South Vietnamese regime. By the end of 1964, the United States Military Assistance Command, now commanded by General Westmoreland, had grown to over 20,000 men.

The Marine contingents in Vietnam showed a corresponding increase in 1964. Of the over 800 Marines in Vietnam, the bulk were in South Vietnam's I Corps Tactical Zone (ICTZ) consisting of the five northern provinces. Sixty Marine advisors were attached to the Army of the Republic of Vietnam (ARVN) units in ICTZ. The SHUFLY unit, reinforced by a Marine rifle company for airfield security, was at the Da Nang Airbase just south of the city of Da Nang in Quang Nam Province. The remaining Marines served as advisors to the Vietnamese Marine Corps (20 Marines served in this capacity), as members of the Marine guard detachment at the U.S. Embassy in Saigon, and with the MACV staff in Saigon.

In May 1964, a Marine radio detachment supported by a reinforced Marine infantry platoon deployed to Tiger Tooth Mountain, north of Khe Sanh in northwestern South Vietnam. This composite force, designated Advisory Team One, later redeployed to Dong Bach Ma, a 3,500-foot mountain 25 miles west-northwest of Da Nang. Advisory Team One returned to Da Nang in September 1964 and then was disbanded. During its short existence, Advisory Team One became the first Marine ground

unit to conduct independent operations in South Vietnam.*

During 1964, the U. S. government examined the possibility of sending U.S. combat troops to South Vietnam for the defense of critical U.S. installations within the country. At that time General Taylor, then the U. S. Ambassador to South Vietnam, warned Washington against overstressing static security and observed that aggressive field operations by the Vietnamese Armed Forces were the best means for restoring law, order, and public safety in the Republic of Vietnam.[1]

In August 1964, tensions between North Vietnam and the United States reached a new high when North Vietnamese torpedo boats attacked two U.S. destroyers, the *Turner Joy* (DD 951) and *Maddox* (DD 731), in the Gulf of Tonkin. On 4 August, the U.S. Joint Chiefs of Staff recommended retaliatory air strikes against several North Vietnamese patrol boat bases and fuel storage areas. The President approved the recommendation and on 5 August Seventh Fleet carrier aircraft carried out bombing missions against selected targets in North Vietnam. On 7 August, the U.S. Congress passed the Gulf of Tonkin Resolution in which it approved and supported ''the determination of the President, as Commander-in-Chief, to take all necessary measures to repel any armed attack against the forces of the United States and to prevent further aggression.''

The possible involvement of American forces was of special concern to the Marine Corps. In the summer of 1964, the most combat ready American troops in the Far East were those of the 3d Marine Division (3d MarDiv) on Okinawa, commanded by Major General William R. Collins, and the 1st Marine Aircraft Wing (1st MAW) at Iwakuni, Japan, and Okinawa, under the command of Major General Paul J. Fontana. These two Marine units were task-organized under several provisional headquarters to support the various contingency plans for Southeast Asia. The largest of the provisional commands was the III Marine Expeditionary Force (III MEF) consisting of the entire 3d Division and the 1st MAW. Components

---

*See LtGen Victor H. Krulak Ret), comments on draft MS, dtd 2Aug77 (Vietnam Comment File) and Captain Robert H. Whitlow, *U. S. Marines in Vietnam; The Advisory and Combat Assistance Era, 1954-1964* (Washington, D. C.: History and Museums Division, HQMC, 1977), pp. 138-41.

of the division and wing could also be combined provisionally into a Marine expeditionary brigade (MEB), essentially composed of a regimental landing team (RLT) and a Marine aircraft group (MAG). Both the air and ground components could be quickly loaded on board Navy amphibious shipping for deployment to South Vietnam or anywhere in the Pacific.

Following the attack against the U.S. destroyers in the Gulf of Tonkin, the U.S. Pacific Command activated the 9th Marine Expeditionary Brigade (9th MEB). The MEB, under the command of the assistant division commander of the 3d Marine Division, Brigadier General Raymond G. Davis, a holder of the Medal of Honor, consisted of the 9th Marines regimental headquarters and three battalion landing teams (BLTs). On 6 August, the 6,000 Marines of the MEB embarked on board Seventh Fleet amphibious shipping. A composite Marine aircraft group (MAG), with headquarters and fixed wing squadrons in Japan and helicopter squadrons on Okinawa, was alerted to support the MEB, but was not embarked. Although the brigade did not land in Vietnam at this time, the August crisis resulted in the transformation of the 9th MEB from a paper organization into an effective force in readiness, capable of landing whereever needed on extremely short notice.

When the Gulf of Tonkin crisis faded, the am-phibious task force carrying the MEB relaxed. Of the three BLTs making up the brigade, one returned to Okinawa, another to the Philippines, and a third remained afloat as part of the Special Landing Force (SLF) of the Seventh Fleet. While General Davis returned to Okinawa, he maintained a skeleton headquarters at Subic Bay on board the U.S. task force command ship, *Mount McKinley* (AGC 7). Brigadier General John P. Coursey relieved General Davis as brigade commander on 16 October 1964.

As 1965 began the Viet Cong had entered a new phase of their insurgency against the South Vietnamese government. The Communists departed from their usual hit and run guerrilla tactics and engaged the armed forces of the Republic of Vietnam (RVNAF) near the village of Binh Gia, 40 miles east of Saigon, in a pitched battle which lasted from 28 December 1964 until 1 January 1965. During the struggle for Binh Gia, two regiments from the *9th VC Division* ambushed and virtually destroyed two battalions of South Vietnamese troops, including the 4th Battalion, Vietnamese Marine Corps (VNMC), and inflicted heavy casualties on relieving armored and mechanized forces. According to General Westmoreland, Binh Gia marked the start of the final Communist offensive, ''it meant the beginning of an intensive military challenge which the Vietnamese government could not meet with its own resources.''[2]

PART I
ESTABLISHING THE ENCLAVES

CHAPTER 1

The Call for Marines

Alert and Realert—Air Retaliation and the Arrival of the HAWKS—Land the Marines—The Landing

---

Alert and Realert

On 22 January 1965, Brigadier General Frederick J. Karch, the assistant division commander (ADC) of the 3d Marine Division and a veteran of several amphibious campaigns during World War II, assumed command of the 9th Marine Expeditionary Brigade. The brigade consisted of two Marine battalion landing teams,* BLTs 1/9 and 3/9, which had been embarked in ships of the Seventh Fleet's Task Force 76 since the beginning of the year in the South China Sea. At this time, the brigade was the U.S. combat force most readily available for deployment to South Vietnam. As General Karch later remarked, "When the temperature went up we got closer."[1]

At this stage of the war the United States was not yet prepared to make the decision to intervene in Vietnam with ground combat units. On 23 January, the U. S. Joint Chiefs of Staff approved a recommendation by Admiral Ulysses S. Grant Sharp, Commander in Chief, Pacific, for a relaxation of the alert status for the 9th MEB. BLT 1/9, then embarked in the ships of Navy Task Group 76.5, 30 miles off Cap St. Jacques, a point 70 miles southeast of Saigon, reverted to a 96-hour reaction time for a landing in South Vietnam while BLT 3/9 resumed normal operations.

Political instability within South Vietnam caused this reprieve to be of short duration. On 22-23

January, Buddhist-inspired antigovernment riots with anti-American overtones rocked Saigon and the former imperial capital of Hue. As a result, the Vietnamese military continued their political version of "musical chairs" and ousted Premier Tran Van Huong on 27 January. BLT 1/9, which had been on its way to Hong Kong, was diverted first towards a position off Da Nang and then back to its former position off Cap St. Jacques. Arriving at its previous location on the 28th, the battalion stood by to land in Saigon if so directed. BLT 3/9, embarked in the ships of Navy Task Group 76.7, reached its assigned position off Da Nang on 29 January. The South Vietnamese formed an interim government and the Marines returned to normal shipboard routine.

The confusing alert status of the amphibious forces resulting from the unstable conditions in Vietnam was the subject of extensive message traffic between General Westmoreland, Commander, U. S. Military Assistance Command, Vietnam (ComUSMACV), and Admiral Sharp. On 30 January, ComUSMACV requested that the Seventh Fleet position one amphibious group off Cape Varella within 24 hours of either Da Nang or Saigon. Admiral Sharp only approved a 72-hour alert status for the forward amphibious group, explaining the disadvantages of maintaining a Marine battalion for an extended period of time in amphibious shipping. In an earlier message to the Joint Chiefs, Sharp observed that since August 1964 the amphibious forces had proven, "we can react quickly as the occasion demands."[2]

While still concerned about possible commitment of Marine forces to South Vietnam, the Pacific Command had made arrangements with the Thai Government for combined maneuvers in Thailand. From 26-30 January, General Karch attended a planning conference at Subic Bay for the MEB-size exercise, JUNGLE DRUM III, scheduled to take

---

*Battalion landing team (BLT) is the basic Marine unit in an assault landing. It is composed of an infantry battalion reinforced by necessary combat and service elements. The reinforcements are usually a battery of artillery; a platoon each of trucks (motor transport), tanks, amphibian tractors, reconnaissance, and engineers; and detachments of communications, shore party, beachmasters, medical, and logistical support. Although BLTs are tailored to meet specific needs, the average strength of a BLT is about 1,500 men.

A Marine HAWK missile launcher is in position at the Da Nang Airfield. The HAWKS are designed to defend against low-flying enemy aircraft.

place in March. On 31 January, both BLTs 1/9 and 3/9 departed for Subic Bay with the latter on 72-hour reaction time for landing in Vietnam. Once more events in Vietnam were to alter training and deployment plans.

Air Retaliation and the Arrival of the HAWKS

On 7 February 1965, the Viet Cong (VC) attacked the U.S. compound at Pleiku in the Central Highlands, a provocation that altered the entire course of the war. In the early morning of the 7th, the Viet Cong attacking force laid down a mortar barrage on the advisors' quarters and airfield, killing 9 Americans, wounding 128 others, and damaging or destroying 122 aircraft. At the urging of the Joint Chiefs of Staff and with the concurrence of Ambassador Taylor, President Lyndon B. Johnson ordered retaliatory air strikes against North Vietnam. Addressing the nation later that day, the

President announced the withdrawal of U.S. dependents from Vietnam and warned that the United States might take further actions. He declared: ''I have ordered the deployment to South Vietnam of a HAWK air defense battalion. Other reinforcements, in units and individuals, may follow.''[3]*

Late on the evening of 7 February, Lieutenant Colonel Bertram E. Cook, Jr., the commanding officer of the 1st LAAM Battalion, which had arrived on Okinawa in December from the U. S., received orders to move one battery to Da Nang. The battalion had originally been slated to deploy to Vietnam

---

*The acronym HAWK stands for Homing-All-the-Way-Killer. The HAWK air defense is a mobile, surface-to-air guided missile system designed to defend against enemy low-flying aircraft. It also has a capability to defend against short-range missiles/rockets. In the Marine Corps, this system is found in the light antiaircraft missile (LAAM) battalions.

in 1964 but the decision was deferred because of facility construction cost. Budgetary considerations on 7 February were of minor relevance; the battalion commander alerted his Battery A, commanded by Captain Leon E. Obenhaus, to prepare for an airlift to an unknown destination. The battery had just completed a firing exercise at Bolo Point, four miles northwest of Kadena, and its equipment was still emplaced there. After a rapid overnight breakdown from "the firing exercise configuration" and delays caused by the morning rush hour, the first echelons of Battery A arrived at Naha Air Force Base, 14 miles to the south of Bolo Point.[4]

Through the night of the 7th and the early morning of the 8th, Lieutenant Colonel Cook had worked out with Colonel Clarence B. Slaughter, commander of the 6315th U.S. Air Force Operations Group, the complicated details of moving a HAWK battery by air from Okinawa to Da Nang. Several years later, he recalled:

> Colonel Slaughter had been a student at the Marine Corps Amphibious Warfare School, Senior Course . . . at the time I was attending the Junior Course. We had been personal friends then and this friendship plus his appreciation of our problems greatly contributed to an extremely smooth, well coordinated operation. His first comment to me upon receipt of his orders to provide aircraft for the airlift was, "How many aircraft of what type do you want and what time do you want them?" He immediately dispatched Air Force loadmaster personnel to work with the 1st LAAM Bn embarkation personnel to iron out possible problem areas. However, 1st LAAM Bn. had participated in several airlift exercises prior to departure from CONUS, and I immediately gave him our requirements—26 C-130 type aircraft and 1 C-124.[5]

The first aircraft took off at 1045 on the morning of 8 February. The LAAM battalion commander planned that the battery would have a "limited" operational capability after the arrival of the 8th or 10th planeload at Da Nang. Lieutenant Colonel Cook remembered, "This was not to be, due to my lack of knowledge that two different models of C-130 were to be used in the airlift and Colonel Slaughter's lack of knowledge that sequential loads were of great importance to our operational readiness." The older C-130A models of the Lockheed Hercules transports held 1,700 fewer gallons of fuel than the newer C-130B models and therefore had to make a refueling stop in the Philippines before flying on to Da Nang. According to Cook, "our sequencing was in trouble. This caused substantial delay (several hours) in achieving both partial and full operational status."

Nevertheless, Battery A was set up on the northwest side of the Da Nang Airfield runway and prepared to fire less than 12 hours after the arrival of the first aircraft. On 8-9 February, the Air Force transports had lifted 52 loads of LAAM personnel and equipment, carrying 309 passengers and 315 tons from Okinawa to Da Nang.[6]

Lieutenant Colonel Cook had attached additional officers to the battery to facilitate the establishment of the battalion at Da Nang and to make liaison with Detachment 1, 619th Tactical Command and Control Squadron, U.S. Air Force, already at the airbase. On arrival, Battery A established radio communication with the Air Force Control and Reporting Post (CRP), located east of the city on top of Monkey Mountain on the Tiensha Peninsula. For missile firing control, the Air Force detachment and the Marines used as their guide a Southeast Asia Standing Operating Procedure (SOP) which had been developed in November 1964 when Major George G. Long, the LAAM battalion executive officer, and USAF 2d Air Division representatives met at MACV headquarters in Saigon "to effect a common understanding." The Air Force determined under what conditions the HAWKs could be used, but employment authority remained with the Marines. On 14 February, Captain Ronald G. Richardson, the battalion operations officer, collocated the Marine Antiaircraft Operations Center (AAOC) with the Air Force CRP on Monkey Mountain.[7]*

On 16 February, the remaining units of the battalion, with the exception of Battery C, which remained on Okinawa, arrived at Da Nang on board the attack cargo ship USS *Washburn* (AKA 108), and the dock landing ship USS *Gunston Hall* (LSD 5). Because the one pier at Da Nang was shallow draft, the cargo of the two ships was lightered from the bay to the military ramp in the port. Trucks transported the Marines of the LAAM Battalion's Battery B and Headquarters and Service Battery and their equipment through the city to the airfield.

Battery B, under Captain Everett L. Cowley, set up a HAWK site in the southwestern sector of the airfield complex in an old bunker area which the

---

* In the following months, the Air Force expanded its CRP facilities and capabilities and redesignated it a Control and Reporting Center (CRC), which reported to the USAF Tactical Air Command Center (TACC) at Tan Nhut Airfield in Saigon.

(Courtesy of Maj Gary W. Parker) USMC Photo A70714

An aerial view of Da Nang Airfield looking toward the northeast. The city of Da Nang is to the right or east of the airfield.

Japanese had built during their occupation of the airfield in World War II. Lieutenant Colonel Cook housed the battalion's command post in an abandoned French military compound adjacent to the airfield located midway between the two firing batteries. The Marine LAAM battalion and Air Force detachment established a communication network, linking the two batteries, the battalion CP, and the AAOC/CRP. On 18 February, Company C, 7th Engineer Battalion, a Force Troops unit of FMFPac, arrived on board the amphibious tank landing ship USS *Vernon County* (LST 1161) at Da Nang from Okinawa to provide construction support for the LAAM battalion. The HAWK deployment to South Vietnam was complete.[8]

Although chances of air retaliation by the small North Vietnamese Air Force were slim, the U.S. Government considered that the deployment of the HAWK missiles in conjunction with the air strike, code named FLAMING DART, on 7 February, would convince Hanoi of American determination to support South Vietnam. The Communists, never-

theless, continued attacks against U.S. installations. On 10 February, the Viet Cong destroyed a U.S. enlisted billet in the coastal city of Qui Nhon, killing 23 U.S. soldiers and wounding 22 others. Once more, President Johnson, on the recommendation of the Joint Chiefs, ordered U.S. aircraft to bomb the north in retaliation. On 11 February, more than 100 Navy carrier planes in FLAMING DART II struck at military targets in North Vietnam.[9]

Land the Marines

During this period, American authorities in Vietnam and Washington were reappraising the U.S. effort in Vietnam. In early February, President Johnson sent a delegation, headed by Presidential Special Assistant McGeorge Bundy, to Vietnam. The President specifically instructed Bundy to discuss with General Westmoreland and Ambassador Taylor the feasibility of air strikes against North Vietnam and the value of such attacks in deterring the Communists. Returning to Washington after the

Pleiku attack, Bundy included in his report the recommendation that the U.S. develop a "sustained reprisal policy" using air and naval forces against North Vietnam. According to Bundy, the situation in South Vietnam was:

> . . . deteriorating, and without new U.S. action, defeat appears inevitable—probably not in a matter of weeks or perhaps even months, but within the next year or so. There is still time to turn it around, but not much. [10]

On 9 February, just prior to the VC attack on Qui Nhon, General Westmoreland offered his appraisal of the war. He recalled that in the past he had considered requesting American combat troops to provide for close-in security of the U. S. bases in Vietnam. This course of action had been rejected for a variety of reasons, not the least of which was that the presence of American forces might cause the South Vietnamese to lose interest and relax. The general was now of the opinion that the attack on Pleiku marked a new phase of the war. With direct Communist attacks on American personnel and facilities, MACV could no longer ignore the question of protecting these troops. Westmoreland believed that this would require at least a division declaring: "These are numbers of a new order of magnitude, *but we must face the stark fact that the war has escalated.*"[11]

Following the Qui Nhon attack, on 11 February the Joints Chiefs of Staff forwarded to the Secretary of Defense a program of reprisal actions to be taken against Communist provocations. The chiefs observed that the retaliatory air raids against North Vietnam had not achieved the intended effect. They recommended in its place a "sustained pressure" campaign to include continuing air strikes against selected targets in North Vietnam, naval bombardment, covert operations, intelligence patrols and cross-border operations in Laos, and the landing of American troops in South Vietnam. On 13 February, President Johnson approved a "limited and measured" air campaign against North Vietnam, which took the code name ROLLING THUNDER. The ROLLING THUNDER campaign was delayed until 2 March because of a combination of bad weather and the instability of the South Vietnamese political situation.[12]

In mid-February, the South Vietnamese were in the midst of another power struggle. The South Vietnamese Armed Forces Council declared on the 15th that it alone had the responsibility for selecting the Premier and Chief of State. While the veteran politician Phan Khac Suu remained as Chief of State, the Council appointed a Saigon physician, Dr. Phan Huy Quat, who had formerly served as Foreign Minister in 1964, as the new Prime Minister. Six days later, a group of senior generals led by Major General Nguyen Van Thieu, the South Vietnamese IV Corps Commander, and Air Vice Marshal Nguyen Cao Ky, Commander of the Air Force, deposed General Khanh, a veteran of other coup attempts, as Commander in Chief of the Armed Forces.

Confronted with both a deteriorating political and military situation, General Westmoreland directed his deputy, Lieutenant General John L. Throckmorton, USA, to determine what American ground forces were needed for base security. After completing his survey, Throckmorton recommended the deployment of a three-battalion Marine expeditionary brigade to Da Nang because of the vital importance of the base for any air campaign against the north and "the questionable capability of the Vietnamese to protect the base." General Westmoreland several years later recalled:

> While sharing Throckmorton's sense of urgency, I nevertheless hoped to keep the number of U.S. ground troops to a minimum and recommended instead landing only two battalions and holding the third aboard ship off shore.[13]

On 22 February, General Westmoreland forwarded this request to Admiral Sharp who in turn informed the JCS that he agreed with Westmoreland's assessment of the situation. Although expressing strong reservations about sending any American ground forces to Vietnam, Ambassador Taylor, in a message to the State Department on 22 February, agreed to placing one Marine BLT at Da Nang "in view of General Westmoreland's understandable concern for the safety of this important base."[14]

By this time, BLTs 1/9 and 3/9 were back on board ship at their former stations near Cap St. Jacques and Da Nang. The Task Force 76 flagship, the USS *Mount McKinley* (AGC 7), with the task force commander, Rear Admiral Don W. Wulzen, and General Karch on board, accompanied the amphibious task group carrying BLT 1/9 off Vietnam. General Karch had met with Westmoreland and the MACV staff in Saigon. The Marines were

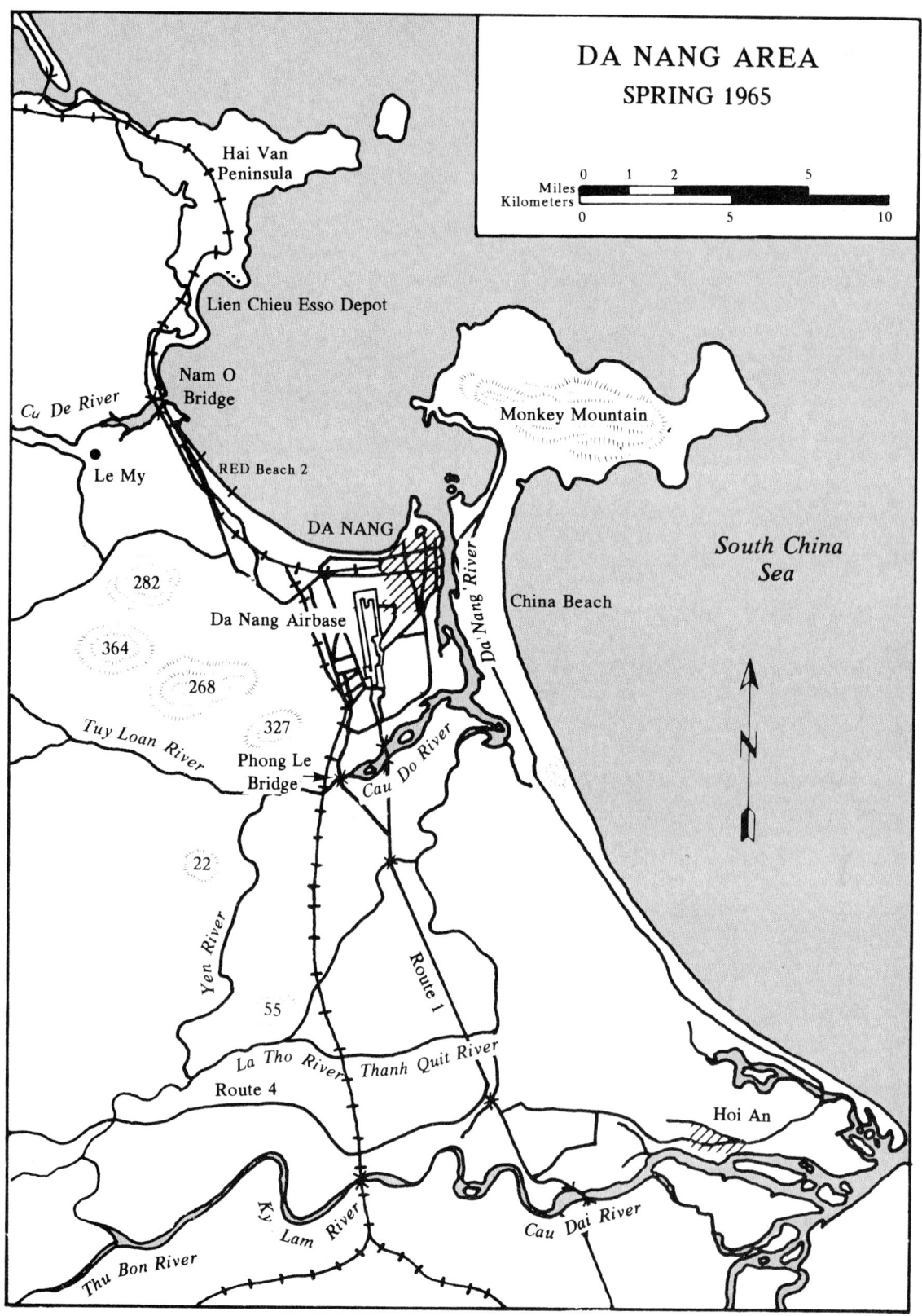

DA NANG AREA
SPRING 1965

prepared for any eventuality and ready to land at Da Nang or Saigon as the situation required.

By the end of February, President Johnson had made the decision to commit a two-battalion Marine expeditionary brigade to Da Nang with the mission of protecting the base from enemy incursion. General Karch and members of his staff once more visited General Westmoreland on 25 February to discuss plans for a Marine landing at Da Nang. The MEB commander left Saigon two days later for Da Nang where he coordinated his plans with the South Vietnamese I Corps Commander, Major General Nguyen Chanh Thi, the virtual warlord of South Vietnam's five northern provinces. Karch later recalled:

> On our way back into Thi's headquarters a jeep came out with a New York Times reporter in it. West-moreland's J-3 [BGen William E. DePuy, USA] turned to me and said, "That is bad news." When he got in he had a phone call from Saigon saying, "Get Karch and his staff out of the country as quickly as posible." [15]

General Karch and his staff immediately departed Da Nang for Subic Bay and then Okinawa.

On 27 February (26 February, Washington time), the Department of State cabled Ambassador Taylor that the Marines were to be landed and that he was to secure approval from the Government of Vietnam for this eventuality. On the afternoon of the 28th, Ambassador Taylor met with Vietnamese Prime Minister Phan Huy Quat to discuss with him the proposed American landing. The following day, 1 March, the Ambassador met with the Minister of the Vietnamese Armed Forces, General Nguyen Van Thieu and the Vietnamese Chairman of the Joint General Staff, General Tran Van Minh ("Little Minh") to discuss the details of the deployment of the 9th MEB. The two Vietnamese officers posed no objections to the proposed commitment of American combat troops. They did, however, express concern about the reaction of the Vietnamese population and requested that the American forces be brought into Da Nang "in the most inconspicuous way feasible." [16]

Evidently this "inconspicuous way" statement had some effect on U.S. officials in Washington. On 3 March, Ambassador Taylor received a message from Assistant Secretary of Defense John T. McNaughton stating that it was desirable to deploy the Army's 173d Airborne Brigade by air from Okinawa instead of the 9th MEB. [17] Some Washington planners obviously believed that the

light infantry of an airborne brigade landing at Da Nang airfield would be a "quieter arrival" than the more formidable appearance of a Marine brigade with its tanks, amphibian tractors, and other heavy weapons arriving in an armada of amphibious ships. General Westmoreland, supported by the American Ambassador, immediately objected to the proposed change. Both considered that the Marines were more self-sustaining. Admiral Sharp, Commander in Chief, Pacific, cabled the JCS:

> Since the origination of OPLAN 32 in 1959, the Marines have been scheduled for deployment to Da Nang . . . contingency plans and a myriad of supporting plans at lower echelons reflect this same deployment. As a result, there has been extensive planning, reconnaissance, and logistics preparation over the years. The CG, 9th MEB is presently in Da Nang finalizing the details for landing the MEB forces in such a way as to cause minimum impact on the civilian populace . . . I recommend that the MEB be landed at Da Nang as previously planned. [18]

The objections to the MEB landing were overruled and on 7 March 1965 (6 March 1965, Washington time) the JCS sent the long-awaited signal to land the 9th MEB at once with two of its three BLTs.

The Landing

The days before the landing were a hectic period for General Karch and the Marines of the brigade. General Karch and his staff had completed 9th MEB Operational Plan 37D-65 for the amphibious landing of a BLT and the airlift of another battalion from Okinawa to Da Nang on 26 February. The MEB staff then conducted a command post exercise (CPX) on Okinawa. According to Major Ruel T. Scyphers, the MEB G-1, the operations order for the deployment of the MEB, "was put together following a non-stop 48 hour CPX . . . we got word about 2000 [27 February] and armed with a staff manual and some borrowed clerks we put together an order and had it boxed about 0300 . . . ." [19]

Still on Okinawa at the beginning of March, General Karch scheduled a two-day map exercise of the Da Nang area beginning on 2 March and a briefing for Lieutenant Colonel Herbert J. Bain,* commanding officer of the 1st Battalion, 3d Marines, whose battalion was slated to fly to Da Nang. On the

---

* Lieutenant Colonel Bain was a combat veteran of World War II. He had earned a battlefield commission in November 1944 and later was awarded the Silver Star for his heroic actions during the Okinawa campaign in 1945.

USMC Photo A183676

Marines from BLT 3/9 came ashore on 8 March 1965 at RED Beach 2, northwest of Da Nang. The heavy surf delayed the landing for an hour.

2d, however, Karch cancelled both the exercise and the briefing when he received orders to proceed immediately to Da Nang. Boarding a Marine KC-130F, the tanker/transport model of the C-130, General Karch and 28 members of his staff departed Okinawa at 2300. The aircraft stopped at Cubi Point to pick up staff members of Navy Task Force 76 and arrived in Da Nang the morning of the 3d. MACV liaison officers met General Karch and his group as they landed and escorted them about the airbase and landing beaches. At 1600, the MEB staff boarded its plane for the return flight to Subic Bay.

The next day, the general issued a warning order to BLT 3/9, which had been off the coast of Da Nang in Navy amphibious shipping since early February, to be prepared ''to administratively land the landing force.'' The BLT commander, Lieutenant Colonel Charles E. McPartlin, Jr., was to land his battalion at RED Beach 2, north of the airbase and west of the

city of Da Nang, and move by truck convoy along Route 1 to defensive positions at the airfield.[20]*

At the same time, the Marines and the Navy made refinements in dispositions of their tactical units. BLT 2/9, embarked on the ships of the amphibious ready group, relieved BLT 1/9 at Subic Bay. The JUNGLE DRUM III exercise was rescheduled for 14-31 March and was scaled down from a MEB-size exercise with only BLT 2/3 slated as the participating unit.

General Karch flew back to Da Nang on 6 March and joined Admiral Wulzen on board the *Mount McKinley*, which was 10 miles off Da Nang with the rest of the task force. As the MEB commander later recalled:

---

* Lieutenant Colonel McPartlin had enlisted in the Marine Corps in 1932. A first sergeant at the outbreak of World War II, he was commissioned a second lieutenant in 1942. He saw combat in both World War II and Korea.

Marines from BLT 3/9 continue landing across RED Beach 2. A member of the beach party (holding flag in foreground) directs traffic.

On 7 March, I was sitting in my stateroom when Admiral Wulzen comes in and says, "Here is a dispatch," which said, "Close Da Nang, land the landing force." I looked at the dispatch, I looked at Admiral Wulzen, and I said "Don, do you think in Washington they know what time it is in Da Nang? This means a night landing if we close Da Nang at this point."

Karch went on to exclaim:

And not only that—we were in the worst weather we had encountered in the South China Sea ever. Visibility was limited to 150-200 yards, and it was about 12 o'clock. The move into the Da Nang harbor from which the landing would be launched was going to take about four to five hours. [21]*

Upon his return to the command ship that evening, General Karch radioed Lieutenant Colonel McPartlin. He assured the battalion commander that Route 1 would be closed to civilians for 36 hours and that McPartlin would control traffic in the beachhead area. The Vietnamese would regulate movement along the rest of the route. The MEB commander concluded: "Unless the situation ashore changes during the night, you can count on an administrative move from beachhead to airfield. Speed in execution is essential . . . ."[22]

---

* A last minute requirement to coordinate the public announcement of the Marine landing with the South Vietnamese may have accounted for the timing of the JCS message. See "Marine Combat Units Go to Da Nang," *Pentagon Papers*, bk 4, sec. IV-C-4, p. 8.

Shortly afterward, General Karch ordered the execution of OPlan-37D. The plan, with H-hour set for 0800, 8 March, scheduled general unloading to be completed by 1600 the next day. Lieutenant Colonel McPartlin planned for Company I to land over the northern portion of RED Beach 2 and Company K over the southern sector. They were to insure that the landing area was secure and provide the advance guard for the movement to the airfield. Company M was designated battalion reserve.

At 0545 on the 8th, the four ships of Amphibious Task Force 76, the flagship *Mount McKinley*, the attack transport USS *Henrico* (APA 45), attack cargo ship USS *Union* (AKA 106), and amphibious transport dock USS *Vancouver* (LPD 2) closed to within 4,000 yards of the Da Nang shore and anchored in the harbor. Admiral Wulzen gave the order "land the landing force" at 0600. At this time, other than an intermittent drizzle, weather conditions were moderate. Visibility was five miles and the wind was blowing at eight knots from the northwest. Near the shoreline, waves were cresting from two to four feet, spilling gently onto the landing beach. Unfortunately, these conditions did not last long.

South Vietnamese children wave at a Marine vehicle heading for the Da Nang Airbase. A South Vietnamese flag flies above the banner welcoming the Marines to Vietnam.

In the transport area, swells reached 8 to 10 feet, playing havoc with the debarkation. It was almost impossible to hold the nets for the troops to debark; several of the lines mooring landing craft to their mother ships snapped under the strain. At 0730 it became impossible to load small boats alongside; Admiral Wulzen postponed H-hour until 0900. At the same time, General Karch left the *Mount McKinley* for the airbase by helicopter. An hour later, the first planes arrived from Okinawa with additional shore party personnel to aid in clearing the beach.

At 0830 the task force commander confirmed the 0900 H-hour. A high surf plan was put into effect which directed that the loads for the smaller landing craft (LCVPs) be rescheduled for larger and heavier landing craft (LCMs). The first wave of assault troops in 11 Marine amphibian tractors (LVTPs) touched down at RED Beach 2 just three minutes late and the fourth and final assault wave of 3/9 landed at 0918.*

On the beach, the commander of I Corps Tactical Zone (I CTZ), General Thi, and the Mayor of Da Nang welcomed General Karch while a group of Vietnamese university students led by a vanguard of pretty girls holding leis of flowers greeted the Marines.** Vietnamese troops secured the beachhead and the route to the airfield. The first echelons of Company L moved out from the beachhead at 0945. Banners in both Vietnamese and English were strung along the route of march welcoming the troops; Vietnamese children lined

---

* The landing craft, mechanized (LCM) is a steel-hulled boat. Two versions exist, the LCM-6 (weight of 29 tons empty which carries 80 troops or 24 tons of cargo), and the LCM-8 (weighs 61 tons empty and carries 200 troops or 60 tons of cargo). The personnel and vehicle landing craft (LCVP) is a wooden-hulled landing craft weighing nine tons and capable of carrying 36 troops or four tons of cargo. The landing vehicle tracked, personnel (LVTP-5) is a steel amphibian tracked vehicle weighing 45 tons and capable of carrying 34 troops or six tons of cargo. The LCM and LCVP are landing craft organic to the Navy while the LVTP-5 is a Marine Corps vehicle.

** The picture shown at upper right appeared in many American newspapers depicting a dour General Karch with a garland of flowers around his neck. Karch later remarked: "That picture has been the source of a lot of trouble for me. People say, 'Why couldn't you have been smiling?' But you know, if I had it to do over, that picture would be the same. When you have a son in Vietnam and he gets killed, you don't want a smiling general with flowers around his neck as the leader at that point." *Karch Intvw.*

Photo courtsey of Associated Press and Wide World Photos
Brigadier General Frederick J. Karch, the Commanding General, 9th MEB, watches the landing bedecked with flowers presented to him by South Vietnamese schoolgirls. This picture received wide distribution in the U.S. press.

both sides of the road, waving and shyly smiling at the Marines. The lead company was followed by Company I, artillery attachments, and Company K, which formed the rear guard of the motor march to the southern portion of the airbase. Company M remained behind as beach security for general unloading.

Simultaneously with the preparations for the landing of the BLT across the beach, the Marines had

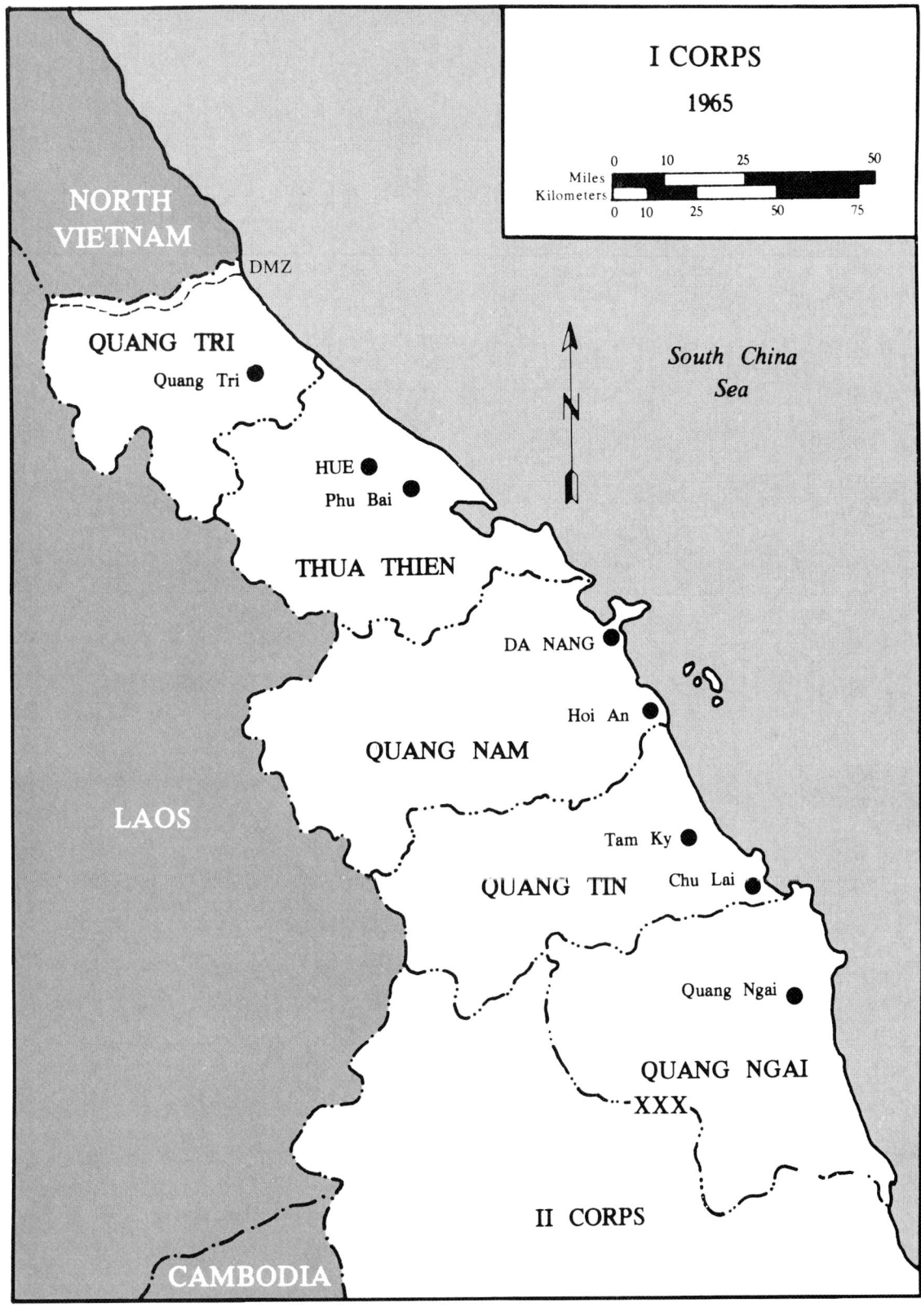

Marines from the 1st Battalion, 3d Marines disembark from U.S. Air Force C-130 transports at the Da Nang Airbase on 8 March. The airlift of the battalion was held up for 24 hours shortly after these Marines arrived.

begun the airlift of Lieutenant Colonel Bain's battalion from Okinawa to Da Nang. On the morning of 7 March, Major General William R. ("Rip") Collins, the 3d Marine Division commander, as directed by a CinCPac message, requested the 315th Air Division of the U.S. Air Force to provide the transportation to move the unit to Vietnam. On Okinawa the 3d Division commander alerted Lieutenant Colonel Bain, and the first elements of the battalion moved from Camp Schwab to the air facility at Futema that night. The BLT was organized into assigned aircraft loads, then moved from Futema to Naha Air Base. At 2200, the Air Force approved the movement orders, establishing 30-minute intervals between launches of the C-130 aircraft.

Shortly after midnight, General Collins radioed MACV headquarters in Saigon for authority to launch the first plane of the airlift which was scheduled to arrive at Da Nang at 0900 on the 8th. Six hours later, MACV granted this clearance but later changed the arrival hour to noon. After a three-hour wait, the first elements consisting of the command group of the battalion and part of Company C left Naha Air Base at 0725. In reporting the move, General Collins observed that the entire lift could take place during daylight if he were allowed to expedite aircraft departures. The MACV Chief of Staff, Major General Richard G. Stilwell, called the CinCPac Command Center and stated that Da Nang could not accommodate two BLTs arriving at the same time. Brigadier General Keith B. McCutcheon, an outstanding Marine aviator of both World War II and Korea then serving as the CinCPac J-3, reminded Stilwell that MACV had already granted clearance for the air movement. General Stilwell replied that conditions had changed and that the airlift would have to be held up. CinCPac so instructed the Commanders, Pacific Fleet and Pacific Air Force.[23]

The first planes carrying the lead elements of the 1st Battalion, 3d Marines, arrived at the Da Nang Airbase about 1300 on the afternoon of 8 March. Although snipers fired at them during their landing approach, the aircraft were undamaged. After the arrival of 13 planes at Da Nang, the airlift was halted with Companies C and B assembled in defensive positions on the western portion of the airfield. Company D, the security company already at Da Nang for protection of the SHUFLY helicopter unit, Marine Medium Helicopter Squadron (HMM) 163, reverted to parent control. Only Company A was left on Okinawa. Lieutenant Colonel Bain later recalled that the "'arbitrary' cutoff [of the airlift] separated the units which had landed from their backup rations."[24]

Although the arrival of the remainder of Bain's battalion was held up, a different airlift occurred on 9 March. The helicopter carrier USS *Princeton* (LPH 5) with HMM-365 (Lieutenant Colonel Joseph Koler, Jr.) on board, arrived off Da Nang shortly after sunrise that morning. Between 0700 and noon on the 9th, all 23 of the squadron's helicopters were transferred to HMM-162,* commanded by Lieutenant Colonel Oliver W. Curtis, whose personnel arrived by Marine KC-130 aircraft at Da Nang from Okinawa the same day. The pilots of HMM-365 returned to the *Princeton* which then steamed for Okinawa to take on replacement aircraft.

That same afternoon, General Karch, who on the 8th had been given operational control of all Marine units at Da Nang, reporting directly to MACV,

---

* The squadron, HMM-162, was no stranger to operations in Vietnam. It had been in the Far East since 1 June 1964 and had been previously assigned to SHUFLY for four months. Much of the intervening time had been spent on board Navy LPHs in Vietnamese waters as part of the Special Landing Force. It had just returned to Okinawa on 4 March from SLF duty. Now, only five days later, the squadron again was in Vietnam. LtCol Oliver W. Curtis had previously commanded this squadron in 1964 when it was assigned to SHUFLY. He was a veteran of both World War II and Korea and had been awarded a Distinguished Flying Cross (DFC) for his actions at Okinawa and later three more DFCs for his aerial feats in Korea.

telephoned General Westmoreland and received permission to resume the airlift of BLT 1/3. The first planes took off from Okinawa shortly after midnight and arrived at Da Nang the morning of the 10th. By 12 March, the rest of the battalion landing team, with the exception of its attached tanks and low priority vehicles, was in Vietnam.

On that date, general unloading of the 9th MEB was completed. Because of a fire fight on the night of 8-9 March between VC elements and Vietnamese Army troops only two miles north of RED Beach, the ships of the amphibious task force had moved to anchorages near the mouth of the Song Han (Da Nang River). The next day unloading continued up the river over a ramp into the city. This too had its limitations as Admiral Wulzen brought out:

> The complete lack of port facilities—cranes, heavy duty fork lifts, cargo nets, and lighterage—coupled with unmarked channels, single small off-loading point (which can only handle two LCMs simultaneously), distance from anchorage to pier (four miles average), lack of staging area at the pier are contributing to slow off-loading.[25]

The administrative landing of the 9th MEB occurred in an uncertain atmosphere; the JCS order directing the landing, bore the laconic title "Improved Security Measures in the Republic of Vietnam." Adding a further surrealistic touch to the Marines' arrival, a few days after the landing General Thi invited the commanders and staff of the 9th MEB to a garden reception, replete with "several orchestras and accompanying nicities." Lieutenant Colonel Bain ironically recalled that the festivities were "followed by a return to my foxhole and C rations."[26]

Nevertheless, a new phase of the Vietnam war had begun. About one-third of the Marine ground forces and two-thirds of the Marine helicopter squadrons in the Western Pacific had been committed to South Vietnam.

CHAPTER 2

The 9th MEB in Vietnam

The First Weeks—Estimate of the Situation—More Marines Arrive—An Expanded Mission—Chu Lai

The First Weeks

Despite the arrival of the 9th MEB, the Marine intervention in Vietnam was still of a limited nature. The Joint Chiefs of Staff made this very clear in their landing order of 7 March which directed that "the U.S. Marine Force will not, repeat will not, engage in day-to-day actions against the Viet Cong." General Westmoreland gave the 9th MEB the responsibility to protect the vital Da Nang Airbase from enemy attack but declared that "overall responsiblity for the defense of Da Nang area remains a RVNAF [Republic of Vietnam Armed Forces] responsibility."[1]

To carry out this limited mission, General Karch had nearly 5,000 Marines under his command, including McPartlin's and Bain's infantry battalions, two helicopter squadrons, and limited logistic and combat support forces. The brigade had absorbed the former Marine Unit Vietnam (MUV), or Task Unit 79.3.5, better remembered as SHUFLY. On 9 March the MUV became Marine Aircraft Group (MAG) 16. Colonel John H. King, Jr., the former MUV commander and veteran Marine aviator who had commanded a helicopter squadron in Korea, assumed command of MAG-16.

The 9th MEB air-ground team at Da Nang faced a difficult logistical situation. General Karch later recalled:

> In late February, Bob Oddy [Colonel Robert J. Oddy, CO, 3d Force Service Regiment] came to me and said, "Your biggest problem is going to be logistics and I am going to find you the best people I have to get you through this test." And bless old Bob, he did just that, otherwise the Brigade would have been flat on its back.[2]

The 3d Service Battalion and Force Service Regiment on Okinawa provided the personnel for the Brigade Logistic Support Group (BLSG). According to Colonel Oddy, "When the time came to embark the Brigade, we split the Service Battalion 50/50, and

supported by personnel from the Force Service Regiment, we were ready to launch the fledging BLSG."[*] Original plans called for a BLSG in excess of 1,000 men, but because the Joint Chiefs imposed a personnel ceiling on the number of Marines who could be brought into Vietnam the group had been cut to 660 men. Colonel Oddy recalled in 1976, "The personnel ceiling resulted in an extremely austere staff group that made service and support a big question mark . . . ."[3] General Karch remarked that there were several contingency plans which fitted the situation in Vietnam better than the one that was used.[4]

The only representatives of the brigade logistic group who participated in the first phase of the landing were the executive officer, Major Pat Morgan, and 11 other Marines. They arrived on 10 March by air with elements of BLT 1/3 and assumed control of the entire logistic operation, but the advance echelon could accomplish very little "except to console the MEB that supplies were on the way."[5]

Despite the activation of the BLSG on 12 March and the arrival of its commanding officer, Lieutenant Colonel George H. Smith, six days later, the first two weeks for the MEB were a logistic nightmare. The entire brigade subsisted on the 15 days of rations that had landed with McPartlin's battalion and an

---

*Colonel Oddy wrote in 1976:" . . . this was a time when unrestricted officers with infantry MOSs could be assigned command of service units. This was fortunate for me as I had previous command experience with infantry platoons, companies and battalions and it seemed unlikely I would command one of the infantry regiments of the Division. Command of a large service organization and the opportunity to formulate from scratch a larger task organized service and support group was certainly a major high point in my career." Col Robert J. Oddy, Comments on draft MS, dtd 25Oct76 (Vietnam Comment File).

emergency airlift from Saigon. Major Morgan later wrote: "Lieutenant Colonel Smith and I almost lost our sanity until matters were straightened out."[6]

On 22 March, the ships carrying the seatail of the 9th MEB entered the port. They were unloaded at the ramp near the base of Monkey Mountain, across the Song Han from the airfield. Since the bridge spanning the river had been destroyed by the Viet Cong the year before, the Marines had to rely on a ferry to carry the supply-laden trucks to the airbase. Despite the complicated unloading, the arrival of its seatail ended the MEB's first logistic crisis.

In this transitional phase of U.S. involvement, some confusion existed as to whether the MEB was to subsist from Marine Corps and Seventh Fleet mount-out stocks, or whether MACV would assume part of the logistic burden. MACV apparently believed that the Marine Corps had received permission from the Department of Defense to use its mount-out supplies, which was not the case. This authority was not given until June. (See Chapters 3 and 12). Marine Colonel Webb D. Sawyer, who headed the MACV J-4 Plans Branch, later provided a MACV perspective of the situation in the following comment:

> When the Marine Brigade landed at Da Nang I had a representative from my J-4 office there, an Air Force Officer, Major Robinson. When Robby returned to Saigon, he brought a very long, very complete, listing of all types of supplies that were being requested by the Marine Brigade. I knew that most of the items were in the Code Plan stocks [mount-out stocks] aboard the shipping that had brought the Marines. I asked Robby why the Marines weren't using the Code Plan supplies. His reply was that the Marines said those supplies were for an emergency. My reaction was that the Marines had just participated in the emergency.[7]

General Karch later recalled that for days the air was filled with messages regarding rations and ammunition. At the end of March, General Westmoreland declared that his command could take on the task of supplying the Marines with basic rations and ammunition for the time being. Although the question was not resolved at this time, the Marines were equipped, armed, and fed; supplies were unloaded and stockpiled; and the MEB was functioning.[8]

During this same period, Colonel King reorganized MAG-16, the air arm of the MEB, to reflect the changes in his command. On 14 March, the headquarters sections became Headquarters and Maintenance Squadron 16 (—) (H&MS-16) under Major John J. McMasters while the housekeeping section became Marine Airbase Squadron 16 (—) (MABS-16) under Lieutenant Colonel Thomas E. Vernon. Colonel King also retained the LAAM battalion as well as the two helicopter squadrons.

The Marine helicopters continued to operate under MAG-16 much the same as they did when under SHUFLY. Most of their missions were flown in support of the South Vietnamese Army (ARVN) forces throughout I Corps. Initially, after the landing of the 9th MEB, most of these flights were made by Lieutenant Colonel Norman G. Ewers' HMM-163. The newly arrived squadron, HMM-162, under Lieutenant Colonel Oliver W. Curtis, became operational on 12 March, but at first was confined to support of the MEB. By the end of March, both squadrons were supporting the Marines and the ARVN.

In support of the ARVN operations, the Marine pilots flew both resupply and strike missions. The former missions, consuming a majority of the flight hours, involved moving troops and cargo to outposts located throughout I Corps. The resupply cargo was a mixture of military supplies, as well as pigs, cows, chickens, and other items required by the sometimes isolated Vietnamese detachments. Strike missions consisted of lifting company- or battalion-size ARVN units in helicopter assault operations.

These strike missions produced the only significant enemy contact experienced by Marines during this period. On 31 March, the group flew helicopter support for ARVN Operation QUYET THANG 512. A force of 17 UH-34Ds from HMM-163, 2 UH-34D SAR/maintenance* helicopters from HMM-162, and 7 U. S. Army Bell UH-1 'Huey' gunships was assigned to lift 465 troops of the ARVN 5th Airborne Battalion. The air task force was to move the ARVN paratroopers from the vicinity of Tam Ky in Quang Tin Province to a landing zone (LZ) about 25 miles south of Da Nang.

Led by Lieutenant Colonel Ewers, the helicopters encountered such heavy antiaircraft fire when they approached the landing zone that Ewers later remarked that the squadron might have flown into a

---

*SAR/maintenance teams are search, rescue, and maintenance teams used to expedite the recovery of downed aircraft. These teams, composed of mechanics and infantry, were placed on board helicopters which remained well above the strike force, or acted as decoys during the initial assault.

trap. In the first lift, Ewers' wingman, First Lieutenant Wendell T. Eliason was killed in the landing zone, but his co-pilot, First Lieutenant Donald R. Wilson, managed to fly the badly damaged craft back to Da Nang. Four other helicopters in this lift also had to be returned to Da Nang for battle damage repair.

The enemy shot down one of the Marine UH-34Ds, whose pilot, First Lieutenant Dale D. Eddy, "was wounded in the neck and initially believed KIA." Eddy's copilot, First Lieutenant James E. Magel, also wounded, was able to make his way to another helicopter, but then died. According to Ewers, Eddy's crew chief, Sergeant Cecil A. Garner, "himself wounded, took his M-60 machine gun with him and joined the firefight on the ground." Another pilot from HMM-163, Major Bennie H. Mann, Jr., landed his craft in the face of the heavy enemy fire and rescued Garner and Eddy. According to Ewers, Mann's crew chief, Staff Sergeant Stanley J. Novotny, "somehow found the strength singlehandedly to lift the concious but paralyzed" six-foot, 200-pound Eddy out of the downed craft. Mann was awarded the Navy Cross and Novotny received the Silver Star for the rescue.[9]

Despite heavy enemy opposition, HMM-163 continued to make three lifts into the zone until the entire 5th Airborne Battalion had been landed. All told, 25 Marine helicopters and 10 U.S. Army helicopters took part in the operation.* Nineteen of the aircraft sustained battle damage. Two Army UH-1s, in addition to the Marine UH-34D, also were shot down. The Army craft were later recovered but Eddy's aircraft was a complete loss. The Marines suffered a total of 19 casualties including the two killed while two U.S. Army personnel required hospitalization. Colonel Thomas J. O'Connor, at the time the 1st MAW Chief of Staff, later wrote: "It was obvious to us in Japan from battle damage and casualty reports of this mission that the VC were really moving into the Da Nang area in strength and that the situation was changing."[10]

In contrast to the helicopter squadrons, the

USMC Photo A183859

Lieutenant General Krulak; Lieutenant Colonel Charles E. McPartlin, Jr., Commanding Officer, 3d Battalion, 9th Marines; Brigadier General Karch; and Lieutenant Colonel Joseph E. Muir, 9th MEB operations officer (left to right) study the terrain from Hill 327 west of Da Nang. This hill was the highest point in the 9th MEB area of operations.

Marine infantry battalions were confined to the approximately eight square miles of relatively unpopulated terrain encompassing the airfield and the high ground to the west which made up the MEB's **tactical area of responsibility (TAOR).**** Within the Marines' TAOR, Bain's 1st Battalion, 3d Marines manned defenses on the airfield while McPartlin's 3d Battalion, 9th Marines moved to forward positions on hill mass 268-327 due west of the base. There, the latter battalion not only protected the airfield but also provided security for Battery B of the LAAM Battalion which moved to Hill 327. To accomplish the mission of airfield defense, Bain's battalion established an extensive system of listening posts forward of the company defensive areas around the

---

*The U. S. Army helicopters belonged to the Utility Tactical Transport Detachment, 68th Aviation Company, USA, also located at Da Nang. This unit provided the armed helicopter escorts for Marine air operations since the Marines did not have their organic fixed-wing attack aircraft support with them at this time.

**According to *Dictionary of United States Military Terms for Joint Usage* (JD), *JCS Pub 1* (Washington: Dec 64), p. 169, a TAOR was "a defined area of land in which responsibility is specifically assigned to the commander of the area for the development and maintenance of installations, control of movement and the conduct of tactical operations involving troops under his control . . . ."

USMC Photo A184119

HAWK missiles move to new positions on Hill 327 from the airfield. The missiles are from Battery B, 1st LAAM Battalion.

airfield perimeter. The battalion was prepared to support these posts with a strong reaction force which could deploy rapidly to any sector of the airfield. The inherent difficulty of the unit's defensive assignment was that the battalion could not establish listening posts or conduct defensive reconnaissance patrols beyond the confines of the airfield.

Although McPartlin's battalion ran patrols into the hills to the west, his Marines encountered no Viet Cong. In fact, the first Americans casualties were inflicted by another Marine when two men from a three-man listening post left their positions to investigate a suspicious movement to their front. The two men apparently lost their way in the dark and came upon their remaining partner from the rear. He turned and opened fire, mortally wounding his two comrades.

Initially, the Marine infantrymen suffered more from the heat and humidity than from the combat situation. In order to reduce the number of heat prostration casualties, General Karch restricted

defensive patrols and heavy work to the cooler hours of the early morning and late afternoon.

Although acclimatization only required time, other problems were not so easily solved. Relations with the South Vietnamese often were difficult. For example, Bain's relief of some ARVN forces at the airfield on 13 March was delayed when the Vietnamese refused to leave their positions. The Marines had to make further liaison with the ARVN headquarters before completing the relief the next day.

McPartlin's battalion recorded a similar experience. The Marines attempted to establish a mutual check point with the Popular Forces (PF), Vietnam's home defense militia.* The PFs showed

---

*Popular Forces were Vietnamese who were recruited and served in their local villages and hamlets. Regional Forces (RFs) were Vietnamese forces recruited within a province and assigned to the province chief. Although comparison with the U. S. institutions is not exact, one could say that PFs were county- or parish-type troops while RFs were state forces.

up at the check point, but then quickly disappeared. These experiences with the PFs led McPartlin to comment, "that the PFs were most unreliable military personnel."[11] To add to the 3d Battalion's problems, fire discipline in an ARVN training camp southeast of the battalion was nonexistent. Periodically, uncomfortable moments occurred as ARVN recruits inadvertently fired towards the unit's positions.

The area south and east of the airbase remained the responsibility of the ARVN because General Thi wanted to keep the Marines away from the populated area, fearing that the Americans might provoke incidents in the villages which would antagonize the local populace.[12] Generals Thi and Karch reached an agreement upon a set of "rules of engagement" which also restricted the activities of the Marines. The Marines were not to fire at persons beyond the defensive wire of the airbase boundary, but they were to report persons outside the wire to the Combined Coordination Center established by the two commands. General Karch made no secret about his unhappiness with the defensive perimeter assigned to the brigade: "Actually this was not a satisfactory arrangement. As a practical matter there is no doubt that the brigade commander would have been held responsible for any successful assault on the airfield."[13]

Estimate of the Situation

When the MEB was in place at Da Nang, General Westmoreland and his staff reexamined the entire American military effort in Vietnam. According to the MACV commander:

We considered it appropriate to undertake a classical

USMC Photo A801078

Colonel Edwin B. Wheeler, Commanding Officer, 3d Marines (center), discusses the tactical situation with Lieutenant Colonel David A. Clement, commanding officer of the newly arrived 2d Battalion, 3d Marines (right). The other officer in the picture is First Lieutenant Marx H. Branum, the forward air controller for the battalion.

Marines from BLT 3/4 on board a Marine helicopter en route to Phu Bai from Da Nang. These troops just arrived in Vietnam.

commander's estimate of the situation to think through in a logical and precise manner, strategy, objectives, enemy capabilities, and our own courses of action before making what may prove to be in the light of history, a momentous recommendation.[14]

By 26 March, Westmoreland had completed his estimate and was prepared to provide the Washington authorities with a resume of recommendations already forwarded to Admiral Sharp and the Joint Chiefs.[15] He saw the military objectives of his command in relatively simple terms. The American goal was to cause the Democratic Republic of Vietnam (North Vietnam) to cease its support of the VC, thus enabling an anti-Communist South Vietnam to survive. To carry out this policy, the American general provided three alternatives.

Under the first, the United States Government would give more aid to the buildup of the Vietnamese Armed Forces, continue and expand air strikes against North Vietnam, and use the resources of the Seventh Fleet to interdict infiltration by sea. General Westmoreland frankly did not believe this was enough. It would not stabilize the Government of South Vietnam and would offer no assurance for the survival of the country.

The second proposal was the deployment of five divisions, including three American, across Vietnam and the Laotian panhandle near the 17th Parallel. This would be coordinated with stepped-up air attacks against the north, while at the same time strengthening the South Vietnamese Armed Forces. Other American and Free World troops would be sent to South Vietnam to deal with the Viet Cong

USMC Photo A184117

Commandant of the Marine Corps, General Wallace M. Greene, Jr., inspects an honor guard at Da Nang during a visit to Vietnam in April 1965. The Commandant later told the press that the Marines would be conducting more aggressive operations.

insurgency. General Westmoreland also rejected this alternative; he did not think that in 1965 the lines of communication or the port facilities in the country could supply and support five divisions strung along the parallel. He feared that by the time this could be done, the war would be lost.

According to the general, this left only one feasible solution. This was to continue the buildup of the ARVN, intensify the air war against North Vietnam, and land the equivalent of two U.S. divisions with their necessary combat and service support in South Vietnam. The American forces would have a three-fold mission: protection of vital U.S. installations; defeat of the Communist efforts to control Kontum and Pleiku Provinces; and the establishment of enclaves in the coastal region. General Westmoreland visualized that the total U.S. reinforcement would consist of approximately 33,000 troops deployed by June. He believed that the insertion of American strength would blunt the Communist offensive in the two northern corps areas and stiffen the backbone of the South Vietnamese forces throughout the country.

Most important for the Marine Corps was the recommendation to reinforce the 4,685 personnel of the 9th MEB. In addition to rounding out the force at Da Nang with a third battalion, Westmoreland suggested that a fourth be stationed at the Hue/Phu

Bai airstrip approximately eight miles south of Hue. The MACV commander later wrote:

> I remained disturbed about possible enemy action against other bases, notably a U.S. Army communications facility [manned by the U.S. Army 8th Radio Research Unit] and a small airfield at Phu Bai, near Hue, not a good field but at the time the best we had north of the Hai Van Pass.[16]

Although Admiral Sharp and the Joint Chiefs had already recommended approval of the Marine deployment to Phu Bai, one influential Marine general opposed this suggestion at the time. Lieutenant General Victor H. Krulak,* then Commanding General, Fleet Marine Force, Pacific (FMFPac) and perhaps the Marine Corps' leading theoretician on counterinsurgency, later commented:

> Here is an example of where dollar economics wagged the tail of the military deployment. Phu Bai is as tactically indefensible as anyone could imagine. General Westmoreland was determined, however, that we should go there because of the existence of the 8th RRU. There was an investment of probably 5 million dollars in the unit. It was firmly locked to the Phu Bai plain and he was determined not to see it move. He was reinforced by the testimony of experts who said its location was particularly good from a ''technical'' point of view. Whether or not this is true and our own . . . people strongly questioned it, he insisted that we go there despite the tremendous land barrier between Da Nang and Phu Bai, difficulty of providing logistical support, and the many better uses to which a Marine BLT could have been put. I believe we would have been better off by far to have moved the 8th RRU to another place and to have kept our forces more concentrated. General Westmoreland felt differently and Admiral Sharp was not prepared to override him.[17]**

In any event, General Westmoreland's J-3,

---

*General Krulak had served as the Special Assistant for Counter-Insurgency and Special Activities for the Joint Chiefs of Staff just prior to his assumption of command of FMFPac. Although as CGFMFPac, General Krulak did not have operational control of any of the Marine units committed to Vietnam, he was responsible for the combat readiness and logistic support of all Marines in the Pacific. A 1934 Naval Academy graduate, the general earned the Navy Cross during World War II. He was affectionately known throughout the Corps as ''Brute,'' a nickname gained by the fact that he is five feet, five inches tall.

**The Center of Military History, Department of the Army, made the following observation in its comments on the draft manuscript, ''General Westmoreland also desired the BLT for the defense of the air strip in that he intended to eventually move the helicopters from Da Nang to Phu Bai to reduce airfield congestion at Da Nang.'' CMH Comments on draft MS, dtd 15Nov76 (Vietnam Comment File).

Brigadier General William E. DePuy, accompanied Ambassador Taylor to hand carry the MACV "Estimate of the Situation" to Washington for a special meeting of the National Security Council. At this 1 April meeting, President Johnson made several far-reaching decisions, two of which were of particular concern to the Marine Corps. He approved an 18,000- to 20,000-man increase in the U.S. forces in Vietnam to include the deployment of additional Marine forces. Furthermore, the President permitted a change of mission for the 9th MEB which would allow the use of Marines "in active combat under conditions to be established and approved by the Secretary of Defense in consultation with the Secretary of State."[18]

More Marines Arrive

Initial Marine reinforcements were to consist of both ground and air units. With growing tension in the Far East, General Krulak had made plans at the beginning of the year for the movement of Marine forces and large-scale preparatory maneuvers. In early February, he alerted two U.S. Marine fixed-

USMC Photo A185086

Brigadier General Karch greets Lieutenant Colonel William C. McGraw, Jr., Commanding Officer, VMFA-531, upon arrival of the squadron at Da Nang. VMFA-531, flying F-4B Phantom II aircraft, was the first Marine fixed-wing tactical squadron to deploy to Vietnam in 1965.

wing squadrons in the United States for deployment to Japan in late March. Coincidentally, the FMFPac commander scheduled the largest landing exercise since World War II to take place on the west coast of the United States in early March. The scenario for the exercise, code named SILVER LANCE, reflected the situation in Vietnam, featuring guerrillas, hard-core aggressor forces, and political-military problems.

In Hawaii, the 1st Marine Brigade, consisting of the 4th Marines and MAG-13, made preparations to reinforce the 1st Marine Division and the 3d Marine Aircraft Wing in SILVER LANCE. With the imminent landing of the 9th MEB in Vietnam, the Pacific Command ordered the curtailment of forces for the exercise at the last minute. At this time, 7 March, the Marines of the 1st Brigade were already embarked in amphibious shipping. Crediting General Krulak for "the amazing coincidence of the readiness of the Brigade" for movement, Lieutenant Colonel Rex C. Denny, Jr., then the Brigade G-3, 11 years later recalled:

> We were on again/off again for Okinawa. Then on precisely the planned sailing date for SILVER LANCE . . . the shipping sailed from Pearl Harbor and turned right instead of left. Perfect timing for the movement to the Far East to be in position for the April troop deployment to Vietnam.[19]

The hastily planned deployments of Marine units from Hawaii and the west coast to Okinawa and Japan went smoothly. The 4th Marines, reinforced by a reconnaissance company, antitank company, and by an artillery battalion, the 3d Battalion, 12th Marines, arrived and reported to the 3d Marine Division on Okinawa by the end of March. At the same time, MAG-13 became part of the 1st Marine Aircraft Wing in Japan.[20]

On 25 March, Marine Attack Squadron (VMA) 311, one of the two squadrons alerted in February, began its air transit from California to Japan, followed two days later by the second air unit, Marine Fighter Attack Squadron (VMFA) 542. According to Lieutenant Colonel Richard A. "Doc" Savage, squadron commander of VMFA-542, the two squadrons refueled in flight from Marine KC-130 tankers, and "in leap frog fashion flew the Pacific in some seven days time." The last elements of VMFA-542 landed in Japan on 2 April, thus ending Operation HAMMERHEAD, the code name for the trans-Pacific flight. Savage wrote in 1976:

> This movement not only marked the largest and

USMC Photo A184344

Marines from the 3d Battalion, 4th Marines have just debarked from helicopters at Phu Bai. The troops in the background, ready to embark in the same helicopter for the return trip to Da Nang, are from the 2d Battalion, 3d Marines.

longest in-flight refueling operation for the Marine Corps at this time, but dramatically illustrated the capability of the Marines to move their air resources rapidly to meet a possible combat situation.[21]

While the units of the 1st Brigade and the two squadrons from the United States arrived in the Western Pacific, plans for the deployment of the Marine reinforcements authorized by the President from Okinawa and Japan to Vietnam were completed. Colonel Edwin B. Wheeler's Regimental Landing Team (RLT) 3, composed of the RLT headquarters and two battalion landing teams, BLT 2/3 from his own regiment, commanded by Lieutenant Colonel David A. Clement, and BLT 3/4 from the newly arrived 4th Marines, commanded by Lieutenant Colonel Donald R. Jones, made up the ground component. Air elements of the reinforcements consisted of Lieutenant Colonels Paul L. Hitchcock's Marine Air Support Squadron (MASS) 2 and William C. McGraw, Jr.'s VMFA-531. The 3d Marine Expeditionary Brigade headquarters, which General Collins had activated on 14 March under Lieutenant Colonel Edward Cook after the landing of the 9th MEB, was to control the movement. On 4 April, the 1st Brigade commander, Brigadier General Marion E. Carl, a World War II

flying ace who had downed 18 Japanese aircraft, assumed command of the 3d MEB. He left Okinawa the following day to join Admiral Wulzen on board the *Mount McKinley* at Subic Bay.

As the *Mount McKinley* weighed anchor for the South China Sea, Task Force 76 and 3d MEB staffs completed embarkation and landing plans. RLT 3, BLT 3/4, and MASS-2 would sail from Okinawa on board five tank landing ships. VMFA-531 would fly its aircraft to Da Nang, while its heavy support equipment would follow in amphibious shipping. Lieutenant Colonel Clement's BLT 2/3 was already on board the ships of Navy Task Group 76.6, having completed the JUNGLE DRUM III exercise in Thailand. On 4 April, while underway for the Philippines, the task group received instructions to move to a position 50 miles off the coast of Da Nang. The amphibious squadron arrived there the next day and awaited further landing instructions.

Landing plans of the 3d MEB directed Lieutenant Colonel Clement, a holder of the Silver Star from the Korean War, to land his battalion over RED Beach 2 while the supplies and heavy equipment of the battalion landing team were unloaded at the LST landing on the Tiensha Peninsula, across the Da

Nang River from Da Nang.* Two companies of BLT 2/3 were to be lifted to Phu Bai and await BLT 3/4. Upon the arrival of Jones' battalion, two of his companies were to land across RED Beach 2 and were then to relieve Clement's force at Phu Bai. The rest of BLT 3/4 would remain on board the transports and the task group would move north to the mouth of the Hue River where the Marines and their equipment would unload into landing craft for the trip to Hue City. Lieutenant Colonel Denny, then the 3d MEB G-3, later recalled:

> . . . coordination for this landing plan had to be worked closely with the 9th MEB, requiring several trips from the *Mount McKinley* to Da Nang. In fact, command relations were not clear to all at this point. The 9th MEB wanted control and those of us on the 3d MEB staff wanted control until the troops were ashore . . . . [22]

It was finally resolved that the 9th MEB would assume control of each unit as it landed.

On the morning of 10 April, Navy Task Group 76.6, joined by the flagship *Mount McKinley*, entered Da Nang harbor. In contrast to the landing of 8 March, the sea was calm with only a light wind blowing from the south. Visibility was unrestricted with a slightly overcast sky.

At 0823, the first of five waves touched down on RED Beach 2. By 1310, the landing was completed. The ships then moved to positions off Tiensha Peninsula and general unloading continued. A provisional task force under Lieutenant Colonel Clement, consisting of Companies F and G of the 2d Battalion, 3d Marines and support elements was helilifted to Phu Bai. At Da Nang, Company H took up positions on Hills 278 and 312 north of the high ground held by the 1st Battalion, 3d Marines while Company E remained on board the ships to assist with the unloading. The next day, Company E joined Company H. General Westmoreland complimented General Karch:

> MACV staff officers who observed the amphibious landing at Da Nang and air movement to Phu Bai of elements of your command on 10 April report the movement was accomplished smoothly and profes-

sionally, reflecting high standards of training, discipline, and esprit. Congratulations to you and others responsible. [23]

On the same day that BLT 2/3 landed, VMFA-531 arrived at Da Nang from Atsugi, Japan. Lieutenant Colonel McGraw's squadron was an all-weather jet fighter/interceptor unit equipped with the Navy/Marine Corps version of the McDonnell Phantom II, the F-4B.** General Westmoreland had requested a Phantom squadron because it was capable of performing both tactical missions within South Vietnam and strike missions against North Vietnam. McGraw had received his deployment orders at 0930 from General Fontana's headquarters and the first flight of four Phantoms was airborne within five hours.*** Refueling in flight from two Marine KC-130s southwest of Okinawa, the planes arrived at Da Nang five and one-half hours after takeoff. Later that afternoon the remaining 11 F-4Bs took off. These aircraft stopped for refueling at the Naval Air Station, Cubi Point, Philippines and arrived in Vietnam the next morning. Most of the squadron personnel and light support equipment arrived the same day in Marine KC-130s of Marine Transport Refueler Squadron (VMGR) 152. The heavy equipment closed on Da Nang 11 days later on board the tank landing ship *Snohomish County* (LST 1126). The entire squadron movement had gone so smoothly that the wing commander, General Fontana, remarked: "it was a splendid demonstration of operation and coordination of all concerned . . . a fine professional performance."[24]

On 12 April, RLT 3 headquarters, which had embarked on amphibious shipping at Okinawa, arrived at Da Nang. Colonel Wheeler, a former Marine raider, had arrived in Vietnam by aircraft a week earlier than his command. This was not his first

---

*According to Major Marc A. Moore, the S-3 of the 2d Battalion, 3d Marines, "The original plan called for unloading BLT 2/3 at the mouth of the Hue River and moving to Hue via the river with flank security on each bank. A specific plan was drawn up to carry out this operation, but was canceled in favor of the plan described in the text."BGen Marc A. Moore, Comments on draft MS, n.d. [Nov76] (Vietnam Comment File).

**Lieutenant Colonel William C. McGraw, Jr. was a veteran of World War II and Korea; in the latter war he had flown 82 combat missions and had earned the Distinguished Flying Cross. In 1962 while serving as a test pilot, he set two world class records in aerial flight in a F-4H Phantom II.

***Colonel Thomas J. O'Connor wrote in November 1976: "The movement of VMFA 531 was impeded somewhat by a last minute question among the major commands involved, as to whether it was appropriate for a combat air unit to deploy directly from a base in Japan to South Vietnam. The delay involved questions of Japan's neutrality in the South Vietnam situation. For this reason, later flights of combat aircraft flew via the Philippines." Col Thomas J. O'Connor, Comments on draft MS, dtd 27Nov76 (Vietnam Comment File).

Marines from the 1st Battalion, 3d Marines hurry to board a waiting helicopter. They will reinforce a reconnaissance patrol south of Da Nang.

visit to Vietnam; he had landed with airlifted Marine elements on 10 March and had remained in Vietnam for 10 days to discuss the possibility of the future deployment of the remainder of the 9th MEB. Now upon his return, Wheeler quickly completed a survey of the areas for which he would be responsible upon the arrival of RLT 3 and BLTs 2/3 and 3/4: the defense of Da Nang Airfield, and the 8th RRU area and airstrip at Phu Bai. He flew to Hue to meet with Brigadier General Nguyen Van Chuan, commanding general of the 1st ARVN Division, to discuss and coordinate Marine activities there. On the 18th, he reorganized his RLT under the 9th MEB structure as the 3d Marines, Reinforced.

While the Da Nang landings presented few problems to the Marines, Hue posed an entirely different situation. On 23 March, a detachment of the 1st Force Reconnaissance Company, under the command of Captain David Whittingham, and a Navy underwater demolition team surveyed landing beaches and movement routes to the Phu Bai area. The intelligence collected indicated that unloading at sea off the coast and then boating up the Hue River (or Song Huong, better known to westerners as the Perfume River) to Hue by landing craft was the most feasible plan. Personnel and equipment could then move south by truck along Route 1 to Phu Bai.

Rear Admiral Wulzen and his staff were not convinced that the Hue River transit was desirable. They believed that there was a lack of detailed information on sandbars, water depth, and most important, VC strength in the area. To overcome the Navy's objection, the 3d MEB commander decided to take a look for himself. General Carl flew to Hue where Brigadier General Chuan provided him with four outboard motor boats. With four ARVN soldiers in both the lead and rear boats, General Carl and his G-3, Lieutenant Colonel Denny, in the second boat, and two American noncommissioned officers in the third, the "armada" set out. They traveled the entire length of the river to the South China Sea and returned to Hue, the trip taking approximately five hours. Although uneventful, the trip provided the desired information. Denny later recalled:

> . . . when the Navy at the next planning meeting brought up the hazards of the Hue River, General Carl said he had personally reconnoitered the river [and] this ended all discussion on the subject and the Navy put the stamp of approval on the landing plans.[25]

On 14 April, BLT 3/4 began landing. The amphibious ships had arrived from Okinawa and anchored in the Da Nang harbor at 0500 that day. Three and one-half hours later, two companies landed across RED Beach 2 and were flown to Phu Bai, where they relieved the task force from the 2d Battalion, 3d Marines that had been positioned there four days earlier. The last elements of the latter battalion departed for Da Nang on the 15th. Colonel King, in the meantime, stationed 10 UH-34Ds at the Phu Bai airstrip to support the 3d Battalion, 4th Marines.

The remainder of the Navy Task Group 76.7 had sailed up the coast to the mouth of the Hue River where the ships anchored late on the evening of the 14th. Before dawn on the 15th, the ships lowered their LCMs and LCVPs; the boats were divided into small groups of four to six craft and the first of these groups departed for Hue, 11 miles inland, at 0640. As the craft approached the landing site in the city, they turned, beached, and lowered their front ramps together. The Marines in full combat gear stepped ashore to be met by an ARVN band and 500 cheering Vietnamese holding aloft a large banner reading "Welcome, U. S. Marines." Dressed in summer white uniforms, the sailors of the Navy beach group supporting the operation also were on hand to greet the Marines. The troops piled into trucks and proceeded south through the city to the base at Phu Bai. The river operation was completed on 19 April. The Navy landing craft made 263 trips, carried 1,371 tons of cargo, and traveled 6,000 miles.

Two other Marine units arrived at Da Nang during April. Lieutenant Colonel Paul L. Hitchcock's MASS-2 debarked during the morning of 16 April. The squadron proceeded to the airfield, where it was assigned to a living area with the LAAM battalion elements west of the runway. The MASS-2 troops immediately began erecting facilities for a direct air support center (DASC) and an air support radar team (ASRT) site.*

The last Marine unit to arrive in Vietnam during the month was Marine Composite Reconnaissance Squadron (VMCJ) 1, less detachments, with six Douglas EF-10B (F3D-2Q) Skynight jets. Lieutenant

---

*DASC provides the tactical air control system required for control and direction of close air support and other tactical air support operations; it is normally collocated with fire support coordination elements. An ASRT is a subordinate operational component of the DASC. These teams vector aircraft to targets and provide ground-controlled precision flight path guidance and weapons release at night and during periods of low ceiling and reduced visibility.

Colonel Otis W. Corman, commander of the unit, led the squadron onto the Da Nang Airfield on 17 April. This squadron, previously based in Japan, was not new to air operations in Southeast Asia. Since 1964, it had provided the Navy and Air Force with electronic countermeasure support. Although administratively assigned to MAG-16 upon arrival, the unit's activities were directed by the U.S. Air Force 2d Air Division. According to Lieutenant Colonel Corman, the directive which placed VMCJ-1 under the operational control of MACV authorized U.S. Navy Forces to use:

> . . . Marine air in accordance with their normal and established practices. . . . It directed MACV to coordinate U.S. Navy and U.S. Air Force requirements for Marine air EW [electronic warfare] support. This coordination was accomplished by designating 2d Air Div as his coordinating authority.[26]

With the arrival of two fixed-wing squadrons, two infantry battalions, and support elements, the MEB reached a strength of 8,878 by the end of April. The brigade now consisted of a four-battalion regiment and a four-squadron Marine aircraft group, as well as artillery and engineer groups and a logistic support group. General Karch was satisfied that he could handle anything that the enemy could throw at him.[27]

An Expanded Mission

As significant as the arrival of reinforcements was the Presidential decision to lift the restrictions on the Marine infantry battalions and permit them to engage in counterinsurgency operations. On 14 April, General Westmoreland provided the MEB with a concept of operations which he divided into four phases: establishment of defensive bases; deep reconnaissance patrols of the enemy's avenues of approach; offensive action as a reaction force in coordination with the Vietnamese; and finally, "undertake in coordination with RVN I Corps, an intensifying program of offensive operations to fix and destroy the VC in the general Da Nang area."[28]

General Karch immediately attempted to implement his new orders. He met with General Thi the same day to negotiate for the realignment of the Marine TAOR in the Da Nang area. After two days of talks, they agreed to a four square mile increase in the Marine area of responsibility, but this still did not include the terrain just south of the airbase. The number of villages in the Da Nang sector under

Marine control increased from one to three, and hamlets from three to 15, with a total population of 11,441.

General Krulak was present at the discussion. He recalled that:

> Thi was opposed to any patrol or offensive action on our part outside the airfield perimeter. With respect to the area south of the field and on the bank of the Da Nang River, he said, "This is enemy country. You are not ready to operate there."[29]

Marine operations in the Phu Bai area were also the subject of discussion with Vietnamese authorities. Colonel Wheeler and Lieutenant Colonel Jones held several informal conferences at Hue and Phu Bai with Brigadier General Chuan, the commanding general of the 1st ARVN Division and the Phu Bai Special Sector, concerning the assignment of the Marines and their mission. It was decided that the Vietnamese would be responsible for the defense of the villages bordering the base on the north and east. Within the Marine sector, the 3d Battalion, 4th Marines would conduct defensive operations "with emphasis on quick reaction offensive moves" within the TAOR.[30] The Marines and South Vietnamese troops of the Phu Bai (Dong Da) Special Sector would establish a combined operations center for the coordination of efforts. Check points along Route 1 in the Marine TAOR were to be manned by ARVN personnel and supported by the Marine battalion.

On 20 April, the Marines began patrol activities beyond their TAORs at Da Nang and Phu Bai, as far as six miles in front of their former positions. These patrols included ARVN troops and Vietnamese civil affairs officers to avoid incidents with Vietnamese villagers. The extended patrolling resulted in the Marines' first fire fights with the VC. On the 22d, a patrol from Company D, 3d Reconnaissance Battalion accompanied by 38 South Vietnamese troops, encountered a Viet Cong force of approximately 105 men near the village of Binh Thai, nine miles southwest of Da Nang. A company from Lieutenant Colonel Bain's battalion was helilifted into the area to reinforce the reconnaissance unit. They pursued the enemy to the south and west, but lost contact and returned to the battalion area. The results of this first engagement were one Viet Cong killed and one Marine slightly wounded. A second engagement occurred two days later when a Marine reconnaissance platoon was attacked on a hilltop 2,000 meters south of Phu Bai by an undetermined number

USMC Photo A184031

Lieutenant Colonel Herbert J. Bain, Commanding Officer, 1st Battalion, 3d Marines (center left), confers with his operations officer, Captain Gaetano F. Squillace (right), and his forward air controller Captain John W. Garriott, in a VC-dominated hamlet south of Da Nang. The arch under which they are standing was built by the Viet Cong.

of enemy. Two Viet Cong and two Marines were killed.

Very little was known about the enemy. A Marine staff officer commented, "intelligence of what the situation was, was non-existent."[31] This of course was an exaggeration; the MEB and MACV staffs had some idea of enemy forces in the area. They credited the VC with seven combat units totaling 560 troops within 25 miles of Da Nang; within 50 miles, 14 enemy combat units, ranging from company to regimental size, with a total of 1,480 personnel. What was lacking was knowledge of the day-to-day movements of the Communist forces, their disposition, and their influence upon the people.

General Karch remarked that, from the day of the landing, reports indicated a continuing enemy buildup in the area. Most of this intelligence had been attained from hired agents who were paid ac-

Marine amphibian tractors move across Route 1 after landing at Chu Lai.

cording to the significance of their information. Their veracity was highly doubtful at best.

Even with the expansion of the Marine mission, contact with enemy forces remained slight. General Karch noted:

> . . . when we had reached the limit of our Phase II TAOR we still had encountered no VC in strength other than undersized platoons . . . . After a few sniper shots were fired at the patrol and [the Marines] moved out to attack, the VC disappeared. Also the only attack . . . at Phu Bai could well have been a mistake . . . or a chance encounter . . . it was broken off immediately after the first exchange of fire.[32]

The Marines had accomplished their basic mission, the defense of the Da Nang and Phu Bai bases, but as General Wallace M. Greene, Jr., the Commandant of the Marine Corps, observed during a visit to the MEB: ''You don't defend a place by sitting on your ditty box.''[33]

Chu Lai

By the end of April, the days of the 9th MEB in Vietnam were numbered. Throughout the month, the question of American participation in the war preoccupied those in authority. On 20 April, a high-level conference convened at CinCPac headquarters in Honolulu attended by Secretary of Defense Robert S. McNamara, his Assistant Secretary of International Security Affairs, John McNaughton, Ambassador Taylor, Generals Wheeler and Westmoreland, and Admiral Sharp. The conferees reached a consensus that the relatively light Viet Cong activity was the lull before the storm and recommended the additional deployment of 42,000 U.S. servicemen to Vietnam, including 5,000 more Marines. These Marine forces, organized into three reinforced battalions and three jet aircraft squadrons, were to establish another enclave at Chu Lai, 57 miles southeast of Da Nang.[34]

The Chu Lai coastal plain lies astride the boundary dividing the two southern provinces of I CTZ, Quang Ngai and Quang Tin. A few miles inland and west of the plain are the heavily jungled and extremely rugged Annamite Mountains. Route 1, an all-weather, macadam road, parallels the sea, bisecting the plain. This national highway, stretching from Saigon to the DMZ, connects the area with Da Nang to the northwest and Quang Ngai City, 20 miles to the south.

The selection of Chu Lai as the base for the next increment of Marine forces resulted from an extended Pentagon debate which lasted over several months concerning the building of an expeditionary airfield south of Da Nang. The proposal for the construction of the expeditionary field originated with General Krulak. Krulak had selected the Chu Lai site on an inspection tour the previous year and gave the future base its name. According to the FMFPac commander, a naval officer accompanying him on the trip remarked that the place looked good, but was not marked on the maps. Krulak replied that the name was ''Chu Lai'' but later explained: ''In order to settle the matter immediately, I had simply given him the Mandarin Chinese characters for my name.''[35] In any event, Krulak suggested that the Chu Lai airfield be built according to a Marine Corps concept still in its early stages which employed metal runways and taxistrips. The program, called short airfield for tactical support (SATS), had been developed to meet Marine Corps requirements for the rapid construction of short expeditionary airfields, in effect shore-based carrier decks. Although the proposed field at Chu Lai would not qualify as ''short,'' it would make use of SATS components including catapults and arresting gear.*

On 30 March 1965, Secretary McNamara tentatively approved the building of the SATS field at Chu Lai but the final decision, according to General Krulak, was not made until late April after the high-level Honolulu Conference. At this conference, representatives from the U. S. Pacific Air Forces command had made a presentation stating that it would take about 11 months to build a concrete airfield. General Krulak then described the SATS concept after which, Krulak remembered:

> [Secretary of Defense] McNamara, in his characteristic bottom line manner, said ''how long?'' I hesitated for a moment and then said, ''25 days.'' Keith McCutcheon had to live with my estimate.[36]

---

*According to Lieutenant Colonel Charles L. Goode, who was the 1st MAW engineering officer: ''The concept of a short Airfield for Tactical Support (SATS) is for a runway 2,000 to 3,000 feet long by 72 feet wide, with a parallel taxiway and the necessary parking space for aircraft. It was envisioned that the Chu Lai field would be required to be in operation for a longer period of time, and would be required to support many more aircraft; therefore, the design was made accordingly. The final design specified a runway 8,000 feet long by 102 feet wide. Obviously this could no longer be termed a Short Airfield for Tactical Support. It was sometimes facetiously referred to as a LATS—a Long Airfield for Tactical Support.'' LtCol Charles L. Goode, Comments on draft MS, dtd 7Oct76 (Vietnam Comment File).

After the McNamara decision of 30 March, Major General Paul J. Fontana, the commander of the 1st Marine Aircraft Wing in Japan, briefed his senior officers about the proposed Chu Lai airfield. He selected the MAG-12 S-1, Major Frank P. Costello, Jr., who had worked with SATS since its inception at Quantico, to be the wing project officer.

On 3 April, Major Costello accompanied General Carl, members of his staff, and the 1st MAW engineering officer, Lieutenant Colonel Charles L. Goode, on a reconnaissance of the Chu Lai site. While making their inspection, the Carl party happened upon some markers apparently placed there by a civilian airfield survey team. According to Lieutenant Colonel Denny, Carl's operation officer:

> I recall that we . . . were to meet a civilian survey party on the beach at Chu Lai. They didn't show. General Carl found some markers . . . and then because we ''had to get on with it'' stepped off the SATS field . . . .[37]

Lieutenant Colonel Goode remembered that the Carl party remained on the site for only two hours and, ''From this very brief reconnaissance and from the available maps and photographs of the area, the location of the runway and supporting facilities was determined and detailed planning commenced.''[38]

After completing the reconnaissance, General Carl reported to General Westmoreland in Saigon and mentioned the survey markers found at Chu Lai. The MACV Commander replied that he did not know the specifics of the civilian survey and suggested that the selection of the exact location for both the SATS field and a later permanent airfield would require further study.

Lieutenant Colonel Goode and Major Costello returned to Japan where they developed the plans for the operating areas of the airbase. It was determined that approximately 1,400,000 square feet of aluminum matting would be required for the runway, taxiways, and supporting areas.** The end results would be an airfield with an 8,000 by 102 foot runway, a 7,916 by 36 foot parallel taxiway, four 300 by 36 foot cross taxiways, and parking and maintenance facilities for three tactical squadrons.

On 25 April, President Johnson approved the recommendation of the Honolulu Conference to land Marines at Chu Lai for the construction of the airfield

---

**The 1,400,000 square feet of matting was every plank the Marine Corps had in the Far East. LtCol Frank P. Costello, Jr., Comments on Shulimson, ''U.S. Marines in Vietnam, pt 2,'' dtd 17Feb70 (Vietnam Comment File).

and the establishment of a third Marine enclave in Vietnam. Three days later, the Marine Corps reactivated General Carl's 3d MEB for the second time within three weeks, its headquarters having returned to Okinawa after completing the RLT 3 and BLTs 2/3 and 3/4 deployments. Colonel O'Connor, the 1st MAW chief of staff, recalled that General Carl at first wanted to employ the former 1st Brigade intact, including both the 4th Marines and MAG-13, for the Chu Lai landings. Carl and Colonel Ralph H. ''Smoke'' Spanjer, the MAG-13 commander, attempted to convince General Fontana, the wing commander, to include MAG-13 as part of the Chu Lai forces. According to O'Connor:

> General Fontana listened patiently to the first presentation, but then informed them that, in view of the considerable planning that had taken place before their arrival, MAG-12 at Iwakuni was the group that would deploy. General Carl and Col Spanjer made at least two appeals of this decision . . . Col Spanjer brought in many visual aids explaining his concept of operation of a SATS field at Chu Lai. General Fontana finally tired of the pressure, and told Spanjer very firmly that MAG-12 was in and MAG-13 was out![39] *

With this decision made, on 29 April General Carl and his staff flew from Okinawa to the Philippines to join Admiral Wulzen on board the amphibious flagship USS *Estes* (AGC 12). The 3d MEB landing forces for Chu Lai were to consist of Colonel Edward P. Dupras, Jr.'s RLT 4 headquarters, two BLTs, BLT 1/4 commanded by Lieutenant Colonel Harold D. Fredericks and BLT 2/4 commanded by Lieutenant Colonel Joseph R. ''Bull'' Fisher, and Lieutenant Colonel Don H. Blanchard's 3d Reconnaissance Battalion. Lieutenant Colonel Alexander Wilson's MABS-12 and Commander John M. Bannister's Naval Mobile Construction Battalion (NMCB) 10 were attached to the MEB for the construction of the airfield. The rest of MAG-12 would arrive after the SATS field was completed.

When General Carl and his staff arrived on board the *Estes*, the MEB commander delegated planning

---

*A former member of MAG-13, Major Gary W. Parker, then a young lieutenant with HMM-161, recalled ''Colonel Spanjer in his attempts to persuade the higher echelons of the merits of MAG-13 had a calling card made up which was distributed throughout the wing. In the upper left hand corner it read-'Have MAG-Will Travel.' at the bottom right hand corner it said-'Wire Smoke-Futema.''' Maj Gary W. Parker, Comments on draft MS, dtd 14Jan77 (Vietnam Comment File).

for the landing to his chief of staff, Colonel Norman R. Nickerson. According to Nickerson, General Carl told him ''to run the show and to report to him daily the progress of planning for the Chu Lai operation.'' Colonel Nickerson stated that despite the fact that time was short and the staff was small, and composed of ''officers that he had not previously known, the Chu Lai Operation Plan/Order was completed on schedule.''[40]

The initial planning concept for the MEB was based on an opposed landing. According to the intelligence available to the planners, the VC operated in strength throughout the Chu Lai area, with approximately 500 Viet Cong living in the local villages and hamlets. The sector included a Communist resupply route from the sea to the VC Do Xa base area, 50 miles to the west. It was estimated that the enemy could mass 2,000 troops in 24 hours and could reinforce with another 2,000 men within 72 hours.

The plan called for RLT 4 to land BLTs 2/4 and 1/4, minus two companies, across the beach; two BLT 1/4 companies would make a helicopter assault of an area inland from the beach. The 3d Reconnaissance Battalion was to follow the two assault battalions across the beach. The planners scheduled a traditional prelanding air and naval bombardment to isolate the beach area. They also planned that the 2d ARVN Division would secure the outer perimeter for an extended period of time.

General Westmoreland was dubious about the landing concept. He believed that two infantry battalions, even if reinforced by a reconnaissance battalion, were an inadequate force to guarantee the permanent defense of Chu Lai. The MACV commander was of the opinion that the 2d ARVN Division, because of its other responsibilities, could not provide adequate perimeter defense for more than a few days. He strongly urged that an additional Marine infantry battalion be added to the Marine brigade. On the other hand, Westmoreland considered the possibility of the enemy opposing the landing to be extremely remote and recommended that the naval and air bombardment be eliminated, although the ships and planes should remain on station. He declared that elements of the 2d ARVN Division would secure the landing site.

General Westmoreland radioed General Collins requesting a meeting in Saigon to iron out the differences. On 30 April, Generals Collins and Fontana departed for Saigon, stopping off at Subic Bay to

South Vietnamese troops secure the Chu Lai area. Their U.S. Army advisors have made a sign to greet the Marines.

confer with General Carl and Admiral Wulzen, the task force commander. General Throckmorton, Deputy ComUSMACV, chaired the conference held in Saigon on 1 and 2 May. He declared that there were three assumptions that everyone present had to accept: the landing would be unopposed; the area at Chu Lai would have been cleared; and that there would be some civilians in the general area of the landing. An agreement among all the participants was finally reached. A third battalion, BLT 3/3, was added to the 3d MEB to be brought ashore after the initial landing was completed. The prelanding air strikes and naval shore bombardment were changed to planned on-call missions to be used only if the enemy opposed the landing. Marine Aircraft Group 16 would provide limited fixed-wing and helicopter support; Navy Task Force 77 aircraft would fly cover for the Marines; and the U.S. 2d Air Division would be available for additional support. The conferrees agreed to postpone the landing until 7 May to allow for further coordination with the Vietnamese authorities.[41]

After the Saigon meeting was over, Generals Collins and Fontana departed for Da Nang. Colonel

Hardy Hay, the 3d Marine Division operations officer, recalled:

> The coverage given the Saigon meeting for the Chu Lai landings was really the major springboard for General Collins and I to remain in Da Nang . . . Up to this point we had, since leaving Okinawa, sort of ignored sending movement reports.[42]

From another vantage point, Colonel O'Connor, the 1st MAW chief of staff, remembered:

> I was aware of the very poor high level command communications. Reports of enemy activity in the Chu Lai area had generated a strong inclination on the part of the sea-based forces to make a conventional preparation of the objective area, in anticipation of an opposed landing.

O'Connor remarked further:

> The air was full of messages about enemy capabilities, friendly plans, and schedules of coordinating meetings at Saigon, Okinawa, Subic Bay and Da Nang. Finally, it was apparent that message traffic was completely out of phase with reality, and the two-day postponement of the landing was invoked to prevent the disaster of an amphibious task force firing on friendly forces in the objective area.[43]

On 3 May, the *Estes* rendezvoused with the rest of the amphibious task force off the coast of South Vietnam and then proceeded to the vicinity of Da Nang where Admiral Wulzen and General Carl met with General Collins to discuss the landing. At the end of these talks, the commander set H-Hour for the amphibious portion of the operation at 0800, 7 May.

Units from the ARVN 2d Division which had secured the Chu Lai area were joined on 6 May by Company K, 3d Battalion, 9th Marines from Da Nang to provide additional beach security. All was ready and the U.S. Army advisors with the ARVN had even prepared their own sign to greet the landing force, ''Ahoy Marines: Welcome Aboard, Area Secured.'' Colonel Edward Cook, who at the time was General Collins' G-2, in 1976 wrote:

> Prior to the landing, I was at General Lam's [Brigadier General Hoang Xuan Lam] headquarters for his briefing on the coordination required between units from his ARVN 2d Division and the Landing Force. I asked him to show me specifically where his units would be and how they would phase their withdrawal as our landing force advanced. He called for a piece of overlay paper, put it over a map and drew a series of phase lines. When he was completed with the clear, concise, and explicit overlay, he gave it to me and said, ''Just like they do it at Quantico.''[44]

Early on the morning of the 7th, the ships of the task force arrived at the transport area off Chu Lai. As planned, at 0800, BLT 1/4 Companies C and D and BLT 2/4 began landing over RED Beach. After crossing the beach, the two companies of the 1st Battalion moved to Landing Zone ROBIN, approximately three miles from the waterline and overlooking Route 1. They quickly secured the LZ and then the helicopters of HMM-161, Lieutenant Colonel Gene W. Morrison commanding, flew in the battalion's remaining two companies from the USS *Princeton*.* The troops met no resistance and occupied their planned objectives. The only casualties were four Marines suffering from the heat and humidity. The scene on the beach was reminiscent of the previous landings the Marines had made in Vietnam. In addition to the usual number of Vietnamese flower maidens and members of the press

---

* HMM-161 supported the RLT-4 landing from the *Princeton* until 7 May. On that day, the Navy changed amphibious assault ships (LPHs), substituting the *Iwo Jima* (LPH-2) for the *Princeton*. Morrison's squadron moved to the *Iwo Jima* which remained positioned off the Chu Lai coast until 12 June. During that period, the squadron provided helicopter support for Colonel Dupras' Marines. On 13 June, the ship moved to a position off the coast from Phu Bai where the squadron unloaded, moved to the Phu Bai airstrip, was placed under the operational control of MAG-16, and began to fly in support of the 3d Battalion, 4th Marines.

Navy Photo 1111513

Troops from the 4th Marines move inland across the soft Chu Lai sand under a welcoming Vietnamese banner. Marine helicopters are seen flying overhead.

corps, Generals Thi, Throckmorton, and Collins were on hand to greet the first waves of troops. The Marines were too busy to pay much attention to the festivities.

By the end of the first day, Colonel Dupras had established his headquarters ashore; his infantry battalions and supporting arms were all in place. The 4th Marines' defensive perimeter extended in an irregular arc from the Ky Ha Peninsula in the north, to the high ground in the west, and from there seaward to a point three miles south of RED Beach. The southern flank was screened by the 3d Reconnaissance Battalion.

The landing of troops and establishment of the defensive lines proved to be the easiest part of the entire operation. The movement of supplies across the beach was a frustrating experience. General Krulak described the Chu Lai Beach area ''as great a challenge as any foreshore that I have ever seen. The sand is of powdered sugar consistency and no wheeled vehicle can negotiate it with success.''[45] Although reducing tire pressure provided some traction, a shortage of beach matting and the fine sand forced the Marines to use tracked vehicles to move material inland. Colonel William M. Graham, Jr., at the time the 3d Marine Division engineering officer, related that a:

> . . . civilian soil consultant was hired to sample the sand

Brigadier General Karch (center, 1st row) poses with members of his 9th MEB staff at Da Nang. The 9th MEB was shortly afterwards deactivated and replaced by the newly formed III MAF.

in the area and report its physical properties so a decision could be made whether to put rubber tired or tracked equipment in the area. The report indicated rubber tired equipment, therefore the "Snafu." I never did find out whether they gave a wrong analysis or took the samples from the wrong site. [46]*

A temporary impasse occurred on 9 May when the attempt was made to unload the airfield matting. The

_____

*Colonel Graham was of the opinion that the markers that the Carl party found during their 3 April reconnaissance of Chu Lai may have been left by the civilian soil party, but General Wallace M. Greene, Jr., suggested that the markers may have been placed there during a reconnaissance of the beach area by the Marine 1st Force Reconnaissance Company. Col William M. Graham, Jr., Comments on draft MS, dtd 18Nov76 (Vietnam Comment File); Gen Wallace M. Greene, Jr., Comments on draft MS, dtd 1Aug77 (Vietnam Comment File). See Chapter 11, Reconnaissance Section, for an account of the 1st Force Reconnaissance Company's beach surveys of the Chu Lai area.

first lift, 68 tons, was placed on flatbed trailers and brought ashore by an LCU. The entire unloading came to a complete standstill; the heavily laden trucks could not move in the deep sand without assistance. The movement of the matting to the airfield site took five and a half hours. To try to expedite the process, the Navy beach group decided to break up the causeway installed on the south end of the beach and use the floating sections as makeshift barges. Approximately 200 bundles of matting could be loaded on one "barge" which could then be floated to a point directly opposite the proposed airfield site, thereby reducing the movement distance. Although this eased the situation, the problem of movement on the beach remained. Finally, on 10 May, the 3d Marine Division provided an additional 2,500 feet of badly needed beach matting which somewhat alleviated the situation.

At noon on 12 May, the amphibious operation

officially came to an end. On this date, the first elements of BLT 3/3, arriving in amphibious shipping from Okinawa, assumed defensive positions on the southern flank, relieving the 3d Reconnaissance Battalion. During the five-day period, 7-12 May, more than 10,925 tons of equipment and supplies had been unloaded and moved across the beach.

With the completion of the Chu Lai amphibious landing, seven of the nine infantry battalions of the 3d Marine Division, supported by most of the 12th Marines, the artillery regiment of the division, and a large portion of the 1st MAW were in South Vietnam. As a result, the 9th MEB was deactivated and replaced by a new Marine organization, the III Marine Amphibious Force (III MAF).*

---

* In the Pacific, one other change in designation of Marine units occurred during May. On the 25th, the 1st Marine Brigade (Rear) at Hawaii consisting of the brigade support elements under the command of Colonel Jack E. Hanthorn was redesignated the 1st Marine Brigade. Colonel Hanthorn relieved General Carl as brigade commander.

CHAPTER 3

Formation and Development of III MAF

The Birth of III MAF—The Le My Experiment—Building the Chu Lai Airfield—III MAF in Transition—The Seeds of Pacification—June Operations in the Three Enclaves

The Birth of III MAF

The birth of III Marine Amphibious Force occurred almost simultaneously with the landing at Chu Lai. On 5 May, the Joint Chiefs relayed Presidential approval for the deployment to Da Nang of a Marine "force/division/wing headquarters to include CG 3d Marine Division and 1st Marine Aircraft Wing."[1] The following day, Major General Collins, who had remained in Vietnam after the Saigon meeting earlier in the month, assumed command of the Naval Component Command and also established the headquarters of the III Marine Expeditionary Force and the 3d Marine Division in Vietnam. The former 9th MEB commander, Brigadier General Karch, resumed his duties as assistant division commander and left for Okinawa to take over the units of the division remaining there. Brigadier General Carl became Deputy Commander, III MAF after the Chu Lai landing.

The III Marine Expeditionary Force became the III Marine Amphibious Force on 7 May. General Westmoreland had recommended to the Joint Chiefs that the Marines select a different designation for their command because the term "Expeditionary" had unpleasant connotations for the Vietnamese, stemming from the days of the French Expeditionary Corps. The Joint Chiefs of Staff asked the Commandant, General Greene, to come up with another name. Although a III Marine Amphibious Corps had existed in the Pacific Theater during World War II, and was a logical choice for the name of the new Marine organization in Vietnam, several of the Commandant's advisors believed that the Vietnamese might take exception to the word "Corps." Consequently, General Greene chose the title III Marine Amphibious Force (III MAF) for the Marine forces in Vietnam and extended this revision to the Marine brigades.[2]

One other major headquarters arrived at Da Nang during this period. On 11 May, Major General Fontana established a forward headquarters of the 1st Marine Aircraft Wing in Vietnam (1st MAW Advance). Four days later, his Da Nang headquarters assumed command of all Marine aviation in the country. The Marine division/wing team was in Vietnam.

The expanded Marine force operated under guidelines provided by General Westmoreland. In his letter of instruction to General Collins, the MACV commander outlined the general mission of the Marines. They were directed to coordinate the defense of their three bases with General Thi; to render combat support to the South Vietnamese; to maintain the capability of conducting deep patrolling, offensive operations, and reserve reaction missions; and, finally, to carry out any contingency plans as directed by ComUSMACV.[3]

The U.S. relationship with the Vietnamese military was a sensitive one. Since the Americans were the guests of the Vietnamese, they could offer advice to their allies, but could not compel action. Means had to be devised so that the two military forces could cooperate, but remain independent entities.

General Westmoreland elaborated further on this relationship between the U.S. and South Vietnamese commands in a message to Admiral Sharp. According to the MACV commander the requirement was for cooperation and agreement among senior commanders of different nationality groups. One of General Westmoreland's more intriguing phrases was that of "tactical direction." In actuality it was identical to operational control, but the general explained that tactical direction was a more palatable term to the Vietnamese. Westmoreland warned: "U.S. commanders at all levels must accommodate to a new environment in which responsibility is shared and cooperatively discharged without benefit of traditional command relationship.'' He emphasized that simple and easily understood plans were a prerequisite for success.[4]

Taking these assumptions into consideration, General Westmoreland observed that American operations would take place in three successive stages: base security, deep patrolling, and finally search and destroy missions.[5] For the Marines in Vietnam at this time base security was of the utmost concern; only at Da Nang had III MAF begun to move into the second stage of operations.

The Le My Experiment

At Da Nang, the most significant development was the beginning of a rudimentary pacification program involving Lieutenant Colonel David A. Clement's 2d Battalion, 3d Marines. Since its arrival

in April, the battalion had been on the high ground in the northwest fringe of the Da Nang TAOR, overlooking the village complex of Le My. The village consisted of a cluster of hamlets located on the southern bank of the Cu De River in the Hoa Vang District of Quang Nam Province, eight miles northwest of the Da Nang Airfield. According to the district chief, there had been little security in this area for over a year. Although the ARVN had conducted several operations, their forces had never remained to root out the Viet Cong political cadre and to provide security for the people.[6] Security was one thing the Marines could furnish. Lieutenant Colonel Clement explained that the occupation of Le My gave him the needed depth of defense around the Da Nang Airbase to carry out his mission.[7]

Beginning on 4 May, the Marines maintained pressure on the VC in the village complex by repeated patrolling of the area. On the 8th, Lieutenant Colonel Clement, accompanied by his S-

USMC Photo A184123

In one of the first extensions of Marine positions into a populated area in May, Marines from the 2d Battalion, 3d Marines move into the hamlet of Le My. Three villagers watch the troops enter the village gate.

USMC Photo A184166

The Marines round up VC suspects in Le My. A South Vietnam Popular Force soldier is in the foreground.

2, Captain Lionel V. Silva, the district chief, Captain Nguyen Hoa, and the battalion's S-2 scouts, visited the hamlets. They surveyed the neighborhood, talked to the villagers, but then came under Viet Cong fire, which killed one of the scouts. This incident confirmed Clement's opinion that in order to secure Le My, he first had to clear it.

On 11 May, the Marine battalion returned in strength. In an opposed fire fight, Clement's Company E "conducted the assault . . . and cleared the hamlets."[8] This time the battalion stayed and took up defensive positions in Le My. The Marines rounded up the male villagers who were put to work destroying punji traps, filling in trenches, and dismantling bunkers. Fifty of the men were sent to Da Nang for further questioning. Three days later, Vietnamese regional and popular forces relieved the Marines in the hamlets and the battalion moved to positions around the village. The actual eradication

of the guerrillas was left to the South Vietnamese, while the Marines saturated the area with patrols and established ambushes to prevent the enemy from moving or massing forces.

To provide the villagers the means of fending for themselves, Clement's battalion trained the Vietnamese local forces, helped to prepare the defenses, and set up medical aid stations. The Marines emphasized self-help projects such as the building of schools and market places so that the local populace could continue on their own. Captain Silva, who was also Clement's civil affairs officer, stated that the battalion's goal was "to create an administration, supported by the people, and capable of leading, treating, feeding, and protecting themselves by the time the battalion was moved to another area of operations."[9]

The Marines also assisted the villagers in rebuilding two bridges, which, according to the battalion's operations officer, Major Marc A. Moore, symbolized the spanning of the "broken link in the road which separated territory previously controlled by the VC from the RVN controlled villages immediately south of Le My."[10] Apparently well aware of this symbolism, a VC main force unit attacked one of the bridges on the night of 20 May. According to Lieutenant Colonel Clement, both the VC and the local population discovered the effectiveness of U.S security: "The attack was repulsed, the bridge unharmed, and four VC were killed and abandoned."[11]

The village held a dedication ceremony the next day at the two newly built bridges. Local government officials made speeches and cut a ribbon strung across the two spans. The festivities also presented grim reminders of the war; the chief displayed the bodies of the VC killed in the attack on the bridges at the gates of the village. This technique had been employed by both the government forces and the Communists to impress on the people what awaited the enemy.

At this early stage of the Marine intervention, the Le My experiment held promise for the future. General Collins stated that the "Le My operation may well be the pattern for the employment of Marine Corps forces in this area."[12] On a visit to III MAF in mid-May, General Krulak described the pacification efforts in Le My as a:

> . . . beginning, but a good beginning. The people are beginning to get the idea that U.S. generated security is a long term affair. This is just one opportunity among many . . . it is the expanding oil spot concept in action.[13]

Building the Chu Lai Airfield

At Chu Lai, the main effort in May was the building of the airfield. On 7 May, Lieutenant Colonel Charles L. Goode, the 1st MAW engineering officer, Lieutenant Colonel Alexander Wilson, the commanding officer of MABS-12, and a small advance party from the MABS arrived at Da Nang from Iwakuni. While at Da Nang, they discussed the Chu Lai airfield problem with Colonel Graham, the III MAF/3d Marine Division engineering officer. According to Goode, he brought Graham "up to date on the runway layout and location as I knew it, including the fact that . . . [the civilian contractor] had not yet provided the coordinates of the runway."[14]

The following morning, Lieutenant Colonel Goode

USMC Photo 185766

A South Vietnamese official stands in front of a bridge at Le My rebuilt by Marines. The VC had destroyed the old bridge.

and the MABS-12 advance party flew to Chu Lai. There they conferred with Commander Bannister, the NMCB-10 commander, and several members of his staff concerning the initial phases of the airfield construction. Commander Bannister informed Lieutenant Colonels Goode and Wilson that he had received a message from Saigon that listed the coordinates for the runway. The two Marines, with Bannister and his operations officer, then toured the area of the proposed location for the SATS field. According to Goode, "the site was completely unacceptable." It was several hundred yards west of the original site selected by General Carl during the reconnaissance of Chu Lai in April. Goode related:

> . . . the line being surveyed at the time was on the west edge of the natural drainage course, which would have placed the cross taxiways, parallel taxiway and the entire operations area in the center of the drainage course. From the signs of water in the area, it was obvious that most of this area would be inundated during the rainy season.[15]

Commander Bannister agreed with Lieutenant Colonel Goode's observations, but stated that he was only following his instructions. The Seabee commander also told Goode that the message from Saigon indicated that a representative of the civilian construction firm would ''be on hand to advise on the specific locations to avoid interference with work on, and operations from, the permanent runway,'' which the civilian firm was to construct. This representative never showed up.[16]

To avoid further delays and to settle the question of the location of the SATS field once and for all, Lieutenant Colonel Goode attempted to contact General Carl on board the *Estes*, only to learn that the general had come ashore. Goode finally located General Carl at the 2d Battalion, 4th Marines CP. With Carl and members of the 3d MAB staff, Commander Bannister and Lieutenant Colonels Goode and Wilson returned to the proposed runway site. According to Carl's Chief of Staff, Colonel Nickerson, ''It was spontaneously determined by all that the intended location was not correct . . . .''[17] General Carl directed that a resurvey be made on the basis of the recommendations that he and the original survey group had made in April. The original site was on a plateau, just inland from a tree line and above the flood waterline, paralleling the sandy berm north of the landing beach. Only a shift of 500 yards

USMC Photo

Seabees lay down aluminum for the SATS field. Two full crews were required for each 12-hour work shift to relieve each other at 30-minute intervals because of the heat and humidity.

USMC Photo A184233

Navy Seabees with their heavy equipment prepare to start on the building of the Chu Lai SATS field. The area to the right will be leveled for the emplacement of the aluminum matting of the runway.

to the north was necessary to avoid a low area just south of the mid-point of the runway. According to Goode, ''This caused no inconvenience because it was just moved to a point that was to be graded for the overrun in any event.''[18]

Following the selection of the SATS site, Lieutenant Colonel Wilson's MABS-12 Marines and Commander Bannister's Seabee construction crews launched an intense struggle against time and nature. The initial planning envisioned an operational airfield by 28 May, 21 days after the landing. The Marines had relocated the 400 civilians who lived on or near the airfield site so that the construction could begin. Heat and humidity quickly sapped the strength of the work crews. Temperatures often climbed over the 100 degree mark and the humidity was not much less. The heavy earth moving equipment could be operated only by alternating crews every 30 minutes. During each 12-hour work shift, at least two full crews were necessary for each piece of machinery, but the work continued on a 24-hour basis.

Sand played havoc with the operation. It worked its way into everything; bearings, brake linings, and clutches were quickly ruined. At times more than half of the tractors and dump trucks were deadlined. Some of the frustrations encountered by the work crews were reflected in an informal log maintained by Lieutenant Colonel Goode:

> 9 May . . . My general impression of the entire day was that there was much wheel spinning, disorganization, and little work accomplished, all compounded by the fact that three of the C.B. TD-24 tractors went out of com-

mission—one because of a front PCV clutch and two for master clutches.

10 May . . . MCB-10 has provided MAG-12 (Adv.) with all the necessities. They even provided one jeep which broke down this afternoon . . . . Because of the continued shortage of tractors, TD-24s, I intend to ask C.O. 3/12 tomorrow if he can provide some to help.

11 May . . . Earth moving on the runway is going slowly. Three of the 6 C.B. TD-24's are deadlined. Two are for main clutches, none of which are available.[19]

Eventually, the 3d Engineer Battalion at Da Nang contributed nearly all of its equipment to the Chu Lai construction, leaving the Marine engineers with only one bulldozer for their own use.

As the equipment situation gradually improved, the major problem for the contruction crews was that of soil stabilization. Initially, it was planned to mix sand and asphalt in order to form a firm base on which to lay the aluminum matting. On 14 May, Lieutenant Colonel Goode wrote: "My biggest concern is the stabilization process. Will the rollers be capable of moving across the asphalt-treated surface? What will be the curing time?" On the 14th, Goode scheduled a test on the asphalt sand mixture in an area adjacent to the MABS command post so that the test site could be used as a helicopter pad after the test. On 15 May, Goode reported: "The test of the asphalt failed completely. Asphalt was shot from a distributor onto the dry sand. There was practically no penetration. Twenty-four hours after the asphalt . . . was put down, it is still not cured." After consulting with Colonel Graham, Lieutenant Colonel Goode decided that the solution for the problem was to stabilize the sand with a six-inch layer of laterite, a red ferrous soil obtained from pits north of the field.[20]

On 16 May, the first piece of runway matting was laid on the north end of the strip. Hauling the red soil was time consuming and it was soon obvious that the runway would not be completed on the scheduled date. The Seabees and Marines were still confident that they could build a usable field by the target date by emplacing the arresting gear for landing and using jet-assisted takeoff (JATO) for the takeoffs. Soon it was evident that even this limited objective was in doubt. On 25 May, Lieutenant Colonel Goode wrote:

As of 1000 this date, there was in place 2,650 feet of matting leaving 650 feet of matting to be placed. One hundred fifty feet of taxiway is in place. A total of 1,200 feet of matting must be placed to meet the goal. Since matting started nine days ago, the average rate was 275 feet per day. The remainder would require that a rate of

USMC Photo A184311

Brigadier General Keith B. McCutcheon, Commanding General, 1st Marine Aircraft Wing, greets Colonel John D. Noble, Commanding Officer, MAG-12. Colonel Noble had just landed the first aircraft at the newly constructed Chu Lai SATS field.

400 feet per day be placed in the next three days . . . It is questionable whether the goal can be met.[21]

The arrival of the first aircraft had to be postponed.

The delay was a short one. By 31 May, the Seabees had completed nearly 4,000 feet of runway and about 1,000 feet of taxiway and the SATS field was prepared to accept its first aircraft. Colonel John D. Noble, Commanding Officer, MAG-12, who had established his CP at Chu Lai on 16 May, recalled that he "caught a logistics flight from Da Nang to Cubi Point . . . so I could bring the first flight of tactical aircraft to Chu Lai."[22] June 1st dawned bright and clear, and at 0810, Colonel Noble led his four-plane division of Douglas A-4 Skyhawks from VMA-225 into Chu Lai. The other three pilots were Lieutenant Colonel Robert W. Baker, commanding officer of VMA-225, and Majors Donald E. Gillum and David A. Teichmann. General McCutcheon, who was at Chu Lai for the landings, recalled, "the NCOIC of the arresting gear cut off the tail of

Noble's skivy shirt, a practice aboard carriers of the Fleet, carried over to our shore-based carrier ops."[23]*

Later in the day, on 1 June, four other A-4s from Lieutenant Colonel Bernard J. Stender's VMA-311 arrived at the field. The Chu Lai-based aircraft flew their first combat sorties that same day. At 1315, the four VMA-225 aircraft, with Lieutenant Colonel Baker in the lead, conducted air strikes in support of ARVN units six miles north of the field.

Although the field was operational, it was still unfinished and soil stabilization would continue to be a problem, especially during the rainy season. Eventually the field had to be rebuilt. Lieutenant Colonel Baker observed:

> . . . for a week or so before the rains came, this aluminum field was as flat and even as a pool table—the smoothest, bump-free surface I ever flew from. Later with rain cavitation the laterite was pumped up through the matting forming a slipping roller coaster effect.

Baker exclaimed:

> But we flew! The Chu Lai operation used every capability my squadron had . . . We were trapped on landings, jato'd on takeoff. Refuelled by our GV's en route to our primary target. Loaded to the hilt with ordnance, we couldn't take off with much fuel. We did close air support . . . in all weather and flew [radar controlled missions] all over the area in foul weather conditions day and night.[24]

The SATS concept worked, but as Colonel Hardy Hay, the III MAF G-3, later remarked: " . . . no one will ever know what the [Chu Lai] project did to men and equipment unless they were there."[25]

III MAF in Transition

The III Marine Amphibious Force and its ground and air components experienced major changes of command within their first six weeks in Vietnam. Generals Collins and Fontana were near the end of their 13-month overseas tours and the Commandant, General Greene, appointed Brigadier General Lewis W. Walt, newly selected for promotion to major general, to replace Collins and Brigadier General

*General McCutcheon also told the story that General Krulak had bet Major General Richard G. Stilwell, the MACV Chief of Staff, a case of scotch that a squadron would be operational within 30 days. General Krulak paid off the bet "on the basis that a full squadron was not operating there in the forecast time, only half of one." McCutcheon, "Marine Aviation in Vietnam," p. 129.

USMC Photo A184616
Major General Lewis W. Walt (left) relieves Major General William R. Collins (right) as Commanding General, III Marine Amphibious Force in an indoor ceremony at Da Nang on 4 June 1965. The ceremony was held indoors because the American colors were not permitted to be displayed outside.

Keith B. McCutcheon, also selected for promotion to major general, to be Fontana's replacement.** Walt looked the part of the football lineman that he was in

**According to Colonel O'Connor, the 1st MAW chief of staff at the time, the question of who was to be CG III MAF was discussed several times. O'Connor recalled that "General Fontana earnestly desired to have that assignment. He and General Collins were both nearing the ends of their overseas tours, and that General Collins would leave first. He talked to General Krulak about the matter several times . . . He [Fontana] even volunteered to extend his overseas tour one year to take command of III MAF. General Krulak was very understanding, but explained that General Greene had already selected General Walt. This did not stop Fontana. He was senior to Walt, and stressed the doctrinal point that either an aviator or a ground officer could be in command . . . Finally he realized that the Commandant's decision would prevail . . . when he realized his time was limited in the Far East, he decided to take his last opportunity to command a wing in combat . . . he would go to Da Nang to command the wing until he was forced to leave." Col Thomas J. O'Connor, Comments on draft MS, dtd 27Nov76 (Vietnam Comment File).

USMC Photo A184614

Major General Walt speaks to troops of the 4th Marines at Chu Lai in June 1965. The new III MAF commander toured all three Marine bases shortly after taking command.

his college days. Upon promotion, he would be the junior major general in the Marine Corps and was one of the Corps' more decorated officers, two Navy Crosses and the Silver Star and combat service in both World War II and Korea. He had just completed a tour as the Director, Landing Force Development Center at Quantico.

In contrast to the physical bulk of Walt, McCutcheon was a short, slim man in appearance, but held equally imposing military credentials. Decorated with the Silver Star and Distinguished Flying Cross and a veteran of both World War II and Korea, McCutcheon was one of the pioneers in the development of close air support and helicopter tactics. In April 1965, he arrived in Japan as the 1st MAW assistant wing commander after completion of his duties as the CinCPac J-3. On 24 May, he assumed command of the wing's headquarters at Da Nang. Two weeks later, McCutcheon assumed command of the entire wing, upon General Fontana's departure for the United States.

After an informal promotion ceremony in the Commandant's office in Washington and a ceremonial battalion parade at Quantico, Major General Walt left for Vietnam at the end of May.[26] On 5 June, he officially relieved General Collins as Commanding General, III MAF and Commanding General, 3d Marine Division.

During this period, there were other command changes. Upon his arrival, General McCutcheon also became Deputy Commander, III MAF, relieving General Carl, who then departed Vietnam as Commander, Task Force 79. On 12 June, General Carl, as assistant wing commander, assumed control of the wing's rear headquarters in Japan after General Fontana's departure. Six days later, General

Karch returned to Vietnam as assistant division commander of the 3d Marine Division while Brigadier General Melvin D. Henderson assumed command of the 3d Marine Division (Rear) on Okinawa. These changes at the top were followed by rapid adjustments in staff assignments. The new layers of command contrasted sharply with the almost spartan simplicity of the old 9th MEB and could not help but cause some initial confusion. One former member of the 9th MEB staff, Major Ruel T. Scyphers, remembered:

> Two full staffs arrived in Vietnam and superimposed authority over the brigade in a very short time. In this connection there wasn't a single moment of liaison or coordination between or among either staff. There was at one time 13 colonels roaming around headquarters without assignments or functions. With the limited space for billeting, messing, and working space—it was a nightmare. [27]*

Perhaps these growing pains were most dramatically reflected in the field of communications. During a visit to Vietnam in May, General Krulak remarked: "I have never seen a worse situation than at Da Nang where a message which has immediate precedence has taken as long as 30 hours to get out of country, some incoming messages do not arrive at all."[28] According to Colonel Hardy Hay, the III MAF G-3:

> We were totally unprepared for the communication load that included an outrageous number of classified messages. Higher echelons simply did not have time to send letters by regular mail. Consequently, letters came by electronic means. [29]

Colonel Nickerson, who had become the III MAF

---

*Colonel Rex C. Denny, from the III MAF G-3 Section, recalled that the fact that General Walt was both the 3d Marine Division and III MAF commander "caused some humorous and often confusing staff work. MAF staff and division staff working on same project or MAF staff doing work division staff rightly should." Col Rex C. Denny, Comments on draft MS, dtd 10Nov76 (Vietnam Comment File). Lieutenant General Leo J. Dulacki, who in 1965 was the III MAF G-2, remarked that "when III MAF was deployed to RVN, it was assumed that the Hqs would be a skeleton Hqs, dependent on the Wing and Division Hqs for *substantial* personnel support and, *in fact, for many of the operational functions.*" Dulacki pointed out that this concept of organization, which had been accepted as standard for years, was for the first time "put to the test." He noted that the subsequent, "*necessary, but agonizingly slow,* growth of the III MAF headquarters in order to perform its tasks would indicate that this concept lacks vitality *especially in a commitment of forces of long duration.*" LtGen Leo J. Dulacki, Comments on draft MS, dtd 24Oct76 and [Jul] 77 (Vietnam Comment File).

G-4, later explained that much of the message backlog was due to periodic power shortages "with the down-time of generators" exceeding "up-time." He commented that the number of classified "dispatches that had not been encrypted or decrypted often exceeded 5,000" and that "manual processing was tedious." Nickerson also remarked on the fact that "higher, comfortable, well-staffed headquarters were firing questions or assigning responsibilities at a prolific rate . . . ."[30] Colonel Nickerson praised the efforts and ingenuity of Colonel Frederick C. Dodson, the III MAF communications officer, and the communications section for reducing the backlog to manageable proportions. Finally Nickerson observed:

> Reading, analyzing, answering, dodging, eliminating these dispatches was a tremendous load. Colonel Regan Fuller, MAF Chief of Staff, challenged, cajoled, and led the staff in his cantankerous manner on a crippling schedule in order to catch up. . . . After many weeks he was successful and he accomplished all of this while ill with a bleeding ulcer.[31]

Communications was only one of the trouble areas caused by the transformation of the command. The troops sent into Vietnam had to be supplied and maintained, and MACV had planned to establish a Da Nang Support Command under the Army's 1st Logistic Command to provide common item supply for III MAF. At the Honolulu Conference in April, this plan was modified and Admiral Sharp directed that the Commanding General, III MAF, in his capacity as Naval Component Commander, would assume the responsibility for common item supply from Marine and Navy sources, as well as the operation of the ports in I Corps. Since the Navy had not yet established a support activity in Vietnam to run the ports, the job had to be done by Marine Corps personnel and equipment. This placed a heavy burden on III MAF.[32]

Following the Chu Lai landings, Colonel Nickerson, the III MAF G-4, held nightly meetings "as the hectic problems spanned the logistic spectrum." These meetings were "designed for liquidating problems, coordinating efforts and insuring that all had the necessary information to do their jobs."[33] On 16 May, Nickerson presented a logistic support concept for the Marine command. While assuming that the Navy would eventually establish a support activity, the concept directed the III MAF to run the ports and at the same time make

Marines from the 2d Battalion, 3d Marines cross the Cu De River in amphibian tractors. The troops later evacuated villagers from the hamlet of Pho Nam Thuong to Le My.

distribution of its supplies through its own force logistic support group (FLSG).[34]

The III MAF FLSG, commanded by Colonel Mauro J. Padalino, was built around the nucleus of the 3d Service Battalion from the 3d Marine Division and reinforced by support elements from the 3d Force Service Regiment on Okinawa. Colonel Padalino, a veteran supply officer who had served in both World War II and Korea, maintained his headquarters at Da Nang while two force logistic support units, FLSU-1 and -2, serviced Chu Lai and Phu Bai. Despite shortages compounded by breakdowns in equipment and a complex peacetime supply system, the FLSG managed to meet the most urgent requirements of

the fully operational MAF.* The logistic situation gradually improved after the Defense Department permitted the Commandant of the Marine Corps to release the emergency FMFPac mount-out supplies for shipment to Vietnam on 5 June.

In spite of the logistic strain, more than 9,000 personnel had been added to the Marine force in Vietnam by mid-June. They were spread over an area of 130 square miles and engaged in a wide variety of tactical, support, and combat support activities. Both the 3d Marines and the 4th Marines

---

* See chapter 12 for a more detailed account of the logistic situation.

USMC Photo A184799

Marines from the 2d Battalion, 4th Marines cross a stream in the northern sector of the Chu Lai TAOR. The Marine in the foreground appears to be able to smile despite a cigarette in his mouth and water up to his neck.

had established their command posts in Vietnam. Elements of the 12th Marines, the division artillery regiment, were located at all three enclaves. The 1st Battalion, 12th Marines under Major Gilbert W. Ferguson supported both Da Nang and Phu Bai, while Lieutenant Colonel Arthur B. Slack, Jr.'s 3d Battalion, 12th Marines provided artillery support for the 4th Marines at Chu Lai. Other supporting units, spread throughout the three enclaves, included major elements of the 3d Motor Transport Battalion, the 3d Engineer Battalion, and the 3d Reconnaissance Battalion. The wing consisted of two aircraft groups, MAGs-12 and -16 with five helicopter squadrons, an equal number of fixed-wing squadrons, and ancillary ground components.

Upon taking command, General Walt had toured the three base areas and familiarized himself with each. Based upon his own observations, supported by available intelligence, he concluded that the VC were building up their forces in the areas contiguous to the Marine enclaves. Walt decided that the Marines had to extend their TAORs and at the same time conduct deeper and more aggressive patrolling. Colonel Hardy Hay, the III MAF G-3, recalled that shortly after Walt's arrival:

> He asked me one night, 'What is our major G-3 problem?' My answer—We have got to convince Saigon that by trying to establish a ring around Chu Lai, Da Nang, and Phu Bai—we will never have enough men and material to adequately do it.

Yet as Hay observed, the Marines were unable to undertake offensive operations because their "hands were tied by ComUSMACV directives."[35]

On 15 June a significant change in the role for the Marines took place when General Westmoreland permitted General Walt to begin search and destroy operations in the general area of his enclaves, provided that these operations contributed to the defense of the bases. The MACV commander further directed that the Marines at Chu Lai conduct operations to the west of their TAOR into the suspected Do Xa VC supply complex.

With this new authority and with the concurrence of General Thi, the I Corps commander, General Walt enlarged the TAORs at all three enclaves. The enlargements gave the units of the division more room for offensive operations and provided distinguishable lines of demarcation on the ground since the trace of the new TAORs followed natural terrain features. At Da Nang, the area occupied by the 3d Marines consisted of 172 square miles and contained a civilian population of over 50,000 persons, but the populated region directly to the south and east of the base still remained the responsibility of General Thi's forces. Within the new Chu Lai TAOR of 104 square miles, there were 11 villages, containing 68 hamlets, and a civilian population of over 50,000. The area of responsibility for the 3d Battalion, 4th Marines at Phu Bai was much smaller, consisting of 61 square miles, but within that area civilian population numbered almost 18,000.

The Seeds of Pacification

Shortly after General Walt assumed command of III MAF he had a survey made which revealed that over 150,000 civilians were living within 81mm mortar range of the airfield, and consequently, the "Marines were into the pacification business."[36] In fact, General Greene later observed:

> From the very first, even before the first Marine

battalion landed in Da Nang, my feeling, a very strong one which I voiced to the Joint Chiefs, was that the real target in Vietnam were not the VC and the North Vietnamese, but the Vietnamese people . . . .[37]

Other than the Le My experiment, in June 1965 Marine pacification consisted largely of an embryonic civic action program which had begun a few months earlier as an offshoot of the former Marine task element's ''people to people'' medical assistance program. In April, the civil affairs officer of the 3d Marines, 1st Lieutenant William F. B. Francis, in cooperation with local officials, established a dispensary in the village of Hoa Phat, known to the Marines as Dog Patch, on the western perimeter of the Da Nang Airbase. A Vietnamese nurse ran the facility, while a Navy hospital corpsman and a lab technician paid occasional visits. Lieutenant Francis begged and borrowed medicines from various U.S. agencies, both military and civilian.

Medical assistance programs of this type expanded throughout the Marine TAORs. Lieutenant Colonel Clement's battalion at Le My established another dispensary and opened sick call to the civilian population every other day, while the 3d Battalion, 3d Marines did the same in its area of operations. The artillery battalion at Chu Lai, the 3d Battalion, 12th Marines, in conjunction with Company B, 3d Medical Battalion, provided daily dispensary service for the local populace. The 3d Battalion, 4th Marines at Phu Bai established a weekly medical service in three small hamlets nearby. In all three Marine enclaves, hospital corpsmen accompanied Marine patrols into the local villages where they dispensed soap and treated minor illnesses.

Civic action, even at this very early stage in its development, encompassed more than merely dispensing medicine. At Chu Lai, the 400 people who were displaced by the airfield were resettled in a new area with the assistance of the 4th Marines and the local district government. The need of much of the rural population for food, clothing, and shelter was apparent to all. The Marines could not hope to eliminate all of the suffering, but they could furnish some assistance. They made contact with private charitable organizations, such as CARE and the Catholic Relief Society, and were able to obtain over 10,000 pounds of miscellaneous supplies to be distributed within their TAORs. The Marines discovered other means besides charity for making life more pleasant for the villagers. In one instance the 3d Marine Division band, marching through Hoa

Phat, suddenly struck up a gay tune, and then, to the delight of hundreds of Vietnamese who had gathered, the band played an impromptu concert for over an hour.

There was a need for overall guidance and direction since civic action was too important to leave to the good will and natural enthusiasm of individual Marines. On 7 June, III MAF published an order which established civic action policy. Major Charles J. Keever, the III MAF Civil Affairs Officer who prepared the directive, had visited hamlets around both Da Nang and Chu Lai to obtain the details of the home life of the Vietnamese villagers, as well as the civic action programs conducted by the Marines. In the order he defined civic action as the ''term applied to the employment of the military forces of a nation in economic and social activities which are beneficial to the population as a whole.''[38] On 14 June, General Walt held a meeting with 25 of his senior officers and reiterated III MAF civic action policies. The goal was to stabilize the political situation and to build up the government by providing it with the respect and loyalty of its citizens.

The Marines attained their first measurable success in the struggle for the people when villagers in two hamlets, five and a half miles northwest of Le My, elected to move into an area under Marine protection. Lieutenant Colonel Clement's battalion had conducted several sweeps along both banks of the Song Cu De, up river from Le My. According to Clement:

> The movement of the people from these two hamlets, of Pho Nam Thuong and Nam Yen, was very important to me because I did not want to extend my defensive posture to include Pho Nam, yet I did not want the VC to have those people. The people were hesitant to move—reluctant to give up their homes; apprehensive about the rice harvest to come; and fearful that association with government forces would mark them for retaliation by the VC.[39]

Clement then decided to convince the villagers that their hamlets were in a combat zone and that ''they would be safer to accept refugee status and relocate near Le My . . . .'' The battalion commander, several years later, recalled:

> I directed that H&I [harrassing and interdiction] fires be brought close in to the hamlet, night after night. The attitude of the people about relocation ''improved'' in time and the relocation operation was scheduled . . . not only did I have to ''convince'' the people of Pho Nam and [Nam Yen] to relocate, but I had to convince the Vietnamese authorities of the necessity of this move since the official policy was to discourage refugees.

On 15 June, Lieutenant Colonel Clement drew up plans for a three-company action in conjunction with the ARVN and Popular Forces. Three days later, the Marine battalion and Vietnamese forces moved through the hamlets and brought out more than 350 villagers, who then moved into the Le My complex. Clement later admitted, ''I suppose given a free choice, the people would not have left their hamlet. I influenced their decision by honesty, sincerity, and a hell of a lot of H&I fires.''[40]

By this time, Le My had become a show case for pacification. Lieutenant Colonel Clement explained:

> . . . by virture of their success and notoriety, the Marines at Le My . . . were not maneuvered around. . . . This permitted the battalion to conduct a counterinsurgency campaign based upon the situation as it appeared to the people on the ground. This privileged position permitted a great deal of person-to-person confidence to develop, and, along with it, a personal commitment to the government cause.[41]

June Operations in the Three Enclaves

With the enlarged TAORs and broader mission in June, General Walt based his concept of operations on the establishment of an elaborate defensive network for the base areas together with forward outposts and extended patrolling in the outlying areas. He envisioned ''the creation of a series of dug-in timbered mutually-supporting defensive positions into which infantry units may withdraw in the event of heavy enemy attack'' as the main defensive line for each enclave. Some 3,000 to 5,000 meters forward of this line, Walt wanted the establishment of a ''lightly fortified combat outpost line'' for a more mobile defense. Concurrently, the III MAF commander ordered all units to continue ''aggressive patrolling'' in all TAORS ''as a means of keeping the enemy off balance, forcing him to deploy, and giving early warning of any attempts to concentrate along TAOR boundaries.''[42]

At Da Nang, the resulting expanded operations resulted in increasing contacts with enemy small units. The 3d Marine Division for the month reported:

> 10 June. In the western sector of the Da Nang TAOR, a company patrol uncovered a VC base camp capable of supporting 150 people. The camp was destroyed . . . .
>
> 21 June. During the morning, 2 reinforced squads from 2/3 were attacked while on patrol in the Da Nang TAOR by an estimated 8 VC, using small arms and grenades.

> One Marine was KIA and 3 WIA, while the VC lost 4 KIA and 2 women captured . . . .
>
> 22 June. In a brief fire fight at an outpost manned by Company C, 1/3, in the southern portion of the Da Nang enclave, two VC were killed with no Marine casualties.
>
> 24 June. Elements of 1/9, under operational control of 3d Marines, and the 1st Bn, 4th ARVN Regiment conducted a combined sweep and clear operation south of Da Nang Air Base along the Song Cau Do . . . 1/9 apprehended 19 suspected VC and the ARVN 1/4 had killed 2 VC. There were no Marine casualties.[43]

The 4th Marines at Chu Lai was equally busy. Lieutenant Colonel Fisher's 2d Battalion, 4th Marines provided security for the Seabees while they constructed the airfield. Shotgun riders from one rifle company were assigned to every vehicle day and night. Two of Fisher's other rifle companies and his headquarters and service company manned the main defensive line, while his fourth rifle company manned forward outposts and conducted patrols.[44] The other infantry battalions at Chu Lai, the 3d Battalion, 3d Marines and the 1st Battalion, 4th Marines, made similar dispositions.

With the consolidation of the Chu Lai base area, Colonel Dupras gradually extended the 4th Marines TAOR so that the air facility was out of range of enemy mortars and light artillery. Lieutenant Colonel Fredericks, the commanding officer of the 1st Battalion, 4th Marines, recalled that initially the Marines had to operate in a very restricted zone and that the enemy was aware of this restriction.[45] With a combination of extended patrolling and civic action within the villages in the TAOR, by the end of June Colonel Dupras was confident that his troops had eliminated the ability of the Viet Cong to mass and attack the airfield. Enemy action was limited to small probes against outposts, sniping, and occasional hand grenade incidents. At the end of the month, the 4th Marines and its supporting units had killed 147 VC while suffering four dead and 23 wounded.

In the Marines' northernmost enclave at Phu Bai, the 3d Battalion, 4th Marines faced a large challenge. General Krulak commented that although the unit was operating aggressively throughout its TAOR, it was too much to expect the base to be safe from enemy mortar attack. He believed that the Marines would require two more battalions and probably a regiment to defend the base properly.[46] The low rolling hills and swampy gullies in the area were divided just to the right of center of the TAOR by a prominent north-south ridgeline dominated at the north end by Hill 180. More disturbing was the fact

USMC Photo A185701

Marines from the 3d Battalion, 4th Marines take cover near Phu Bai. Their patrol had just been fired upon by the VC.

that the area directly to the north and east of the airstrip, designated Zone A, was not included in the Marine area of responsibility.

Lieutenant Colonel William W. ''Woody''

Taylor,* the battalion commander, was unhappy with the tactical arrangements and commented that the VC could apparently come in and shoot up the villages with impunity while the Marines were not permitted to operate in Zone A.[47] On 21 June, General Nguyen Van Chuan, the 1st ARVN division commander, incorporated the sector into the Phu Bai TAOR, and at the same time gave Lieutenant Colonel Taylor limited operational control of the five South Vietnamese Popular Force platoons in Zone A. This eventually led to the development of the highly successful Marine and South Vietnamese combined action company. (See Chapter 9)

By the end of June, the stepped-up activity in all three Marine enclaves had placed a heavy strain on III MAF, in terms of both men and material. During the month, General Walt requested the remaining battalions of the 3d Marine Division on Okinawa.** It was now obvious in both Saigon and Washington that more American forces were needed and the entire subject of the total U.S. troop commitment to the war in Vietnam was undergoing reconsideration.

---

* LtCol Taylor relieved LtCol Jones when the latter suffered a heart attack on 28 April 1965.

** On 11 June, 1/9 arrived and relieved 3/9, which returned to Okinawa for transfer back to the United States. This exchange of units was in line with the peacetime battalion transplacement system then in effect and could not in any sense be considered a reinforcement.

CHAPTER 4

Reinforcement and Expansion

The Need for Further Reinforcements—The Establishment of the Qui Nhon Enclave—The Attack on the Airfield—Expansion to the South—Further Reinforcements

---

The Need for Further Reinforcements

Despite increasing U. S. involvement, the major Viet Cong effort bypassed American concentrations during the spring of 1965. Most of the contacts between the Marines and the VC were the results of American initiative. Other than sporadic harassment, the Communists generally left the U.S. troops alone, and reserved their major efforts for the Vietnamese Armed Forces. Apparently the Communist strategy was to finish off the South Vietnamese before more American forces could be deployed to South Vietnam.

In many respects, the moment for concentrated VC action appeared opportune; the South Vietnamese government's war against the Communists was in disarray. According to the government's campaign plan for 1965, the South Vietnamese had established as their objectives the defense of bases and lines of communications, the harassment of VC bases and lines of communications, surveillance of border and coastal areas, and most important, support of the *Chien Thang* ("Struggle for Victory") pacification program. Promulgated in early 1964 and based on the "spreading oil" concept, the *Chien Thang* program placed priority on the consolidation of the secure populous area by a combination of military, paramilitary, police, economic, and social reform activities. At the heart of the program was the "New Life" hamlet, a variation of the planned community. Although similar in many respects to the abortive "Strategic Hamlet" program of the Diem regime, the *Chien Thang* campaign was supposedly better planned and more realistic, in that security was to be "restored in one area prior to going to another." These secure areas were then to serve as "springboards to pacify the areas" which were insecure.[1]

Once more the South Vietnamese pacification plans proved to be too ambitious. In I Corps, for example, where the 1965 campaign plan called for pacification of the coastal plain inland to the railroad in Quang Nam and Quang Ngai Provinces, the situation had deteriorated by the end of March 1965 to the extent that the government controlled only the areas surrounding the provincial capitals. Only in the Saigon region, where the South Vietnamese had begun an intensive pacification campaign in 1964, code named HOP TAC, did the government enjoy a modicum of success in its efforts against the Communists during the spring of 1965.[2]*

Compounding the difficulties for the South Vietnamese, the government, at the end of May, was in the throes of another internal crisis. Head of State Suu and Prime Minister Quat disagreed over the makeup of the cabinet and were unable to resolve their differences. They both stepped down and handed the reins of power to a military directorate presided over by Generals Thieu and Ky. As one study on pacification concluded, this entire period was marked by governmental instability and "as a consequence, Saigon's military efforts and related pacification programs sputtered both at the national and local levels," and there was "neither the time nor the inclination on the part of the various

---

* Coincident with the *Chien Thang* program, the South Vietnamese, at the urging of MACV, launched the HOP TAC (Working Together) campaign in mid-1964 with the aim of linking together the six rural provinces surrounding Saigon. Using Saigon-Cholon as a hub, the provinces were divided into four concentric zones. The idea was to first pacify the closer zones and then move outward until all six provinces were pacified. A special HOP TAC directorate was formed with U.S. advisors to coordinate the military, police, social, and economic activities of the program. In 1965, an effort was made to use the HOP TAC example in other Corps areas. See the Ngu Hanh Sonh section in Chapter 9 for the effects of this effort in I Corps.

USMC Photo A194964
Major General Walt provides Admiral Ulysses S. Grant Sharp, Commander-in-Chief, Pacific, with an inflight briefing on III MAF operations in Vietnam. The trace of the Marine area of operations can be seen on the briefing map.

governments in Saigon to deal with anything but the most urgent military threats.''[3]

The VC spring-summer offensive, which opened on 30 May, caught ARVN units widely dispersed in support of the *Chien Thang* campaign. As a result, the enemy was able to chew up the ARVN battalions piecemeal. In I Corps, the *1st VC Regiment* ambushed the 1st Battalion, 51st ARVN Regiment outside of the small hamlet of Ba Gia, 20 miles south of Chu Lai. Of the 500 men in the battalion, only 65 soldiers and 3 U.S. advisors were able to break through the Communist lines. General Thi threw in his last reserves, the 39th Vietnamese Ranger Battalion and the 3d Vietnamese Marine Battalion. Marine F4Bs from VMFA-531 flew close support for the South Vietnamese units. When the battle ended on the 31st, the South Vietnamese had lost 392 men killed and missing, as well as 446 rifles and carbines, and 90 crew-served weapons. They claimed to have killed 556 Viet Cong and captured 20 weapons. Two battalions of U.S. Marines had been alerted, but were not committed.

The question arose concerning the circumstances under which U.S. combat troops would go to the aid of the South Vietnamese. It was answered on 8 June when the White House issued the following statement:

> If help is requested by the appropriate Vietnamese commander, General Westmoreland also has authority within the assigned mission to employ these troops in support of Vietnamese forces faced with aggressive attack when other effective reserves are not available and when in his judgment, the general military situation urgently requires it.[4]

Despite his new authorization, there was little General Westmoreland could do to alleviate the situation. Other than III MAF in I Corps, he could only call on one other U.S. infantry formation, the U.S. Army 173d Airborne Brigade, which had arrived at Bien Hoa near Saigon in May. During June, the South Vietnamese Army was losing the equivalent of one infantry battalion a week to enemy action.

General Westmoreland had come to the conclusion that the South Vietnamese, by themselves, were incapable of holding back the Viet Cong, who were being reinforced by North Vietnamese regulars. In a message to the Joint Chiefs on 7 June, the MACV commander painted a stark picture depicting enemy strength and corresponding ARVN weakness. Westmoreland told the JCS, ''I believe that the DRV [Democratic Republic of Vietnam] will commit whatever forces it deems necessary to tip the balance and the GVN cannot stand up successfully to this kind of pressure without reinforcement.'' Specifically, General Westmoreland asked for the immediate approval for the deployment to Vietnam of those forces already being considered in various plans. These forces included the remaining two battalions of the 3d Marine Division, as well as two Army brigades and an airmobile division. In addition, Westmoreland requested the deployment, already under consideration, of a Republic of Korea division to South Vietnam, as well as the possible deployment of more American forces at a later date.[5]

In an exchange of messages between MACV, CinCPac, and JCS, units were added and deleted to the ''shopping list'' that MACV had proposed in the 7 June request. By 22 June, the Joint Chiefs, in a message to Admiral Sharp and General Westmoreland, cited an eventual 44 battalion-size force in South Vietnam exclusive of the South Vietnamese Armed Forces. These 44 battalions were to be largely U.S. Army and Marine Corps, although supplemented by units from South Korea, Australia, and New Zealand. In this same message, the Joint Chiefs discussed the immediate approval of a 23 U.S. battalion commitment to South Vietnam, but failed to mention the two battalions of the 3d Marine Division on Okinawa. They also remarked on the possibility of returning the 173d Airborne Brigade to Okinawa after the scheduled July arrival of the 1st Brigade, 101st Airborne Division. Finally, the JCS wanted to know if Westmoreland and Sharp thought that the 44-battalion force "would be enough to convince the DRV/VC they could not win."[6]

In his reply two days later, General Westmoreland opposed any decision to withdraw any U.S. units and objected to any suggestion that 23 U.S. Army and Marine battalions were the upper level of the U.S. commitment. In response to the JCS inquiry on the adequacy of a 44 battalion-size force, Westmoreland answered, "I saw 44 battalions as no force for victory, but as a stop-gap measure to save the ARVN from defeat." In his message to the Joint Chiefs, he stated: "The premise must be that we are in for the long pull . . . it is time all concerned face up to the fact that we must be prepared for a long war which will probably involve increasing numbers of U.S. troops."[7]

By the end of the month, the Joint Chiefs informed ComUSMACV and CinCPac that the U.S. forces that Westmoreland had asked for in his 7 June and subsequent requests had been approved. This decision allowed for the movement of 8,000 more Marines to Vietnam including the 9th Marines headquarters. It also permitted deployment of the airmobile division, then being formed at Fort Benning, Georgia, as well as the already approved deployments of the 101st Airborne Brigade and a brigade from the 1st Infantry Division.

The same time that he requested more troops, General Westmoreland also asked for the authority to employ American forces in offensive operations against the enemy. He claimed that the:

> . . . enemy's shift to big unit war was drawing ARVN troops away from the heavily populated regions . . . American and Allied troops . . . would have to assume the role of fighting the big units, leaving the . . . ARVN free to protect the people. No more niceties about defensive posture and reaction . . . we had to forget about enclaves and take the war to the enemy.[8]

This concept was soon to be known as the search and destroy tactic, with the aim of searching out and destroying the main force units. On 26 June, Westmoreland received permission from Washington to commit U.S. forces to battle "in any situation . . .

when in ComUSMACV's judgment, their use is necessary to strengthen the relative position of GVN forces."[9] This in effect gave the MACV commander a relatively free hand to employ his forces.

General Westmoreland's particular concern at this time was the military situation in South Vietnam's II Corps. Intelligence reports indicated that North Vietnamese regular units were infiltrating through the Central Highlands in the western provinces of Kontum and Pleiku, while the coastal provinces of Binh Dinh and Phu Yen remained major sources of enemy manpower and food. Westmoreland placed the highest priority on preventing the linkup of the North Vietnamese regulars in the mountains with the VC on the coast. The key to the entire area was Route 19, which runs from the city of Qui Nhon to Pleiku City where it joins with Route 14 which continues north to Kontum.

In making his plans to counter the expected Communist offensive, General Westmoreland relied heavily on the arrival of the 1st Cavalry Division (Airmobile) which had been specifically designed as a mobile force "that could be moved from one trouble spot to another."[10]* As early as April, Westmoreland contended that such a division was ideally suited to conduct helicopterborne operations in the Central Highlands. The MACV commander maintained that the division could be supplied overland from the coastal logistic bases at Qui Nhon and Nha Trang via Route 19, and augmented by aerial supply. Finally, Westmoreland argued, "If the VC choose to mount a major campaign against Highway 19, this is a better place than most for a showdown."[11]

---

*During the spring of 1965, the Army formed the 11th Air Assault Division (Test) at Fort Benning, Georgia, for final testing and evaluation. "The decision to activiate the test division as part of Army force structure and to subsequently deploy it to Vietnam required the reorganizing, retraining and reequipping of the division in a period of 90 days. Activated as the 1st Cavalry Division (Airmobile) on 1 July 1965, the division was composed of the men and equipment of the air assault division and the 2d Infantry Division, plus aviators procured from Army units worldwide." As reorganized for deployment to Vietnam the newly formed 1st Cavalry Division (Airmobile) consisted of three brigades which included eight infantry battalions, an air cavalry squadron, an aerial artillery battalion, three helicopter battalions, and three 105mm howitzer battalions. The division had a strength of over 15,000 men and was equipped with 1600 vehicles and 434 helicopters. CMH, Comments on draft MS, dtd 15Nov76 (Vietnam Comment File).

USMC Photo A185286

General Walt greets Marines from the 2d Battalion, 7th Marines at the newly established Qui Nhon enclave. The 2d Battalion had just relieved the SLF battalion, BLT 3/7.

Within the defense establishment, there was some opposition to the deployment of the airmobile division so far from its logistic bases. Admiral Sharp, supported by Ambassador Taylor and some members of the Joint Chiefs, wanted the airmobile division based in the Qui Nhon area:

> Until both Route 19 and the vital coastal area had been secured, primarily out of concern that the logistical backup for the Division, 600-800 tons per day, would severely overtax the existent limited airlift and airfield facilities if the ground supply route should be closed off.

After further study, according to Admiral Sharp, General Westmoreland agreed to base the division at An Khe, 35 miles west of Qui Nhon. From this base, which could be resupplied by road, the airmobile division could launch operations ''into the Pleiku Highlands as well as into the surrounding countryside of Binh Dinh Province.'' Despite this compromise, the deployment of the airmobile division so far inland would be a departure from the earlier Marine deployments in secure coastal enclaves.[12]

The Establishment of the Qui Nhon Enclave

Because of the serious situation in II Corps in June, General Westmoreland had to make difficult decisions. Faced with the fact that the 1st Cavalry Division would not arrive until September, he considered, but finally rejected, moving two III MAF Marine battalions into the Central Highlands. Moreover, the MACV commander was concerned that the security for the Army's Qui Nhon logistic base was no longer adequate and so informed

Admiral Sharp on 21 June. In his message, he stated that he could not divert units from III MAF, or from the 173d Airborne Brigade at Bien Hoa, for base defense in II Corps. Although a brigade from the Army's 1st Infantry Division was to arrive at Qui Nhon in mid-July, Westmoreland feared that the existing U.S. Army logistic buildup there offered too lucrative a target for the VC. Consequently, he requested that a Marine battalion be flown to Qui Nhon from Okinawa as soon as possible.

Admiral Sharp agreed to the request for reinforcement, but suggested a modification to the deployment of the Marine battalion. During June, the 7th Marines, a 1st Marine Division regiment, had arrived at Okinawa from Camp Pendleton with all three of its battalions. The regiment's arrival permitted the Navy and Marine Corps to embark one battalion on amphibious shipping and reconstitute the special landing force (SLF) of the Seventh Fleet. Sharp proposed that the SLF land at Qui Nhon, rather than redeploy another battalion by air. This alternative would allow the Marines to reembark in their own shipping when they were relieved by the Army's 1st Division brigade. The Joint Chiefs agreed with Sharp and ordered him to land the SLF at Qui Nhon on 1 July.

During the period 24-26 June, Lieutenant Colonel Charles H. Bodley's BLT 3/7 and Lieutenant Colonel Norman G. Ewer's HMM-163 embarked on board the amphibious ships *Iwo Jima* (LPH 2), *Talladega* (APA 208), and *Point Defiance* (LSD 31).* The ships sailed for Vietnam on the 26th. Lieutenant Colonel Bodley, who had been on a staff visit to the Philippines and to Vietnam, recalled, "our return flight to Okinawa arrived just in time to permit us to wave down a local helicopter and still be able to catch the departing SLF at sea."[13]

On 30 June, the amphibious task group arrived off Qui Nhon; ashore General Westmoreland was on hand to greet the Marines. Lieutenant Colonel Bodley flew ashore by helicopter to meet Westmoreland, who, according to Bodley, "wanted to personally brief me and resolve on the spot any landing/operating problems existing or anticipated." The MACV commander offered to support the SLF

---

* There had been no Seventh Fleet SLF since mid-May. The helicopter squadron, HMM-163, had just returned from Vietnam on 21 June where it had been replaced by Lieutenant Colonel Mervin B. Porter's HMM-261. See Chapter 13 for a further discussion of the SLF.

Captain Michael F. Welty, Commanding Officer, Company F, 2d Battalion, 7th Marines, (kneeling) discusses the tactical situation with his battalion commander, Lieutenant Colonel Leon N. Utter, (seated) at Qui Nhon. Master Sergeant E. J. McCarthy, the Company F First Sergeant, is seated in the middle.

battalion with rations, ammunition, and other common items of supply. Bodley recalled that when General Krulak was notified of this offer, he "disapproved declaring that Marines would be self-sufficient."[14]

According to plan, on 1 July, Lieutenant Colonel Bodley landed three of his infantry companies and the attached 107mm Mortar Battery from the 3d Battalion, 11th Marines. The fourth infantry company, Company L, and other attachments remained on board ship as the BLT reserve. By 1700 the amphibious phase of the operation was over and the battalion had established positions on the high ground south of the city.

The SLF battalion's stay at Qui Nhon was shorter than anticipated. On 2 July, General Westmoreland advised Admiral Sharp that, with the mounting enemy offensive in II Corps and northern III Corps, he believed it was necessary to release the 173d Airborne Brigade from its static mission of protecting the Bien Hoa airfield and use it as a mobile reserve. He recommended that the 1st Infantry Division brigade scheduled for Qui Nhon be diverted

(Courtesy of Major Gary W. Parker) USMC Photo A707619

Marine helicopters from HMM-161 approach Qui Nhon airfield from the northwest. The base area of the 2d Battalion, 7th Marines was located four miles to the west of the airstrip.

to Bien Hoa and that one of the Marine battalions slated to reinforce III MAF relieve BLT 3/7 at Qui Nhon so that the SLF could once again function as a floating reserve. The incoming Marine battalion would remain at Qui Nhon until relieved by Republic of Korea (ROK) troops scheduled to arrive later in the year. Admiral Sharp approved the request and General Krulak assigned Lieutenant Colonel Leon N. Utter's BLT 2/7 for the Qui Nhon mission.[15]*

The Marines of BLT 2/7 had been embarked in the

---

*2/7 was substituted for 3/9 to go into Vietnam because the latter battalion had just arrived on Okinawa from the U.S. under the battalion transplacement system. Under this system, a battalion from the 1st Marine Division in California relieved a battalion of the 3d Marine Division in the Western Pacific, exchanging designation and mission. Thus the 2d Battalion, 5th Marines when it arrived on Okinawa at the end of June became the 3d Battalion, 9th Marines. In the movement of the 7th Marines battalions there was no change in designation since they actually reinforced the 3d Marine Division.

dock landing ship *Alamo* (LSD 33) and the attack transport *Okanogan* (APA 220) at Okinawa since 30 June, awaiting permission to deploy to South Vietnam. When the battalion received its new mission, the ships sailed, arriving off Qui Nhon on the evening of 6 July. The selected landing area, GREEN Beach, was south of the city and had been secured by Bodley's battalion. At 0800 the next morning, the first troops landed and the relief was completed by that evening. Supplies and equipment of Utter's battalion were brought ashore during the night and the entire operation was over by daybreak. BLT 3/7 reembarked in its own shipping on the afternoon of the 8th, but the amphibious squadron remained off Qui Nhon for several days in position to reinforce BLT 2/7 if the need arose.

Upon arriving at Qui Nhon, Lieutenant Colonel Utter's battalion came under the operational command of III MAF. General Walt directed the battalion to deploy its forces about ''the key terrain in Qui Nhon in order to reinforce the RVNAF and to defend the airfield, port, logistic facilities, and U.S. supporting installations.''[16]

To fulfill the requirements of his mission, on 6 July Lieutenant Colonel Utter issued his three-phased concept of operations; the first phase was completed on the afternoon of the 7th with the relief of BLT 3/7, the second began on the 8th with the occupation of Hill 586, the dominant ridge line running north and south, while the third phase was to consist of aggressive patrolling of the TAOR. The defensive perimeter consisted of three concentric areas: close-in defensive positions around the airfield, a defensive zone out to mortar range, and an outer zone to the limit of organic artillery range.

The establishment of the Qui Nhon enclave made General Walt's mission in I Corps more difficult. Not only did he lose the services of one infantry battalion, which could have been used either at Phu Bai or Da Nang, but also he had to position a detachment of 10 UH-34s from HMM-161 at Qui Nhon to provide helicopter support for the Marines there. The need for still more Marines in I Corps became disturbingly evident in July.

The Attack on the Airfield

On 1 July, a Viet Cong mortar and ground attack on the Da Nang airfield exposed the vulnerability of the base to enemy hit-and-run tactics. The Communists had carefully planned and rehearsed this operation for over a month, taking advantage of the fact that the entire area south of the perimeter fence was the responsibility of the South Vietnamese forces. On the night of 30 June, an 85-man enemy force, armed with automatic weapons, demolitions, grenades, one 57mm recoilless rifle, and four 81mm mortars, crossed the Cau Do River south of Da Nang. The attack force, a VC special operations company and a mortar company, reinforced by a 13-man North Vietnamese sapper team reached the southeastern perimeter of the base by midnight.

The enemy mortar company divided into two sections; the first section was to fire on the helicopter parking area, the other was to support the demolition team. Two rifle squads took up blocking positions to counter any reaction force, while the recoilless rifle team backed up the mortars. At approximately 0115, the 13 men of the demolition team tunneled under

USMC Photo A194609

Marines from Company H, 2d Battalion, 9th Marines stop a Vietnamese civilian bus on Route 1, 12 miles south of Da Nang in a search for VC guerrillas. The troops are checking civilian ID cards and looking for unauthorized weapons and ammunition.

the outer defensive wire, crossed the open area, and cut a hole in the inner perimeter fence.[17]

Lieutenant Colonel Verle E. Ludwig's 1st Battalion, 9th Marines was responsible for airfield defense. All four companies and the battalion CP had been located on the airfield, but ''there were continuing talks and plans between and among myself [Ludwig], Colonel Wheeler, and General Walt to use 1/9 to increase the offensive capability in the Da Nang area.'' As a result, Companies B and D, the CP, and most of Headquarters and Service Company had been moved to a more forward base area to begin a series of sweeps south of Da Nang. Two companies, A and C, augmented by MAF Logistic Support Group troops and Ontos [106mm recoilless rifles] strong points, provided the defense of the airfield proper. Ludwig later observed that these two companies were responsible for the same area that the entire battalion had previously covered and ''This meant, of course, that our positions were spread out, with the spaces between covered with roving sentries. This was the situation in the area penetrated by the sappers.''[18]

The night of 30 June had been quiet, with the exception of two minor probes on the extreme western portion of the Marine TAOR. About 0130 on 1 July, one of the Marine sentries near the fence heard a suspicious noise and threw an illumination grenade. At the moment the grenade burst, the enemy opened fire. Under the protection of concentrated covering fire and grenades, ten sappers ran onto the field. The 3d Division journal contains the following description of the initial confusion at the base:

> 0130—Heard incoming at the airfield
>
> 0142—Counter-mortar radar is oriented toward BTOO-77
>
> 0143—Counter-radar is working but we don't have anything yet. Sounds like we are getting more incoming now.
>
> 0150—Called G-3. Major Foster said a F-102 and C-130 are burning. Lieutenant Colonel Muir said incoming all seemed to be on Air Force side of field in area of F-100s and C-130s.
>
> 0208—3d Marines just got permission to fire 81mm illumination. [19]

Some of the infiltrators managed to throw their satchel charges on the Air Force aircraft, destroying a Convair F-102 and two C-130s, and damaging two F-102s and one C-130. Company C immediately sent two squads to the vicinity of the attack to reinforce the sentries on post. In the minutes it took for the additional Marines to arrive, the sappers were already withdrawing in the same direction from which they had arrived. As the reinforcing squads approached the southern fence, enemy small arms fire wounded two of the Marines; a 57mm shell hit the top of a concrete bunker and wounded the guard inside.

The Marines could not cut off the demolition team, but the enemy had not escaped unscathed. Troops of Ludwig's battalion found blood trails leading from the airfield, and Lieutenant Colonel Muir picked up a pistol at the cut in the wire during his early morning reconnaissance. Fifty minutes after the attack, Marine artillery opened fire on suspected enemy avenues of escape. Company D and a platoon from Company B arrived to reinforce the defenders. Two companies of the 2d Battalion, 3d Marines deployed along Route 1 to block any attack from the west and northwest.

General Walt, several years later, recalled that from the time the attack began that he was:

> . . . in an amphibian tractor out in the rice paddies west of the Air Base. This tractor was my combat command post where I slept at night. I had both wire and radio communication capability. I directed Colonel Wheeler (CO 3d Marine Regiment) to commit our Air Base reserve company and to personally go to the Air Base and direct the defense, which he did immediately. [20]

Colonel Wheeler called in Lieutenant Colonel Ludwig at 0300. They outlined a plan to find the retreating enemy force. Assisted by ARVN units, Company B, 1st Battalion, 9th Marines was to sweep

the northern bank of the Cau Do, under operational control of the 3d Reconnaissance Battalion which would search the area south of the river. The commanders planned to start the mission at first light, but all units were not in place until 0700. One platoon of Company B, in LVTs, patrolled the river and remained ready as a mobile reserve. The other platoons of the company deployed along the road north of the Phong Le Bridge, a mile and a half south of the airbase. At 1700, the operation ended. The Marines returned to the base with 14 suspects, but none proved to have been involved in the attack. The South Vietnamese were more fortunate. They found a wounded North Vietnamese who turned out to be the intelligence officer of the sapper team. He identified his parent unit as the *3d Battalion, 18th NVA Regiment*.

Although the damage on the airfield was not extensive and there were a few casualties, the spectacular nature of the VC attack caused worldwide publicity and renewed command attention to the vulnerability of the American bases. General Walt, in 1977, remarked:

> During the period of 0200 to 0400 I received phone calls from MACV Hq, CinCPac Hq, FMFPac Hq, Headquarters US Marine Corps, Secretary of the Navy's Office, Secretary of Defense Office and from the White House "Watch Officer" *not* President Johnson. All of the callers wanted to know *all* about the attack and *what* I was doing about it. Fortunately I had given instructions to Colonel Wheeler before the phone started ringing. This points out one of the hazards (for a commander) of having present day instantaneous communications to the battlefield, all over the world. [21]

General Walt ordered Brigadier General Karch to conduct an investigation concerning the circumstances surrounding the attack. In his findings, Karch concluded that the counter-mortar radar installation failed to function properly, thus hampering the Marines in their effort to locate the enemy mortar position. Nevertheless, the reaction force from Ludwig's battalion had responded rapidly. [22] Ludwig, himself, later wrote:

> It was my understanding all along that the division of my battalion . . . was a bit of a calculated risk with Colonel Wheeler and General Walt. Yet both believed that the need for more sweeps and offensive action justified this thinning of the airfield defense. [23]

Colonel Hardy Hay, the III MAF G-3, later remarked:

> I believe what really got us going and extending our patrols was the attack on the Da Nang air base. We then

began to seriously hunt and destroy the enemy before he could bring his weapons to bear on our enclaves.[24]

Reinforcing Colonel Hay's observation, General Krulak remembered: "I landed at Da Nang at 0800 that day, and it was already acknowledged that we had better get moving off the airfield perimeter, or there would be more of the same kind of attack."[25]

Expansion to the South

The basic weakness in the airfield defense remained that the Marine TAOR at Da Nang did not extend south or east of the airbase. General Walt later acknowledged that the enemy's sapper assault had been a "surprise," but that he and his staff members had been "worried about such an attack." Walt stated that General Thi, the I Corps commander, "was concerned about incidents" between Marines and South Vietnamese civilians in the densely populated areas south and east of the base. The III MAF commander repeatedly had asked General Thi "for permission to put some type of defense outside the airbase on the east and south side," but each time the I Corps commander had

A Marine from the 2d Battalion, 9th Marines moves through a Vietnamese hamlet south of Da Nang. The Marines found war in the hamlets to be difficult and frustrating.

answered "that action be delayed until the people of Da Nang become more used to the Marine presence."[26]

Despite General Thi's reluctance to have American troops operate in populated areas, General Walt, accompanied by General Krulak, met with the I Corps commander on 2 July, to renew his request to extend the Da Nang TAOR. Recognizing that the present defense arrangements gave every advantage to the enemy, General Thi gave his tentative approval for the expansion, but asked that General Walt put his request in writing. The I Corps commander still had reservations about the presence of Marines in the populated area and remarked to General Krulak, "You are still not ready to try and search out the VC."[27]

On 5 July, General Walt, in a letter to General Thi, formally asked that the Marine boundary be expanded approximately four miles south of the Cau Do and that it include as well, the Tiensha Peninsula east of the airbase. At the same time, Walt requested that the Marine reconnaissance zone be extended to Hai Van Pass, 19 miles north of Da Nang.

The Vietnamese general then directed his staff to study what effect the enlargement of the Marine TAOR would have on the following:

> (1) The "anti-Communist spirit" of the local population.
> (2) Administration and territorial security.
> (3) Coordination with ARVN forces in the area.
> (4) The lack of experience on the part of the U.S. Marines in distinguishing the civilian population from the Viet Cong.

This last qualification apparently was uppermost in the minds of the ARVN officers. On 20 July, realizing the importance of the security of the Da Nang base and the limited capability of the South Vietnamese to provide this protection, General Thi officially approved the boundary extensions in a letter to General Walt. The Vietnamese general cautioned that the Marine occupation of the new area should be divided into several phases and urged that the Marines thoroughly coordinate their planning and operations in the area with the Vietnamese military forces.[28]

III MAF designated the territory between the Cau Do and the southern boundary of the base as Zone A, and the area to the south of the river as Zone B. The Marines were to occupy Zone A immediately, and, at the same time, begin combined operations with ARVN forces south of the river. As in most

Marines from Company B, 1st Battalion, 3d Marines are seen in Operation BLASTOUT I southwest of Da Nang. The 1st Battalion, 9th Marines conducted its search of the Cam Ne village complex, four miles to the north, in conjunction with this operation.

operations emphasis was on coordination and cooperation; the Americans were to be careful not to give the appearance of occupation troops. General Thi remarked that he hoped the expansion would be carried out "by both parties in a spirit of friendly cooperation in order to obtain good results."[29]

Even the smoothest of relations could not disguise the need for more Marines at Da Nang. The increased demands for airfield security and the expanded Da Nang TAOR, as well as the deployment of BLT 2/7 to Qui Nhon, forced General Walt to scrap his original plans to reinforce Phu Bai with a regiment. Instead, most of the Marine reinforcements authorized by the JCS, with the exception of BLT 2/7 at Qui Nhon and the 4th Marines (Rear) which was slated for Chu Lai, arrived at Da Nang on 6 July. These included all of RLT-9 headquarters, BLT 2/9, the remainder of the 12th Marines, and support units of the 1st MAW and 3d Marine Division.

With the arrival of the last units of the 3d Division, General Walt made some adjustments in the disposition of his infantry at Da Nang. While the 3d Marines retained operational control over the battalion at Phu Bai and responsibility for the defense of the western and southwestern perimeters of the Da Nang Base, Walt assigned the defense of the airfield and the southern portion of the TAOR to Colonel Frank E. Garretson, the 9th Marines commander.

Lieutenant Colonel Ludwig's 1st Battalion, 9th Marines was retained as the airbase defense battalion, but reverted to parent unit control, while the 2d Battalion, 9th Marines, under Lieutenant Colonel George R. Scharnberg, was given the responsibility of expanding Marine control to the south.

To free the 1st Battalion, 9th Marines from a static role on the airfield itself, General Walt ordered the establishment of a provisional airbase defense battalion to be formed from the personnel of the various service units at Da Nang. Lieutenant Colonel William H. Clark, the executive officer of the 9th Marines, was assigned as the provisional battalion commander. The provisional battalion was to be organized as a conventional infantry battalion with a headquarters and service company and four infantry companies and a total strength of 38 officers and 911 enlisted men. On 19 July, Clark activated his new command. Three days later his newly formed Company A relieved one of Ludwig's companies on the airfield perimeter, and on 1 August, Company B relieved another 1st Battalion company.

The formation of the provisional base defense battalion released infantry companies from the airfield security mission, but the organization had a debilitating effect on the support and service units of III MAF. Too many specialists needed on their own jobs were serving as infantrymen. As early as 17 July, Lieutenant Colonel Clark had recommended

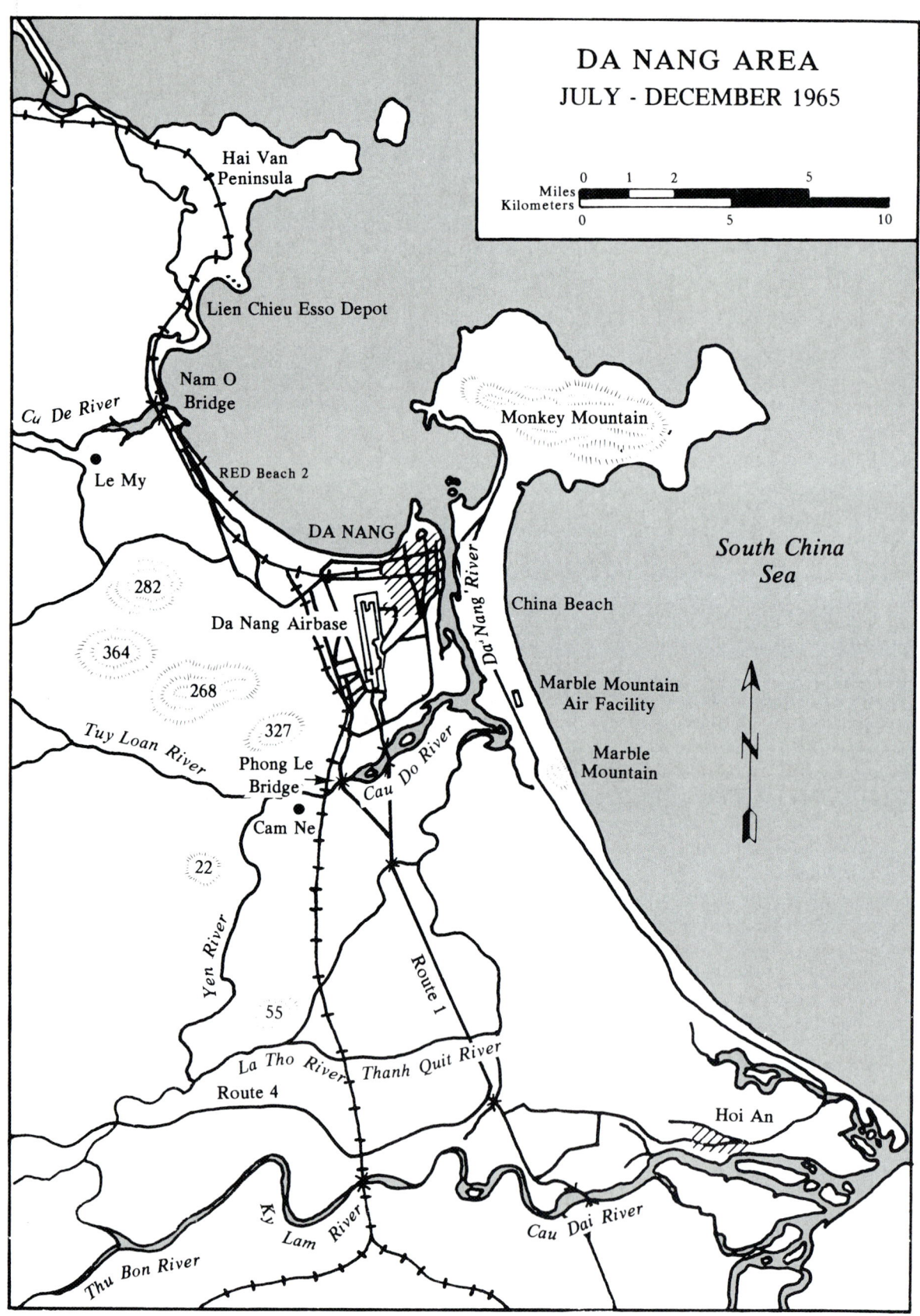

DA NANG AREA
JULY - DECEMBER 1965

against activating his own command, arguing that ''The overall effect of the creation of the Provisional Base Battalion is uneconomical from personnel, equipment, and airfield security viewpoints.''[30] Although this recommendation was rejected, it soon became apparent that he was right. Clark later recalled that during General Walt's 7 August morning briefing, Colonel Edward Cook, the commanding officer of the 3d Motor Transport Battalion:

> Reported a significant number of vehicles deadlined for lack of drivers or for required maintenance. Seems the drivers and mechanics were TAD [temporary additional duty] for their 60 days with the ADB [airfield defense battalion]. General Walt said deactivate.[31]

Although the order to deactivate came on 7 August, the provisional battalion remained in existence for two more weeks, sharing the airfield defense mission with the two companies of the 1st Battalion, 9th Marines and later with the newly arrived 3d Battalion, 9th Marines. The 3d Battalion assumed the entire mission of base defense on the formal deactivation of the provisional battalion on 22 August.

The provisional battalion had served its purpose, in that the 9th Marines was able to begin the occupation of its new TAOR. Of particular concern was the area to the south of the Cau Do. The 9th Marines area of responsibility now extended to the South China Sea on the east, the Yen River on the west, and approximately three and a half miles to the south of the Song Cau Do, about 30 square miles in all. This entire region was densely populated with innumerable clusters of villages and hamlets. The term ''village'' in Vietnam denoted an administrative unit, while the true local community was the hamlet, several hamlet clusters making up a village. An example of the confusion this caused for III MAF staffs was the fact that in the 9th Marines TAOR there were six hamlets with the name of Cam Ne and three Duong Sons, identified only by a parenthetical number after the hamlet name. Often the hamlets had different names from that of their administrative village, while clusters had no names at all, or none that the Americans could determine.

Prior to the extension of their TAOR, the Marines had only limited contact with the Vietnamese civilian population and then only in areas such as Le My where the people had shown basic loyalty to the government cause. This was not the case in the region south of the Cau Do. It was difficult to build loyalty to the Government of South Vietnam where fathers, brothers, and relatives were part of the VC structure and had been for a generation. A Buddhist priest who lived in one of the Duong Son hamlets furnished the Marines with some basic intelligence of the VC strength and organization, typical of the area. He revealed that the Viet Cong maintained a roadblock near the railroad tracks between Duong Son (2) and (3) manned by a four-man squad. A 40-man VC force which lived in his village was contructing bunkers, foxholes, punji traps, and setting in booby traps. Enemy political cadres were also active and VC tax agents collected 270 piastres annually from each family living in the area. The priest laconically summed up: ''The attitude of the people is generally friendly to the VC and unfriendly to the government forces.''[32]

With General Thi's concurrence, the Marines entered the new TAOR on 12 July; Lieutenant Colonel Scharnberg's 2d Battalion moved into the vicinity of Duong Son (1), a mile south of the Phong Le Bridge. While two companies formed a perimeter defense around the hamlet, Company B, 1st Battalion, 9th Marines, moved through the hamlet. The Marines from Company B met strong resistance; three men were killed and four wounded. Further south, Company D, 3d Reconnaissance Battalion, attached to the 2d Battalion for the operation, came under sniper fire; eight were wounded. Most of the enemy fire appeared to be coming from the direction of Cam Ne (1), approximately 1,800 to 2,000 yards northwest of the jumping-off point. The Marines pulled back and called for close air support. F-4Bs from MAG-11 answered the request and blasted the enemy positions. An aerial observer in an O-1B confirmed six VC dead and secondary explosions in a minefield.

With Duong Son (1) secured, Lieutenant Colonel Scharnberg established a forward command post under his executive officer, Major John A. Buck, in ''the old French reinforced concrete bunker at the northwest end of the Phong Le Bridge,'' to control the two companies remaining in the hamlet. Buck recalled that he maintained ''almost daily contact with . . . [the] village chief of Duong Son,'' believing this ''liaison was essential in order to obtain raw information . . . and in general to develop a rapport without which the Marines could not achieve their full potential.''[33] Nevertheless, the two Marine

USMC Photo A184783

A Marine searches for caches of VC weapons in a hamlet south of Da Nang. The five small children in the background appear to be unconcerned about the presence of the American Marines.

companies in Duong Son (1) continued to receive fire from Cam Ne (2) directly to the west and from Duong Son (2) to the south. Throughout July and into August, the Marine units encountered resistance in the area.

An incident that perhaps best mirrored the perplexities which faced the 9th Marines was a mission conducted in the Cam Ne village complex on 3 August by Company D, 1st Battalion, 9th Marines. It was planned in conjunction with a 3d Marines' operation, BLASTOUT I, carried out by the 1st Battalion, 3d Marines and an ARVN battalion four miles south of the Cam Ne complex along both banks of the Yen River. The 3d Marines battalion would provide a blocking force to the south while Company D cleared the Cam Ne complex.

Cam Ne was a well-known VC stronghold and its residents were long-time Communist sympathizers, dating back to the time of the French. American intelligence officers estimated that VC local and main force troops were present in company size in the village complex.

According to Lieutenant Colonel Ludwig, the 1st Battalion, 9th Marines commander, his orders were "to search out the VC and to destroy them, their positions, and fortifications." Captain Herman B. West, Jr., the Company D commander, briefed his platoons to the effect that if they received fire from a "a position, hedgerow, trench line, bunker, spider trap, hut, or any other location," they were "to overcome and destroy."[34]

The company was to embark in a platoon of LVTs at the northern end of the Phong Le Bridge, navigate the Cau Do to its junction with the Yen River, and land opposite the Cam Ne complex, 1,200 yards downstream. The Marines were to attack east and occupy Cam Ne (1) and Cam Ne (2), two and a half miles from the line of departure. A forward battalion command post was to be established on the northern bank of the Song Cau Do. The attack was to begin at 1000 with the Marines scheduled to reach their objectives at 1500 that afternoon.

Complications arose at the very beginning. Three of the LVTs stuck in the mud of the Cau Do. Two tractors were able to get free, but the troops in the third had to transfer to another vehicle. The entire company did not arrive at its line of departure until 1040.

The objective area consisted of a maze of open rice paddies, tree lines, hamlets, and hedgerows. When the Marines dismounted from the tractors, they were greeted by occasional small arms fire from the tree line in front of the builtup area to the southeast. The troops quickly advanced on a 1,000-foot front, all three platoons were on line. It took the company approximately 10 minutes to cross the open paddy land and reach the cover afforded by the nearest treeline. One Marine was wounded during this phase of the attack. As the Marines edged foward, the VC withdrew into the hamlets. The hedgerows around the hamlets caused other difficulties. As the LVTs bore forward and crushed the thick hedgerows they set off several boody traps. No one was injured and the Marines proceeded into the cluster of thatched huts. The VC, however, refused to fight and disengaged. These tactics added to the frustrations of the Marines who were spoiling for a fight.

The entire Cam Ne complex favored the enemy hit-and-run methods. The innocent looking collection of crude structures harbored punji sticks, spider holes, interconnecting tunnels between houses, and an uncooperative civilian population.

USMC Photo A184852

Secretary of Defense Robert S. McNamara (center) and General William C. Westmoreland, Commander, United States Military Assistance Command, Vietnam (right), discuss the situation in I Corps with the I Corps commander, Major General Nguyen Chanh Thi (back to the camera), in July 1965. Secretary McNamara was in Vietnam to review the U.S. military commitment to South Vietnam with General Westmoreland.

The Marines would search one hut, only to have a VC sniper turn up behind them, shoot, and disappear. Troops from one of the platoons began to burn the huts from which they had received fire. The platoon commander, Second Lieutenant Ray G. Snyder, claimed that Cam Ne was an "extensively entrenched and fortified hamlet." Lieutenant Colonel Ludwig explained, that "in many instances burning was the only way to ensure that the house would not become an active military installation after the troops had moved on past it."[35]

By midafternoon, Captain West realized that his men would not be able to reach their objective area by nightfall. The company uncovered 267 punji stick traps and pits, 6 Malayan whips,* 3 grenade booby traps, 6 anti-personnel mines, and 1 multiple booby-

trapped hedegrow. The troops demolished 51 huts and 38 trenches, tunnels, and prepared positions, yet they had only progressed a quarter of the distance to their final objective.

Not knowing the strength of the enemy and realizing that the situation could deteriorate after dark, Captain West ordered a withdrawal to the Yen. When the Marines were once again in the open, the Viet Cong returned to the tree line and opened up with automatic and small arms fire upon the Americans. This time the Marine company called on Battery D, 2d Battalion, 12th Marines and the battalion 81mm mortar section for cover. Twenty-four 105mm shells and 21 mortar rounds struck the VC positions in four-to-five minutes. The troops were not able to observe the results, but the Viet Cong fire stopped and the Marines boarded their tractors.

During this engagement it had been impossible for

---

*A Malayan whip is a bent bamboo fence which, when tripped, whips pointed stakes into the intruder.

the Marines to determine accurately how large an enemy force they had encountered. Estimates of the size of the Viet Cong unit varied from 30 to 100; the Marines believed they accounted for at least seven enemy. The withdrawing VC had carried off their dead, wounded, and weapons, leaving no vindication for the four Marines wounded in the day's fighting.

When the tractors entered the Cau Do they were fired on from the southern bank. The Marines returned fire and the enemy rifles were once again silenced. Some thought had been given to going back to the Phong Le Bridge and again attacking southward into Cam Ne (1) and (2), where the company could be supported by the 2d Battalion, 9th Marines, but Lieutenant Colonel Ludwig knew it was too late to accomplish the mission in the remaining daylight. He called off the operation.

The company had not attained its final objective, but the Marines had learned some valuable lessons. They realized that one company could not cover the area and reach its target in the time allotted. Beyond the tactical lessons learned, Cam Ne forcibly brought to the attention of the American command both the political and military dilemmas inherent in the Vietnam War where the enemy could and did use the civilian population as a shield. Among the casualties at Cam Ne were a dead 10-year-old Vietnamese boy and four wounded villagers, who were caught in the crossfire between the Viet Cong and the Marines.

The nastiness of the village war was dramatized for millions of Americans on their television screens. A CBS television crew had accompanied the Marine company into Cam Ne and American viewers saw a Marine casually set a hut on fire with his cigarette lighter while an old woman pleaded for the preservation of her home. The CBS film version of the action showed the Marines meeting little or no resistance, and indeed, Morley Safer, the CBS reporter, who narrated the film, bluntly stated that "If there were Viet Cong in the hamlets they were long gone." Taking exception to the CBS report, the Marine Corps argued that Cam Ne was a fortified Viet Cong village and that Captain West's Marines had received small arms fire, including automatic weapons, from an estimated VC platoon as Company D attempted to enter the hamlets. The editors of the *Marine Corps Gazette*, perhaps best stated the Marine Corps position:

> War is a stupid and brutalizing affair. This type of war perhaps more than others. But this does not mean that those who are fighting it are either stupid or brutal. It does mean that the whole story should be told. Not just a part of it.[36]*

Realizing that extending the Marine TAOR into the heavily populated hostile area south of the Cau Do would cause trouble, General Walt, as early as 10 July, had issued a written directive to keep noncombatant casualties to a minimum. He stated:

> It is imperative that all officers and men understand the nature of the Vietnamese conflict, the necessity of winning the support of the people, and the primary importance of protecting and safeguarding civilians whenever possible . . . the indiscriminate or unnecessary use of weapons is counterproductive. The injury or killing of hapless civilians inevitably contributes to the Communist cause, and each incident of it will be used against us with telling effect.

But the general made it clear that this order was not to infringe upon "the inherent right of an individual to defend himself from hostile attack."[37] Rather, the emphasis was on discretion by the Marines to employ the necessary force to accomplish their mission. General Westmoreland, also concerned about civilian casualties, reiterated his interest on 5 August with an order to all commands for increased emphasis on the subject.

On 18 August, the Marines returned to Cam Ne, this time in greater strength. The 1st Battalion, 9th Marines established its command post south of the

---

*In 1977, General Walt remembered that he gave Morley Safer a lift into the Cam Ne area in his personal helicopter on 3 August. According to Walt, he gave permission to the battalion and company commanders "to burn those thatched houses which hid or camouflaged pill boxes," and that Mr. Safer heard him give this permission. Walt considered that the television account of the incident was a misrepresentation of the facts. Gen Lewis W. Walt, Comments on draft MS, dtd 10Aug77 (Vietnam Comment File). Lieutenant Colonel Charles Ward, who in 1965 was the 9th Marines S-2, recalled that in a conversation about the Cam Ne incident with *Newsweek* correspondent Francois Sully in 1968, Sully told him that "the Marines' orders and efforts to avoid antagonizing and to try to win the cooperation of the local populace were misplaced in regard to the people of Cam Ne, and breaking up the group and levelling of the village structures were the only feasible actions short of a military assault." Ward concluded his comments with the observation that the Marines operated in the area south of Da Nang with "salient gaps" in their knowledge "regarding the people" and very often without the cooperation of the local authorities stating, "too often the Marines had to blunder their way through the early critical encounters with the people as well as with the enemy." LtCol Charles Ward, Comments on draft Ms, dtd 27Oct76 (Vietnam Comment File).

Cau Do and prepared to reinforce the 2d Battalion, 9th Marines which sent two of its companies from Duong Son (1) westward into the Cam Ne complex. For two days, the Marines searched and cleared the entire village without encountering difficulties; the Viet Cong were not to be found.

During this period the 9th Marines also took over the new TAOR on the Tiensha Peninsula east of the airbase, extending from Monkey Mountain south to the north face of Marble Mountain. The Seabees had begun construction of an helicopter air facility there for MAG-16 to relieve congestion at the main airbase. Lieutenant Colonel Ludwig had begun to move his battalion into this area at the end of July. By the end of August he had secured the entire peninsula. Ludwig's 1st Battalion then tied to the west with the 2d Battalion whose area extended to the Yen River.

Further Reinforcements

During July, the Johnson Administration concluded its internal debate concerning the manpower level of U. S. forces in Vietnam and made some far-reaching decisions for the future. Secretary of Defense McNamara decided to visit Vietnam to discuss with the field commanders the various alternatives. The Secretary, accompanied by the outgoing U. S. Ambassador to RVN, Maxwell D. Taylor, and his successor, Henry Cabot Lodge, who was beginning his second tour as U. S. Ambassador, arrived in Saigon on 16 July. During a four-day period, McNamara and the MACV commander made a complete review of the military situation. Westmoreland stated that the ARVN troops were no longer able to hold critical rural areas and were unable to cope with the VC threat and that it was obvious that unless further American and allied forces were deployed, ''there was little chance of arresting the trend.'' Apparently the MACV commander convinced McNamara, for, on 28 July, President Johnson announced to the American people that the U.S. force level in Vietnam would be raised to 125,000 and that General Westmoreland would receive reinforcements as needed.[38]

During the first week in August, another conference was held in Honolulu, attended by representatives of the Joint Chiefs, CinCPac, and ComUSMACV to determine what units would be deployed and when. The troops to arrive in Vietnam during 1965 were referred to as Phase I forces. For the Marine Corps, the immediate result of the conference was the decision to reinforce III MAF with the 7th Marines regimental headquarters and the remaining two battalions on Okinawa, the 1st Battalion, 7th Marines and the 3d Battalion, 9th Marines. The arrival of the 7th Marines at Chu Lai on 14 August was to signal the beginning of the first major Marine offensive against a main force Viet Cong unit.*

---

*The regimental headquarters and BLT 1/7 landed at Chu Lai on this date. BLT 3/9 arrived at Da Nang and relieved the 1st Battalion, 9th Marines of the responsibility for airfield defense.

PART II
THE BIG BATTLES

CHAPTER 5

STARLITE: The First Big Battle

Intelligence and Planning—The Battle—The Aftermath

Intelligence and Planning

Throughout July evidence had accumulated showing a VC buildup in southern I Corps, especially in the area south of Chu Lai. By the 21st, General Westmoreland's intelligence staff, assessing enemy capabilities, stated that the Viet Cong could attack Chu Lai with as many as three regiments. The American command doubted that the enemy was ready to risk such a large concentration of forces against American firepower; a more likely course of action would be a sudden hit-and-run attack against the Marine base in regimental strength.

On 30 July, General Westmoreland told Walt that he expected the Marine commander to undertake larger offensive operations with the South Vietnamese against the enemy at greater distances from his base areas. General Walt reminded Westmoreland that the Marines were still bound by the 6 May Letter of Instruction that restricted III MAF to reserve/reaction missions in support of South Vietnamese units heavily engaged with an enemy force. The MACV commander replied "these restraints were no longer realistic, and invited General Walt to rewrite the instructions, working into them the authority he thought he needed, and promised his approval."[1]

On 6 August, General Walt received official permission to take the offensive against the enemy. With the arrival of the 7th Marines a week later, he prepared to move against the *1st VC Regiment*. In early July, the *1st VC Regiment* had launched a second attack against the hamlet of Ba Gia, 20 miles south of Chu Lai. The garrison had been overrun, causing 130 casualties and the loss of more than 200 weapons, including two 105mm howitzers. After the attack on Ba Gia, American intelligence agencies located the *1st VC Regiment* in the mountains west of the hamlet. Disturbing reports indicated that the enemy regiment was once more on the march.

According to Colonel Leo J. Dulacki, Walt's experienced intelligence officer:

Early in August, we began receiving countless low-level reports from the numerous intelligence collection organizations concerning the movement of the *1st VC Regiment*. The sources for most of these reports were of doubtful reliability and, indeed, many were contradictory, nevertheless, it was decided to plot all of the hundreds of reported movements, regardless of credibility, on a map, and an interesting picture developed. When the many "aberrations" were discounted, it appeared that the *1st VC Regiment* was, in fact, moving towards Chu Lai. Although most of the intelligence experts, including ARVN and the U.S. Army I Corps Advisory Group, discounted such a possibility, I briefed Colonel Edwin Simmons, III MAF G-3, on what appeared to be developing and suggested the consideration, if further indicators developed, of an offensive operation in the area south of Chu Lai.[2*]

Acting on this intelligence, the 4th Marines conducted a one-battalion operation with the 51st ARVN Regiment in search for the *1st VC Regiment* south of the Tra Bong River. Code-named THUNDERBOLT, the operation lasted for two days, 6-7 August, and extended 7,000 meters south of the river in an area west of Route 1. The ARVN and Marines found little sign of any major VC force in the area and encountered only scattered resistance. In fact, the Marines suffered more from the 110 degree temperature than at the hands of the enemy, sustaining 43 heat casualties and only two wounded. Nevertheless, Colonel James F. McClanahan,** who had relieved Colonel Dupras as commander of the 4th

---

* Both Colonels Dulacki and Simmons had arrived in Vietnam and assumed their new duties in July. Colonel Dulacki, who served in World War II and commanded the 1st Battalion, 7th Marines in Korea, had an extensive intelligence background, including two tours with the Defense Intelligence Agency. Colonel Simmons, also a veteran of World War II and Korea, and holder of both the Silver and Bronze Stars, had just finished a tour with the Strategic Plans Branch of the G-3 Division, HQMC.

** Colonel McClanahan was a veteran Marine of nearly 30 years of enlisted and commissioned service. He was commissioned in June 1942 and was awarded the Silver Star for his actions on Guadalcanal. He came to Vietnam after serving as Commanding Officer of Camp H. M. Smith in Hawaii.

Marines on 25 July, remembered that at the time the "operation was considered a successful experiment in command and control."[3]

Eight days after THUNDERBOLT, the allies finally comfirmed the location of the *1st VC Regiment*. On 15 August, a deserter from the enemy regiment surrendered to the South Vietnamese. During his interrogation at General Thi's headquarters he revealed that the regiment had established its base in the Van Tuong village complex on the coast, 12 miles south of Chu Lai. It planned to attack the American enclave. The prisoner told his interrogators that the *1st VC Regiment* at Van Tuong consisted of two of its three battalions, the *60th* and *80th*, reinforced by the *52d VC Company* and a company from the *45th Weapons Battalion*, approximately 1,500 men in all. General Thi, who personally questioned the prisoner and believed the man was telling the truth, relayed the information to General Walt. At about the same time, Colonel Dulacki's G-2 section received corroborative information from another source. Convinced of the danger to the airfield, Colonels Dulacki and Simmons advised a spoiling attack in the Van Tuong region.[4]

Agreeing that the situation called for action, General Walt flew to Chu Lai and held a hurried council of war with his senior commanders there: General Karch, who had become the Chu Lai Coordinator on 5 August, Colonel McClanahan of the 4th Marines, and Colonel Oscar F. Peatross, the newly arrived 7th Marines commander.* According to Peatross, "General Walt laid the situation out rather plainly . . . ." The III MAF commander remarked that "General Thi thought this was the best information he's had in the corps area throughout the whole Vietnam War." Two obvious courses were open to the Marines: they could remain within their defenses and wait for the enemy to attack, or they could strike the VC before the enemy was ready to move. The latter course of action meant reducing the defensive forces manning the Chu Lai perimeter, but the arrival of the 7th Marines

and BLT 1/7 on the 14th made the risk acceptable. Walt told the assembled officers:

> At most, all we're going to dig up is two battalions. If we dig up as many as two battalions, we've got to have the amphibious means of making a [landing] and our ultimate action depends upon how we come to grips with this thing.

He then turned to Colonel Peatross, and according to the latter stated, "Pete, you're the only one available." General Walt then returned to Da Nang and made the final decision to go ahead with the operation after further consultations with his staff and, "going to General Westmoreland for permission to carry out the plan."[5]

In a hectic two-day period, the III MAF, division, wing, and 7th Marines staffs assembled forces and prepared the plans for the attack. The concept for the operation, code-named STARLITE,** dictated a two-battalion assault, one battalion to land across the beach and the other to land by helicopter further inland. The division reassigned two battalions previously under the operational control of the 4th Marines to Colonel Peatross as the assault battalions, Lieutenant Colonel Fisher's 2d Battalion, 4th Marines and Lieutenant Colonel Joseph E. Muir's 3d Battalion, 3d Marines. General Walt, who wanted a third battalion as a floating reserve, requested permission to use the SLF. Admiral Sharp approved immediately. At the time of the request the amphibious task force was located at Subic Bay, 720 miles away. Based upon its transit time to the operational area, the planners selected 18 August as D-Day.

Colonel Peatross, in the meantime, had borrowed General Walt's helicopter and, accompanied by Lieutenant Colonels Muir and Fisher, made an aerial reconnaissance of the 10-square mile objective area. They saw relatively flat terrain occasionally broken by small wooded knolls and numerous streams. The many hamlets were surrounded by rice paddies and

---

*See Chapter 8 for the establishment of the Coordinator and ADC Command Group at Chu Lai. Colonel Peatross was a veteran of several amphibious operations during World War II including the Makin Island Raid and Iwo Jima. For his actions on Makin Island, he was awarded the Navy Cross. Colonel Peatross had served previously as a battalion commander under General Walt when the latter commanded the 5th Marines in Korea.

**Colonel Don P. Wyckoff, the 3d Marine Division G-3, designated the code name SATELLITE for the operation, but as the division plan was being typed, the electrical generators failed and the typing was completed using candlelight. Inadvertently, the clerk typed STARLITE instead of SATELLITE throughout the document. The next morning the error was discovered, but there was insufficient time to correct the error. Many accounts of the operation have mistakenly spelled the code name for the operation as STARLIGHT. LtCol Richard J. Johnson intvw by Hist&Mus Div, HQMC, dtd 24Mar73 (OralHistColl, Hist&Mus Div, HQMC).

USMC Photo A185826

A Marine Ontos patrols a beach area during Operation STARLITE. The South Vietnamese fishermen go about their business despite the war.

dry crop areas. The Marine commanders noted two suitable amphibious landing sites, one beach between two peninsulas northeast of the Van Tuong Complex (Nho Na Bay) and another beach 4,000 meters to the south, north of the coastal hamlet of An Cuong (1).

While airborne, Colonel Peatross and his commanders selected the amphibious assault landing site, as well as the helicopter landing zones (LZs). They chose the more southerly beach, later designated GREEN Beach, for the landing. A force there would block VC avenues of escape to the south. Three LZs, RED, WHITE, and BLUE, were selected four to five miles east of Route 1 and roughly one mile inland from the coast. LZ BLUE, about 2,000 meters west of GREEN Beach, was the southernmost of the landing zones. WHITE was 2,000 meters west-northwest of BLUE, while RED was 2,000 meters north of WHITE. From these positions, the Marines were to move northeast to the South China Sea.

Fortunately for the 7th Marines, the ships of Amphibious Squadron (Phibron) 7, which had brought the regiment to Vietnam, were at Chu Lai unloading BLT 1/7 and Da Nang disembarking BLT 3/9. Colonel Peatross later wrote:

> On the evening of 16 August the Amphibious Group Commander, Captain W. [William] R. McKinney, USN, under whose command most of the ships operated, had to

be informed of the operation. Colonel Peatross sent his RLT S-4, Major Floyd J. Johnson, Jr., out to Captain McKinney's flagship to inform him of the operation and to brief him on the plans as we knew them. This was a timely move as one of the ships had just sailed from Chu Lai and was on its way to Hong Kong. Captain McKinney was able to turn this ship around and return it to Chu Lai just in time to make the tight schedule laid out for the earliest possible D-Day.[6]

On the morning of the 17th, McKinney's staff joined the Marine aviation and ground planners ashore and the plans were completed. Lieutenant Colonel Muir's 3d Battalion was to land across GREEN Beach at 0630, 18 August with Companies I and K abreast, K on the right. Company L, the battalion reserve, was to follow as the lead companies swerved to the northwest. The remaining company, Company M, was to make an overland movement from Chu Lai to a ridgeline blocking position in the northern portion of the operations area, four miles northwest of the landing beach and one mile inland from the sea, closing off the VCs' retreat. Soon after H-Hour, UH-34s from Marine Medium Helicopter Squadrons 261 and 361 were to shuttle Fisher's 2d Battalion into the three LZs. The two battalions were to join forces when Company H from LZ BLUE linked up with Company I outside the hamlet of An Cuong (2), 1,800 meters inland from GREEN Beach.

From there, the Marines were to sweep to the sea through the Van Tuong village complex and over the Phuoc Thuan Peninsula. Artillery batteries at Chu Lai were to provide artillery support while two U.S. destroyers, the *Orleck* (DD 886) and the *Prichett* (DD 561), and the cruiser *Galveston* (CLG 3) were available for naval gunfire. Aircraft from MAGs-11 and -12 were to fly close support for the operation. The planning phase was short; Colonel Peatross later remarked, "there just wasn't enough time for anyone to bring up any problems."[7]

The Battle

With the completion of planning, the Marines began preparations for the operation. Lieutenant Colonel James P. Kelly's 1st Battalion, 7th Marines took over the defensive positions of Muir's 3d Battalion in the Chu Lai TAOR, while two companies, one each from the Da Nang and Phu Bai enclaves, were flown in to man the perimeter held by Fisher's 2d Battalion. At 1000 on the 17th, Company M, 3d Battalion, 3d Marines boarded LVTs at Chu Lai and moved along the coast to the Trung Phan Peninsula; then the company marched four miles south where it established its blocking position. The Marines of Company M met only minor resistance, an occasional sniper and booby traps. One man tripped a mine and suffered superficial wounds; no one else was injured. Before dawn on the 18th, the company reached its objective and dug in. Marine patrols had been active in this area for some time and to the casual observer the company's activity was just another small unit movement.

At 1700 on 17 August, the rest of Lieutenant Colonel Muir's 3d Battalion, 3d Marines, with Colonel Peatross and his staff, embarked on the three ships of the amphibious task group, *Bayfield* (APA 33), *Cabildo* (LSD 16), and *Vernon County* (LST 1161). Three M-67 flame tanks attached to the 7th Marines and a platoon of five M-48 tanks assigned to Fisher's battalion boarded two LCUs, which then sailed independently towards the amphibious objective area, timing their arrival to coincide with that of the troop transports. That night at 2200, the larger ships were under way. The task force first sailed east to deceive any VC in sampans in the coastal waters. Once over the horizon, the ships changed course to the southwest, arriving in the amphibious objective area shortly after 0500. There they were joined by

the *Galveston* and the *Orleck*, which were to cover the landing.*

At 0615, 15 minutes before H-Hour, Battery K, 4th Battalion, 12th Marines, which had displaced to firing positions on the northern bank of the Tra Bong River in the Chu Lai TAOR the night before, began 155mm preparation fires of the helicopter landing zones. The artillery was soon reinforced by 20 Marine A-4s and F-4s which dropped 18 tons of bombs and napalm on the LZs. The Marines limited their preparation of GREEN Beach to 20mm cannon strafing runs by MAG-12 A-4 Skyhawks, because of the proximity of An Cuong (1) to the landing site.

As the air and artillery fires lifted, the ground forces arrived. Lieutenant Colonel Muir's Companies I and K, in LVTs, landed across GREEN Beach at 0630 and pushed inland according to plan. A charge exploded to the front of Company I, but caused no casualties. The troops quickly spread out and moved into An Cuong (1). After a futile search for VC, the company continued advancing to the west. Company K received sniper fire from its right as it crossed the northern portion of GREEN Beach. Two platoons quickly moved northward and the enemy fire ceased. The third platoon secured the northern half of An Cuong (1). Fifteen minutes after H-Hour, Company G landed at LZ RED. Company E and Fisher's command group landed at LZ WHITE and Company H arrived at LZ BLUE 45 minutes later. On the beach, Lieutenant Colonel Muir, who had moved his CP ashore, was joined at 0730 by Colonel Peatross and his staff. Tanks and Ontos rolled off the LCUs and LCMs and made their way forward to support the assault companies. Company L came ashore and established perimeter security for the supply area at the beach.

Most of the Marine companies met only light resistance as they moved into the attack. Company G searched two hamlets in the vicinity of LZ RED and then advanced to the northeast and linked up with Company M without incident. At LZ WHITE south

---

*The *Prichett* did not arrive to support the operation until D plus 1. Colonel Floyd J. Johnson, Jr., the 7th Marines S-4 for STARLITE, believes the Marines were able to achieve the element of surprise because the ships used in the operation were the same ones that brought RLT-7 to Vietnam and "When we backloaded and sailed so soon after arrival, it's very possible the VC paid little attention, since the ships were due to leave anyway." Col Floyd J. Johnson, Jr., Comments on draft MS, dtd 29Nov76 (Vietnam Comment File).

of LZ RED, Company E encountered stiffer opposition from the Viet Cong. The enemy manned firing positions on a ridgeline east and northeast of the LZ, employing mortars, machine guns, and small arms. After dogged fighting, the Marines cleared the hills. By midmorning, Company E began moving northeast. At one juncture, the Marines spotted about 100 VC in the open and asked for artillery fire. The 107mm Mortar (Howtar) Battery, 3d Battalion, 12th Marines, helilifted into the position held by Company M, shelled the enemy force. Fisher, who later flew over the impact area in a helicopter, estimated that the artillery mission had accounted for 90 enemy dead. Company E continued to push forward, finding only occasional opposition.

Along the coast, Company K had advanced to Phase Line BANANA, 2,000 meters north of the landing beach. There a VC force, entrenched on a hill overlooking the Marine positions, blocked the advance of the company. Lieutenant Colonel Muir, who had established his forward CP with Company K, ordered Company L forward. By midafternoon, the two Marine companies, aided by supporting arms, carried the high ground and set up night defenses.

The major action developed in the south near LZ BLUE, at the junction of Fisher's and Muir's units. This area, roughly one square kilometer, was bound by the hamlets of An Thoi (2) on the north, Nam Yen (3) on the south, and An Cuong (2) to the east.

USMC Photo A184967

A Marine helicopter from HMM-361 brings ammunition to a howtar position during Operation STARLITE. The howtar is a 107mm mortar tube mounted on a pack howitzer chassis, hence the name howtar.

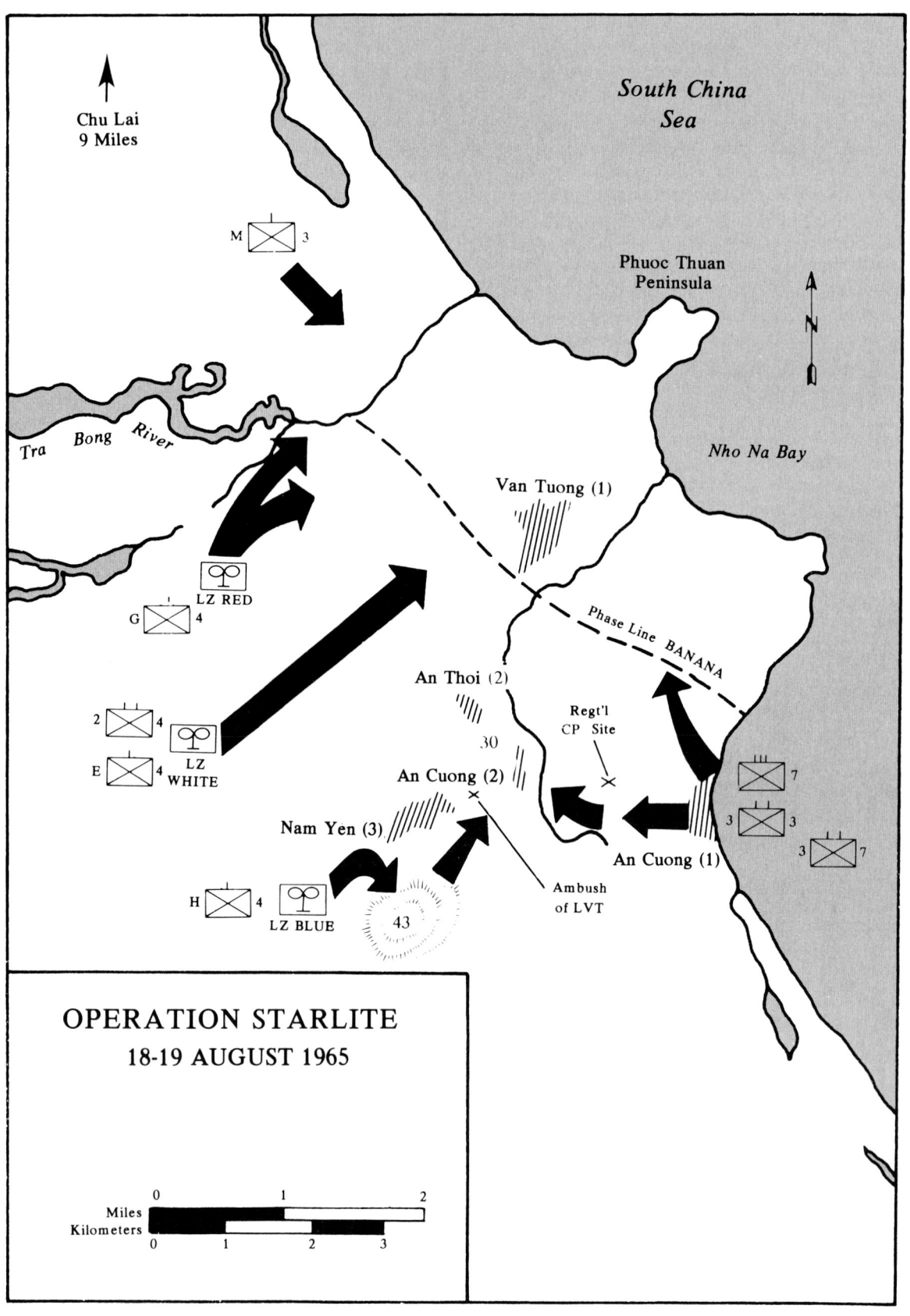

OPERATION STARLITE
18-19 AUGUST 1965

It was a patchwork of rice paddies, streams, hedgerows, woods, and built-up areas, interspersed by trails leading in all directions. Two small knolls dominated the flat terrain, Hill 43, a few hundred meters southwest of Nam Yen (3), and Hill 30, 400 meters north of An Cuong (2). LZ BLUE was just south of Nam Yen (3), between Hill 43 and the hamlet. Company H's LZ was almost on top of the *60th VC Battalion*. The enemy allowed the first helicopters to touch down with little interference, but then opened up as the others came in. According to one of the helicopter pilots, Captain Howard B. Henry from HMM-361, "You just had to close your eyes and drop down to the deck."[8] Three U.S. Army UH-1B Huey gunships from the 7th Airlift Platoon, took the VC on Hill 43 under fire while the infantry company formed a defensive perimeter around the landing zone.

The Company H commander, First Lieutenant Homer K. Jenkins, was not yet aware of the size of the enemy force. He ordered one platoon to take the hill and the rest of the company to secure Nam Yen (3). Both attacks soon stalled. The platoon attacking Hill 43 was still at the bottom of the hill when Jenkins called back his other two platoons from the outskirts of Nam Yen (3) in order to regroup. He requested air strikes against both the enemy hill position and Nam Yen (3). He then renewed the attack, but this time, Jenkins moved all three of his platoons into the assault on the hill. The VC fought tenaciously, but the Marines, reinforced by close air support and tanks, were too strong for the enemy. One Marine platoon counted six dead VC near a heavy machine gun position and more bodies scattered throughout the brush. Jenkins' men took one prisoner and collected over 40 enemy weapons.

The airstrikes called by Jenkins against enemy positions at Nam Yen (3) momentarily halted the advance of Company I, 3d Battalion, 3d Marines at a streambed east of Nam Yen (3). Bomb fragments slightly wounded two Marines. After the bombing run, Company I moved north along the stream for 500 meters to a point opposite An Cuong (2). Under fire from the hamlets, Captain Bruce D. Webb, the company commander, requested permission to attack An Cuong (2), although it was across the bank in the area of responsibility of the 2d Battalion, 4th Marines. Lieutenant Colonel Muir approved the request, after consulting with Colonel Peatross.

An Cuong (2) was a fortified hamlet, ideally suited to Viet Cong combat tactics. Major Andrew G. Comer, Muir's executive officer in charge of the 3d Battalion's rear command group at the 7th Marines CP, described the area surrounding the hamlet as heavily wooded with severely restricted fields of fire. The only open areas were the rice paddies and "even these were interspersed with hedgerows of hardwood and bamboo thickets."[9] An Cuong (2), itself, consisted of 25-30 huts, fighting holes, and camouflaged trench lines connected by a system of interlocking tunnels. As the company cleared the first few houses, a grenade exploded, killing Captain Webb and wounding three other Marines. No sooner had the grenade exploded, than two 60mm mortar rounds fell on the advancing troops, inflicting three more casualties. First Lieutenant Richard M. Purnell, the company executive officer, assumed command and committed the reserve platoon. The company gained the upper hand and the action slackened as the troops secured the hamlet. Making a hurried survey of the battlefield, Purnell counted 50 Viet Cong bodies. He then radioed his battalion commander for further instructions.

Muir ordered Purnell's company to join Company K, which was heavily engaged at Phase Line BANANA, 2,000 meters to the northeast. Company H remained near Nam Yen (3) to clean out all enemy opposition there and then planned to link up with Muir's battalion.

As Company I was preparing to move from An Cuong (2), a UH-1E gunship from Lieutenant Colonel George F. Bauman's VMO-2 was shot down by enemy small arms fire northeast of the hamlet. Lieutenant Colonel Muir ordered Purnell to leave some men behind to protect the helicopter. The lieutenant ordered two squads and three tanks to stay with the helicopter until the craft was evacuated. As the company departed, its members could see that Jenkins' Company H had left Hill 43 and was advancing on the left flank of Company I.

At 1100 Jenkins led his unit, augmented by five tanks and three Ontos, from the Hill 43 area into the open rice paddy between Nam Yen (3) and An Cuong (2). Jenkins bypassed Nam Yen (3) as he mistakenly believed that Company I had cleared both hamlets. Suddenly, from positions in Nam Yen (3) and from Hill 30, the VC opened up with small arms and machine gun fire, catching the Marine rear guard in a murderous crossfire. Then mortar shells began bursting upon the lead platoons. Company H was taking fire from all directions, and tracked vehicles, Ontos and tanks, were having trouble with the muck of the paddies. Jenkins drew his armor into a tight circle and deployed his infantry. One squad moved to the northwest of Nam Yen (3) and killed nine VC who were manning a mortar, but were driven off by small arms fire and had to withdraw to the relative security of the tanks.*

Lieutenant Jenkins saw that his position was untenable, and after radioing for supporting arms, he ordered his force to withdraw to LZ BLUE. Artillery hit Nam Yen (3) while F-4s and A-4s attacked Hill 30. About 1400, the company tried to move back to the landing zone. The lead platoon was forced to alter course when medical evacuation helicopters tried to land in the midst of the unit. As it maneuvered off to the flank of Company H, this platoon became separated from Jenkins' main body and was engaged by the Viet Cong. At this juncture, the platoon unexpectedly linked up with Purnell's helicopter security detail which had started to move toward its parent company after the downed helicopter had been repaired and flown out. The small force was quickly engaged by a Viet Cong unit, but together the two Marine units fought their way to An Cuong (2).** Meanwhile, Jenkins and his other two platoons fought a delaying action and withdrew to LZ BLUE, arriving there at 1630. Lieutenant Colonel Fisher directed Jenkins to establish a defensive perimeter and await reinforcements.

The expected reinforcements never arrived; they had been diverted to help a supply column that had been ambushed 400 meters west of An Cuong (2). Just before noon, Lieutenant Colonel Muir had ordered Major Comer to dispatch "our mobile (LVT) resupply" to Company I, which, at the time, was only a "few hundred yards" in front of Comer's command group. Major Comer recalled that he briefed both the five LVTs and the section officers of

_____

*Lance Corporal Joe C. Paul, a fire team leader in Company H, was posthumously awarded the Medal of Honor for his gallant actions during the engagement near Nam Yen (3). A copy of his citation is printed in Appendix D.

**Company I senior squad leader, Corporal Robert E. O'Malley, killed eight VC single-handedly that day. For his action, O'Malley became the first Marine to receive the Medal of Honor in Vietnam although Captain Frank S. Reasoner was later posthumously awarded the medal for an action in July 1965. See Chapter 11. Copies of both citations are printed in Appendix D.

the three flame tanks, the only tactical support available at the time, on the location of the company and marked the routes they were to follow on their maps.[10]

The supply column left the CP shortly after noon, but got lost between Nam Yen (3) and An Thoi (2). It had followed a trail that was flanked on one side by a rice paddy and on the the other by trees and hedgerows. As the two lead vehicles, a tank and amtrac, went around a bend in the road, an explosion occurred near the tank, followed by another in the middle of the column. Fire from Viet Cong recoilless rifles and a barrage of mortar rounds tore into the column. The vehicles backed off the road and turned their weapons to face the enemy. Using all of the weapons at their command the troops held off the closing VC infantry. The rear tank tried to use its flamethrower, but an enemy shell had rendered it useless. Throughout the bitter fighting, the convoy was still able to maintain communications with the command post.

At the rear CP area, Major Comer received "word on the LVT command net . . . that the column was surrounded by VC and was about to be overrun." Comer recalled:

> The LVT radio operator kept the microphone button depressed the entire time and pleaded for help. We were unable to quiet him sufficiently to gain essential information as to their location. This continued for an extended period, perhaps an hour.

Major Comer relayed the information about the ambush to Lieutenant Colonel Muir. The battalion commander replied that he was returning Company I to the rear CP and that Comer "was to gather whatever other support . . . [he] could and to rescue them as rapidly as possible." Major Comer told Colonel Peatross about the proposed rescue mission. The regimental commander, well aware of the vulnerable positions of both Company H and the supply column and fearing that the enemy was attempting to drive a salient between the two battalions, heartily approved and provided Comer with "the single available M-48 tank for support."[11]***

When Company I arrived at the rear CP, Comer held a hurried briefing with Lieutenant Purnell and

_____

***Colonel Peatross later stated that the enemy force which ambushed the supply column may have been getting ready to hit the regimental CP when the LVTs rumbled into them. Peatross, "Victory at Van Tuong," p. 9.

USMC Photo A185824

Marines from the 2d Battalion, 4th Marines assemble near a small hamlet during Operation STARLITE. The unit pictured is a command group; note the number of radio antennas.

the other leaders of the improvised rescue force. The plan was to use "a rapidly moving tank, LVT, and Ontos column through the previously cleared An Cuong (2) area." Before the meeting broke up, one of the flame tanks which had been in the supply column arrived at the CP. According to Comer, "The crew chief, a staff sergeant, reported to me that he had just passed through An Cuong (2) without being fired upon and that he could lead us to the LVT supply column."[12]

Shortly after 1300, Comer's force moved out. Just after cresting Hill 30, the M-48 tank was hit by recoilless rifle fire and stopped short. The other vehicles immediately jammed together "and simultaneously mortar and small arms fire saturated the area." Within a few minutes, the Marines suffered 5 dead and 17 wounded. The infantry quickly dismounted and the Ontos maneuvered to provide frontal fire and to protect the flanks. Major Comer called for artillery fire and air support. With the response of supporting arms, the enemy fire diminished but did not stop. According to Comer, "It was obvious that the VC were deeply dug in, and

emerged above ground when we presented them with an opportunity and withdrew whenever we retaliated or threatened them."[13]

With the letup of the action on Hill 30, Comer ordered Company I to resume its advance toward An Cuong (2) leaving a small rear guard on Hill 30 to supervise the evacuation of the casualties. The company entered An Cuong (2) against surprisingly little resistance, but Comer and the command group were caught by intense fire from a wooded area to their right front and forced to take what cover they could in the open rice paddies. At the time, the Marines came upon the two reinforced squads from Company I which had been left to guard the downed Huey and the platoon from Company H. The two squads from Company I fought their way to Hill 30 where they were evacuated while the Company H platoon remained with Comer in the rice paddies. At this point Comer recalled:

When it became obvious that I could not move the "B" group [the command group] in either direction . . . I radioed instructions to Lieutenant Purnell to extricate the supply column as rapidly as he could as I deemed that the most urgent matter, and that I would support him from my present position as best I could . . . I also advised Lieutenant Colonel Muir of our situation as I had been doing all day.[14]

While Company I maneuvered through An Cuong (2) encountering periodic strong enemy resistance, Colonel Peatross committed one company of his reserve battalion to the battle.* A ship of the special landing force, the LPH *Iwo Jima* with Companies I and L, 3d Battalion, 7th Marines and HMM-163 on board, arrived offshore shortly after 0930. As the intensity of the battle increased, Colonel Peatross ordered a halt to the advance of the units from LZs RED and WHITE and along the coast to prevent the overextension of his lines. He ordered Company L, 3d Battalion, 7th Marines, commanded by Captain Ronald A. Clark, to be landed. This company was helilifted to the regimental CP at 1730. There it was placed under operational control of Lieutenant Colonel Muir, who ordered Clark to reinforce Comer's group and then join Company I in the search for the supply train.

Supported by two tanks, Clark's force moved out. As the company advanced through the open rice paddies east of An Cuong (2), it came under heavy fire, wounding 14 and killing four. The Marines persevered and the VC broke contact as night fell.

The addition of a third Marine company to the area, coupled with the weight of supporting arms fires available, evidently forced the *60th VC Battalion* to break contact. The Marines radioed the *Galveston* and *Orleck* requesting continuous

---

*Major General Peatross recalled that at the time he did not have the authority to commit the SLF battalion. General Walt could not delegate this decision without first receiving permission through command channels, himself. General Walt had arrived at the 7th Marines CP earlier in the day, but had departed before the heavy fighting broke out. At this time, Lieutenant General Krulak, CGFMFPac, who was in Vietnam on an inspection visit, flew into the CP by helicopter while "rifle and recoilless rounds were flying around." General Karch, who was also present, told Peatross "to keep him [Krulak] aboard the helicopter and then fly to the command ship of the SLF, and then obtain permission to employ 3/7." General Krulak later remarked that he was not entirely successful in this mission: "We watched the confusion then took off, only to have to land with a hit in our chopper's gas tank." Colonel Peatross, nevertheless, received permission to employ both the SLF infantry and squadron since "the number of helicopters seemed to be reduced by the hour." MajGen Oscar F. Peatross, Comments on draft MS, dtd 26Oct76 (Vietnam Comment File), and Lt Gen Victor H. Krulak, Comments on draft MS, dtd 2Aug77 (Vietnam Comment File).

illumination throughout the evening over the Nam Yen-An Cuong area.** As darkness fell, Colonel Peatross informed General Walt that the VC apparently intended to defend selected positions, while not concentrating their forces.[15]

Lieutenant Colonel Muir decided that it was too risky to continue searching for the supply column that night, especially after having learned that the column, although immobilized, was no longer in danger. Muir ordered Captain Clark's Company L to move to Phase Line BANANA and join Companies K and L, and establish a perimeter defense there. He also ordered Company I to return to the regimental CP. For all intents and purposes, the fighting was over for Company I; of the 177 men who had crossed the beach, 14 were dead, including the company commander, and another 53 were wounded, but the company could claim 125 dead VC.

During the night of 18 August, Colonel Peatross brought the rest of the SLF battalion ashore. Company I, 3d Battalion, 7th Marines arrived at the regimental CP at 1800 followed shortly by Lieutenant Colonel Bodley and his command group. Just after midnight, Company M landed across GREEN Beach from the *Talladega*. With the arrival of his third battalion, Colonel Peatross completed his plans for the next day.

The regimental commander's concept of action remained basically the same, squeeze the vise around the VC and drive them toward the sea. As a result of the first day's action against the *60th VC Battalion*, he readjusted the battalions' boundaries. At 0730, Lieutenant Colonel Muir's battalion, with Companies K and L abreast and Company L from Bodley's battalion following in reserve, was to attack to the northeast from Phase Line BANANA. Simultaneously, Fisher's unit, with Companies E and G, was to drive eastward to the sea, joining Muir's force. Jenkins' Company H, Comer's group, and Company I were to withdraw to the regimental CP.*** The remainder of Lieutenant Colonel Bodley's 3d Battalion, 7th Marines was to fill the gap. Companies I and M of his unit were to move out of the regimental CP, extract the ambushed supply column, and then move toward An Thoi (2) to

---

**At about 0530 the next morning, the ships ceased firing; their magazines had been emptied of star (illumination) shells.

***Company H had accounted for 156 dead VC and sustained 45 evacuated casualties; 15 killed and 30 hospitalized.

Marines from Company E, 2d Battalion, 4th Marines move out from LZ WHITE during Operation STARLITE. Shortly after this picture was taken, the company met stiff resistance from Viet Cong entrenched to the right of the photograph.

establish a blocking position there which would prevent the VC from slipping southward. Company M, 3d Battalion, 3d Marines was to hold its blocking positions further north. The enemy was to be left no avenue of escape.

On the 19th, the SLF battalion moved into its zone of action which included the area of the fiercest fighting of the day before. The VC were gone. At 0900, Companies I and M of Bodley's battalion left the regimental CP, and moved through An Cuong (2), meeting no enemy resistance. They brought out the supply convoy* and by 1500 had established their assigned blocking position at An Thoi (2).

Although much of the enemy resistance had disappeared, Fisher and Muir still found pockets of stiff opposition when they launched their combined attacks at 0730. The terrain was very difficult. The

compartmented rice paddies, ringed by dikes and hedgerows, hindered control, observation, and maneuverability. The VC were holed up in bunkers, trenches, and caves which were scattered throughout the area. Marines would sweep through an area, only to have enemy snipers fire upon them from the rear. In many cases, the Marines had to dig out the enemy or blow up the tunnels. By 1030, Company E had linked up with Company K and the two battalions, continued their advance to the sea. By nightfall, the 2d Battalion had completed its sweep of the Phuoc Thuan Peninsula. Enemy organized resistance had ceased.

The Aftermath

Although the cordon phase of STARLITE had been completed, General Walt decided to continue the operation for five more days so that the entire area could be searched systematically. He believed that some of the enemy had remained behind in underground hiding places. Fisher's and Muir's

---

*Of the 23 Marines assigned to the convoy, five were killed and several others wounded. Only nine men remained in action throughout the three-hour period they engaged the VC. The enemy left 60 bodies behind.

A MAG-16 helicopter evacuates STARLITE casualties, while a Marine M-48 tank stands guard. The Marine on the left carries a M-79 grenade launcher.

battalions returned to Chu Lai on the 20th and Lieutenant Colonel Kelly's 1st Battalion, 7th Marines moved into the objective area and joined Bodley's battalion and units from the 2d ARVN Division for the search. The Marines killed 54 more VC in the Van Tuong complex before STARLITE came to an end on 24 August. The Marines had killed 614 VC, by body count, taken 9 prisoners, held 42 suspects, and collected 109 assorted weapons, at a cost of 45 Marines dead and 203 wounded.

The exploits of the infantry battalions were only part of the story of the battle. Colonel Peatross had high praise for both the tank and engineer detachments attached to his command. He observed the engineers were particularly helpful in destroying enemy fortifications, "mostly trenches and caves during the heat of battle and many more during the

five days that followed the mop up." The regimental commander later claimed that "the tanks were certainly the difference between extremely heavy casualties and the number that we actually took. Every place the tanks went, they drew a crowd of VC."[16]

Another factor in the outcome of the battle was the vast amount of firepower that the Marines brought to bear against the enemy. Elements of Lieutenant Colonel Page's artillery group at Chu Lai, supporting the operation, fired over 3,000 rounds of high-explosive, white phosphorous, and illumination. Fifty-eight missions were called in by artillery forward observers. The remainder consisted of preparation fires, marking concentrations, and harassing and interdiction missions. On five occasions, aerial observers reported secondary explosions in fortified villages. The 107mm Mortar Battery from the 3d Battalion, 12th Marines operating with Company M, 3d Battalion, 3d Marines and Battery K, 4th Battalion, 12th Marines provided most of the artillery support for the 7th Marines, firing over 2,400 rounds.*

The ships *Orleck, Galveston,* and *Prichett* fired 1,562 rounds in support of STARLITE. One of their most effective fire missions occurred on 19 August when 100 VC were spotted on a beach trying to escape. The destroyer *Orleck* engaged the target with rapid salvos from her 5-inch guns with excellent effect. In addition, the *Orleck* sank seven sampans in which VC were attempting to flee.

Close air support provided by Colonel Robert F. Conley's MAG-11 and Colonel John D. Noble's MAG-12 was a vital adjunct to the Marines on the ground. Seventy-five Marine F-4Bs and A-4s from five squadrons flew air support missions, at times dropping ordnance within 50 meters of friendly positions.** The fixed-wing planes of the 1st MAW flew a total of 78 sorties on the first day of the operation and expended 65 tons of bombs, 4 tons of napalm, 523 2.75-inch rockets, and 6,000 rounds of 20mm ammunition. Over 290 sorties were flown during the entire operation.

Colonel Leslie E. Brown, the Wing Operations Officer, recalled:

> . . . The Marines were in trouble . . . and our airplanes were literally just staying in the flight pattern and they'd land and rearm and take off and be right back again in a few minutes just dropping and strafing and firing rockets as fast as we could rearm them . . . in the three day period, we flew more sorties than in the history of any other attack group before or since, in support of that one operation which took place . . . in an area probably about two miles square . . . . Air control was pretty racy. People were congested and the helicopters were bouncing in and out. Helicopters were being struck and helicopters were burning. So it was a pretty exciting two or three days.[17]

---

*The Chu Lai artillery group, under the command of Lieutenant Colonel Leslie L. Page, established a forward fire direction center (FDC) with Battery K on the northern bank of the Tra Bong. Other Chu Lai artillery units which provided support for the operation were Battery C, 1/12; Battery M, 4/11; the 3d 155mm Gun Battery (SP); and a platoon, two guns, of the 1st 8-inch Howitzer Battery (SP). The 105mm howitzer and 107mm mortar batteries embarked with the SLF were not committed.

**The A-4s were from VMA-214, VMA-225, and VMA-311 while the F-4s were from VMFA-513 and VMFA-342.

General Walt later stated:

> I was near the front lines when this close air support action was taking place. It was an outstanding professional performance of the highest order. Strafing was done within 200 feet of our pinned down troops and was a very important factor in our winning the battle. I have never seen a finer example of *close* air support.[18]

The helicopters of Colonel Thomas J. O'Connor's MAG-16 furnished the infantry with maneuverability and the capability of quick resupply and casualty evacuation. A task force of 24 UH-34s from HMM-361 and -261 escorted by Marine and U.S. Army 'Huey' gunships brought the 2d Battalion, 4th Marines into battle. After the first landings, the eight helicopters from Lieutenant Colonel Mervin B. Porter's HMM-261 returned to Da Nang, leaving Lieutenant Colonel Lloyd F. Childers' HMM-361 to carry the burden of resupply and evacuation. Fourteen of Childers' 16 helicopters were hit by enemy fire. After the SLF arrived, Lieutenant Colonel Ewers HMM-163 was able to assume part of the load. During the entire operation, the helicopter squadrons flew over 500 sorties in support of the ground troops.***

Logistics for STARLITE became strained as the operation was extended, nevertheless, every critical demand was met. Major Floyd J. Johnson, the 7th Marines S-4 for the operation, later wrote that Colonel Peatross had directed "that we not maintain

---

***Colonel O'Connor assumed command of MAG-16 from Colonel King on 7 August. He wrote: "I left Da Nang about an hour before dawn in a UH-1E, in company with HMM-361 and HMM-261, and flew to the pickup zones west of Chu Lai. At this time MAG-16 was based at crowded Da Nang airfield, and the hazards of getting [the] squadrons airborne and en route to the objective area in darkness were apparent. The flight time to Chu Lai for a helicopter was about 50 minutes." Colonel O'Connor also remarked on the poor marksmanship of the VC gunners: "One feature of battle damage stood out. Most of LtCol Lloyd Childers' helicopters took extensive small arms fire but it was not crippling. Most of the bullet strikes occurred in the tail booms aft of the passengers compartments. This indicated poor training of VC gunners on moving targets. Most of these hits occurred when the helicopters were approaching or leaving landing zones, at airspeeds under 60 knots." Colonel Thomas J. O'Connor, Comments on draft MS, dtd 7Nov76 (Vietnam Comment File). Colonel Mervin B. Porter commented that when his squadron, HMM-261, returned to Da Nang, it "received word of the heavy action and 261 returned to the STARLITE area with all available aircraft and supported operations there until about 2000 or 2030." Col Mervin B. Porter, Comments on draft MS, n.d. [Nov 76] (Vietnam Comment File).

a big logistic support area'' in order not to lose mobility and to ''reduce the need for security.'' Johnson stated that he kept in the logistic support area ''one days rations and two days of ammunition.'' To insure ''continuous and responsive logistic support,'' the 7th Marines stockpiled supplies on the helicopter deck of the LSD *Cabildo*. Johnson explained, ''A special communication link was created between the RLT CP and the ship and most of the resupply to the battalions was made by helo direct from what was really a large floating dump.''[19]

One of the greatest demands was for water. Over 1,500 gallons of water per day were supplied to the troops ashore from the *Cabildo*, causing the ship to go on short water rations; even so, high temperatures and high humidity caused several cases of heat prostration. An effective means was devised for bringing the water from the ship to shore. LVTs loaded with empty cans were floated into the well deck of the *Cabildo* where a two-inch water hose was lowered into the tractors and the cans were filled in place without having to manhandle them. The heavy cans still presented a problem; they had to be carried from the regimental collection point to the operating units. As a result, Colonel Peatross recommended that plastic water containers replace the impractical bulky cans and that in the future, infantry battalions carry enough water to supply each man with four gallons per day.

Civilians in the combat zone presented complications. The first attempts to evacuate them were difficult; the people were frightened and did not trust the Marines. Eventually most of the local populace were placed in local collecting points where they were fed and provided with medical attention. Although attempts were made to avoid civilian casualties, some villages were completely destroyed by supporting arms when it became obvious that the enemy occupied fortified positions in them. Colonel Peatross commented:

> No . . . [supporting fires] were utilized unless called for by one of the units and each had a forward air controller, naval gunfire teams and forward observer. All weapons were controlled and no fire ashore was conducted unless it could be observed; consequently, neither aircraft nor naval gunfire made any judgments on ''military necessity.'' Only ground units being supported made such judgment.[20]

There could be no doubt, however, that the hamlets in the area were used by the Viet Cong as staging areas for their operations. Lieutenant Colonel Kelly provided the following description of Van Tuong (1):

> The village was encircled with a trench line and double apron fence. The streets had punji traps for personnel and vehicles, as well as spider traps. There were numerous hand-painted anti-American signs. There were numerous caves throughout the village . . . .[21]

Accumulated evidence indicated that this hamlet had served as the CP of the *1st VC Regiment*. The Marines found communication equipment, numerous documents, munitions, rice, and propaganda leaflets in Van Tuong (1).

During Operation STARLITE, III MAF severely punished the enemy regiment. According to prisoners, the Marines completely destroyed the *60th VC Battalion* and badly mauled the *80th*. General Krulak credited intelligence as the primary reason for the Marine success. He later wrote, ''The Marines, ground and air, just behaved like they were supposed to behave.'' According to the FMFPac commander, it was ''the confluence of all of the many information sources in a credible picture of what was happening,'' that was the ''decisive factor in STARLITE.''[22]

The reaction to the Marine victory was not altogether what would be expected. General Westmoreland reported that several ARVN general officers on the Joint General Staff made some rather disparaging remarks about the Marine operation. The MACV commander attributed their attitude to the extensive press coverage that the Marines received and suggested that on future occasions that Vietnamese units be included on operations so they could receive their share of plaudits. Moreover, none of the Vietnamese General Staff, except for General Thi and Lam, had been informed about the operation until after it had started. Colonel Don P. Wyckoff, the 3d Marine Division G-3, recalled that none of the Vietnamese were told, at the insistance of General Thi. According to Wyckoff:

> General Walt, concerned about the reaction of ARVN forces in the area when a large scale operation flared up unexpectedly, convinced Thi that General Lam had to know ahead of time to keep his own forces in rein. To my recollection, this was done on a person to person basis from Thi to Lam and Lam kept the information in strict confidence until the battle began.[23]

General Walt later stated that he received his ''instructions from General Westmoreland. I had requested that the 'need to know' among the Vietnamese be limited to the very minimum,'' and

USMC Photo A801265

General Walt, Commanding General, III MAF, congratulates Colonel Oscar F. Peatross, Commanding Officer, 7th Marines, upon the awarding of the Navy Unit Commendation to the 7th Marines for the regiment's participation in Operation STARLITE. Lieutenant Colonel Charles R. Bodley, Commanding Officer, 3d Battalion, 7th Marines, looks on.

recommended that only "Generals Thi and Lam be told. General Westmoreland concurred and approved my action."[24]

Regardless of laudable press reports or restrained Vietnamese reaction, the Marines came out of STARLITE with a renewed faith in their ability. They had passed the first big test. What they did not fully appreciate may have been the cause for the less-than-enthusiastic Vietnamese response. The veteran RVN commanders had seen more than one enemy unit supposedly destroyed, only to reappear on the battlefield at full strength a few months later. The *60th* and *80th VC Battalions* had taken a beating, but they would be back.

CHAPTER 6

The Enemy Refuses to Give Battle: September-November Operations

Operation PIRANHA—Much Ado About CS, Operation STOMP—October-November Operations

Operation PIRANHA

After Operation STARLITE, III MAF entered a new stage of operations aimed at striking at enemy main force units. Having eliminated the threat posed to the Chu Lai base by the *1st VC Regiment*, General Walt considered the time opportune to complete the destruction of the enemy regiment. His intelligence sources indicated that its remnants had withdrawn to the Batangan Peninsula, eight miles south of Van Tuong. After consulting with General Thi, General Walt issued a warning order on 26 August to Colonel Peatross for the 7th Marines to plan for a coordinated operation in the area.*

In contrast to STARLITE, the planning and preparations for the new operation were extensive. From 31 August through 2 September, Marine and naval commanders travelled between Da Nang and Chu Lai. They were briefed by the III MAF staff and prepared detailed plans. Captain McKinney and Colonel Peatross once more were to be the respective

---

*Colonel Wyckoff, the 3d Marine Division G-3 at the time, recalled that following STARLITE, he worked closely with Major Charles T. Williamson, the Division G-2, to locate the *1st VC Regiment*: "The Division G-2 staff sought for indicators in two general areas: the eastern edge of the mountains coming down toward Chu Lai and the cave-dotted Batangan Peninsula. In the latter they found a 'V' of older field fortifications pointing inland with its open end toward the sea. Kept under visual and photographic surveillance, a second 'V' of new positions, inland of the older ones showed under development. A series of transparent overlays was made up, showing the progression of activity over several days. General Walt concurred in the analysis and a staff team was flown down to Saigon to brief General Westmoreland, using the same set of maps and overlays." Col Don P. Wyckoff, Comments on draft MS, dtd 16Oct76 (Vietnam Comment File).

commanders of the amphibious task force and landing forces. They coordinated their activities with the the South Vietnamese and on 3 September the plans were complete. That date, the 7th Marines published Operation Order 423-65, codenamed PIRANHA.

The concept of operations for PIRANHA was similar to that of STARLITE. Two Marine battalions, Lieutenant Colonel Kelly's 1st Battalion, 7th Marines and Muir's 3d Battalion, 3d Marines, would be embarked on Seventh Fleet shipping, while another battalion, Lieutenant Colonel Bodley's 3d Battalion, 7th Marines, would conduct a heliborne assault of the objective area.** On D-Day, Kelly's battalion would land across WHITE Beach, north of the Batangan Peninsula, and push south, while Bodley's helilifted Marines would set up blocking positions 4,000 meters inland. Muir's battalion would remain at sea as a floating reserve. Participating Vietnamese battalions, the 2d Battalion, 4th ARVN Regiment and 3d Vietnamese Marine Battalion, would be moved by helicopter into the region south of Bodley's position. There the South Vietnamese would conduct a search and clear mission on the An Ky Peninsula which was separated from Batangan by the Sa Ky River.

On 6 September, Captain McKinney's task group, consisting of the attack transport *Bayfield*, two dock landing ships, *Belle Grove* and *Cabildo*, and three tank landing ships, sailed for the amphibious objective area. They arrived early the following morning and were joined by the naval gunfire ships, the cruiser *Oklahoma City* (CLG 5), and two

---

** BLT 3/7 joined III MAF on 1 September when it landed at Chu Lai. The battalion had been replaced in the SLF by BLT 2/1.

Lieutenant Colonel Charles H. Bodley, Commanding Officer, 3d Battalion, 7th Marines, writes an order for one of his units during Operation PIRANHA. The operation took place on the Batangan Peninsula, eight miles south of where Operation STARLITE took place.

destroyers, *Prichett* and *Orleck*. In addition, the high-speed destroyer transport *Diachenko* (APD 123) stood offshore prepared to provide direct fire.

Small boats from the South Vietnamese Navy's Junk Division 15 screened the local fishing craft from the American naval task group. By 0500 on the morning of 7 September, all amphibious forces were in position, except for the amphibious assault ship *Princeton* with Muir's 3d Battalion embarked. It arrived later that day.

Two days after the operation had started, the *Oklahoma City* was replaced by the cruiser *Galveston* and the *Orleck* by the destroyer *Braine* (DD 630). An additional destroyer, the *Walke* (DD 723), also arrived. The *Princeton* had stopped off the coast of

Chu Lai to unload newly arriving elements of Colonel William G. Johnson's MAG-36 before proceeding southward.

Air operations over the objective area began with the 0520 arrival of a Marine KC-130, configured to function as an airborne DASC until one could be established ashore. Shortly afterwards a USAF Fairchild C-123 Provider flare plane reported on station to provide illumination. Under the light of the flares, eight A-4s from Colonel Noble's MAG-12 strafed the landing beach with 20mm cannon fire from 0555 to 0615. A lone A-4 laid a smoke screen to cover the assault of the landing force. Marine pilots next turned their attention further inland. Beginning at 0620, eight F-4s and four A-4s dropped eight tons of ''Daisy Cutter'' bombs to prepare the helicopter landing zones.*

While the aircraft bombed the LZs, the first waves of the 1st Battalion, 7th Marines landed across WHITE Beach at 0635. Two LVTE-1s** came ashore to clear enemy mines on the beach. These two amphibian tractors were followed by the assault elements of Companies A and C. The troops dismounted at the water's edge and deployed. The enemy reaction was a few sniper rounds.

The entire battalion was ashore within 20 minutes and enemy resistance continued to be very light. The tractors proved their worth in ploughing paths through the numerous hedgerows where any boobytraps were likely to be hidden. One of the tractors slightly damaged its dozer blade when it detonated a VC boobytrap buried in the sand. This was the first use of the LVTE-1 tractors in combat.

As Kelly's battalion was securing its beachhead, 40 UH-34Ds from MAG-16 helilifted the assault elements of Bodley's 3d Battalion to their objective area, LZ OAK, four miles to the west. The Marines encountered no opposition in the landing zone and completed the helilift in less than three hours.

---

*''Daisy Cutter'' is a term given to bombs equipped with a nose probe which causes the bomb to explode above ground. This causes a clearing by blowing-away the vegetation with a minimum of cratering. These daisy cutters were of the 250- and 500-pound varieties.

**The LVTE-1 is an amphibian tractor equipped to clear a path through minefields. It fires a string (line) of demolitions to its front; these demolitions then explode on the ground setting off mines. The tractors are also equipped with a front dozer blade. Only one of the tractors was able to fire its line chargers without difficulty, but the beach was not mined.

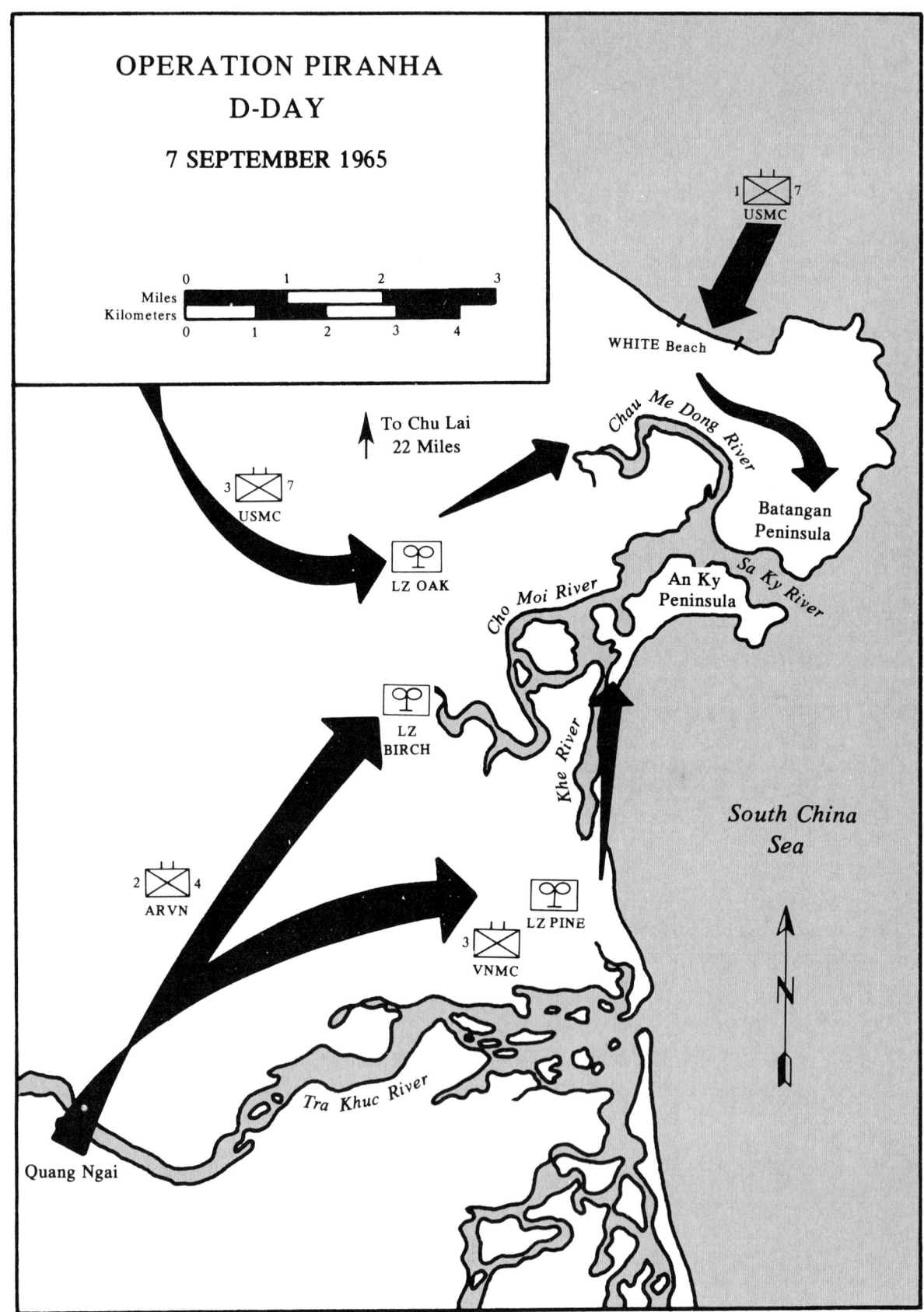

OPERATION PIRANHA
D-DAY

7 SEPTEMBER 1965

Miles
Kilometers

To Chu Lai
22 Miles

WHITE Beach

Chau Me Dong River

Batangan
Peninsula

Sa Ky River

USMC

LZ OAK

Cho Moi River

An Ky
Peninsula

LZ
BIRCH

Khe River

South China
Sea

ARVN

LZ PINE

VNMC

N

Quang Ngai

Tra Khuc River

A Marine whistles while searching a hamlet for VC during Operation PIRANHA as two Vietnamese boys watch him. The Marines encountered relatively little resistance during the operation.

Lieutenant Colonel Bodley established his command post and set up his blocking positions on the high ground.

After inserting the 3d Battalion, 16 of the UH-34Ds flew to Quang Ngai and began shuttling the two South Vietnamese battalions into their landing zones, LZs BIRCH and PINE. This was the only opposed helicopter landing of the day. Four U.S. Army Huey gunships escorting the troop carriers and two of the Marine helicopters were hit by ground fire. As the Vietnamese troops moved out of the landing zones, the firing stopped.

During the three-day operation, only Lieutenant Colonel Kelly's 1st Battalion found a significant number of enemy. On 8 September, Kelly's Company B discovered a VC field hospital in a large cave near the center of the Batangan Peninsula. The Marines captured four prisoners, but then came under fire from other VC in the cave. Kelly's men

returned the fire and attempted to convince the enemy inside to surrender. Marine engineers then placed explosives in the cave. After the detonation, the Marines counted 66 Viet Cong bodies inside. They also found medical supplies, some small arms, and a small amount of ammunition. While searching the cave, six of the Marines were overcome by oxygen starvation. One of them, a lieutenant, died of asphyxiation.

During PIRANHA, allied forces killed 178 VC, seized 20 weapons, and captured or detained 360 enemy and suspected enemy. Lieutenant Colonel Kelly's battalion accounted for 106 of the enemy dead. Allied losses were two Marines and five South Vietnamese killed, 14 Marines and 33 Vietnamese wounded.

The low level of artillery and naval gunfire required during PIRANHA further underscored the enemy's absence. During the first 24 hours of the

USMC Photo A185340

Marines uncover an enemy underground position during Operation PIRANHA. One Marine can be seen inside the tunnel searching for enemy documents and supplies.

operation, the two artillery units, the 107mm Mortar Batteries from the 3d Battalions of the 11th and 12th Marines, fired only 10 missions totaling 110 rounds from positions on Batangan.* The second day they fired 111 rounds. The naval gunfire ships fired 1,052 rounds, but only two illumination missions of 127 rounds for the American forces. Marine air-naval gunfire liaison teams (ANGLICO) attached to the South Vietnamese battalions called in the remainder of the naval support.

Another reason for the limited use of supporting arms fire was the elaborate precautions the Marines took to safeguard the civilian population. The following excerpts from Lieutenant Colonel Kelly's operation order furnish some evidence of this:

> . . . All naval gunfire, artillery, mortar, and close air support must be approved explicitly by this headquarters (FSCC) fire support coordination center prior to being fired. . . . Once approved, all artillery, mortar, and naval gunfire will be fired on forward observer's command. . . . Supporting fires on populated areas will be approved only when organized resistance is being encountered therefrom. Sniping does not constitute organized resistance. . . . No houses or villages will be burned or destroyed as a retaliatory measure.[1]

Lieutenant Colonel Kelly noted that despite the attempt of the Marines to assure the local populace

that no harm would come to them, the villagers remained aloof and made no friendly overtures.[2]

Considering the magnitude of the allied effort, PIRANHA hardly could be called a success. The target of the operation, the *1st VC Regiment*, had withdrawn from the Batangan Peninsula before the operation began. Local villagers told the Marines that Viet Cong units had been in the area but had left, some less than 24 hours before PIRANHA started. Intelligence reports later indicated that the enemy regiment began leaving the area on 4 September, coinciding with the increased movement of the amphibious ships at Chu Lai and the increased activity of the South Vietnamese naval junk force.

The Marine experience in Operation PIRANHA pointed to the need for the development of tactics to clear VC out of caves and enclosed areas. After the operation, Lieutenant Colonel Kelly recommended to General Walt that Marines be authorized to use riot-control gas to save both American and enemy lives. This suggestion touched on the very sensitive political subject of gas warfare; there was no response, for the moment.**

Much Ado About CS, Operation STOMP

The U.S. and South Vietnamese commands had suspended the use of riot-control ammunition, including tear gas, in the spring of 1965 after a public outcry in the United States against such tactics. When Secretary of Defense McNamara visited Saigon in July, he told General Westmoreland that public opinion would not support the use of gas in any form. Despite this statement, during the continuing deployment of U.S. forces to South Vietnam and the reorganization of the American Command in Vietnam, not all echelons of MACV received word of the prohibition. In II Corps, Lieutenant Colonel Leon N. Utter's 2d Battalion, 7th Marines, which on 5 August came under the operational control of Army Major General Stanley R. (Swede) Larsen's

---

* Two South Vietnamese artillery units, a four-gun 105mm howitzer battery, and a two-gun section of 155mm howitzers, supported their portion of the offensive.

** Lieutenant Colonel Kelly later commented: ''It was apparent from this operation that the enemy could not be talked out of the caves and therefore some techniques had to be devised that would enable the Marines to cope with him in his underground hide-out and at the same time minimize as much as possible the risks involved.'' LtCol James P. Kelly, Comments on Shulimson, ''USMC Ops Jul-Dec65,'' dtd 28May71 (Vietnam Comment File).

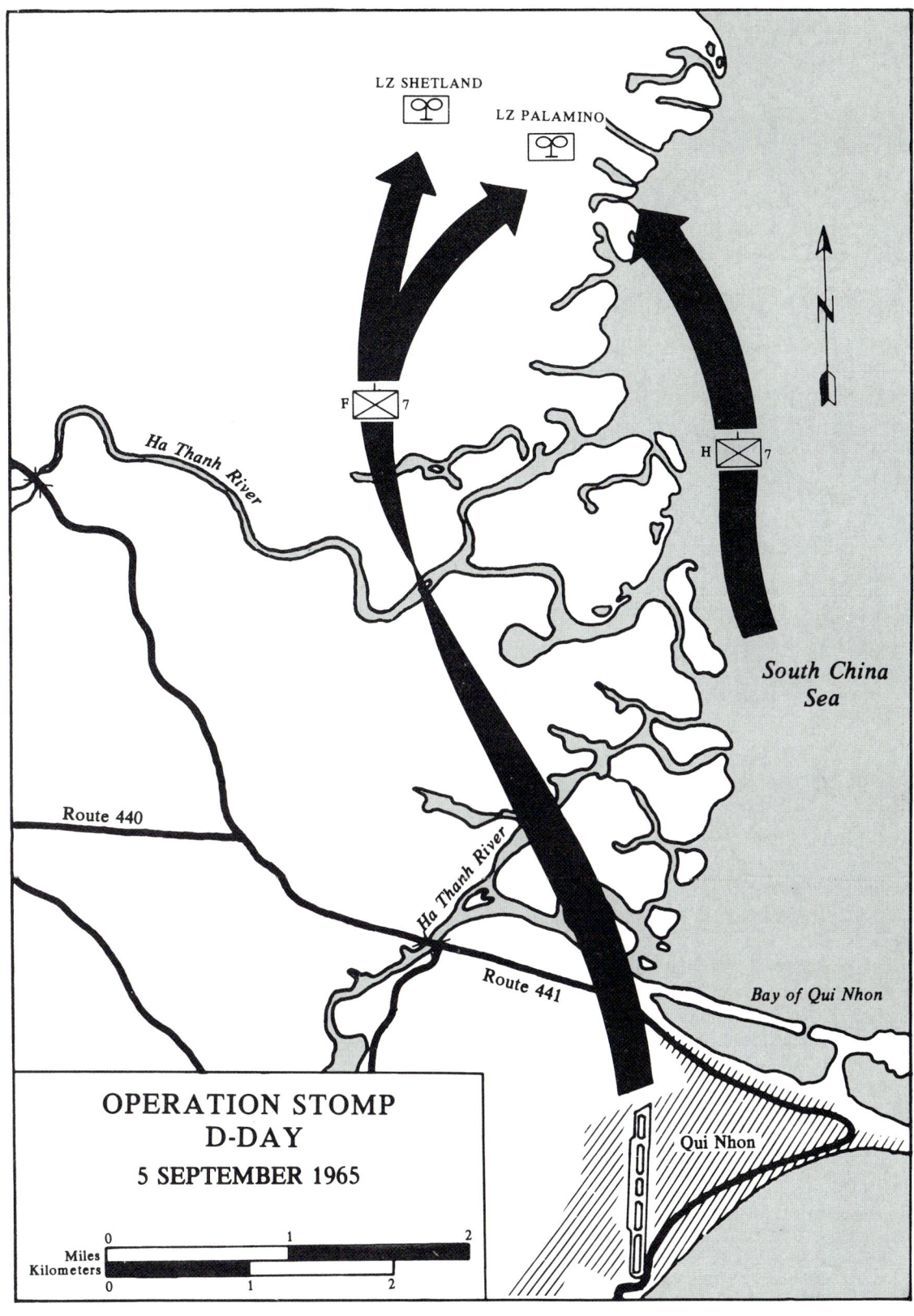

LZ SHETLAND

LZ PALAMINO

F ⊠ 7

H ⊠ 7

Ha Thanh River

South China Sea

N

Route 440

Ha Thanh River

Route 441

Bay of Qui Nhon

Qui Nhon

**OPERATION STOMP
D-DAY**

5 SEPTEMBER 1965

Miles

Kilometers

0   1   2

0   1   2

(Courtesy of Major Gary W. Parker) USMC Photo A707622

An aerial view of the Operation STOMP area of operations north of Qui Nhon. Smoke from artillery preparatory fires can be seen in the left center of the picture.

Task Force ALPHA,* was unaware of the ban. The Marine battalion employed tear gas (CS) near Qui Nhon during an operation codenamed STOMP, which took place from 5-7 September, just before PIRANHA.

Major Raymond W. Wilson, Utter's executive officer, curious about a suspected Communist stronghold some 10 miles north of Qui Nhon, visited a Special Forces camp on Ky Son Mountain which overlooked the region in early September. From intelligence reports, Wilson concluded that the surrounding area was an operating base for a VC

---

* Task Force ALPHA was the forerunner of Field Force, Vietnam, which was established on 25 September with Larsen as commander. Major General Larsen had much the same responsibility for U.S. forces in II Corps as General Walt had for I Corps. See chapter 8 for further discussion of these command relations.

main force unit. He learned that the terrain was honeycombed with a network of tunnels. Major Wilson then suggested to his battalion commander that their unit conduct a search and clear operation through Ky Son and its surrounding countryside. Utter agreed and, after General Larsen gave his permission, the battalion prepared for a two-company sweep of the Ky Son area. Lieutenant Colonel Utter assigned Major Wilson as the commander of the operation and the battalion S-3 officer, Captain Alvin J. Doublet, as second in command. The Marines planned to envelop the Communist forces, with one company landing by LVTs and the other by helicopter.

The basic problem was to kill or capture the Viet Cong, who blended with the civilian population, without harming the innocent. Captain Doublet had been attached to the 7th Marines during STARLITE where he observed several occasions when CS or CN riot-control ammunition could have been most effectively employed in routing the VC from shelters and tunnel complexes. He suggested the use of tear gas for this purpose when he and Wilson briefed Lieutenant Colonel Utter on STOMP. When a thorough review of his orders and message traffic revealed nothing prohibiting the use of such munitions, the battalion commander approved and ordered the execution of the operation.

Operation STOMP unfolded according to plan. Company H made its LVT assault through the mud flats of Qui Nhon bay while Company F landed by helicopter to cut off the VC avenues of retreat. The two companies closed their cordon around the Viet Cong, killing 26 and capturing three. With escape denied, the enemy went underground, taking many local peasants with them for use as human shields. During the mop-up of the area, a much-publicized action occurred. As the Marines slowly and methodically searched out a complex of tunnels, they threw in tear gas grenades to flush out the occupants. Seventeen VC were forced from hiding in this fashion, as well as more than 300 women, children, and old men, not one of whom was harmed.

When the story broke, the Communist propaganda machines went to work. Radio Hanoi broadcast on 8 September that the "U.S. Marines imprudently used toxic gas, killing or seriously affecting many civilians."[3] Both the Communist China News Agency and Russian TASS organization made similar charges.

USMACV headquarters in Saigon was surprised by the news. One of General Westmoreland's subordinates stated that although BLT 2/7 had not been told that tear gas was prohibited, nonetheless, "Everyone knew how Westy felt about it and had permission been asked to employ it, such permission would have been denied." Lieutenant Colonel Utter, fearing the worst, later recalled that he "already had his farewell remarks to his troops in mind."[4]

General Larsen's headquarters conducted an investigation following which the general backed the battalion commander's decision. Larsen declared that had he been asked about the use of tear gas in this operation, he not only would have approved, he would have directed that it be used. He went on to state that the use of tear gas was the most humane way to handle the tactical situation and that he was in receipt of no restrictions on its use. Major Wilson

later wrote that the order for the operation had been "submitted to and approved by General Larsen's headquarters prior to enactment. Although in all fairness, it is doubtful that it was read by anyone other than [the] 2/7 liaison officer to the task force."[5]

A *New York Times* editorial of 11 September perhaps best expressed U.S. public opinion, declaring:

> If the government prohibits the use of tear gas it will thereby order to certain death or injury more Americans and Vietnamese than the absolute necessities of war demand. Nonlethal riot-control gases can be far more humane and will cause far less casualties than many of the weapons now being used in Vietnam.[6]

By the end of the month, the Washington authorities acceded to a request from General Westmoreland that U.S. forces be permitted to use riot-control ammunitions in tunnel-clearing operations. In October while on a visit to Qui Nhon, General Westmoreland told Lieutenant Colonel Utter that it was the successful use by his battalion of nontoxic gases that had altered world opinion to accept their employment in combat.[7]

October-November Operations

In I Corps, III MAF increased the number of battalion-size operations against VC main force elements outside of the Marine TAORS, but with disappointing results. For the next two months, the Viet Cong refused to give battle, except on their own terms. During October, the Marines mounted six attacks far afield from their enclaves, but they resulted in few Communist casualties. Typical of these were Operation RED SNAPPER and LIEN KET-10.

Operation RED SNAPPER was a coordinated USMC/ARVN search and clear operation conducted on the Phu Gia Peninsula overlooking Dam Lap An Bay, 20 miles north of Da Nang. From this region, the Viet Cong threatened Route 1, the vital main road link between Da Nang and Phu Bai.*

The operation involved two companies of Lieutenant Colonel Clement's 2d Battalion, 3d Marines and one company from the 3d Battalion, 4th

---

*The strategic Nam O Bridge, which was Da Nang's only northward link over the Cu De River, the Esso storage facilities, and the Hai Van Pass were all on this route, all good targets for the VC.

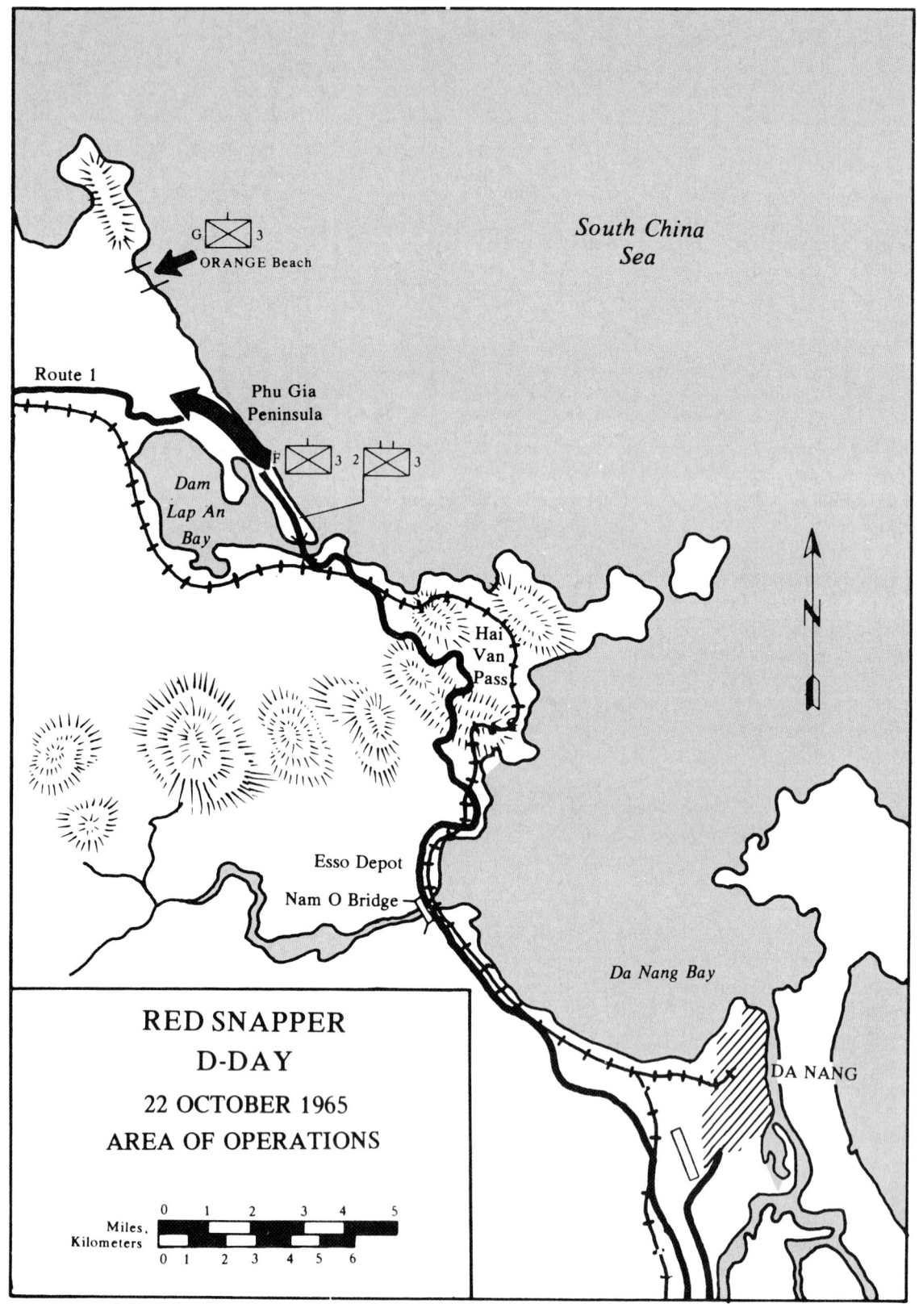

South China
Sea

G ⊠ 3
ORANGE Beach

Route 1

Phu Gia
Peninsula

F ⊠ 3   2 ⊠ 3

Dam
Lap An
Bay

N

Hai
Van
Pass

Esso Depot

Nam O Bridge

Da Nang Bay

DA NANG

RED SNAPPER
D-DAY
22 OCTOBER 1965
AREA OF OPERATIONS

Miles,
Kilometers

0 1 2 3 4 5

0 1 2 3 4 5 6

Marines from the 3d Battalion, 3d Marines cross a beach in the second phase of BLUE MARLIN. Vietnamese fishing boats are in the background.

Marines. The South Vietnamese provided two ARVN battalions, one ARVN ranger battalion, and four Regional Force/Popular Force companies for the offensive. RED SNAPPER began on 22 October when Clement loaded his command group and Company F into trucks and left Da Nang in a motorized column for the Phu Gia promontory. Coinciding with Clement's arrival, his Company G landed from two LCUs over ORANGE Beach halfway up the eastern coast of the peninsula. Concurrently, the ARVN forces deployed along Route 1, west of the Marines, in order to block the withdrawal of any Viet Cong moving away from the two-pronged Marine attack.

Both Marine elements moved into the objective area as planned without encountering any opposition. The next day the company from Phu Bai was helilifted into the operation to reinforce Clement's Company F. At the same time, Clement's Company G conducted a second amphibious landing by LCU further north along the coast and then pushed inland. RED SNAPPER ended on 25 October with meager results; the VC had left before the landing began. Marines captured 1 VC, 4 weapons, and 90 pounds of TNT; ARVN forces killed seven VC, captured five, and seized four weapons.

Operation LIEN KET-10 was equally disappointing. This operation, mounted by Lieutenant Colonel Rodolfo L. Trevino's 2d Battalion, 4th Marines and the 3d Battalion, 6th Regiment of the

ARVN 2d Division, took place in the hills 12 miles west of Chu Lai in the eastern part of the Viet Cong's Do Xa base area. On 29 October, after preparation of the two landing zones by Marine air and artillery, 26 helicopters lifted the two battalions into their respective zones. The Marines encountered no enemy, but did find several deserted huts and a 200-pound rice cache. The second day, Trevino's force captured an enemy courier carrying a brief case of documents. There was little doubt that the combined force had entered a recently evacuated VC staging area, but neither Trevino's battalion nor the ARVN were able to find the enemy. The operation ended that afternoon when III MAF received warning of an imminent attack on the Chu Lai airfield. Trevino's battalion was ordered back to reinforce the TAOR; the attack never materialized.*

Although the VC avoided combat, the Marines were not discouraged and continued their offensive forays during November. During Operation BLACK FERRET, elements of the 1st and 3d Battalions, 7th Marines joined forces in a coordinated effort with two

---

*Lieutenant Colonel Trevino, who replaced Lieutenant Colonel Fisher on 16 October as battalion commander, commented that he believed that had the operation continued, it would have resulted in contact in the region adjacent to and in the western portion of the LIEN KET-10 TAOR. The VC prisoner captured during the operation later committed suicide in the Chu Lai compound. Col Rodolfo L. Trevino, Comments on Shulimson draft MS, "USMC Ops, RVN, Jul-Dec65," n.d. (Vietnam Comment File).

USMC Photo A186116

Marines from the 2d Battalion, 7th Marines debark from Navy landing craft in Operation BLUE MARLIN. The troops are deploying from Qui Nhon to Chu Lai.

battalions of the 2d ARVN Division's 4th Regiment in a search and destroy operation 10 miles south of the Chu Lai airfield, just north of the Song Tra Bong. On 3 November, the Marines opened the operation, attacking southward toward the river from an assembly point on Route 1. While the ARVN patrolled the south bank of the Tra Bong, two platoons of the Marines' 1st Reconnaissance Battalion were helilifted into screening positions on the northern and western edges of the battle area, LZs CONDOR and ALBATROSS. The 3d Battalion, 11th Marines furnished artillery support with a battery of six 105mm howitzers, a battery of six 107mm mortars (howtars), and two sections of 155mm howitzers. Allied intelligence sources reported the presence of a VC main force battalion in the region and the

BLACK FERRET scheme of maneuver envisioned the Marines pushing the enemy southward toward the river where the VC would be trapped between the two allied forces.

Once more the allies were disappointed. No VC battalion materialized, just occasional snipers and booby traps. On the second day of the operation, 4 November, a Marine patrol triggered a booby trap consisting of a M-26 grenade and an 81mm mortar shell. In the ensuing blast newswoman Dickey Chapelle, who had covered Marine operations since World War II, was killed and six Marines were wounded. During the entire operation, the Marines suffered 1 KIA and 13 WIA, while killing at least 2 VC, capturing 6, and taking 79 suspects into custody.

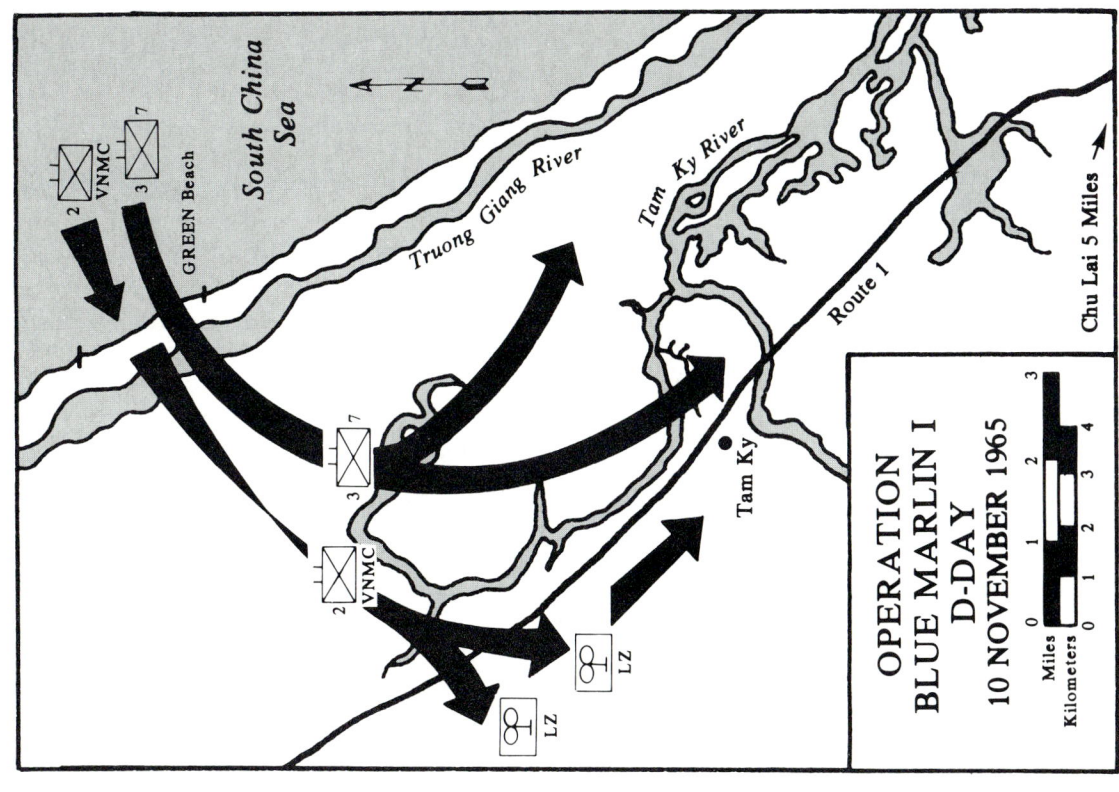

OPERATION
BLUE MARLIN I
D-DAY
10 NOVEMBER 1965

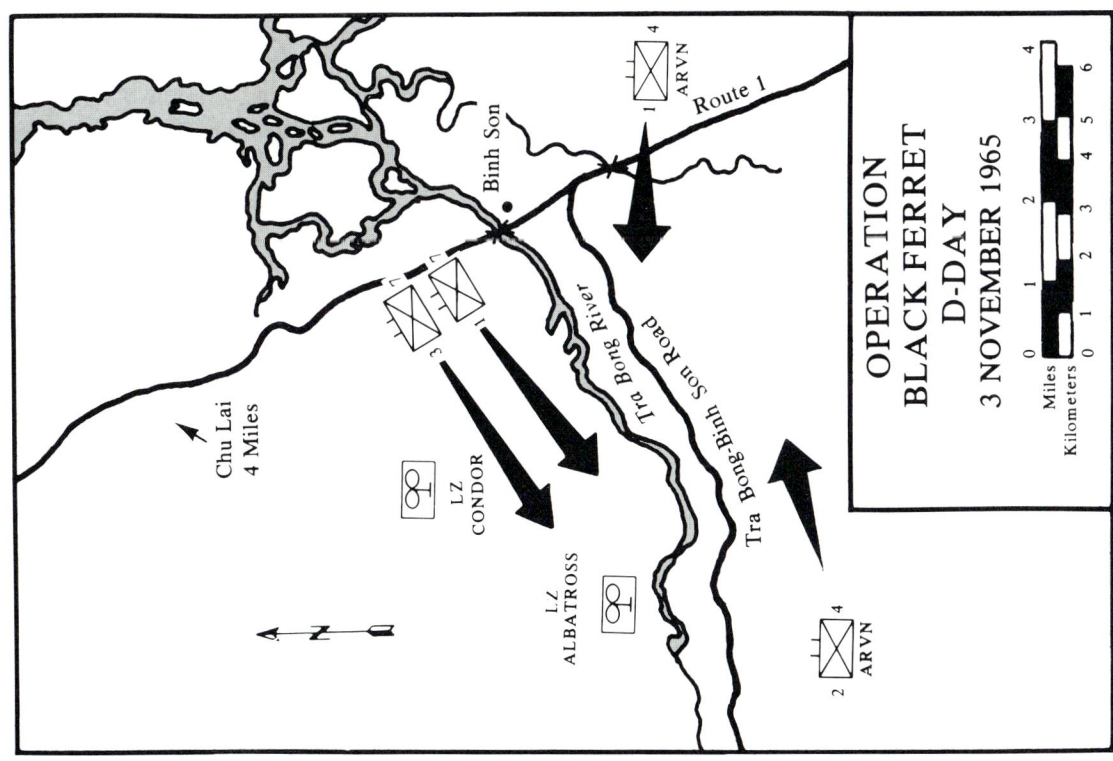

OPERATION
BLACK FERRET
D-DAY
3 NOVEMBER 1965

USMC Photo A186113

Marines from the 2d Battalion, 7th Marines use a Vietnamese fishing boat to cross a river during BLUE MARLIN. Other Marines wait their turn to cross.

There were still many positive results of the operation. The Marines had entered an area where the inhabitants had long been sympathetic to the enemy. Since the Marines indicated that they would be frequent visitors, the ARVN decided to establish a permanent outpost on the southern bank of the Tra Bong. In addition, Marine firepower may have hurt the VC more than the statistics of the operation indicated. Marine aircraft hit several enemy craft on the Tra Bong River and a Marine artillery mission, fired at a suspected VC concentration area, produced secondary explosions.

The last large operation initiated in November was the two-phased BLUE MARLIN. This offensive was the outgrowth of a realignment of forces and an abundance of available amphibious shipping, a combination which offered an excellent opportunity to conduct search and clear operations between the coast and Route 1 in the 50-mile littoral corridor between Da Nang and Chu Lai. Responding to a U.S. appeal for troop assistance from its SEATO allies, the South Korean government dispatched its famed "Tiger Division" to Vietnam's Binh Dinh Province in II CTZ during October. This deployment of forces freed Lieutenant Colonel Utter's BLT 2/7 from its mission at Qui Nhon. General Walt decided to return Utter's unit to its parent regiment at Chu Lai and to move the 3d Battalion, 3d Marines from Chu Lai to its parent regiment at Da Nang. Walt received approval from Seventh Fleet to use the ships of Amphibious Squadron 5 (PhibRon-5) which were then in Korean waters embarking the "Tiger" troops. He then designated Colonel Thell H. Fisher, the deputy chief of staff of III MAF, as the BLUE MARLIN landing force commander and sent him to

Pusan, Korea. On the voyage southward, Colonel Fisher and Captain William J. Maddocks, USN, the amphibious squadron commander, completed the preliminary planning for the operation.

After the Korean troops had relieved Lieutenant Colonel Utter's BLT 2/7 on 4 November, the task group sailed northward to Chu Lai where the 3d South Vietnamese Marine Battalion also boarded the ships. On 10 November, the 190th birthday of the U.S. Marine Corps, the combined USMC/VNMC force* landed according to plan 15 miles north of Chu Lai. Helicopters from Colonel Johnson's MAG-36 ferried the South Vietnamese inland from the beach to landing zones west of Route 1. The combined force then swept southward along both sides of the road. BLUE MARLIN I ended two days later when the allies reached the Chu Lai TAOR. Except for numerous booby traps, no other enemy presence was encountered.

The second phase of BLUE MARLIN followed a similar pattern. After Phase I ended, the amphibious task group returned to Chu Lai where Lieutenant Colonel William H. Lanagan, Jr.'s 3d Battalion, 3d Marines embarked on the ships. Lieutenant Colonel Lanagan had assumed command of the battalion five days after Lieutenant Colonel Muir's death during an operation south of Da Nang.** On 16 November, the battalion landed over beaches 22 miles south of Da Nang, and pushed north. The area of operations for Lanagan's force was a corridor bounded by the Truong Giang River to the west, the Cua Dai River

---

*Major Richard E. Romine accompanied the South Vietnamese Marines in BLUE MARLIN. He recalled: "We had a bad time getting on the beach with the Amtracs due to the extremely rough surf. . . . we landed north of Tam Ky and swept towards Chu Lai." On 10 November, he remembered that he celebrated the Marine Corps Birthday with "a beer that an H-34 pilot dropped to me that evening." Romine added, ". . . although enemy contact was very light, the snipers seemed to single me out from the Vietnamese Marines I was near." LtCol Richard E. Romine, Comments on draft MS, dtd 25Oct76 (Vietnam Comment File).

**The 3d Battalion, 3d Marines had flown from Chu Lai to Da Nang on 10 September to support a 9th Marines operation. On the early morning of 11 September, Lieutenant Colonel Muir stepped on a 155mm shell rigged as a mine and was killed with his radio operator. Four other Marines were wounded in the blast. This occurred on Hill 55, a strategically located elevation 8,000 meters south of the Cau Do. The 3d Battalion returned to Chu Lai on 14 September. In the interim, Major Comer, the executive officer, was the acting battalion commander until relieved by Lieutenant Colonel Lanagan. See Chapter 8.

to the north and the South China Sea to the east. Two ARVN ranger battalions conducted a coordinated search and destroy mission west of the Truong Giang. During the three-day operation, the combined forced killed 25 Viet Cong. In addition, 15 VC were captured, 79 suspects apprehended, and 9 weapons were seized. Friendly casualties were two ARVN killed, and one ARVN and three Marines wounded. At the conclusion of the operation, the 3d Battalion, 3d Marines moved to Da Nang by amphibious shipping and helicopters where it assumed the mission of division reserve.

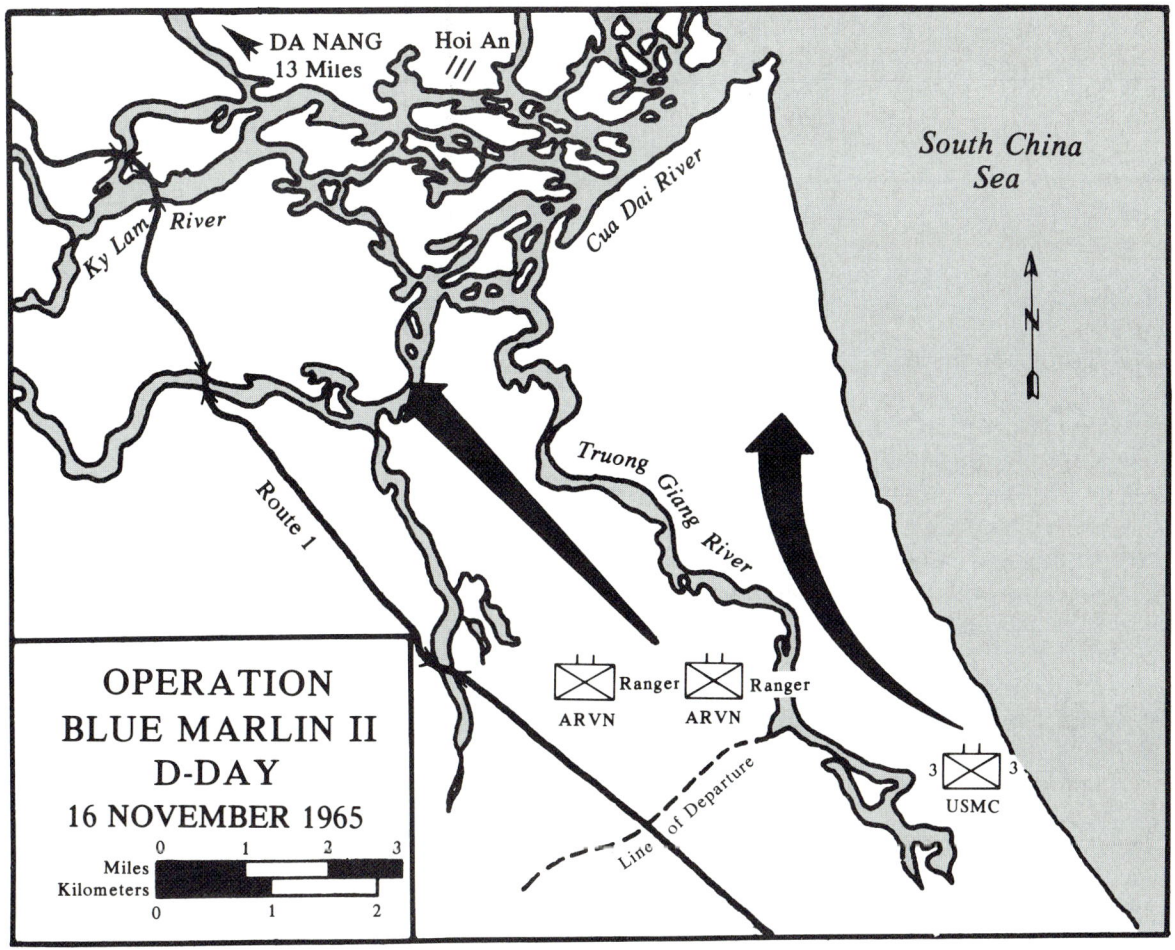

CHAPTER 7

The *1st VC* Again—
Operation HARVEST MOON

The Abandonment of Hiep Duc—Activation of Task Force DELTA and Planning the Operation—The VC Strike and the Marines Are Committed—The Search of the Phouc Ha Valley—The Fight at Ky Phu—The Wrap-Up

---

The Abandonment of Hiep Duc

In November, the *1st VC Regiment*, obviously recovered from the beating received during Operation STARLITE, attacked the South Vietnamese outpost located at Hiep Duc, 25 miles west of Tam Ky.* This district capital, situated on the headwaters of the Song Thu Bon, was the western gateway to a fertile mountain valley which later became known to Marines as the Nui Loc Son Basin, named for a rugged, narrow hill that protrudes from the center of the valley floor. Also known as the Que Son Valley, the broad, heavily populated expanse of farm land constituted one of the more strategic areas between Da Nang and Chu Lai. During the northeast monsoon season, heavy rain clouds shrouded the valley and its western approaches, thus allowing the enemy freedom of movement without being observed from the air.

On the evening of 17 November, the enemy regiment, with all three of its battalions, the *60th, 80th,* and *90th,* overran the small Regional Force garrison. Enemy units were identified later from captured documents and by interrogation of a VC defector. Hiep Duc District leaders reported 174 of the 433 defenders missing and 315 weapons lost.

** Colonel Wyckoff, remarked in his comments on the draft that he was unconvinced that the *1st VC* ever recovered from STARLITE. He believes that its "resurgence as a fully active unit was the result of reinforcement by North Vietnamese Regulars." Colonel Wyckoff recalled message traffic at the time in which the VC main forces were "notifying the local guerrillas to stick it out on their own until help came down from the north; that their current role was to be assistance to the main force, not vice versa." Col Don P. Wyckoff, Comments on draft MS, dtd 16Oct76 (Vietnam Comment File).*

Soon after reports reached Da Nang of the loss of Hiep Duc, F-4B Phantoms from MAG-11 and A-4 Skyhawks from MAG-12 arrived over the outpost and conducted strikes against enemy positions in the surrounding hills. At the same time, the two helicopter groups, MAG-16 and MAG-36, prepared to helilift two South Vietnamese battalions into the battle area.

Colonel Thomas J. O'Connor, the MAG-16 commander and airborne coordinator for the operation, Lieutenant Colonel Robert J. Zitnik, the commander of VMO-6, and the South Vietnamese infantry commander made an early morning reconnaissance flight over the fallen base on 18 November "to look over the area and select a landing zone." O'Connor remembered as they looked down:

> The area was ominously quiet. We didn't see a living soul. There was much evidence of the fight the day before. The typical triangular-shaped French fortification in the village had been penetrated in several places. There were several corpses hanging on barbed wire around a few of the outposts across the Song Thu Bon.[1]

In their search for a suitable landing zone, the three officers rejected a rice paddy about 500 meters north of Hiep Duc because of the potential of an enemy ambush. Instead, the South Vietnamese commander selected a small hill, about 80 meters high, 700 meters southeast of the village. With this decision made, the three returned to Tam Ky where the transport squadron commanders were organizing the lifts to Hiep Duc.

The site chosen for the landing zone would create problems. It was quite small and could only accommodate two helicopters at one time. Furthermore, the hill on which the landing zone was situated was the western end of a ridgeline stretching

USMC Photo A186279

Captain Richard E. Theer, Commanding Officer, Company B, 2d Battalion, 7th Marines, describes the battle situation to General Walt. The scene is near the base of Hill 407 in the Que Son Valley.

about 4,000 meters east of Hiep Duc with some peaks over 200 meters high. Unknown to the allies, the VC had emplaced 12.7mm machine gun positions on this hill mass which dominated the landing zone.

The enemy gunners allowed the first helicopters to land on 18 November, but then opened fire on the following waves.* Colonel O'Connor, who was airborne with Lieutenant Colonel Zitnik over Hiep Duc during the landing attempt, stated that, "they [the enemy gunners] were actually firing down on the landing helicopters." Several of the aircraft were

hit and, according to O'Connor, "It became obvious that we had to knock out those guns on the peaks or suffer unacceptable helicopter losses." Colonel O'Connor recalled:

> I stopped the oncoming helicopter flights, and directed them to circle their positions about 3 miles east of the hill mass. Then, A-4's and F-4's from MAG 12 and MAG 11 began a thorough neutralization of gun positions on the hill under control of some Army light fixed-wing observation aircraft.
>
> We took a risk in stopping the helicopter lift, because we had landed less than a company in the zone. Enemy ground movement was observed after the first helicopter had landed. They [the enemy troops] began to displace from their original positions north and west of the paddy we had scouted, and moved into the village toward the landing zone. Bob Zitnik and I were fired upon while circling Hiep Duc observing these movements. But we had to give the jets a good clear shot at the gun positions, and they did their job.[2]

After a 20-minute wait for the Marine jets to

---

*It was later learned that the intense and well directed 12.7mm antiaircraft fire was delivered by the *NVA 195th* [also known as the *9th*] *Antiaircraft Battalion*. This North Vietnamese unit had been formed from elements of the *NVA 308th Division* early in the spring of 1965, and moved south via the Ho Chi Minh Trail through Laos and arrived in South Vietnam during September. It had joined the *1st VC Regiment* in the Que Son-Hiep Duc Region on 20 October 1965. III MAF ComdC, Dec65.

knock out the enemy antiaircraft emplacements, Colonel O'Connor resumed the troop lift. Although the VC ground forces were converging on the landing zone, ''we landed a superior force in the zone without further opposition.'' For the operation, the Marines had employed 30 UH-34s, 17 of which were hit, and 3 badly damaged. One Marine crewman was killed and three others wounded.[3]

The relief force had its work cut out for it, but with Marine close air support and determined fighting, the ARVN gained the advantage. By the end of the 19th, the South Vietnamese reoccupied Hiep Duc, but the *1st VC Regiment* still controlled the critical terrain to the northwest. The two ARVN battalions killed 141 VC and captured 87 weapons while suffering 33 killed and 73 wounded themselves. American advisors with the ARVN estimated that Marine air support had accounted for another 300 VC killed.

General Thi now had to make a major decision: either regarrison the district capital with the ARVN force, or abandon the outpost. In spite of rainy weather and poor flying conditions, Lieutenant Colonel Bodley's 3d Battalion, 7th Marines at Chu Lai was ready to reinforce the ARVN should the need arise. The Communists actually decided the issue when they attempted to overrun an isolated outpost, Thach Tru, in southern I Corps.* Forced to commit more forces to this action, Thi ordered the two ARVN battalions withdrawn from Hiep Duc.[4]

Instead of reinforcing Hiep Duc, Bodley's battalion was committed to the Thach Tru engagement, 16 miles south of Quang Ngai. The attacking force was identified as North Vietnamese, the *18th NVA Regiment* reinforced by the *45th VC Heavy Weapons Battalion*. Although the Marines arrived on 22 November, the day after the attack had begun, their help was never really needed. The defenders, two RF companies and the 37th ARVN Ranger Battalion, repulsed the attack, inflicting heavy casualties on the enemy. Dense cloud cover over the area hampered close air support, but two U. S. destroyers provided

---

*Advance elements of Bodley's 3d Battalion were actually helilifted to Hiep Duc area on 21 November, but the bad weather prevented the unit from landing. The battalion had planned to start Operation QUICK FIRE that day in the Hiep Duc region in support of the ARVN's ongoing Operation QUYET THANG 485; the Marine plans were cancelled the next day when the 3d Battalion, 7th Marines went to Thach Tru.

USMC Photo A801116

Brigadier General Melvin D. Henderson, Commanding General, Task Force DELTA (left), and Lieutenant Colonel Leon N. Utter, Commanding Officer, 2d Battalion, 7th Marines (right), discuss the commitment of Utter's battalion into Operation HARVEST MOON. Utter's Marines were inserted after the VC struck the 5th ARVN Regiment.

much needed fire support during the engagement. Two U.S. Marines advisors to the 2d ARVN Division, flying over the battlefield in O-1B observation aircraft, directed the 5-inch guns of the *O'Brien* (DD 725) and *Bache* (DD 470) against enemy formations. The ARVN Ranger commander credited these two ships with breaking the back of the enemy attack.[5] During the three-day battle, the ARVN, supported by naval gunfire and Marine air, killed 175 enemy and captured 136 weapons. Bodley's force accounted for another three enemy dead and took 17 prisoners. Unfortunately, one Marine UH-34D and its four crew members were lost during a troop lift sortie. The 3d Battalion, 7th Marines was helilifted back to Chu Lai on the 24th, after being relieved by the 11th ARVN Ranger Battalion at Thach Tru.

USMC Photo A186281

A Marine helicopter brings in supplies to a forward company during Operation HARVEST MOON. The Marine in center of the picture is making landing signals to the pilot.

The two actions at Hiep Duc and Thach Tru typified the enemy's monsoon strategy. Moving during periods of poor weather which hampered air operations, the Communists attacked isolated outposts and then established ambushes to trap any relief forces. At Thach Tru the enemy had miscalculated, but at Hiep Duc, in forcing the ARVN to abandon control there, the *1st VC Regiment* was in excellent position to enter the strategic Nui Loc Son Basin, threatening ARVN outposts at Que Son and Viet An.

To counteract this threat, on 17 November General Westmoreland ordered General Walt to hold two battalions on a 12-hour alert so that they could be deployed rapidly as a mobile reserve. Five days later, he issued a new letter of instruction in which he reaffirmed his previous verbal order to Walt that III MAF should "conduct search and destroy operations against more distant VC base areas to destroy or drive the VC out."[6]

At about the same time, General Krulak, though not in the official operational chain-of-command, commented on the need for the Marines to recapture the initiative. General Krulak made several suggestions including the idea of enticing the VC to attack a supposedly weak position which was actually "loaded for bear." The place the general mentioned was Hiep Duc.[7]

General Walt, concerned about the enemy's growing control in the Nui Loc Son Basin, met with General Thi on 4 December to discuss the mounting threat. According to intelligence reports, the enemy had moved northeast from Hiep Duc and was threatening the ARVN outposts at Que Son and Viet An. Both commanders concurred in the need to launch a sizeable attack against the VC before the enemy unit was able to establish a firm base of operations. The result of this agreement was Operation HARVEST MOON/LIEN KET 18.*

Activation of Task Force DELTA and Planning the Operation

On 5 December, III MAF activated a temporary command, codenamed Task Force DELTA, under the Assistant Division Commander, 3d Marine Division, Brigadier General Melvin D. Henderson, to control the upcoming operation.** Two battalions, Lieutenant Colonel Utter's 2d Battalion, 7th Marines from Chu Lai and Lieutenant Colonel Joshua W. Dorsey's 3d Battalion, 3d Marines from Da Nang, were assigned to the task force.*** A provisional artillery battalion was formed from elements of the 11th and 12th Marines, consisting of two 105mm howitzer batteries. In addition, III MAF had received permission to use the SLF as the task force reserve.

By 7 December, General Henderson had completed planning efforts with his ARVN counterpart, Brigadier General Hoang Xuan Lam, commander of

---

*This operation should not be confused with the rice harvest operations, also named HARVEST MOON, conducted during September-October. These pacification efforts are discussed in Chapter 9.

**At this time there were two assistant division commanders of the 3d Marine Division. General Henderson was stationed at Da Nang while Brigadier General Jonas M. Platt, who had relieved General Karch on 9 November, was assigned to Chu Lai and also acted as base coordinator there.

***LtCol Dorsey had relieved LtCol Lanagan as battalion commander on 1 December. During HARVEST MOON, the 3d Battalion, 3d Marines had only one of its own companies, Company L, but had attached Company E from 2d Battalion, 9th Marines and Company G from 2d Battalion, 4th Marines for the operation.

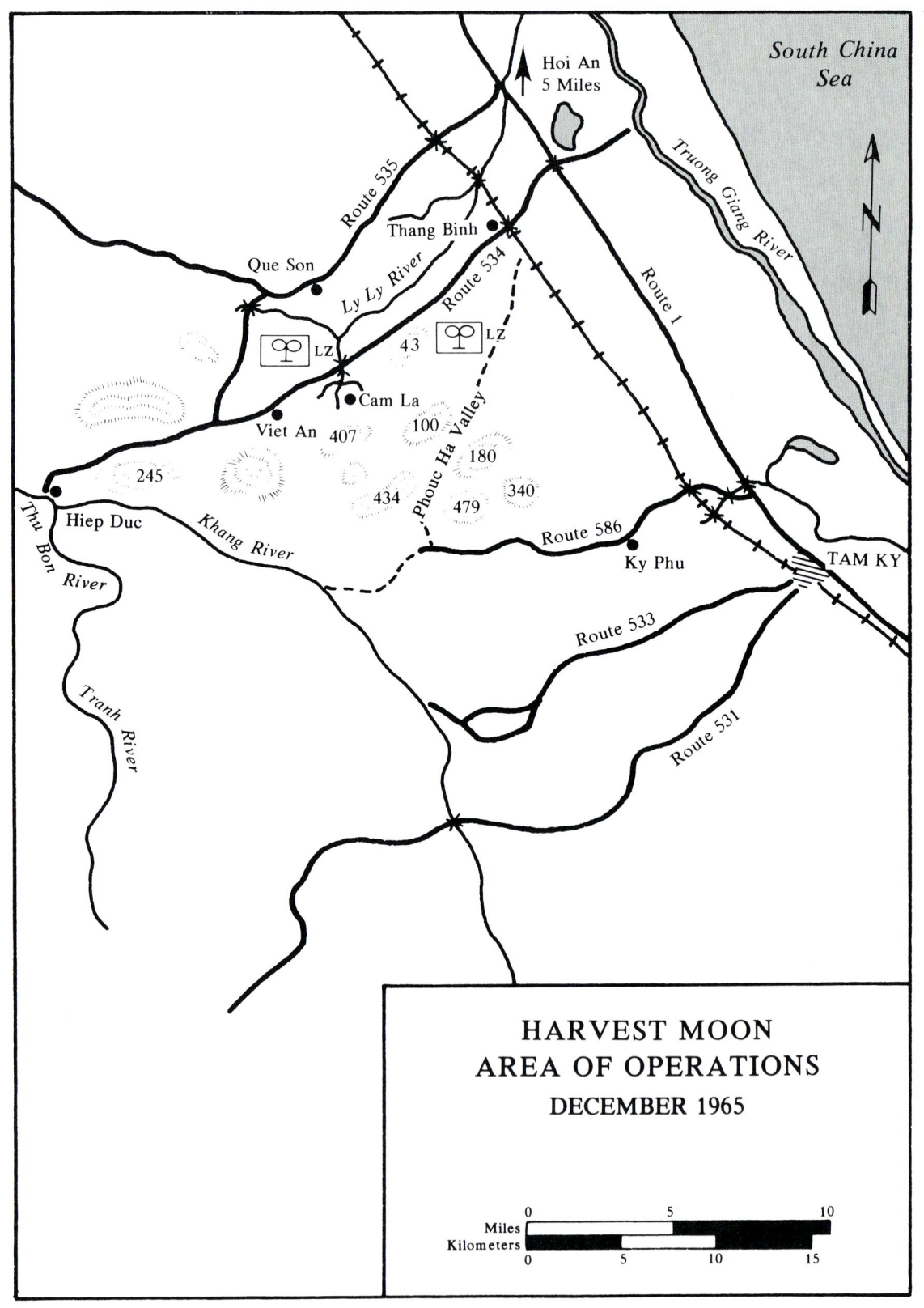

**HARVEST MOON
AREA OF OPERATIONS
DECEMBER 1965**

Marines from Company E, 2d Battalion, 9th Marines receive a briefing before boarding helicopters during Operation HARVEST MOON. The helicopters wait in the background.

the 2d ARVN Division. General Lam, ''a figure familiar to the Marines in his black beret with silver badges, tanker's jacket, and swagger stick,'' would establish his operational CP at Thang Binh, while Henderson would locate his near the artillery positions at Que Son.[8] The largest combined operation since the arrival of the Marines was about to begin.

The plan for Operation HARVEST MOON/LIEN KET 18 directed the 5th ARVN Regiment, consisting of the headquarters group and 1st Battalion, and the 11th Ranger Battalion, to enter the Que Son Valley along the Thang Binh-Hiep Duc road on 8 December. The objective for the first day was a point south of the village of Que Son, eight miles southwest of Route 1. According to allied intelligence sources, the *1st VC Regiment* was west of this area; contact was not expected until the second day. On 9 December, Lieutenant Colonel Utter's battalion was to be inserted behind the enemy to force them eastward into the advancing ARVN. Lieutenant Colonel Dorsey's battalion would then be inserted to reinforce Utter's unit when needed.

The VC Strike and the Marines Are Committed

The 5th ARVN Regiment left Thang Binh on schedule with the 11th Ranger Battalion on the right of the road, and the regiment's 1st Battalion on the left. During the first few hours, the advance was

uneventful. At 1330 about halfway to Que Son, the ranger battalion was ambushed by the *70th VC Battalion*.* The enemy allowed the ARVN to close within 20 meters and then opened fire. In the first 15 minutes of the battle, the rangers lost nearly one third of their personnel and were overrun. According to an American advisor who was with the ARVN force, ''They attacked in a mass and hit us from all sides. . . . People were dropping around us right and left.''[9]

The badly mauled ranger unit was able to withdraw to a position 1,200 meters to the northwest and

---

* The *70th*, although not organic to the *1st VC Regiment*, was attached during this period. IntellRept, Encl 2, *TF DELTA AAR*, p. 1-2. Lieutenant Colonel Ralph E. Sullivan, at the time a member of the TF DELTA staff, recalled that information on the operation was severely restricted. According to Sullivan, the 5th ARVN regimental commander, ''was told his mission was to be a routine 'sweep and clear' along highway 1 to the vicinity of Ky Lam. On reaching the vicinity of Thang Binh, [the regimental commander] was brought to the 'bunker' at Da Nang about 1500 on 7 December and apprised of his actual mission. General Thi warned us not to discuss the operation with any of the ARVN except for a select few in his own headquarters and that of General Lam's. The fact that at 1330, 8 December the 11th ARVN Ranger Battalion walked into a *prepared* ambush is *prima facie* evidence that if [the regimental commander] was kept in the dark, the commander of the *1st VC Regiment* was not.'' LtCol Ralph E. Sullivan, Comments on draft MS, dtd 28Oct76 (Vietnam Comment File).

Marines move through a Vietnamese village in Operation HARVEST MOON. Each of the riflemen is carrying two 60 mm mortar rounds in additon to his own weapon and ammunition.

then called in Marine air support. Skyhawks from MAG-12 at Chu Lai attacked the Communist positions, while Marine helicopters evacuated many of the casualties. The 1st ARVN Battalion attempted to reinforce the rangers, but was unable to cross the road because of enemy mortar fire and U.S. air strikes. Later in the afternoon, General Lam, using 10 UH-34Ds from Lieutenant Colonel Rex C. Denny, Jr.'s HMM-161, moved the 1st Battalion, 6th ARVN Regiment from Tam Ky to reinforce the surviving rangers. This battalion replaced the rangers and established a night defensive perimeter.

The next morning, the 5th ARVN Regiment command group and its 1st Battalion bore the weight of the VC attack. Although the battalion had been probed during the night, it had not seen heavy action. On 9 December, about 0645, the *60th* and *80th VC Battalions* struck. In the heavy fighting that followed, both the 1st Battalion and regimental command group were overrun. The ARVN regimental commander was killed and the ARVN force was scattered to the south and east. At about the same time, another VC battalion attacked the 1st Battalion, 6th ARVN Regiment to the northeast, but this ARVN unit managed to hold its ground.

At that point, General Henderson decided to commit his Marines. At 1000, UH-34Ds from Denny's HMM-161 and Lieutenant Colonel Lloyd F. Childers' HMM-361 lifted Utter's 2d Battalion from Tam Ky to a landing zone 5 1/2 miles west of the

General Jonas M. Platt (second from the left) discusses plans with III MAF staff officers and officers from the 2d Battalion, 7th Marines. The objective areas are outlined on the map overlay.

ARVN troops. After the landing, the battalion moved northeast, securing a hill mass 2,500 meters from the landing zone by late afternoon. Utter's Marines encountered only a few Viet Cong and one of his platoon leaders later complained: ''The enemy always seemed one step ahead of us.''[10] The same afternoon, General Henderson directed Dorsey's 3d Battalion, 3d Marines to land 1 ½ miles southeast of the 5th ARVN Regiment's 1st Battalion and then move to link up with the shattered South Vietnamese unit.

Lieutenant Colonel Dorsey's Marines had left Da Nang by motor convoy that morning and were at the logistics support area (LSA) on Route 1, three miles north of Thang Binh. Lieutenant Colonel Mervin B. Porter's HMM-261, the SLF helicopter squadron on board the LPH *Valley Forge*, was assigned the mission of ferrying the battalion into a landing zone southeast of the 5th ARVN Regiment's command group and its 1st Battalion. The 3d Battalion landed at 1400, and an hour and half later, the battalion's lead unit, Company L, made contact with elements of the ARVN battalion and then pushed northwestward toward Hill 43, 1 ½ miles from the landing zone. Before the Marines could reach the hill, they ran into a force of 200 VC. The firefight raged into the early evening. Supported by Marine air and artillery, Dorsey estimated that his battalion had killed 75 VC. Eleven Marines were dead and 17 wounded. The VC broke contact as darkness fell and the battalion established night positions. The next morning, the Marines took Hill 43, where they joined 40 South Vietnamese soldiers from the 1st Battalion, 5th Regiment.

On the 10th, General Henderson ordered Utter to drive east and Dorsey to push northwest to compress the enemy between them. The avenue of escape to the south was to be closed by Lieutenant Colonel Robert T. Hanifin Jr.'s 2d Battalion, 1st Marines, the SLF battalion which would be lifted into the area by Porter's HMM-261.

At 1100, 15 UH-34Ds from the *Valley Forge* lifted the assault elements of Company F to a landing zone near the hamlet of Cam La, five miles southeast of Que Son. As the helicopters landed they came under heavy 12.7mm machine gun fire from emplacements on Hill 407, 2,000 meters to the south. The intense, heavy caliber enemy fire surprised the Marines. Colonel Michael R. Yunck, the 1st MAW G-3, who had volunteered to act as Tactical Air Controller (Airborne) for the assault mission, remembered: "We thought the LZ was far enough from the hill to the south to nullify effective fire from that distance and had pretty well scrubbed the immediate area of the LZ." As the assault helicopters lifted off, Yunck maneuvered his UH-1E over the landing zone to locate the enemy gunners, but in the process was wounded by a 12.7mm round. His co-pilot, Major Edward L. Kuykendall, took control of the air operation and directed the remaining helicopters carrying Lieutenant Colonel Hanifin's command group and Company G to land in another landing zone further west.*[11]

Company F at the first landing site was in trouble. The enemy kept the Marines under continuous machine gun fire and then opened up with mortars and small arms fire. The company took what cover it could in the open rice paddies and waited for reinforcements. Since the rest of the battalion had landed to the west, the task force commander ordered a company from Lieutenant Colonel Utter's battalion

to move south to aid the hard-hit unit. Company E, 2d Battalion, 7th Marines pushed southward towards Hanifin's Company F, but was hit on its right flank by enemy fire. With some difficulty, Company E reached an area from which it could support the stranded company. Company F began withdrawing under the relief force's covering fire. Ten hours after the first helicopter had landed, Hanifin's battalion command group, Companies G and F, and Company E from Utter's battalion joined forces. Both companies E and F had suffered substantial casualties during the day, 20 dead and over 80 wounded.**

As darkness fell on the battlefield that day, General Walt relieved General Henderson. Brigadier General Jonas M. Platt became head of Task Force DELTA. General Platt, appraised of the battle situation, ordered another of Utter's companies to reinforce the 2d Battalion, 1st Marines. Company G, 2d Battalion, 7th Marines arrived at Hanifin's position at 0300 the next morning.

The Search of the Phouc Ha Valley

On the 11th, Task Force DELTA maneuvered to consolidate its position and General Platt, airborne in a helicopter, studied the terrain from which the Marines of Company F and helicopters of HMM-261 had received such extensive fire on the 10th. The general, surprised that his craft did not draw enemy fire, surmised that the Viet Cong must have abandoned their positions on Hill 407 during the night. Platt, therefore, ordered Lieutenant Colonel Utter to seize the hill, a task which the 2d Battalion, 7th Marines accomplished without opposition.[12]

In the interim, Lieutenant Colonel Dorsey's 3d Battalion searched the area to the north of Hill 407, while the remaining two companies of Hanifin's 2d Battalion, 1st Marines were helilifted from the ARG ships to join the battalion.*** By the end of the day,

---

*Colonel Yunck was the 1963 Marine Aviator of the Year. He was awarded his second Silver Star for his actions during HARVEST MOON. His leg had to be amputated as a result of the wound he suffered during the battle.

**One of the casualties was Captain James E. Page, Company F commander, who had been pronounced dead on the battlefield. The next day medical personnel checking the bodies detected a faint heart beat and evacuated Captain Page to a hospital. The captain recovered.

***When the SLF was assigned to HARVEST MOON on 7 December, Companies E and H on board the APA *Montrose* were en route to Okinawa and the ship had to be diverted to Vietnam. It arrived offshore from the objective area at about 1600 on the 10th.

USMC Photo A186243

Lieutenant Colonel Joshua W. Dorsey III (left), Commanding Officer, 3d Battalion, 3d Marines, confers with Brigadier General Jonas M. Platt (right), Commanding Task Force DELTA. Dorsey's battalion is about to enter the Phouc Ha Valley, a known VC main base area.

it was apparent that the enemy, except for a few snipers, had vanished. General Platt suspected that the regiment had retreated into the Phouc Ha Valley, a smaller valley paralleling the Que Son Valley, five miles to the southeast. The Phouc Ha Valley was a known VC base area. When General Thi was questioned about going into the valley after the Communists, the I Corps commander replied, "be very, very careful."[13] On the afternoon of the 11th, Brigadier General Platt was visited by Brigadier General William E. DePuy, USA, General Westmoreland's J-3, who suggested that USAF B-52 Boeing Stratofortresses from Guam could strike the objective area before the Marines entered. General Platt accepted the offer and the first of several B-52 raids occurred on the morning of the 12th.

General Platt, on board a UH-1E piloted by the Assistant 1st MAW Commander, Brigadier General

Carl, observed the first strike and directed Lieutenant Colonels Dorsey and Hanifin to move their battalions in to exploit the bombing mission. During the afternoon, Hanifin's battalion deployed south of the valley, while Dorsey moved along two ridges, Hills 100 and 180, overlooking northern entrances to the Phouc Ha Valley. During the night of 12 December, General Platt ordered Dorsey to move 1,000 meters to the north so that the USAF B-52s could strike the valley again.*

---

*General Platt had received a message from General Westmoreland's staff that ground troops should be no closer than 3,000 meters from a B-52 strike, the reason for Dorsey's move. *Platt interview, Jan 70.* General Platt observed in his comments on the draft that General DePuy had previously told him "1,000 meters off the line of flight." MajGen Jonas M. Platt, Comments on MS, dtd 7Oct76 (Vietnam Comment File).

The next morning, after the second B-52 strike, the two Marine battalions entered the valley from both the north and south. While searching the target area, Dorsey's battalion did not find the *1st VC Regiment*, but discovered large amounts of enemy supplies and equipment. The two battalions remained in the valley for the next few days, but encountered little organized resistance.

The Fight at Ky Phu

While the two Marines battalions were operating in the Phouc Ha Valley, Lieutenant Colonel Utter's battalion sought the VC along the northern bank of the Song Chang, also known as the Khang River, seven miles south of Que Son. The battalion then turned eastward toward Tam Ky, sweeping the southern boundary of the HARVEST MOON objective area. The Marines had more trouble with the weather than the enemy. Except for occasional snipers, the enemy could not be located, but the monsoon rains harassed the Marines' every step. During the prolonged search, the battalion slogged over 20 miles through extremely rugged terrain, varying from flooded rice paddies to jungle-covered hills.

On 18 December, the 2d Battalion, 7th Marines, on the last leg of its long trek, encountered the *80th VC Battalion* in strength. Earlier that morning, after evacuating 54 Marines suffering from immersion foot,* the battalion had moved out in a column formation with Company G in the lead, followed by Company F, Headquarters and Service Company, and Company H, 2d Battalion, 9th Marines.** The Marines moved along a narrow road which wound through hedgerow-bordered rice paddies. The Viet Cong allowed the lead company to pass through the village of Ky Phu, four miles from Route 1, before opening fire on the Company G advance guard. At

first, Lieutenant Colonel Utter thought that the enemy force consisted only of a few snipers, and ordered Company G to clear the area south of the road and moved Company F forward.

Company F had just passed through the east end of Ky Phu when enemy mortar rounds dropped on H&S Company, still in the open paddies west of the hamlet. Two Viet Cong companies tried to enter the gap between Company F and H&S and envelop Utter's command group and the H&S Company. First Lieutenant Nicholas H. Grosz, Jr., the commander of H&S Company, recalled that he crossed the area between his company and the battalion command group and told Lieutenant Colonel Utter of the ''H&S deteriorating situation.'' Realizing that he was engaged with a major enemy force, the battalion commander ordered Company F to turn and attack the ''main VC positions on the H&S right flank.''[14]

Supported by ''Huey'' gunships and accurate artillery fire from Battery M, 4th Battalion, 11th Marines, the Marines counterattacked. Company F rolled up the VC from the rear while H&S Company fought its way into Ky Phu. According to Grosz, who accompanied the lead elements of Company F in the attack, ''Once we got them going, the VC just broke and ran. It was just like a turkey shoot.''[15]

At the rear of the column, Company H remained in contact with the enemy; a VC company struck the Marines from both flanks and the rear. Both the company commander and his radio operator were mortally wounded. First Lieutenant Harvey C. Barnum, the attached artillery forward observer, did what he could to save the two dying Marines, strapped the radio on his back and assumed command. The young officer rallied the company and the Marines established a defensive position on a small hill north of the road. After four hours of heavy fighting, Barnum led Company H into Ky Phu and rejoined the battalion.***

By nightfall the fight at Ky Phu was over. The *80th VC Battalion* broke, leaving 104 bodies on the

---

* Immersion foot is an extremely painful foot condition, a symptom of which is swelling which takes on a puffy, wrinkled look. This malady was caused by prolonged wear of wet footgear and continued to plague the Marines throughout the war.

** Company H, 2d Battalion, 9th Marines had been attached to Utter's battalion on 13 December, replacing Company E which had taken heavy casualties. Company H, 2d Battalion, 7th Marines was not with the column. It was providing security for the 107mm Mortar Battery, 1st Battalion, 12th Marines.

***Lieutenant Barnum was performing temporary duty in Vietnam from his permanent duty station at Marine Barracks, Pearl Harbor. He had volunteered for 60 days of ''on-the-job'' training under the FMPac combat indoctrination program. For his heroic exploits in this engagement, Lieutenant Barnum was awarded the Medal of Honor.

USMC Photo A186280

Marines from the 2d Battalion, 7th Marines move along a dike across a flooded rice paddy during HARVEST MOON. The battalion suffered several cases of immersion foot during the operation.

battlefield, 76 of them killed by the artillery fire.* Lieutenant Colonel Utter's command had sustained 11 killed and 71 wounded.

The Wrap-Up

The next day, the 19th, all three of the Marine battalions completed their movement out of the operation area. For all practical purposes the operation was over, but Operation HARVEST MOON/LIEN KET 18 ended officially on the 20th when all allied forces returned to their enclaves. The combined USMC-ARVN operation had accounted for 407 enemy killed, 33 captured, and 13 crew-served and 95 individual weapons seized. In addition, 60 tons of food and ammunition were taken in the Phouc Ha Valley. Marine casualties were 45 killed and 218 wounded. General Lam's forces suffered 90 killed, 91 missing, and 141 wounded, most occurring during the first two days of the operation.

Despite the poor flying conditions, airpower played a major role in the outcome of the battle for the Nui Loc Son Basin. The F-4 Phantom pilots from Colonel Emmett O. Anglin, Jr.'s MAG-11 at Da Nang and A-4 Skyhawk pilots of Colonel Brown's Chu Lai-based MAG-12 flew numerous tactical support missions under marginal flying conditions.** During the 12-day operation, Marine F-4 pilots (Lieutenant Colonel Clyde R. Jarrett's VMFA-115 and Lieutenant Colonel Andrew W. O'Donnell's VMFA-323) logged 227 flight hours on 205 sorties, striking enemy targets with 215 tons of bombs and 628 rockets. The A-4 pilots from Lieutenant Colonel William E. Garman's VMA-211, Lieutenant Colonel Keith O'Keefe's VMA-214, and Lieutenant Colonel Thomas E. Mulvihill's VMA-224 delivered another 235 tons of ordnance in support of HARVEST MOON/LIEN KET-18. During the operation, Marine attack aircraft were credited with killing 95 of the enemy.

---

*Lieutenant Grosz observed that, ''we counted 76 enemy KIA in the arty impact area to the H&S right flank (south)'' but believes that a portion of the number must be credited to the Marine ground attack. Maj Nicholas H. Grosz, Jr., Comments on draft MS, dtd Dec76 (Vietnam Comment File).

** Colonel Anglin had replaced Colonel Conley as CO, MAG-11 on 3 November.

Marine helicopters made an equally important contribution to the operation. The seven helicopter squadrons of Colonel O'Connor's MAG-16 and Colonel Johnson's MAG-36, and Lieutenant Colonel Porter's HMM-261 flew 9,230 sorties, carried 12,177 troops, and transported 638 tons of supplies.* Besides providing battlefield mobility to the infantry, the pilots of these aircraft accomplished medical evacuation, reconnaissance, resupply, and other operational and administrative missions. The UH-1Es of Marine Observation Squadrons 2 and 6, armed with 7.62mm machine guns and 2.75-inch rockets, provided valuable close air support when fixed-wing aircraft could not attack targets due to low visibility. These Huey gunships also served as escorts for truck convoys and UH-34D helicopters and performed a number of medical evacuations. Lastly, these squadrons provided the airborne "eyes" for the commanders of HARVEST MOON; two UH-1Es were continuously assigned to the Task Force DELTA commander for command and control purposes.

The six-plane detachment of Sikorsky CH-37C heavy-lift helicopters attached to Headquarters and Maintenance Squadron 16 proved invaluable for lifting 105mm howitzers into the battle area. Two U.S. Army CH-47 Chinook helicopters, "on loan" to the Marines from the 1st Cavalry Division (Airmobile), supported the operation by retrieving several downed helicopters. During the course of the operation, Marine helicopter pilots reported over 100 occasions in which they received enemy fire. Fifty-three helicopters sustained battle damage, and the Marine crews suffered 1 killed, 12 wounded, and 2 helicopters destroyed.

A significant contribution to the success of the operation was the establishment of a logistic support area near Thang Binh on Route 1. Truck convoys from Da Nang and Chu Lai brought in supplies which could then be quickly helilifted to the using units. A company from the 3d Engineer Battalion, attached to Task Force DELTA, had the mission of

keeping Route 1 open and trafficable. Lieutenant Colonel Nicholas J. Dennis, commander of the 3d Engineer Battalion, later wrote:

> Culverts, bridges, earth fill, and equipment were transported in daily convoys down Route 1. We repaired many road cuts or sites where the road was blown. I visited the task force CP daily, and performed helicopter recons.[16]

Artillery also was moved out of the TAORs into the battle area to provide support for the infantry units. Five Marine artillery batteries fired 6,386 rounds during HARVEST MOON.** The mortar battery, using helicopter mobility, deployed to hilltops in a leapfrog manner.*** HARVEST MOON furnished reinforcing evidence that Marine artillery could both move and be resupplied by rotary wing aircraft.

HARVEST MOON was not without its problems. The hastily established provisional headquarters, the fast moving ground situation, poor weather conditions, and the large number of tactical aircraft operating over the Que Son Valley caused coordination and control difficulties. Colonel Leslie E. Brown, who had relieved Colonel Noble as commander of MAG-12 on 19 September, believed that better advance planning prior to the operation could have alleviated some of the problems encountered by his pilots. His group operated throughout HARVEST MOON "with practically no coordination with supported units except that which was accomplished in the air over the target area." As an example, on 10 December his group launched 32 sorties under an alert declared by Task Force DELTA, but when the attack aircraft arrived over the objective area, control was so poorly synchronized that many of the aircraft were unable to drop their ordnance.[17] At other times, fixed-wing and rotary-wing aircraft maneuvered at the same altitude in the same general area. Still, even with these difficulties, Marine aviation significantly influenced the results on the battlefield. Through these

---

*MAG-16 squadrons participating in HARVEST MOON were Bauman's VMO-2, Denny's HMM-161, Clark's HMM-263, and Childers' HMM-361. MAG-36 squadrons were Lieutenant Colonel Robert J. Zitnik's VMO-6, Lieutenant Colonel James Aldworth's HMM-362, and Lieutenant Colonel William R. Lucas' HMM-364.

**Artillery support was furnished by Batteries A, 1/11; F, 2/12; M, 4/11; L, 4/12 (from 11 December); and 107mm Mortar Battery (only three tubes), 1/12.

***According to General Platt, the displacement of artillery units during HARVEST MOON was "a crude forerunner of the fire base concept" in that the deployed units were always in range of some form of artillery. *Platt PhonCon, Jun71.*

problems, Marines learned valuable lessons in air-ground coordination for future operations.*

HARVEST MOON/LIEN KET 18 was the last of the Marines' big battles in 1965. These large-scale

---

*Colonel Roy C. Gray, Jr., who relieved Colonel Yunck as G-3 of the 1st MAW, agreed with Colonel Brown's remarks on coordination. He later wrote: ''The Wing G-3 Section subsequently assigned a senior experienced aviator to TF headquarters on operations such as HARVEST MOON and Air/Ground preplanning and coordination was given greater emphasis.'' Col Roy C. Gray, Jr., Comments on draft MS, dtd 31Oct76 (Vietnam Comment File). Although agreeing with Colonel Brown's observations, Colonel Peatross attributed the lack of coordination to too much secrecy and inexperience on the part of the HARVEST MOON planners, stating ''there could be no better advance planning without experience on the part of the planners.'' MajGen Oscar F. Peatross, Comments on draft MS, dtd 26Oct76 (Vietnam Comment File).

efforts had become a regular feature of the war for General Walt's forces. During the last half of its first calendar year in country, III MAF conducted 15 operations of battalion-size or larger. American intelligence agencies indicated that during 1966, General Walt's forces would face even larger enemy forces as North Vietnamese troops entered South Vietnam to join their Viet Cong comrades. The big unit actions were only one aspect of the Marine war, nevertheless, in I Corps. According to General Krulak:

. . . we cannot be entrapped in the dangerous premise that destruction of the VC organized units *per se* is the whole answer to winning the war, any more than we can accept the erroneous view that pacification and civic action will solve the problem if major enemy forces are free to roam the countryside.[18]

PART III
THE CONTINUING WAR

CHAPTER 8

Defending and Expanding the Base Areas

The Evolution of a Strategy—Further Deployments and Realinements—Refinement of Command Relations—Expanding the TAORs—Attacks on the Airfields and Hill 22—Base Defense—Extended Patrolling

The Evolution of a Strategy

During the second half of 1965, the American command in Vietnam began to formulate basic operational concepts for fighting the Vietnam War. With President Johnson's approval of General Westmoreland's request for U.S. reinforcements and for an expanded role for U.S. ground troops, the MACV commander had completed his overall plan for the employment of these forces by the end of August. He divided the war into three phases. The first, to end in 1965, was simply ''commit those American and allied forces necessary to halt the losing trend.'' Beginning in 1966, the second phase, allied forces were to take the offensive in selected high priority areas. At an undetermined date, the allied forces were to begin phase three, the total destruction of enemy forces and base areas. For the remainder of 1965, General Westmoreland planned to employ American combat troops ''to protect developing logistical bases, although some might have to be committed from time to time as 'fire brigades' whenever the enemy's big units posed a threat . . . .''[1]

Based on general directives from ComUSMACV and its own experience gained during this period, III MAF developed a concept of operation for I Corps. Essentially, the Marines stressed the ''oil spot'' approach, in which III MAF was to secure its coastal enclaves and gradually extend them as manpower and material became available. The 21 November MACV Letter of Instruction, which superseded the amended 6 May directive, prescribed five missions for III MAF. These were: to defend and secure its base areas; to conduct search and destroy operations against VC forces which posed an immediate threat to these bases; to launch other search and destroy operations against more distant enemy base areas; to

extend clearing operations in selected areas contiguous to the major bases; and finally to execute any contingency plan in I Corps or elsewhere in Vietnam as directed by ComUSMACV.[2] Given these all encompassing objectives, the Marines produced what they called the ''Balanced Strategy'' to fight the war. Basically it consisted of a counterguerrilla campaign within the TAORs, search and destroy operations against enemy main force troops outside the TAORs, and a pacification campaign within the hamlets to eradicate the VC ''infrastructure'' and win the loyalty of the people to the government's cause.*

Although both MACV and III MAF used the same terminology in defining their strategies, by the end of 1965 there was a decided difference in perception as to where the enemy posed the greatest danger. Confronted with the pervasive VC guerrilla strength, especially in the rich and heavily populated rice lands south of Da Nang, General Walt insisted that his first priority was to clear out this region. He recognized the threat of the VC main force units, but he wanted good intelligence before denuding his base area defenses to go after them. General Westmoreland, on the other hand, perceived the growing NVA and VC main force to be the main target for U.S. forces. Brigadier General Karch, General Walt's assistant division commander, recalled that

---

*General Westmoreland has stated that the term search and destroy ''has been fully distorted.'' He explained that he adopted the term in 1964 as a ''teaching aid to the South Vietnamese'' when he believed the South Vietnamese Army ''was static and the enemy was taking full advantage of the situation.'' Search and destroy simply meant offensive operations against enemy main force units. The former MACV commander observed that he dropped the terminology in 1968 when he ''realized that it was being distorted.'' Gen William C. Westmoreland, Comments on draft MS, dtd 5Nov77 (Vietnam Comment File).

USMC Photo A185832

General Walt speaks to the men of the newly arrived 1st Battalion, 1st Marines at Da Nang. The III MAF commander tells the troops: "We need you here; our job is just beginning."

this difference in priorities was evident as early as July when MACV required the Marines to report "Battalion Days in the Field." Karch remembered that he first heard of this report, "at the usual morning briefing for General Walt." When the III MAF commander asked the reasons for the "disparity of Army versus Marine 'Days in the Field,' the briefing officer explained that battalions engaged in pacification operations were not counted as battalions in the field."[3]

General Westmoreland reiterated his emphasis on the big unit war, on 10 December, in a letter to a subordinate commander. He wrote: "I am increasingly concerned about the fact that we are not engaging the VC with sufficient frequency . . . to win the war in Vietnam." Although relatively satisfied with the American counterguerrilla effort, he believed, "we have not yet proved that we have mastered the art of finding and destroying major VC forces through sustained campaigns against them in a given area." The MACV commander recognized the validity of the Marines' concern with

pacification, but he wanted General Walt to create a two- or three-battalion force capable of moving quickly into enemy-dominated regions, to join with the ARVN in operations of sufficient size to punish the enemy's big units and disrupt bases and supply caches. In his memoirs, General Westmoreland declared that he had no desire "to precipitate an interservice imbroglio," and recognized that:

> General Walt had a mission-type order which by custom afforded him considerable leeway in execution. Rather than start a controversy, I chose to issue orders for specific projects that as time passed would gradually get the Marines out of their beachheads.[4]*

Lieutenant General Krulak claimed that the difference between what was called at the time "the Army Strategy" and "the Marine Strategy" was more a matter of emphasis than of substance; both formulas were sound. Krulak believed that the "Army maneuver technique" was correct in the area around Plei Me in the Central Highlands, but observed, "You cannot shoot anything that moves in the rich area south of Da Nang, where the population runs as high as 1,000 per square mile." The FMFPac commander argued that in I Corps the enemy was mixed in with the civilian population and "we have to root him out, and separate him from the people; which is to say, fight a guerrilla/counterinsurgency war, and clean the area up a bit at a time." In any event, to fight both the big unit war and the war in the enclaves, the Marines needed more men.[5]

Further Deployments and Realinements

In the summer of 1965, General Walt informed MACV that III MAF required a force of two Marine

---

*General Westmoreland qualified his views in the following comment: "There was a recognized difference in the deployment of troops between the I and the II Regions because of terrain, roads, population dispersion, Vietnamese political and psychological considerations. To try to make a big point of a difference in strategy is to take an unreasonable and narrow view . . . . In the final analyses, the strategy and tactical operations of the war obviously required both pacification and military Main Force units. The degree of emphasis between these two types of operations varied as a function of the local situation." The former MACV commander observed "The I Corps Region was more vulnerable to attack by Main Force units than any other region because of its proximity to North Vietnam." Gen William C. Westmoreland, Comments on draft MS, dtd 22 Jul77 (Vietnam Comment File).

USMC Photo A185789

A South Vietnamese interpreter questions a farmer and his wife about the VC as Marines watch. The hamlet is located in the heavily populated area south of Da Nang.

divisions supported by a reinforced Marine aircraft wing to carry out its mission in I Corps. Furthermore, the III MAF commander stated that if he were to be responsible for the entire area from Quang Ngai Province to the DMZ, he would need three more battalions.[6]

These new force requirements would have repercussions throughout the Marine Corps. In August, the Marine Corps was authorized a 30,000-man increase, for a total strength of 223,000, to support the Vietnam effort. By October, HQMC furnished the Secretary of Defense with plans for obtaining another 55,000 Marines to allow for the formation of the 5th Marine Division in California, 18 infantry battalions in Vietnam, and 3 battalions on Okinawa. This plan was approved and funded by the end of the year.[7]

The reinforcement of III MAF during this period caused continuing realinement and readjustment of personnel and units in the Western Pacific. On 24 August, the 1st Marine Division, under Major General Lewis J. Fields, established its CP on Okinawa, as did the 1st Marines. Only one regiment of the division, the 5th Marines, remained at Camp Pendleton. As noted earlier, one battalion of the 1st

Marines, Lieutenant Colonel Hanifin's 2d Battalion, relieved BLT 3/7 as the SLF battalion of the Seventh Fleet, and at the end of August Lieutenant Colonel Bodley's 3d Battalion rejoined its parent regiment, the 7th Marines, at Chu Lai. At the same time, Lieutenant Colonel Donald V. McCloskey's 1st Battalion, 1st Marines arrived at Da Nang and relieved the 1st Battalion, 3d Marines, which returned to the United States. Another battalion from the United States, the 3d Battalion, 5th Marines, was moved to Okinawa to become the new 1st Battalion, 3d Marines. This relief ended the intertheater battalion transplacement system.

The end of the battalion rotation between East Pac and West Pac caused the institution of an individual personnel replacement system for all units of III MAF. Under the designator Operation MIXMASTER, Marines in Vietnam were transferred between units so that everyone in each unit would not have the same overseas tour expiration date. This homogenization process involved thousands of Marines and took place over several months.*

With the termination of the intertheater transplacement system in September 1965, FMFPac immediately began planning for the rotation of battalion landing teams from Vietnam to Okinawa, then to the Seventh Fleet, and back to Vietnam again. This program was designed to allow BLTs to refit and retrain in a non-combat environment where emphasis could be placed on training rather than operations. The intratheater rotation began in November when the new BLT 1/3 relieved the 2d Battalion, 3d Marines at Da Nang. The latter unit

---

*This process did not always go smoothly. In November 1965, the 9th Marines regimental commander stated that there was a lack of replacements which resulted in a personnel shortage throughout the regiment. 9th Marines ComdC, Nov65, p. 1-1. The following excerpt furnishes an example of how Operation MIXMASTER worked: "On 19 November, Company E, 2/7 was exchanged with Company A, 1/4 and on 30 November Company A, 1/7 was exchanged with a company from 3/4." 7th Marines ComdC, Nov65, p. 3. Colonel Nicholas J. Dennis, who at the time commanded the 3d Engineer Battalion, wrote that MIXMASTER "was a two edged sword for my battalion, We could only infuse with the 7th Engineers and the 1st Engineers. In the case of the 7th, except for 'Charlie' company, the rest had arrived in RVN on the same date. The mixing with the 1st Engineer Battalion was more practical, however, it provided a one on one situation." Col Nicholas J. Dennis, Comments on draft MS, dtd 3Nov76 (Vietnam Comment File).

reformed as BLT 2/3 and became the Seventh Fleet SLF ground force in late December, replacing BLT 2/1 which replaced the 3d Battalion, 4th Marines at Phu Bai.

There were other reinforcements and read-justments in Vietnam during this period. In August, the 7th Engineer Battalion and the rear echelon of the 3d Division headquarters battalion arrived, as well as the 7th Marines. During September, MAG-36, a helicopter group, and the 2d LAAM Battalion were established at Chu Lai. In November, Lieutenant Colonel Utter's 2d Battalion, 7th Marines left Qui Nhon to reinforce Colonel Peatross' 7th Marines at Chu Lai. The return of Utter's unit to III MAF control allowed General Walt to reinforce units at Da Nang by transferring the 3d Battalion, 3d Marines there from Chu Lai.

By the end of December, there were six infantry battalions at Da Nang, five at Chu Lai, and one at Phu Bai. At Da Nang, the 9th Marines controlled the southern and southeastern sectors of the TAOR with four battalions, all three of its own battalions and the attached 3d Battalion, 3d Marines. The 3d Marines was responsible for the western and nor-thern portions of the TAOR with two battalions, the 1st Battalion, 1st Marines and the 1st Battalion, 3d Marines. The battalion at Phu Bai also reported to the 3d Marines. At Chu Lai the TAOR was divided between the 4th and 7th Marines. The 7th Marines controlled the southern sector with its own three battalions while the 4th Marines operated to the north with its 1st and 2d Battalions.

In addition to the infantry units, by the end of the year III MAF had a reinforced artillery regiment, eight fixed-wing squadrons, and eight helicopter squadrons. Since the beginning of July, III MAF had

USMC Photo A184953

The village chief of Thuy Phu points out to General Walt an artillery-targeted impact area in the Phu Bai TAOR. Lieutenant Colonel William W. "Woody" Taylor (left) looks on.

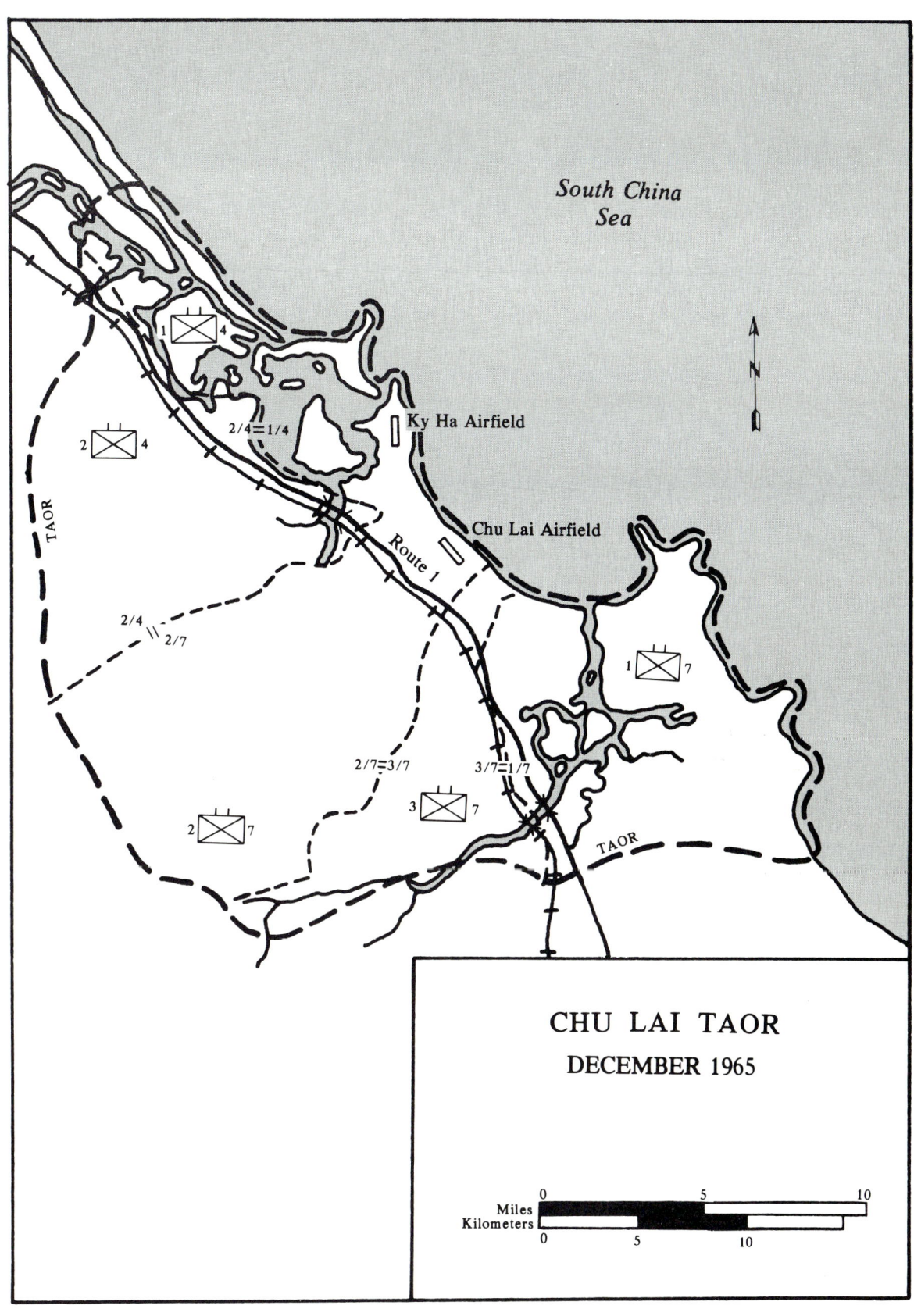

South China
Sea

Ky Ha Airfield

Chu Lai Airfield

Route 1

TAOR

TAOR

CHU LAI TAOR

DECEMBER 1965

Miles
Kilometers

USMC Photo A185897

Marines from the 3d Battalion, 9th Marines move through a village south of Da Nang. The Vietnamese farmer continues with his hoeing, apparently ignoring the Marines.

received over 25,000 reinforcements for a total of approximately 45,000 Marine and Navy personnel.

Refinement of Command Relations

With the buildup, command relationships became increasingly important; any conflict of interest had to be resolved. For III MAF, this applied not only to its association with MACV, but with the U.S. Army in II Corps, civilian and military Vietnamese authorities in I Corps, the U.S. Navy, and the U.S. Air Force's 2d Air Division.

General Walt was well aware of the possible pitfalls that lay before him in this sensitive area. When he split his division staff and established the coordinating headquarters at Chu Lai under General Karch on 5 August, part of the rationale was:

> . . . to anticipate and alleviate actual possible conflicts of interest before irreversible action, plans, or commitments are taken that would adversely affect: A. Another command or commands. B. Relationships with the Vietnamese Government. . . .[8]

Until August General Walt had dealt with the Vietnamese only in relation to Marine operations, but the 6 August MACV amendment to the III

MAF Letter of Instruction also made General Walt the Senior U.S. Advisor to I Corps, responsible for the U. S. military advisory effort in the five northern provinces. The significance of this authority is indicated in the following excerpt pertaining to the responsibilities of the I Corps Advisory Group:

> To advise, assist and support the RVN military and para-military units and staffs in all combat, support, and combat service support operations and training; to assist the RVN in developing and maintaining an effective conventional and counter-insurgency military capability; to exercise operational control of all assigned U.S. units; and to perform liaison among U.S., RVN, and international Military Assistance (third country) Force Commanders.[9]

On 7 August, General Walt assumed his new responsibility and Colonel Howard B. St. Clair, USA, the former senior advisor, became his deputy.

The influx of large numbers of U.S. Army forces caused General Westmoreland to reexamine the basic command structure within MACV. He told the Joint Chiefs of Staff that he desired the option of placing III MAF under Field Forces, Vietnam if the war escalated to the proportions of the Korean conflict, but saw no advantage to changing the

An aerial view of the Da Nang Airfield looking north. The airfield and the buildup of III MAF forces at Da Nang made the airbase a prime target for VC hit-and-run attacks.

present command relations as long as the Marines operated only in I Corps. In October, the MACV commander established an interservice steering committee to study the problem. The committee reported on the 19th and recommended that the command structure remain basically the same; General Walt, as Commanding General, III MAF would report directly to General Westmoreland for operations in I Corps while General Larsen would retain a similar responsibility in II Corps.[10]

Command relationships with the South Vietnamese were just as sensitive. Here, too, no basic change was made in the fundamental understandings that had been worked out with the South Vietnamese. In the new Letter of Instruction furnished to subordinate commands in November, Westmoreland continued to stress coordination and cooperation. The MACV commander told the Joint Chiefs of Staff that any mention of a combined headquarters was politically infeasible at the time. Colonel Wyckoff, the 3d Division G-3, recalled that after briefing General Westmoreland on one occasion, the general

> . . . gave quite an extensive rundown on his feeling regarding the conduct of the war where his major thrust was getting the GVN and the ARVN on their own feet with the proper leadership and the proper attitude so they could carry on the war more as a unilateral thing, rather than depending on the support of the United States.[11]

Under the guidelines furnished by Com-USMACV, III MAF developed its own special expedients for operating with the South Vietnamese. The Marines made few formal agreements with their Vietnamese counterparts, but, on the other hand, several informal understandings emerged. There was nothing in the MACV directives that prevented temporary ''tactical direction'' of Vietnamese forces by U.S. commanders under certain circumstances. One of the more important ingredients of the Marine relationship with the Vietnamese authorities of I Corps was the mutual understanding and friendship which formed between General Thi and General Walt. The Marine general realized that the ARVN desired American assistance and cooperation, as long as the Vietnamese retained their pride and face. The Marine Corps concept of operations was based on these factors.[12]

Expanding the TAORs

An indication of the growing coordination between the III MAF and the I Corps commands was the continued extension of the Marine tactical areas of responsibility. From the eight square miles around the Da Nang Airbase that constituted the Marine area of operations on 8 March, III MAF had extended its influence into the rich coastal plain in all three enclaves, containing a total area of 804 square miles. This area was populated by 506,732 people living in more than 100 villages which included nearly 550 hamlets. Most of this population lived in the fertile farming area south of the Da Nang Airbase.

By the end of August, the 9th Marines had completed its TAOR extension south of the Cau Do according to the terms of General Thi's letter of 20 July.* On 13 September, General Walt asked the I Corps commander for a further extension of the Marine Da Nang TAOR. This time Walt requested that the Marine area of operations be extended to the La Tho and Thanh Quit Rivers, three kilometers south of the former boundary. Walt pointed out that the Marines would have the advantage of a natural boundary and would be in position to help the South Vietnamese drive the Viet Cong out of the rice-rich region.[13] Eight days later, General Thi granted permission for the larger Marine TAOR, but cautioned General Walt to closely coordinate his forward movement with local Vietnamese authorities and forces. The I Corps commander noted that the area was densely populated and he wished to ''avoid deplorable incidents to the local people.''[14]

Anticipating the enlargement of its TAOR, the 3d Marine Division began an adjustment of lines. In August, the 3d Marines, now under Colonel Norman R. Nickerson, the former III MAF G-4 who assumed command on the 16th, positioned the 2d Battalion, 3d Marines to cover the movement of the 1st Battalion, 1st Marines south of the Tuy Loan River. The following month, the 9th Marines, now under Colonel John E. Gorman,** began Operation RICE STRAW, which was the first of a three-phase move in which the regiment eventually planned to reach the Ky Lam River. It was during this operation

---

* See Chapter 6 for the details of this letter.

** Colonel Nickerson recalled that he and Colonel Gorman were platoon leaders of sister platoons in Company A, 1st Parachute Battalion in the capture of the island of Gavutu during World War II and now some 23 years later, ''both officers were in command of sister regiments at the same time.'' Col Norman R. Nickerson, Comments on draft MS, dtd 27Oct76 (Vietnam Comment File).

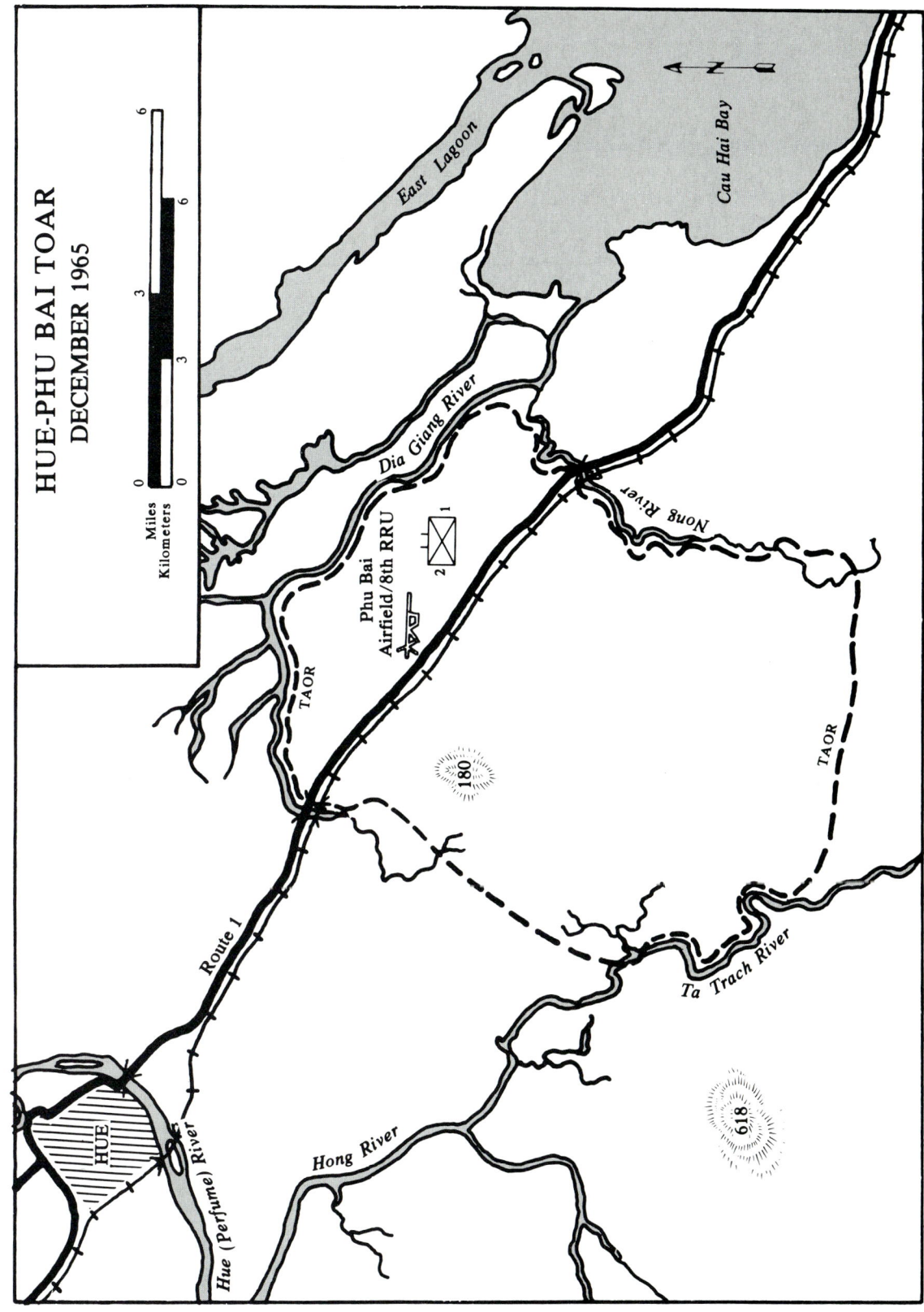

HUE-PHU BAI TOAR
DECEMBER 1965

Miles
Kilometers

East Lagoon

Cau Hai Bay

Dia Giang River

Nong River

Phu Bai
Airfield/8th RRU

TAOR

TAOR

180

Route 1

Ta Trach River

618

HUE

Hue (Perfume) River

Hong River

Marines clean up the debris after the sapper attack on Marble Mountain. Helicopter parts are being salvaged.

that Lieutenant Colonel Muir, whose 3d Battalion, 3d Marines had arrived at Da Nang from Chu Lai to act as a blocking force, was killed on 11 September.*

By the middle of November, both regiments had made appreciable advances to the south. The 1st Battalion, 1st Marines established defenses 3,500 meters south of the Tuy Loan and its combat patrols covered over 13,000 square meters. The 9th Marines' forward battalions had formed a defensive line roughly five miles south of the Cau Do River. On the 20th, the Marines incorporated the former reconnaissance zone, the three-mile area between the La Tho and Ky Lam Rivers, into the TAOR. The 9th Marines then established new defenses along the line of the La Tho and Thanh Quit Rivers and made plans to advance to the southern boundary of the TAOR.

At Chu Lai, the Marines also expanded their TAOR, but to a more limited extent. On 8 October, General Thi approved an extension of approximately six square miles to the northwest, and Colonel McClanahan moved his 4th Marines into this area. There was no further expansion of the TAOR in 1965, but Colonel Peatross prepared plans to extend

the frontline of his 7th Marines southward to the Tra Bong River.**

A different situation existed around the northern enclave at Phu Bai, where the one battalion, the 3d Battalion, 4th Marines, was spread very thin. The Marines had incorporated the populated area immediately north and south of the base into the battalion's TAOR by the end of September. The terrain to the west consisted of rolling hills with very little vegetation or population; both aerial and ground observation were excellent.

Lieutenant Colonel Sumner A. Vale, who assumed command of the battalion on 1 October, later commented:

> . . . gradual increases were made as the result of a cat and mouse game played between the Marines and the VC. The VC would determine the general boundaries of the TAOR by plotting the sites where they were engaged by Marine ambushes. Then the VC would move their

---

*See Chapter 6.

**Since 13 September, one company of 1/7 already operated south of the river, maintaining a combat base on the Trung Phan Peninsula. General Peatross stated that the lines of the 7th Marines were on the Tra Bong in October, but after the attack on the Chu Lai airfield (see next section), ''the lines of the 7th were pulled back by General Walt.'' MajGen Oscar F. Peatross, Comments on draft MS, dtd 26Oct76 (Vietnam Comment File).

avenue of approach to north and south to avoid the TAOR. The Marines countered by setting up ambushes outside the TAOR (with the permission of the CO, 3d Marines and the CG, 1st ARVN Division). The CG, 1st ARVN Division would then arrange to have the TAOR enlarged to encompass these ''new operating areas.''[15]

Attacks on the Airfields and Hill 22

Despite the Marines' extension of their TAORs, the enemy still had the ability to mount well-coordinated hit-and-run attacks, similar to the 1 July Da Nang raid. On the evening of 27-28 October, the VC struck the newly built Marble Mountain helicopter facility on the Tiensha Peninsula and the Chu Lai SATS field.

At Chu Lai, the infiltrators entered the Marine base from the northwest and split into two groups. According to the MAG-12 commander, Colonel Leslie E. Brown, the first knowledge the Marines had of the attack was when they heard machine gun fire and satchel charges blowing up. Brown recalled:

> . . . a couple of the airplanes were on fire, and the sappers had gotten through intact . . . . they were barefooted and had on a loin cloth and it was kind of a John Wayne dramatic effect. They had Thompson submachineguns and they were spraying the airplanes with the Tommy guns and . . . throwing satchel charges into tail pipes . . . Some went off and some didn't, but the net effect was that the machine gun fire caused leaks in the fuel tanks, so that JP fuel was drenching the whole area . . . . and in the middle of that, the airplanes were on fire.[16]

The Marines killed 15 of the force of 20 VC, but not before the attackers had destroyed two A-4s and severely damaged six more. General Karch, the Chu Lai Base Coordinator, remembered that when he arrived ''Les Brown . . . was on the scene [and] the armament crews were going up and down the flight line disarming bombs . . . I couldn't give Brown too much credit for the job he and his crews did there that night—it was fabulous.''[17]

The Communist attack on Marble Mountain was larger and better coordinated. A VC raiding party of approximately 90 men quietly assembled in a village just to the northwest of the Marble Mountain Air Facility. Under cover of 60mm mortar fire, four demolition teams struck at the Marble Mountain airstrip and a hospital being constructed by the Seabees. At least six of the enemy, armed with bangalore torpedos and grenades, reached the MAG-

16 parking ramp. Colonel O'Connor, the MAG-16 commander, remembered:

> I awoke to the sound of explosions shortly after midnight . . . arriving at the group command post, I received a phone call from General McCutcheon. He was warning me that the airfield at Chu Lai had been attacked and to be on the alert. I told him no one was asleep at Marble Mountain, as we had also been under attack for about 15 minutes.[18]

After leaving the command post, Colonel O'Connor drove to the aircraft parking ramp where ''Helicopters were burning all over . . . .VMO-2 was practically wiped out.'' Before the VC could be stopped they destroyed 19 helicopters and damaged 35, 11 of them severely.* Across the road, much of the hospital, which was nearing completion, was heavily damaged. After 30 minutes, the Viet Cong withdrew, leaving behind 17 dead and four wounded. American casualties were three killed and 91 wounded.[19]

During the attack, Lieutenant Colonel Verle E. Ludwig's 1st Battalion, 9th Marines, south of Marble Mountain, came under small arms fire, but apparently this was a feint designed to fix the unit in its defensive positions. All units at Da Nang went on full alert, but the damage had been done.

The VC attacking forces at both Chu Lai and Da Nang were not ordinary guerrillas. There were indications that these troops were from hardcore main force VC units, although the VC unit which attacked Marble Mountain was better trained than the one which hit Chu Lai. Captain Hoa, the Hoa Vang District Chief, believed that the enemy group which attacked Da Nang was North Vietnamese, but the four prisoners captured by the Marines there came from small hamlets in Quang Nam and Quang Tin Provinces.[20]

The enemy had been well equipped for the mission. At Marble Mountain, Marines recovered a considerable stock of fragmentation, concussion, and thermite grenades, as well as three bangalore torpedoes, several Chinese Communist B-40 antitank rockets, and miscellaneous ammunition. The American troops also captured several weapons, a

---

*Colonel O'Connor observed that the destruction of the helicopters at Marble Mountain resulted in ''a 43 percent loss of division mobility'' and that it ''put a crimp in division plans for several months afterward.'' Col Thomas J. O'Connor, Comments on draft MS, dtd 27Nov76 (Vietnam Comment File).

An aerial view of the damage caused by the VC sapper attack on Marble Mountain. Nearly one-third of the Marine helicopers were destroyed or damaged during the attack.

7.62mm AK assault rifle, two .45 caliber automatic weapons, and a 7.62mm Tokarev automatic pistol.[21]

One of the more significant aspects of the events of 28 October was an attack which did not occur. The enemy had also planned to hit the main airfield at Da Nang. Two separate occurrences may have frustrated this attack. General Walt's staff received word on 27 October that a VC main force battalion was moving out of its base in "Happy Valley," 10 miles south-

west of Da Nang, and heading towards the base. At 1930, division artillery fired 680 rounds into the area. Later intelligence reports indicated that the shells hit the VC unit, forcing it to disperse.

Shortly afterward, a 9th Marines squad ambushed a strong VC force near the An Tu (1) hamlet, five miles south of Da Nang. The Marine patrol, 11 Marines and a Navy corpsman from Company I, 3d Battalion, 9th Marines, had arrived at the ambush

USMC Photo A185986

Sergeant John A. Anderson describes his squad's patrol action. His squad was credited with preventing a major attack on the Da Nang Airbase.

site after dark. By 1945 they had established their positions; only 15 minutes later the Marines heard movement along the trail. The squad leader, Sergeant John A. Anderson, ordered his troops to hold fire until the enemy was at pointblank range. Seven VC had passed the site of the most forward Marine before Anderson triggered the ambush. At this moment, the VC were only six to seven feet away from the Marine's M-60 machine gun position. The machine gunner initiated the engagement with a long burst, followed by heavy fire from all the

weapons of the rest of the squad. This volley killed all seven VC.[22]*

The seven dead were only the advance party for a larger enemy force which moved forward to engage the Marines. Sergeant Anderson fired several M-79 rounds at the muzzle flashes of the approaching VC. The firefight continued for another minute, but then the enemy began to disengage. Sergeant Anderson realized that his troops had to get out of the area; he was outnumbered. The squad leader ordered his men to count the dead VC before leaving; they counted 15. The Marines moved out to their battalion's position, but during the return two squad members were wounded by Viet Cong firing from a dike. Anderson called for fire support and after 60 rounds of 81mm mortar fire hit on the enemy position, the VC stopped firing. At first light the next day, 28 October, Company I sent two platoons to search the ambush site more thoroughly. Of the 15 known VC dead only two bodies were found.[23]

General Walt and his staff believed that Sergeant Anderson's patrol probably had foiled an attack on the airbase. Apparently the patrol had intercepted a VC company from the same unit that carried out the Marble Mountain attack:

> This belief is supported by the fact that the company was moving in the direction of the Da Nang base, and time and distance being considered, the time of the attack on the Marble Mountain Air Facility.[24]

Two days after the airfield attacks, the Viet Cong attempted another probe of the Marine defenses, not at the base area, but against the defensive perimeter on Hill 22, south of the Tuy Loan River, manned by the Marines of Company A, 1st Battalion, 1st Marines. The action began at 0100, 30 October,

---

*Captain Charles Ward, at the time the 9th Marines S-2, debriefed the Anderson patrol. He recalled that the VC advance party had been preceded by a point element carrying candles and flashlights to give the appearance of villagers returning home. According to Ward, Anderson's men had seen the point men but "were uncertain as what to do—after all, the men wore villagers' clothing, held lighted candles, and the ambush location was on a well-travelled trail leading to Highway 1 only 200-250 meters away and was only 100 meters from occupied huts. The question became academic when the main body traipsed into the squad's position. So surprised was Anderson by the unexpected appearance of the column of men on the trail, he almost forgot to give the order to the machine gunner." Ward concluded his remarks with the observation that "reportedly this was Sgt Anderson's *first* combat patrol." LtCol Charles Ward, Comments on draft MS, dtd 27Oct76 (Vietnam Comment File).

when 10-15 VC walked into a squad ambush 1,000 meters south of the hill. The Marines opened fire and killed three of the enemy, but the squad had not been able to maintain communications with the company and was unable to notify the company commander of the contact. All was quiet for about two hours, when suddenly approximately 25 enemy enveloped the Marine squad, killing three and wounding six.[25] At 0315 the rest of the VC force attacked the main Marine positions on Hill 22. Enemy troops, supported by two recoilless rifles, penetrated about a third of the northwestern perimeter, capturing three M-60 machine guns, two 3.5-inch rocket launchers, and one 60mm mortar. They also gained access to the company's ammunition bunker.

Lieutenant Colonel Harold A. Hatch, who had assumed command of the 1st Battalion on 27 September, immediately sent reinforcements and ammunition to Company A. One resupply helicopter was "so fully loaded that it barely could get off the ground" and its "rotor wash blew the supply tent down." The battalion commander also called for supporting artillery fire and close air support.[26]

About 45 minutes after the enemy had launched the main attack on Hill 22, three UH-34s landed Sergeant Russell L. Kees' 13-man squad from Company C on the hill. Kees stated, "The VC were everywhere; in the tents, on the tents, and in the trenches."[27] Supported by air, artillery, and mortars, the Company A commander, Captain John A. Maxwell, rallied the Marines; they counterattacked and drove off the enemy. Marines casualties were 16 dead and 41 wounded, while the Communists left behind 47 bodies and one wounded.[28]

Marine air accounted for a few more enemy when the VC unit tried to cross the eastern bank of the Song Yen three miles south of Hill 22. The Marine pilots reported destroying 10 boats and seeing 10 bodies in the water.[29] Villagers in the area told the American troops that the Viet Cong forced them to

USMC Photo A184893

Two young Vietnamese boys assist a Marine in directing traffic through a checkpoint. The boys are the sons of a South Vietnamese Air Force sergeant.

USMC Photo A185921

A Marine from the 1st Battalion, 9th Marines mans a defensive position on top of an old French fort in the Marble Mountain area. The Marines used the fort to store supplies.

bury several bodies, apparently casualties of the Hill 22 fight.[30]

The VC had planned the operation thoroughly. They hit the critical portions of the perimeter and knew exactly which bunker contained ammunition. American intelligence sources discovered that the VC unit involved in the attack was the *R-20 Battalion* which had just completed training. The Hill 22 attack was apparently its final training exercise.[31]*

Base Defense

The enemy attacks on the airfields and on Hill 22 gave added impetus to the improvement of base defenses. After the dissolution of the provisional defense battalion in August, one Marine infantry battalion was kept on the Da Nang Airbase as the airfield defense battalion. On 21 August III MAF assumed direct control of the airfield defense bat-

---

*The enemy battalion also was known as the *Doc Lap Battalion*. According to General Simmons, it was not "a new battalion, but one which had just been filled up with new recruits, most from the city of Da Nang, and retrained." BGen Edwin H. Simmons, Comments on Shulimson, "USMC Ops RVN Jul-Dec65," dtd 12 May 71 (Vietnam Comment File).

talion, Lieutenant Colonel Robert J. Tunnell's newly arrived 3d Battalion, 9th Marines, which relieved the 1st Battalion, 9th Marines on the airfield. Lieutenant Colonel Clark still retained the position of base defense coordinator. His job, according to his successor, was to collect statistics on Marine "saturation-type patrolling" and to inform the battalion commander "where to alternate the emphasis" in the airfield defense battalion's patrolling effort.[32]

The main physical security problem of the airfield, other than keeping the Viet Cong out, was overlapping American and Vietnamese authority. There was a heterogeneous mixture of U.S. and Vietnamese units at Da Nang, each responsible for its own internal security. The 41st Fighter Wing, VNAF was responsible for its defensive perimeter, while U.S. Air Police and Vietnamese MPs controlled the main gate. This situation was further complicated when the Marble Mountain Air Facility east of the main airfield opened in September. At Marble Mountain, MAG-16, the Seabees, and support troops provided their own security. The various security forces both at Da Nang and Marble Mountain integrated their efforts as much as possible with the plans of the airfield defense battalion. General Walt exercised "a sort of presuptive authority over the tenants."[33]

Obtaining a clear decision for relations between the various commands was a continuing problem. On 4 October, the III MAF staff proposed that General Walt ask ComUSMACV for permission to activate a base defense command to exert "coordinating authority over the internal security provided by the various commands and units at Da Nang."[34]

General Walt expanded the authority of the base defense coordinator and appointed Colonel George W. Carrington to this position in place of Lieutenant Colonel Clark. After the enemy attacks at the end of October, the new coordinator visited the Da Nang airfield tenants to ensure that an integrated defense did exist. He also planned the trace of a fence around the airfield. Carrington's duties also included advising, coordinating, and drawing together the defensive measures of the other two Marine enclaves.

According to Colonel Carrington, his responsibility extended to and:

> . . . included field artillery battery positions (but I could not infringe upon command responsibilities of the artillery regimental commander), water points, bridge and

USMC Photo A185856

A VC prisoner leads a Marine squad to a weapons cache. The prisoner claims that the VC are using the Buddhist Pagoda in the picture to store their arms.

ferry crossing sites, LAAM sites on mountain peaks, ammunition dumps, supply dumps, and units of the MAW. I arranged for rotation of the war dogs, temporary augmentation from scarce infantry assets to help in night-time guarding or patrolling, or improvement of the physical barriers. I withheld infantry assistance on occasion for our assets were too thin. We had to tell some sailors, soldiers, Marines, even civilians, to ''do the best you can, to be alert.'' [35]

Security coordinators were established at all Marine airfields. The commanding officer of the 9th Marines assumed the additional title of Marble Mountain airfield coordinator with the responsibility of overseeing the defense for the helicopter field. After the October raid, the 3d Engineer Battalion, with the assistance of MAG-16 personnel, built a barrier of minefields and barbed wire.[36] Similar measures were taken at the other installations.

Each Marine enclave developed its own procedures for providing internal airfield security. At Da Nang, one infantry battalion provided security; each of its four companies was assigned a defensive area from 2,100-3,400 meters wide. The battalion conducted patrols outside the airfield perimeter to add depth to the Marine defense, as well as to prevent the VC from setting up mortar and recoilless rifle firing positions.[37] The Vietnamese Air Force defense sector remained separate from the battalion's area of operations. At Chu Lai, the Marines also assigned one infantry battalion to airfield security, but only two of the battalion's companies were deployed on the airfield perimeter. These two companies were

reinforced by two provisional rifle companies composed of personnel from MAG-12, the Seabees, and the 2d LAAM Battalion.[38] At Phu Bai, the 3d Battalion, 4th Marines developed the combined action company to deal with the unique situation existing there.

III MAF experimented with several techniques to ensure the security of the major airbases. These included the use of dogs and sophisticated electronic devices. In August, 11 sentry dogs and their Marine handlers arrived at Da Nang from Japan. After three weeks of intensive training, the dogs were assigned to posts at ammunition supply points, LAAM battery sites, and Marble Mountain. In November, some of the dogs accompanied Marine patrols along the airfield perimeter. The Marines learned that the dogs were most effective when employed in remote areas where few people worked or lived. The dogs were extremely valuable at the LAAM battery site on secluded Monkey Mountain, but proved to be unsatisfactory at the ammunition supply point where Marines worked around the clock. The continuous activity at the latter site only confused the animals.[39]

In November and December 1965, III MAF received 600 seismic detection sets for perimeter defense. These electronic devices were extremely sensitive to ground vibrations and relayed seismic disturbance signals to Marine-monitored control boxes. These instruments operated well, but, as Colonel Carrington pointed out:

> We had known in the first place that there were always plenty of human beings out there in front of us in the paddies, huts, jungles, and hills. No tricky devices or stunts, however, could help Marines determine friend from foe.[40]

Even so, the Marines found the devices useful. As one battalion commander explained:

> We used the seismic devices in each one of these situations, very successfully so. We shot a few water buffalo and a few dogs . . . [the devices allow] you, of course, to maintain and secure a much greater perimeter with a lot less people.[41]*

---

*Colonel Carrington recalled one rather humorous use of the seismic device: '' . . . a senior USMC officer was concerned that sappers might be tunneling under our MAF headquarters. Use of seismic detectors to confirm this was inconclusive, but after resort to bull dozers to dig futilely for the assumed tunnel, I was chatised by another senior USMC officer for allowing destruction of a projected, ceremonial parade ground.'' Col George W. Carrington, Jr., Comments on draft MS, dtd 24Nov76 (Vietnam Comment File).

Extended Patrolling

Throughout the latter half of 1965, Marine units concentrated on small unit operations. General Walt referred to such actions as the "bread and butter of my command."[42] A month-by-month comparison of the number of patrols, ambushes, listening posts, and other activities of Marine platoons and squads shows a steady increase in the tempo of operations. In October 3d Marine Division units at all three enclaves conducted 2,877 patrols and 1,061 ambushes which resulted in 70 contacts with the enemy. In December, the division reported a total of 9,698 offensive operations which resulted in 510 contacts.[43]* One battalion commander observed that each of his platoons conducted two night patrols and one daylight patrol during an average 24-hour period.[44]

III MAF developed and modified techniques and tactics for the employment of small Marine units. The Marines experimented with specially trained and equipped sniper teams. Fifty of the best marksmen were selected from each of the regiments. These troops were divided into four-man teams and equipped with Winchester Model 70 rifles and telescopic sights. After training, the teams rejoined their regiments. During November and December, 20-30 teams operated in the Marine TAORs daily. On 23 November, a sniper team at Phu Bai killed two VC and wounded another at a distance of more than 1,000 meters.

Aggressive small unit patrolling continued to pay dividends. On 5 December, a platoon from Company C, 1st Battalion, /th Marines surprised 70 VC on the

---

*These statistics must be used with care. They are reliable for showing general trends, but are not absolutely accurate. As an example, CG FMFPac's staff stated that in October the Marines conducted 3,900 patrols of squad and platoon-size, in addition to 1,361 ambushes which resulted in 323 contacts. III MAF, on the other hand, reported 3,520 small unit actions resulting in 287 VC contacts for the same period. III MAF ComdC, Oct65 and FMFPac, *III MAF, Ops, Oct 65.* In the text, the figures provided by the division are used in that it furnished both III MAF and FMFPac with the figures they used. On the general subject of reporting, Brigadier General Edwin H. Simmons observed that as III MAF G-3 he "spent 60 percent of my time reporting or generating reports (in two directions: Hawaii and Saigon) . . . ." BGen Edwin H. Simmons, ltr to Col George W. Carrington, dtd 2Dec76 (Vietnam Comment File).

Trung Phan Peninsula, six miles southeast of the Chu Lai airfield. The platoon, operating from its company's combat base, had been assigned the mission of searching the Tuyet Diem (1) hamlet on the banks of the Moi River. The platoon had established an ambush site 2,000 meters south of the hamlet. At 0300, four VC walked into the trap and were killed by a burst of Marine fire. First Lieutenant Charles D. Jones, the platoon commander, fearing that the noise had compromised his position, ordered two of his squads to deploy to the left and right of the village while he led the third squad into the hamlet. At 0600 the 3d squad entered Tuyet Diem (1) and caught the VC completely unaware. According to one report: "At that time it [the hamlet] became alive with VC. They ran into the streets, some of them naked; all of them carrying weapons, and of course the squads on the right and left took them under fire."[45]

At the same time, the 3d Squad pushed the enemy toward the river where the platoon killed 30 VC and captured seven more. A search of the area turned up a squad leader's diary, three weapons, and a medical kit.[46]

Several hours later there was a sequel to this action. Lieutenant Colonel James P. Kelly, the battalion commander, ordered Company A to move into the same area. Kelly believed that there was a good chance that VC might still be there.[47] He was correct. The Marines of Company A killed eight VC and captured three more weapons.

Another significant engagement occurred in the Da Nang TAOR on 27 December when a 17-man patrol from Company B, 1st Battalion, 9th Marines engaged a large enemy force near the small hamlet of Quang Ha, 11 miles south of the base. As the Marines approached the hamlet they were fired on from a tree line to their front and from their right flank. The first burst killed the patrol's radioman, destroyed his radio, and damaged one of the two M-60 machine guns. The heavy fire lasted about 15 minutes, seven members of the patrol were hit, and one Marine died of wounds.

Earlier the patrol leader, First Lieutenant James P. Weller, had sent a fire team to a sandy ridge on his right flank to cover the patrol's approach. The main body of the patrol and the flanking fire team immediately returned fire. The enemy launched a frontal attack. The VC were caught in a crossfire between the main body and the fire team on the right flank. The Marines killed nine of the attackers, but 40 to 50 more VC moved into positions behind the ambush site. Lieutenant Weller set off a smoke grenade, the prearranged signal to the battalion for help in case of radio failure. After 30 minutes, the Americans heard a shrill whistle and the enemy fire diminished. The Marines continued to fire 60mm mortar rounds. At this point, Marine reinforcements, including two Ontos and two tanks, arrived. According to Lieutenant Weller, fire from the tanks caused another 13 VC casualties. An armed helicopter covered the Marines as they withdrew

from the area, while artillery fire was placed on the suspected enemy escape routes. The engagement resulted in 41 confirmed enemy dead and another 15-20 probable kills. The Marines suffered seven casualties, all during the initial burst of fire.[48]

As small unit patrolling expanded into the populated ricelands of the growing Marine enclaves, III MAF soon realized the futility of such actions unless the Viet Cong infrastructure there was destroyed. Several programs were established to accomplish this end. They had many different labels, but pacification was the true name of the game.

CHAPTER 9

Pacification

*The Combined Action Program—Protection of the Harvest: GOLDEN FLEECE—Cordon and Search:
The Seeds of COUNTY FAIR and Population Control—Civic Action—The Ngu Hanh Son Campaign
and the Frustrations of Pacification*

The Combined Action Program

Fighting guerrillas was not a new experience for the Marine Corps. General Walt recalled that as a young officer he learned the fundamentals of his profession ''from men who had fought Sandino in Nicaragua or Charlemagne in Haiti.''[1] Based on earlier experiences in the Caribbean republics, in 1940 the Marine Corps published the *Small Wars Manual*, which contains the statement:

> In small wars, tolerance, sympathy, and kindness should be the keynote of our relationship with the mass of the population . . . . The purpose should always be to restore normal government . . . . and to establish peace, order, and security. . . .[2]*

General Walt expressed much the same sentiment when he described pacification, The name doesn't matter, the idea does: sympathy, understanding, regard for the people.[3]

The Marines recognized the close interrelationship between defense of the base area and the extension of Marine influence into the countryside. This was clearly demonstrated at Phu Bai where the 3d Battalion, 4th Marines faced the situation of

defending an expanding area of operations with a limited number of troops. They responded by developing the Combined Action Program. When Zone A,** the 10-square-mile built-up area directly north and east of the airfield, was incorporated in the Marine TAOR on 21 June, Lieutenant Colonel William ''Woody'' Taylor expected reinforcements from the 3d Marine Division to control the added area, but the diversion of Utter's battalion to Qui Nhon forced Taylor to make do with the forces he had on hand.

At the suggestion of Captain John J. Mullen, Jr., the battalion adjutant and civil affairs officer, Taylor decided to tap a neglected resource, the South Vietnamese Popular Forces (PF). There were six PF platoons in the Phu Bai TAOR; one each in the villages of Thuy Luong, Thuy Tan, Phu Bai, and Loc Son, and two guarding the railroad and Highway 1 bridges. In July, Lieutenant Colonel Taylor was granted limited operational control of the PF units in Zone A by General Chuan, the 1st ARVN Division commander. Major Cullen C. Zimmerman, Taylor's executive officer, developed plans for the incorporation of Marines into the PF units. Lieutenant Colonel Taylor then discussed the concept with Colonel Wheeler, still commander of the 3d Marines, and General Walt. Colonel Wheeler assigned a young, Vietnamese-speaking officer from his staff at Da Nang, First Lieutenant Paul R. Ek, the responsibility for establishing the program at Phu Bai. Ek was to integrate a Marine squad into a PF

---

*A former III MAF staff officer in 1965 and, later, a battalion and combined action group commander, Colonel John E. Greenwood, cautioned that the relationship between Marine Corps counterinsurgency theory and the earlier Marine experience in the Caribbean can be overdrawn. Colonel Greenwood remarked that during the Kennedy era ''guerrilla warfare expertise'' was one of the ''popular 'in' topics,'' and the ''hundreds of Marine officers,'' including himself, ''attended Army schools and studied the doctrine developed and articulated by the British and by the U.S. Army.'' He made the point that for officers of his generation, as opposed to the senior commanders such as General Walt, ''our insights in war of this kind came from this nearly contemporary effort, not from Marine Corps experience 30 years previous.'' Col John E. Greenwood, Comments on draft MS, dtd Nov77 (Vietnam Comment File).

**Zone A consisted of the ARVN Dong Da training camp, a series of hamlets, and low, wet rice lands extending to the waterways which formed a semicircle around the Marine base. The rivers in the area roughly defined the boundaries for the entire Marine TAOR: the Ta Trach in the west, the Dai Giang to the north and east, and the Nong to the east and south. See Chapter 3 for the incorporation of Zone A in the TAOR.

133

At Phu Bai, 1st Lieutenant Paul R. Ek, commander of the Combined Action Company (holding the rifle), inspects a combined squad of Vietnamese Popular Force troops and U.S. Marines.

platoon, forming what was then called a "joint action company," patterned along the lines of the British companies used in Malaya during the 1950s.*

The Marine Corps had established its own pacification precedents in the Caribbean and senior Marine officers, as early as February 1963, considered adapting this experience to the Vietnam situation. General Greene, then chief of staff at HQMC, met with Edward H. Forney, a retired Marine general, home on leave from his post in Saigon where he was the Public Safety Advisor with the U.S. Operations Mission. Forney, a Naval Academy graduate and a veteran of both World War II and Korea, had served two years with the 1st Marine Brigade in Haiti during the early 1930s. According to General Greene, Forney believed that:

> The Marine Corps should get into the Vietnam job with both feet and that it should be a real grass roots level operation, not tied in with the MAAG; but rather an effort to be linked with the Civil Guard, the Self-Defense Corps, and the local Militia in the village and boondock level. This would be similar to the Guardia effort in Nicaragua or the Gendarmerie operation in Haiti and Santo Domingo. Forney thinks that this is the type of operation around which the common people of South Vietnam would rally; that this is the big deficiency in the

---

*General Walt made the following statement concerning the origins of the Combined Action Program: "I can unequivocally state that the original suggestion was made by Captain John J. Mullen, Jr., the first plans made by Major Cullen C. Zimmerman, with the approval of the Commanding Officer of the 3d Battalion, 4th Marines (Regiment), Lieutenant Colonel William W. Taylor." Walt, *Strange War, Strange Strategy*, p. 105. According to Captain Paul R. Ek, the first commanding officer of the Combined Action Company, the Province Chief of Thua Thien Province, Lieutenant Colonel Khoa "indicated to Lieutenant Colonel Taylor that there should be only one commander for all troops, Marines and Popular Forces, in the area." *Ek MR, 10Nov72.*

USMC Photo A185800

Lieutenant Paul R. Ek (on the right) discusses the situation with a South Vietnamese officer (left). The South Vietnamese soldier in the center with the floppy wide-brim hat is the interpreter.

present operation and the one in which the USMC could make a solid contribution.[4]

Unlike the *Guardia Nacional* in Nicaragua or Haitian *Gendarmerie*, the joint action company was to be a cooperative effort rather than a Marine-officered native constabulary. The first, and perhaps most important, task was the selection of the Marines for the program. All of the Americans were hand-picked by Ek, and, as far as he was concerned, they were the best men available. They were highly motivated volunteers. The Marine lieutenant spent a week teaching his recruits about Vietnamese customs and the political structure in the countryside. The men were to live in the surrounding hamlets and they needed to know their exact place in this society. In Ek's words, they had to know "whom to call 'sir' and whom to call 'you'."[5]

When the school period was over, each of Ek's four Marine squads was assigned to a PF platoon. The Marine squad leader became the platoon commander while the Vietnamese commander became his assistant. A Marine fire team was the nucleus of each combined squad with Marines filling most of the leadership billets, but with Vietnamese counterparts. This relationship existed on the company level as well; Vietnamese Warrant Officer Nyugen Diem Duong was to be Ek's executive of-

ficer. The company headquarters included a Marine first sergeant and three Vietnamese radio operators who manned the ARVN radio nets. These nets included the hamlet chief as well as the 3d Battalion's fire direction center. At first, Ek's headquarters served only as an administrative and coordinating center for the activities of each platoon, but, in time, the headquarters controlled company-size operations in which the combined unit operated with Regional Force and ARVN units.

The command structure was flexible. Although Lieutenant Colonel Taylor had operational command, the Vietnamese district chief retained administrative responsibility for the PF. Correspondingly, in each village where the joint action platoons were garrisoned, the village chief kept his administrative civil responsibilities, while the combined force was responsible for military security. A great deal depended on the tact and resourcefulness of each Marine, especially the platoon commander who had to maintain harmonious relations among his subordinates, the village chief, and his PFs.

Ek's concept of operations for the employment of the PF with Marines was patterned on the organization of the VC infrastructure, using "assistance rather than terror to win the people's loyalties." He believed that as the PFs and Marines built their "infrastructure . . . they would be destroying that of the Viet Cong." The combined force would have several basic assignments: "security, counter-intelligence, obtaining the good will of the people . . . . These formed the spokes of the wheel while training was the hub of the entire program."[6]

Training was accomplished jointly. The Vietnamese taught local customs, Vietnamese language, local terrain peculiarities, and furnished information about the VC in the area. The Americans taught tactics, discipline, and civilian population control.

On 1 August, the joint action company was formally established and two days later the first platoon made a reconnaissance of its assigned village. During the first week, the platoons entered the villages only during daytime. At first the Marines ignored the villagers and worked solely with the PFs. The Americans had to learn the terrain and local patterns. Each Marine carried a small notebook in which he recorded the daily habits of the people in the hamlets, such as what time the buffalo boys took their animals out to the fields and when the people

USMC Photo A185799

A Combined Action Company patrol moves across a dike near Phu Bai showing the complete integration of Marines and PF.

got up in the morning. He was to pay particular attention to all deviations from the daily pattern. When there was a break in the routine, it was his job to find out the reason why. Eventually the Marines were able to talk with the people, at first using a combination of sign language, and then "pidgin" Vietnamese and English.

The main obstacle to the establishment of mutual trust between the Marines and the Vietnamese was the *sub rosa* control that the VC maintained in the area. They did not rule with a tight rein, but would come into the villages several nights a week to distribute propaganda, make speeches, and collect taxes. According to Ek, the understrength Vietnamese territorial forces were unable to cope with the VC. The government troops appeared to lack the initiative to go after the Communists. Ek suspected that some of the Vietnamese village chiefs and the VC commanders had reached informal, unwritten agreements, not as a conspiracy, but as an understanding of the realities of the situation. The Communist troops had the freedom to move during the night, and, in turn, offered no interference to government operations during the day.

Once Lieutenant Ek's combined force began to enter the hamlets, much of the collusion stopped. During the first weeks, the joint platoons saturated the area with patrols, day and night. They introduced several innovations in population control. One of the most successful was accomplished with the aid of the

local Vietnamese National Police. The PFs and Marines would enter a hamlet just before dawn and gather the people in the village street. The troops would first apologize to the inhabitants for disturbing them, but then state that it was necessary to check their identification cards in order to protect them from the Communists. The actual identification and questioning of the people was done by an accompanying force of policemen.

The allied commands were unsure how the VC would react to the U.S. Marines living in the hamlets. Ek believed that the Communists had two alternatives. They would either attack the hamlets and wipe out the joint platoons, or ignore the Americans altogether. The VC chose the latter course. As the Marines lived among the people, in time the Americans were able to sense if they were welcome or not. They had to be especially careful in hamlets where the inhabitants were overly friendly. That usually meant that the people had something to hide, and that something usually turned out to be VC.

The first significant engagement between a combined action unit* and the Viet Cong occurred

---

*The name of the joint action company was changed to combined action company by III MAF in October since "joint" pertains to two or more services of the same country and "combined" means services of different countries. See *Mullen Study*, p. C-H. Captain John J. Mullen, Jr., became the commanding officer on 25 September when Lieutenant Ek completed his overseas tour and left Vietnam.

USMC Photo A185740

Marines and PF troops of the Combined Action Company patrol the Nong River near Phu Bai in Vietnamese boats. The two Marine swimmers are apparently searching for any VC who may be hiding under the water.

on 29 November during a successful ambush near Phu Bai. As a VC platoon started to cross a bridge into the hamlet, a combined action squad opened fire on the VC, killing four and capturing one of the enemy troops. The enemy platoon fled to the south where it was engaged by another combined action squad and then forced to turn west through blocking artillery fires. There were no Marine or PF casualties. One of the dead VC was later identified as the enemy unit commander, Phan Van Thuong.[7]*

The combined action platoons did not kill many VC during this early period, but by protecting their assigned hamlets they accomplished the primary mission for which they had been formed. In addition, the platoons furnished the Marine battalion with defense-in-depth protection of the base at Phu Bai.

---

* Thuong, a member of the Communist party, was born only a few miles from where he died and was a veteran of the Viet Minh War against the French.

The enemy was duly impressed by this factor. According to Lieutenant Colonel Vale, who had relieved Lieutenant Colonel Taylor, a report found on a VC body read ''There were at least 4,000 Marines in the area. You could not move anywhere because Marines were always in the way.''[8]

The platoons also became an important source of information. The combined action troops soon learned about the VC organization in the area. They knew that it was led by a man named Vo Dai, who, although born in the Phu Bai area, had lived in North Vietnam for several years. The Marines and PF troops discovered where Vo Dai's mother and wife lived and paid frequent visits to the two women. The combined action units never captured Vo Dai, but they managed to keep him on the run.

Indicative of combined action effectiveness was the close bond forged between the Marines and the local villagers. When Vale's battalion was replaced at Phu Bai by Lieutenant Colonel Hanifin's 2d Battalion, 1st

Marines in December, 40 of the 66 Marines assigned to the combined action company at Phu Bai volunteered to extend their tour with the PFs rather than return to Okinawa with their battalion.[9]

Marines in the other sectors of I Corps also experimented with the employment of local Vietnamese defense forces. On Ky Ha Peninsula, north of Chu Lai, the local chief, with the cooperation of Lieutenant Colonel Robert J. Perrich's 1st Battalion, 4th Marines, established a self-defense corps in September, composed entirely of local village volunteers. Their duty was to patrol the five hamlets which made up Ky Ha village during the night. On the 25th, members of this force began accompanying Marine patrols in the area. In the sectors of both the 4th and 7th Marines at Chu Lai, PF units were brought into the battalion sectors for introduction and training. At Da Nang, two Regional Force companies' operations were coordinated with the Marine regiments, the 3d and 9th Marines. In addition, both regiments also used PF units during offensive operations to serve as guides and interpreters. Where PF defensive positions were near to those of the Marine battalions, close coordination was maintained for mortar and artillery fires, night ambushes, patrols, and listening posts.

General Walt watched the Marine employment of local forces with intense interest. He realized that the PF soldier had the poorest training and worst equipment of the South Vietnamese armed forces, but he considered him to be a vital link in the process of providing real security for the population. He noted:

> He had a signal advantage over all others; he was defending his own home, family, and neighbors. The Popular Force soldier knew every person in his community by face and name; he knew each paddy, field, trail, bush, or bamboo clump, each family shelter, tunnel, and buried rice urn. He knew in most cases the local Viet Cong guerrilla band, and it was not uncommon for him to be related to one or more of them by blood or other family ties.[10]

During November, the III MAF commander persuaded General Thi to release eight PF platoons at Da Nang to the operational control of the 3d Marine Division. Seven of the PF units were assigned to the airfield defense battalion and the eighth to Lieutenant Colonel Ludwig's 1st Battalion, 9th Marines, operating south of Marble Mountain.[11] Marine and PF troops patrolled the defensive perimeters of the airfield area together. Reports of innocent people

Two Marines from the 1st Battalion, 9th Marines stack newly harvested bags of rice inside a Marine amphibian tractor in Operation GOLDEN FLEECE. The rice is to be taken to a central collection point for safe keeping and marketing.

being detained at the airfield decreased considerably, and the PFs received valuable combat training. On 5 January 1966, General Walt asked General Thi to extend combined action operations between PFs and Marines to all three enclaves, which Thi agreed to do on 28 January.[12]

Protection of the Harvest: GOLDEN FLEECE

The expansion of the 9th Marines TAOR into the populated area south of Da Nang during Operation RICE STRAW coincided with the autumn rice harvest and resulted in another task for the Marines, rice harvesting protection. The most publicized effort involved the 1st Battalion, 9th Marines along the eastern perimeter of the 9th Marines' area of operations.

USMC Photo A186015

A Marine guards a Viet Cong prisoner during Operation GOLDEN FLEECE in September 1965. The Viet Cong had taken a percentage of the rice harvest for their own use for years in this area south of Da Nang prior to the arrival of the Marines.

In mid-August, the battalion was released from duty as the airfield defense battalion and was assigned to the area south of Marble Mountain bordering the South China Sea. Operating from a central base area, Lieutenant Colonel Ludwig sent out small patrols to bait the VC. When these units made contact, a mobile reaction force, composed of Marines mounted on tanks, Ontos, and amtracs, sped to the point of contact. At the same time, the battalion commander attempted to enlist each of the four village chiefs in his area of operations to support his efforts against the Viet Cong.[13]* The chiefs were wary until the

*One of Ludwig's company commanders was an Australian exchange officer, Captain Michael J. Harris of the New South Wales Light Infantry, who had served with the British forces in Malaya and gladly shared his experiences with the Americans. He suggested the formation of an area security council consisting of the four chiefs, a program which Ludwig later implemented. *Ludwig intvw.*

Americans proved themselves, which did not take long. On 29 August, the battalion defeated a Viet Cong company, killing 12, capturing 12 more, and dispersing the remainder.

Impressed by this action, Huynh Ba Trinh, chief of Hoa Hai village, contacted the battalion intelligence officer the next day and reported that his villagers had told him that more than 30 of the enemy had been killed in that engagement.** Trinh then asked that the battalion provide security for the villagers when they began harvesting their rice on 10 September. The chief explained that the VC came each year and took what they considered to be their share of the harvest. According to South Vietnamese and Marine intelligence sources, the Viet Cong had already moved one battalion and several companies into the 9th Marines TAOR to accomplish their rice collection.[14] Trinh proposed that the Marines help the farmers bring the rice to central collection points where it could be stored in warehouses. He would then give the people receipts for their crops and distribute the rice when the need arose.***

Lieutenant Colonel Ludwig did not believe that the local chiefs could administer such a large undertaking. He suggested that a meeting be held with the four chiefs on 7 September. The battalion commander had lunch that day with the chiefs and proposed that the Marine battalion, through active patrolling, ambushes, and sweep operations, screen the VC from the people, freeing the peasants to harvest their rice. The farmers could keep the rice in their homes and the Marines would try to keep the VC out. The chiefs were agreeable and Ludwig, borrowing from Greek mythology, labeled the operation GOLDEN FLEECE. General Walt cleared the operation with General Thi, the I Corps Com-

**The 9th Marines S-2, Major John A. Buck, commented: "Regardless of the accuracy of the reported 30 VC KIAs—which is not an improbable total for the action referred to—the fact that the village chief accepts this figure is, in itself, important." 9th Marines Intelligence Summary No. 54, dtd 1Sep65, 9th Marines S-2 Section, Journal and Intelligence Summaries, Sep65.

***The 9th Marines intelligence summary of 1 September indicated the significance of Trinh's proposal: "Hoa Hai village has a population of over 3,000 and has been considered VC controlled territory. If the villagers are now willing to risk possible VC reprisals by refusing to pay the usual rice tax, it would indicate a confidence and firmness heretofore lacking in this locality."

USMC Photo A185845

Marines of the 1st Battalion, 9th Marines help South Vietnamese farmers load bags of rice into a Marine LVT. Note that the Vietnamese have hung the bags on their traditional carrying pole.

mander, and on 9 September, Colonel John E. Gorman, the 9th Marines commander, ordered both his forward battalions, the 1st and 2d, to render all possible assistance to the Vietnamese in the protection of the harvest.[15] The 3d Battalion, 9th Marines later replaced the 2d Battalion.

The campaign produced results quickly. About noon on 12 September, Chief Trinh told Lieutenant Colonel Ludwig that a VC main force unit had moved into a hamlet south of Marble Mountain to collect its rice tax. The battalion commander immediately sent a two-company attack force, supported by Ontos, tanks, and amtracs into the area. The Marines met strong opposition from VC mortars and recoilless rifles. Shortly after dark, the enemy broke contact and fled. The next morning the Marines found no enemy bodies, but later learned that the VC had

taken refuge during the night in a leper hospital, five miles south of Marble Mountain. The Viet Cong had taken medicines and supplies from the leprosarium and moved out of the area. Ludwig believed this battle broke the back of the VC tax collection organization in his battalion's TAOR.[16] After this encounter, the 1st Battalion Marines met only sporadic resistance as GOLDEN FLEECE continued through the rice harvesting season.

Rice protection was not only the preserve of the 9th Marines. In the northwestern portion of the Da Nang TAOR, Lieutenant Colonel Clement's 2d Battalion, 3d Marines conducted a similar harvest protection operation in the Cu De Valley near the hamlets of Pho Nam Thuong Ha and Nam Yen. When the peasants of this region voluntarily left their homes to resettle in the pacified village of Le My, they agreed to do so only if the Marines would protect their autumn harvest. Lieutenant Colonel Clement accepted this condition and fulfilled his promise in September.[17] On the 15th, the battalion intelligence officer, Captain Lionel V. Silva, discussed plans for the harvest with the district chief. A Marine helicopter flew a group of farmers from Le My to their fields near their former homes to survey the crops. By 18 September the battalion and South Vietnamese had completed preparations and the harvest began in earnest on the next day. During the period 18-23 September, the Marines moved approximately 150 villagers to their fields for the harvest. Marine helicopters and LVTs brought over 12,000 pounds of harvested rice into Le My, as well as some civilians who had decided to resettle there. The helicopters flew 14 sorties while the LVTs logged 800 miles in this GOLDEN FLEECE operation.*

In October, rice protection operations were extended to two other areas of operations. At Da Nang, Lieutenant Colonel Hatch's 1st Battalion, 1st Marines, in the southwestern portion of the Da Nang TAOR, assisted the villagers of Hieu Duc District in their harvest of over 71,000 kilograms of rice. During this same month, Lieutenant Colonel Fisher's 2d Battalion, 4th Marines conducted two operations labeled HARVEST MOON** in "Western Valley," five miles west of Chu Lai airfield. The village chief of Ky Ha (2) reported that the battalion protected the harvesting of over 102,000 kilograms of rice.[18]

On 26 November, Lieutenant Colonel Clement submitted a study for General Walt evaluating the GOLDEN FLEECE Operations.*** Using figures furnished by the Vietnamese village chiefs, he declared that, "512,410 pounds of rice, threshed, was denied the VC. At the accepted rate of 1.5 pounds per person per day, this could have subsisted 1,900 VC for the six months until next harvest."[19]

.* The battalion did not call its operation GOLDEN FLEECE, but this name was soon adopted to refer to all rice harvesting protection missions.

**III MAF records indicate that 2/3 also conducted a rice harvest operation named HARVEST MOON. The early HARVEST MOON operations should not be confused with the multi-battalion combat operation HARVEST MOON conducted by Task Force DELTA in December.

***Lieutenant Colonel Clement was detached from 2/3 on 10Nov65 and assigned to the III MAF G-3 Section.

USMC Photo A185783
A Marine officer assists a South Vietnamese woman gather the rice into a shock while another Marine stands guard during Operation GOLDEN FLEECE.

Clement concluded that the operation was both a psychological and economic success, it had kept the rice in the hands of the people while denying it to the VC. General Walt, confident of further success, ordered that plans be drawn up to implement GOLDEN FLEECE II for the spring harvest.

Cordon and Search: The Seeds of COUNTY FAIR and Population Control

During this period, III MAF started what was to become the COUNTY FAIR technique, a cordon and search operation with psychological overtones. Although the 9th Marines was to give the technique its name, the concept evolved from the experience of several units and techniques they had developed to meet local conditions. In the 3d Marines TAOR, southwest of the airfield, several operations were conducted, initially by the 1st Battalion, 3d Marines and later by the 1st Battalion, 1st Marines, during which one company would surround a hamlet while another would search it for VC. In the Le My area, the regiment's nothern TAOR, the 2d Battalion, 3d

USMC Photo A413090

Major Charles J. Keever was the III MAF Civil Affairs Officer in 1965. He was the author of the III MAF Civic Action Order.

His [Colonel Thanh, the I Corps Chief of Staff] solution was to react with fire at the first hostile action. I got the distinct impression that I Corps preferred a dead villager to a live refugee.[21]

Although the 9th Marines plan, which in effect was a blueprint of future COUNTY FAIR operations, was not immediately adopted, Lieutenant Colonel Ludwig's 1st Battalion tried a similar operation during GOLDEN FLEECE I. When a company from the battalion entered a village, all the people were gathered at a collection point. The Marines fed them and a Navy corpsman held sick call, while the village chief checked identity cards and attempted to identify any VC. Ludwig later admitted that these sweeps were too ambitious. At times, the Marines had more than 1,000 people from various hamlets collected in one location, but they had neither the time or personnel to properly screen all of them.[22]

By the end of year, nevertheless, the 9th Marines S-2, Captain Charles Ward, and the S-3, Major Vincente T. Blaz, had improved the COUNTY FAIR concept to the degree that it was ready to be implemented on a regular basis in 1966. It would become a sophisticated procedure, combining civic action, population control, and psychological operations. Captain Ward stated: ''COUNTY FAIR operations were distinguished by two features: the pre-eminence given to the role of the GVN, and the protraction of the duration of the cordon and search to surface the hidden enemy.''[23]*

Civic Action

All of these battlefield tactics were coordinated with an ever increasing civic action program, what General Walt sometimes referred to as the ''Velvet Glove.''[24] Civic action programs were basically Marine efforts to assuage the effect of the ravages of war, poverty, and sickness upon the population. There was more to the concept than just pure

Marines conducted a ''similar type operation . . . in conjuction with RVN civic action personnel provided by the Province Chief and National Police.''[20]

Prior to reentering Cam Ne after the ''Zippo'' lighter incident, the 9th Marines planned to use loudspeakers to call the villagers out of the hamlets to a holding area where they would be fed and given medical treatment. Marines, reinforced by local forces, would then enter the empty hamlets to search for VC. The difficulty lay with obtaining the cooperation of the local South Vietnamese authorities. Colonel Edwin H. Simmons, the III MAF G-3, met with the I Corps chief of staff to discuss the problems of operating in the villages south of Da Nang, but failed to reach any agreement on methods. Simmons recalled:

*Lieutenant Colonel Ward remembered that the Hoa Vang District Chief, who had always found a ready excuse ''when participation of his people was concerned,'' became much more cooperative after his wife's vehicle was shot at in late 1965. The chief wanted a sweep of the hamlet from which the shot was fired and his ''insistence, and his promises of future cooperation if the Marines would assist him in this action, finally convinced the 9th Marines that this might be the opening they were seeking.'' LtCol Charles Ward, Comments on draft MS, dtd 27Oct76 (Vietnam Comment File).

USMC Photo A185777

Navy Lieutenant James R. McMillian, the surgeon for the 3d Battalion, 4th Marines, examines a South Viet-namese infant. The child is the 10,000th Vietnamese patient treated by the battalion's medical team.

benevolence; it was to be used as a weapon. General Walt and his staff hoped that American civic action would sever the populace from Viet Cong control and perhaps induce popular loyalty to the government.

The Marines knew that the entire effort could be dissipated through lack of direction. In addition to the III MAF civic action program, several U. S. civilian agencies,* administered by the United States Operations Mission in Vietnam (USOM),

dispensed American aid throughout South Vietnam. On 25 August General Walt met with Mr. Marcus J. Gordon, the regional director of USOM in I Corps. He suggested that a council be established to coordinate American participation in the Vietnamese Rural Construction Program.** Mr. Gordon agreed

*These agencies included representatives from AID, JUSPAO, and CIA.

**The South Vietnamese pacification program changed names frequently during 1965-1966. The program was originally known as "rural pacification" until 5 April 1965 when it was changed to "rural construction." In May 1966, the name was changed again to "revolutionary development." These were simply other names for "pacification."

and, on 6 September, the I Corps Joint Coordinating Council (JCC) came into being. Both Mr. Gordon and General Walt hoped to bring the South Vietnamese into the council, but only American representatives attended the first session: Mr. Gordon; Colonel St. Clair, the Deputy Senior Advisor to I Corps; and the III MAF Civil Affairs Officer, Major Charles J. Keever.[25]

Apparently, the Vietnamese authorities took a wait-and-see attitude before joining in the council's deliberations. On 28 September, General Walt visited General Thi and prevailed upon him to send a representative to the next council meeting. The I Corps commander appointed a representative from his staff to attend the October session, and he became a permanent member of the JCC.[26]*

The I Corps JCC soon became the coordinating hub for "the Vietnamese government's rural construction plan" in the northern five provinces. Most of the important work was done by committees; and by January 1966, six were functioning. These were: public health, education, roads, food distribution, psychological warfare, and the Port of Da Nang. In November, General Walt further underscored the importance of the progress of the council by appointing Brigadier General Keith B. McCutcheon, Deputy Commanding General, III MAF as his personal representative. He was subsequently elected chairman of the council. Mr. Gordon later declared:

> The fact that senior officers from all military commands under General Walt . . . sat together every Tuesday morning with the Regional Directors of Civilian Agencies contributed greatly to facilitating coordination. But to me the most important fact about the JCC was that "the word went out" through all command channels. All commands were working on a seven-day week basis around the clock. The desire to cooperate was there, but coordination required special effort. The existence of the JCC stimulated coordination at all levels.[27]

During this same period, General Walt also concentrated on internal coordination of the civic action program within III MAF. On 29 October, he changed the designation of his III MAF general staff G-5 Section from plans and programs to civic action. More significantly, the new organizational designation was reflected throughout III MAF with the creation of division and wing G-5 and regimental and battalion S-5 sections.

III MAF developed some tentative conclusions. In October, the Marine command noted that programs of commodity distribution to the people and medical and dental care were most successful in reaching hamlet inhabitants. The emphasis was on short-term, high-impact, low-cost projects. The Marines had perceived that long-term projects, which required continual supervision and large amounts of material, failed to have the desired effect; the people did not see any immediate results.[28] One of the most important reasons why the Marines emphasized short-range activities was the fact that the battalions just did not have the time to attempt more ambitious programs.** The Marines primary tactical duties left very little time for action in direct support of the local government or rural construction.[29]

The Ngu Hanh Son Campaign and the Frustrations of Pacification

During the autumn of 1965, the South Vietnamese revamped their pacification program in I Corps. Earlier in the year, MACV had urged the South Vietnamese to prepare new pacification plans in each corps area based on the HOP TAC campaign in the Saigon region.*** The idea was for each corps commander to select a critical region and develop plans for coordinating and focusing both the military and civilian activities in an intensive pacification campaign in the selected area. At a meeting of South Vietnamese corps commanders in April, the Joint General Staff directed them to make such plans. The following month, at a follow-up meeting, General Thi, the I Corps commander, declared that his pacification efforts would be centered in the area south of Da Nang in Quang Nam Province.[30]

---

*Colonel Keever wrote in his comments: "The Vietnamese military leadership (and MACV for that matter) tended to overlook the vital importance of the civil side of pacification. The support of General Thi and GVN military leadership in I Corps for the so-called people-to-people program was the result of General Walt's leadership and persuasive powers." Col Charles J. Keever, Comments on draft MS, dtd 20Dec76 (Vietnam Comment File).

**There were some exceptions to the above: the 7th Marines and 4th Marines help in the construction of the "new life" village of Chu Lai; the 9th Marines reconstruction effort at Cam Ne; and the Le My effort in the 3d Marines TAOR. All of these met with varying degrees of success, depending on the degree of security the Marines and the local government could provide.

***For a description of the HOP TAC program see Chapter 4.

In October, Lieutenant Colonel Le Trung Tuong, the Quang Nam Province Chief, developed the Ngu Hanh Son (Nine Villages) pacification campaign in a nine-square-mile area of Hoa Vang District, south of the Cau Do River.* Tuong divided the objective area into two sectors, one consisting of a five-village complex west of Route 1 and the other, a four-village complex east of the highway. Taking advantage of the protective screen afforded by the 9th Marines' advance south of Da Nang, the province chief proposed to pacify the western sector by the end of the year. This area included the villages of Cam Ne, Duong Son, and Yen Ne where the 9th Marines first encountered organized VC resistance during July and August. Lieutenant Colonel Tuong planned to insert a political action team (PAT) and a Regional Force company from the 59th Regional Forces Battalion into each of the five villages of this sector.** He then hoped to recruit 1,000 Popular Forces troops to relieve the RF companies. Tuong intended to station one PF squad in each hamlet and a platoon in each village. The 9th Marines was to coordinate its activities to provide additional security for the pacification efforts, as well as furnishing some material resources.[31]

The VC were quick to realize the threat of the new program, but the enemy also quickly found a vulnerability. The program for the PFs and the RFs was too ambitious. PF recruiting policy had not

---

*Lieutenant Colonel Tuong was also Assistant Commander of the Quang Nam Special Sector, which was established on 1 September 1965, and reported directly to I Corps. As such, he as umed responsibility for rural construction in both Quang Nam Province and Da Nang Special Sector. The Quang Nam Special Sector, a military command, controlled all ARVN forces in Quang Nam Province. The authority of the Quang Nam Special Sector commander often overlapped that of the Quang Nam province chief, which was one reason why Tuong was the assistant commander of the special sector as well as province chief. By combining both responsibilities, he remained in the chain of command for the military aspects of pacification, while retaining authority over the political and administrative functions of the province.

**The political action teams were American-trained pacification cadre. While part of the teams provided limited security within the hamlets, the other members assisted the villagers in building up the local economy and meeting community needs. Colonel Simmons, the III MAF G-3, later observed that the formation of the 59th Regional Forces Battalion ''actually was an innovation. RF Companies had not previously been combined into battalions.'' BGen Edwin H. Simmons, Comments on draft MS, dtd 26Sep76 (Vietnam Comment File).

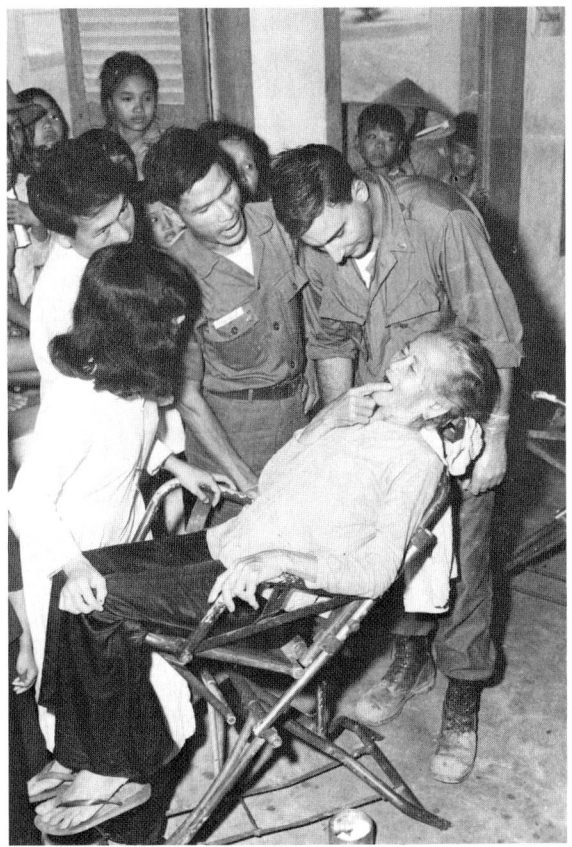

USMC Photo A186322
As part of their civic action program, the Marines provided dental care to the South Vietnamese villagers. This makeshift dental clinic near Da Nang is obviously very popular.

showed the hoped-for success. The PFs, the RFs, and PATs offered lucrative targets; the VC were quick to take advantage. By the end of November, about 10 to 15 percent of the PAT members had resigned, fearing reprisals from the VC, forcing the 9th Marines to increase its involvement in the area to offset VC gains.

The 9th Marines provided security for nearly a quarter of the campaign area during December, but the Viet Cong avoided the Marine-held territory and continued their offensive against the PFs. During the last week of the year they halted almost all government progress. On 21 December, the enemy attacked one of the PAT units, killing four of its members. Later that afternoon, 60 VC, sheltered for two days by the peasants of Cam Ne and Yen Ne, struck the 593d RF Company, whose sole mission was to protect the PATs. The government force suffered heavy casualties. During the next week, the VC systematically continued their campaign against local defense forces. The Marines could do little to prevent it. The PFs were to provide continuous security in the hamlets, but events had proved conclusively that they were incapable of carrying out their mission. Instead of strengthening their security forces the Vietnamese authorities changed leaders. The Ngu Hanh Son Program was allowed to drift until March 1966.

As early as September, 1965 General Krulak observed that ''the Marines have never felt that the war stands to be won by the grand maneuvers of large forces, by brilliant marshalship in the Tannenberg or Chancellorsville image, '' but rather in the villages.[32] The problem, was to provide security in the hamlets, and, in this, the Marines were not always successful. On the night of 25 October, a VC terrorist squad threw a grenade and fired a submachine gun into the house of Chief Trinh of Hoa Hai Village, the village chief who had cooperated with Lieutenant Colonel Ludwig's battalion in GOLDEN FLEECE. The chief and four of his family were wounded.* General Walt took the occasion to order all regimental commanders to insure the personal protection of village and district chiefs in their TAORs.[33] This was more easily said then done. On 24 December, in the supposedly secure Le My area, Lieutenant Colonel Dickey reported that the Viet Cong tortured and buried alive the assistant chief of Hoa Hiep.[34]**

---

* Lieutenant Colonel Ludwig later commented: ''we moved Trinh and his family into a special tent complex in our battalion CP. The family remained safe, and Trinh 'went to work' each day in the village. But his intelligence was never as good after that.'' Col Verle E. Ludwig, Comments on draft MS, dtd 8Oct76 (Vietnam Comment File).

**Colonel Clement, who had commanded the 2d Batttalion, 3d Marines in the Le My area, commented: ''It was security that failed. In the absence of firm security, there will be a VC intrusion every time.'' Col David A. Clement, Comments on draft MS, dtd 5Oct76 (Vietnam Comment File).

USMC Photo A800917

A South Vietnamese interpreter with a Marine patrol talks with a South Vietnamese boy. The boy's father had been killed by the Viet Cong.

The following excerpt from the 3d Battalion, 7th Marines command chronology at Chu Lai graphically depicts the Marines' frustrations:

> 12 December: Marines from 3/7 were invited to attend the celebration . . . After the religious ceremony the Marines participated at the banquet with the hamlet chief and elders in the local village of Tri Binh (1).
>
> 13 December: A flag raising ceremony was conducted in the local village of Tri Binh(1). The hamlet chief invited Captain Long, the District Chief, and representatives from 3/7.
>
> 24 December: 3/7 Civil Affairs teams conducted a Christmas party in the local villages of Tri Binh(1) . . . .
>
> 25 December: The CO 3/7 invited the children of the local villages of An Thien and Tri Binh(1) to attend the Christmas celebration at the Battalion CP.
>
> 31 December: Hamlet chief of Tri Binh(1) was shot and killed by an unknown assassin. . . .[35]

The best that could be said for the III MAF pacification effort by the end of 1965 was that the Marines had realized the problems and had started to challenge the VC control of the countryside. There was still much to learn and do.

PART IV

SUPPORTING THE TROOPS

CHAPTER 10

Marine Aviation in Vietnam

Deployments—Control of Marine Aviation—Fixed-Wing Operations—
Helicopter Operations—Air Defense Responsibilities

Deployments

The 1965 buildup of Marine aviation in Vietnam paralleled that of the III MAF ground forces. Following the landing of the 9th MEB in March, two Marine fixed-wing squadrons, VMCJ-1 and VMFA-531, later relieved by VMFA-513, joined MAG-16 at Da Nang in April. MAG-16 had been, until that time, the MEB's composite helicopter group.* In May, the wing established its forward headquarters in Vietnam, and the next month MAG-12 arrived at the newly built SATS airfield at Chu Lai. On 14 July, MAG-11 headquarters assumed operational control of the fixed-wing squadrons at Da Nang from MAG-16. These now included the photo reconnaissance

---

*Colonel Thomas J. O'Connor, the 1st MAW chief of staff in the spring of 1965, recalled: "The arrival of VMFA-531 and VMCJ-1 marked the end of a long period of planning, coaxing, cajoling, begging, and outright pressure to obtain space for these units to operate out of Da Nang . . . . During the early planning stages, high level commands battled in the Pentagon, CinCPac, and in the Far East over who would conduct air operations out of Da Nang. Navy and Marine commands invoked the nebulous authority of Marine Air Ground task forces. But these plans . . . were overtaken by events. The Air Force was there—and, they invoked the military equivalent of squatters rights . . . they occupied the entire east side of the airfield. The USAF was extremely unwilling to move around and vacate more space for the deploying Marine fixed-wing air units . . . .Finally under the weight of plans approved at high levels, and with Marine deployment dates irrevocably approaching, the Air Force finally gave in. Some promises about future construction to enlarge their area, commitments of Marine support of various projects, and a lot of sweet talk did the trick." Aircraft facilities remained overcrowded until the helicopter field at Marble Mountain was opened and the expansion construction of Da Nang Airfield was completed. O'Connor observed: "The final area occupied by two Marine fighter squadrons and the VMCJ-1 squadron was of such restricted size that effective operations were only marginally possible . . . .The three units were like three peas in a pod, but they were operational." Col Thomas J. O'Connor, Comments on draft MS, dtd 27Nov76 (Vietnam Comment File).

squadron, VMCJ-1, and two F-4B Phantom II squadrons, VMFA-513 and VMFA-542, the latter squadron having arrived on 11 July. After the President's 28 July proclamation announcing further reinforcement, the Joint Chiefs of Staff authorized the deployment of a second helicopter group, MAG-36, and another missile battalion, the 2d LAAM Battalion. The first elements of the helicopter group arrived on 31 August. The LAAM battalion followed 10 days later.

On 2 September, Colonel William G. Johnson, the MAG-36 commander, established his headquarters on the Ky Ha peninsula, north of the SATS field, where construction had begun on a helicopter facility for the Chu Lai base. When the group arrived, "the helicopter pad had been fully graded and about one-third or more of the matting laid . . . ."[1] The MAG-36 squadrons remained at Da Nang until Ky Ha was operational. By the end of the month, most of the MAG-36 units, including HMM-362, HMM-364, VMO-6, H&MS-36, and MABS-36, were at Ky Ha. The only exception was HMM-363 which had relieved a detachment from HMM-161 at Qui Nhon.

The other Marine helicopter group in Vietnam, MAG-16, also had moved into new facilities. Colonel Thomas J. O'Connor, who relieved Colonel King as group commander on 7 August, established his headquarters at Marble Mountain Air Facility on Tiensha Peninsula, across the Da Nang River from the main base. The group's aircraft were operating from Marble Mountain by the end of August. In August 1965 MAG-16 consisted of three medium helicopter squadrons, HMM-261 and -361 at Da Nang and HMM-161 at Phu Bai with a 10-plane detachment at Qui Nhon, one observation squadron, VMO-2, and two support squadrons, MABS-16 and H&MS-16. In September a six-plane detachment of Sikorsky CH-37C heavy-lift helicopters from HMH-462 was attached to H&MS-16. There was a continuing rotation of helicopter squadrons between

South Vietnam, the Seventh Fleet, and Okinawa, but no change in the total group strength.

Marine fixed-wing squadrons, as well as the helicopter units, continued to deploy to Vietnam. MAG-11, under the command of Colonel Robert F. Conley and his successor in November, Colonel Emmett O. Anglin, Jr., made three more squadron changes during 1965. On 15 October, VMFA-115 replaced VMFA-513, which rotated back to Japan. VMFA-323 relieved VMFA-542, which also returned to Japan on 1 December, and on 19 December, a F-8 Crusader squadron, VMF(AW)-312, joined MAG-11 at Da Nang. Lieutenant Colonel Richard A. Savage, at the time commanding VMFA-542, later commented: "These rotations were used to refurbish and change aircraft and train new aircrews as overseas tours drew to a close."[2]

MAG-12, under the command of Colonel John D. Noble, 16 May-18 September, and later Colonel Leslie E. Brown, 19 September through the end of the year, operated from the SATS airfield at Chu Lai. Three A-4 Skyhawk squadrons, VMA-225, VMA-311, and VMA-214, made up the aircraft group in July 1965. A fourth squadron, VMA-211, joined MAG-12 on 11 October. Although the group remained at basically the same strength, there was a rotation of squadrons between Iwakuni and Chu Lai.

The fixed-wing squadrons of MAG-12 engaged in the rotation program during this period were VMA-224 for VMA-225, 30 September-4 October, and VMA-223 for VMA-311, 14-19 December. At the end of the year, Brown's group consisted of VMA-211, VMA-214, VMA-223, and VMA-224.

By the end of 1965, most of the elements of the 1st Marine Aircraft Wing had arrived, although a rear headquarters remained in Japan. Brigadier General Marion E. Carl, the assistant wing commander, arrived at Da Nang on 31 August to assist the wing commander, Brigadier General Keith B. McCutcheon, who also was Deputy Commanding General, III MAF. Colonel Harry W. Taylor assumed command of the rear headquarters (1st MAW Rear) at Iwakuni on that date; he still controlled a sizeable organization. MAG-13 with three fixed-wing squadrons remained in Japan, and one helicopter squadron was on Okinawa. One transport squadron, VMGR-152, and elements of a second, VMGR-352 (Fwd), with several service and supply elements of the 1st MAW, also remained under the rear headquarters' operational control. In addition to these units, two Marine helicopter squadrons, one attached to the Seventh Fleet SLF and the other to the U.S. Army's Field Force Vietnam in II Corps, were not available to III MAF. In spite of these exceptions,

USMC Photo A184074

Marine F4B Phantoms from VMFA-531 arrive at Da Nang in April 1965. The drag parachute in the foreground helps to slow the aircraft's landing rollout.

Colonel William G. Johnson, Commanding Officer, MAG-36, speaks to one of his officers on board the Princeton *(LPH 5). Colonel Johnson is about to establish the newly arrived helicopter group's headquarters at Ky Ha in the Chu Lai TAOR.*

the preponderance of General McCutcheon's operational units were in South Vietnam supporting General Walt's ground forces. By December, 9,402 of the 12,655 officers and enlisted men of the 1st MAW were in South Vietnam.

Control of Marine Aviation

Control of Marine aviation in Vietnam was a very sensitive issue. Many Marine aviators remembered their experience in Korea where the 1st MAW had been under the operational control of the Air Force. They believed that Marine aircraft had been used unwisely, at least from a Marine point of view, and had not furnished the Marine infantry with the close air support that could have been provided if the Marine command had retained control of its aviation.[3] Marine generals were determined not to allow the Korean experience to repeat itself.

In 1964, when air operations were undertaken over Laos and North Vietnam, Admiral Sharp authorized General Westmoreland to designate the senior U. S. Air Force commander in Vietnam as coordinating

authority, since both Air Force and Navy air units were participating in these operations. When the decision was made to land Marines at Da Nang in 1965, it was natural for Admiral Sharp to direct that a similar arrangement be devised to coordinate the fixed-wing aviation of the 9th MEB. General Karch reported directly to ComUSMACV and coordinating authority was granted to the Air Force component commander, Major General Joseph H. Moore, for matters pertaining to tactical air support and air traffic control.

This emphasis on coordinating authority was reaffirmed by CinCPac in late March 1965, just before the assignment of a Marine fighter squadron to the MEB. General Westmoreland had wanted to put the Marine F-4 squadron under the operational control of General Moore, but Admiral Sharp immediately objected and repeated his earlier guidance.[4]

One month later, Admiral Sharp published a directive on the conduct and control of close air support. He stated that close air support was the chief mission of U.S. aviation in South Vietnam and that

USMC Photo A184307

A Douglas A-4 Skyhawk from VMA-225 makes the first landing at the Chu Lai SATS field. Colonel John D. Noble, Commanding Officer, MAG-12, piloted the aircraft.

top priority was to go to ground troops actually engaged with the enemy. Sharp maintained that such support should be directly responsive to the ground combat units. The directive also noted that "nothing herein vitiates the prior CinCPac provision that ComUSMACV's Air Force component command shall act as coordinating authority for matters pertaining to tactical air support and air traffic control in South Vietnam."[5]

After receiving CinCPac's instruction, General Westmoreland ordered that a revision be made to his air support order. The new MACV directive, published on 13 July 1965, reiterated CinCPac's appointment of General Moore as the coordinating authority. In addition, the order charged him with the responsibility of insuring that coordination was established between his service and the other allied commanders. General Walt retained operational control of Marine aviation, but to insure maximum use of all aircraft, the III MAF commander was to notify the 2d Air Division daily of those aircraft available in excess of his requirements so that additional sorties could be allocated.* Finally, Walt, as Naval Component Commander, Vietnam, was charged with preparing joint operating instructions, in coordination with General Moore, to insure an integrated air effort.[6]

Concurrently, with the revision of MACV's air directive, General McCutcheon met with Major General Moore to coordinate air efforts as related to

air defense operations. Moore wanted operational control of all air defense, but McCutcheon pointed out that the F-4B Phantom II was a dual-purpose plane, capable of both close air support and air-to-air defense. To relinquish these aircraft would deprive the Marine ground commanders of an important supporting arm.

Nevertheless, General McCutcheon recognized the necessity of having one overall air defense commander. After several meetings between the generals and their staffs, it was decided to publish a memorandum of agreement to set forth the basic policies, procedures, and responsibilities. Under this agreement, the Air Force had overall air defense responsibility. McCutcheon designated those Marine forces that would participate in air defense. He agreed that the U. S. Air Force had the authority to handle alert aircraft, designate targets, and control HAWK missile readiness status, including firing orders. Generals Moore and McCutcheon signed the document in August 1965.[7]**

The revised MACV air directive and the memorandum of agreement provided the basic policy for command, control, and coordination of Marine aviation, an arrangement completely satisfactory to General Walt. These arrangements were to remain unchanged until 1968, when General Westmoreland received approval from higher authority to establish a single management system for tactical air control.

Fixed-Wing Operations

The system of close air support which was employed by the Marines in South Vietnam in 1965 was born during the island campaigns of World War II. Since then, Marine air support doctrine had been continuously modified to keep pace with technological advances.

Marine attack aircraft were required to fly close air

---

*Colonel Roy C. Gray, Jr., the 1st MAW G-3, commented, "At the wing G-3 level it was always extremely difficult to identify those air assets that were in excess of III MAF needs. Generally both III MAF and the Air Force wanted far more than the wing could muster." Col Roy C. Gray, Jr., Comments on draft MS, dtd 28Sep76 (Vietnam Comment File).

**Colonel O'Connor recalled that he "was present at the key meeting of this series in Da Nang . . . . I observed General McCutcheon cross swords with General Moore. The Air Force general used every argument at his command. He appealed across service lines, as aviator to aviator, enumerating the advantages of centralized control of aviation in a theater of operations. But General McCutcheon held his ground. He had his orders from III MAF and CGFMFPac. He was also buttressed by several policy directives [from] CinCPac. . . ."Col Thomas J. O'Connor, Comments on draft MS, dtd 27Nov76 (Vietnam Comment File).

USMC Photo A184866

Admiral Ulysses S. G. Sharp, Commander in Chief Pacific (left), Brigadier General Keith B. McCutcheon, Commanding General, 1st Marine Aircraft Wing (center), and Major General Walt are seen inside a Marine helicopter. Admiral Sharp supported the Marine position on air control.

support missions against enemy troops who were as close as 15 meters from friendly lines. To reduce the risk to allied infantry, close air support strikes were controlled either by a tactical air controller (airborne) (TAC (A)) in a high performance aircraft; a forward air controller (airborne) (FAC (A)) in a light spotter plane or UH-1E gunship; or a forward air controller (FAC) on the ground. In addition, many of the III MAF aerial observers (AOs) flying in light observation aircraft were qualified air controllers and directed air strikes, as well as artillery and naval gunfire.

The airborne controllers, familiar with the tactical situation on the ground, remained on station for extended periods of time. They maintained contact with the supported infantry unit on a FM tactical radio net while directing the attack aircraft over a UHF net. Communications for the control of air support was a flexible arrangement, depending on the circumstances and ground radio availability. Frequency-modulated (FM) radios of infantrymen could not net with ultra-high frequency (UHF) radios of jet aircraft; usually the UHF radios at the infantry battalion level were not available for use by the company or smaller unit commanders in contact with the enemy. After the controller relayed pertinent target information and mission requirements to the attack pilots on station, he then marked the target with a white phosphorus rocket or a colored smoke grenade. When he was sure the attack pilot had properly identified the target, the controller cleared the pilots to make their firing runs.

At this time, the lead pilot rolled in toward the smoke marker and dropped his ordnance. Using the lead pilot's "hits" as a reference, the controller furnished the second plane in the flight with whatever corrections were necessary and cleared the second aircraft target run. The same procedure continued until all of the attack aircraft in the flight, usually two aircraft per strike, had completed their missions.

Two basic types of close air support strikes were flown by Marine aviators in South Vietnam, preplanned and on-call. The preplanned mission was a complex process. A Marine battalion commander would submit a request for fixed-wing aircraft through his air liaison officer the afternoon before his battalion was to begin an operation. The request would go to the direct air support center (DASC) and to the tactical air direction center (TADC) of the wing at Da Nang. At this level, all the requests were assimilated and orders were issued to both MAGs-11 and -12, the fixed-wing groups. The groups then scheduled flights for the next day and issued mission requirements to the individual squadrons. This procedure required approximately 20 hours from the initial time of request to the delivery of the ordnance on the target.

On-call missions could be processed and executed almost instantaneously. These missions were flown either in support of troops in contact with the enemy, or against targets of opportunity located by airborne or ground controllers. In the case of an emergency, the TADC or DASC could divert in-flight aircraft from their original missions to a new target. The TADC could also call upon aircraft which each group maintained on an around-the-clock alert for just such contingencies.

Marine air provided this combat support for other

than Marine units. During the battle of Ba Gia in June 1965, the A-4s of Colonel Noble's MAG-12 took off on their first night launch from Chu Lai to provide support for the embattled outpost 20 miles to the south. For three days, the MAG-12 A-4 Skyhawks and the F-4B Phantom IIs of Da Nang-based VMFA-513 bombed and strafed the enemy positions around the clock. Four months later, the F-4Bs of Colonel Anglin's MAG-11 and the A-4s of Colonel Brown's MAG-12 flew 59 sorties in support of U.S. and South Vietnamese troops at the Plei Me outpost, 20 miles southwest of Pleiku in northwestern II Corps. The attack against the outpost resulted in a major engagement, the Battle of Ia Drang Valley, in which the U.S. Army's 1st Cavalry Division (Airmobile) killed 1,238 enemy in 12 days.

In the 3d quarter of 1965, the two Marine air groups flew 4,614 sorties in support of Marine units and 1,656 sorties for the ARVN. Six hundred thirty-five of these sorties in support of the ARVN were close air support attacks supporting friendly forces engaged in close combat.[8] In the month of December, in spite of poor flying conditions, 1st MAW fixed-wing aircraft still flew 119 close air support missions for ARVN troops.[9]

Marine attack aircraft performed several other duties in addition to their primary task of close air support. Both the F-4Bs and A-4s flew direct air support missions. Similar in some respects to close air support, these strikes were not conducted in the immediate vicinity of friendly lines and did not require integration with the ground unit's fire support plan, although coordination did take place at an echelon of command above that of the maneuver unit. The aim of the direct air support strikes was to isolate the enemy from the battlefield and destroy his troops and support bases.*

The two MAGs also played a vital role in protecting the MAG-36 and -16 helicopters. For a typical helicopter landing zone preparation, Marine

---

*Strictly speaking, this definition of direct air support applies to deep support missions. The Marines used the term direct support, as defined in the text, to differentiate between interdiction missions and ground support missions. Even so, Colonel Gray remarked that the distinction between close air and direct support was at times vague since, "The powers to be always wanted missions logged as close air support where possible to weigh in the right direction when assessing Marine air support operations." Col Roy C. Gray, Jr., Comments on draft MS, 28Sep76 (Vietnam Comment File).

USMC Photo A185852

Major General Walt climbs into the back seat of a Marine F-4B Phantom II jet at Da Nang for a reconnaissance flight. The aircraft is piloted by Lieutenant Colonel Walter C. Stewart, Commanding Officer, VMFA-513.

jet aircraft, in coordination with other supporting arms, would cover the landing area and surrounding region with bombs, napalm, rockets, and cannon fire. As the transport helicopters approached the LZ, armed UH-1Es, acting as escorts, would take over suppression of light small arms fire. Meanwhile, Marine fixed-wing close air support aircraft would orbit overhead, prepared to attack any enemy offering heavy resistance.[10]

Besides landing zone preparation, the attack aircraft from Da Nang and Chu Lai were called upon to provide armed escort for helicopters. Lieutenant Colonel Norman G. Ewers, who commanded HMM-163 in 1965 and whose squadron developed a close working relationship with VMFA-531, remarked, "Some people commented that using F-4s to escort helos was like driving tacks with a gold plated sledge hammer. That may be. All I know is that it worked, and worked very well."[11]

While most of the combat strikes of the 1st Marine Aircraft Wing were flown within South Vietnamese air space, Marine pilots also crossed the DMZ. On 6 May, Captain Don K. Hanna led a flight of four F-

USMC Photo A185339

A ground crew member arms the bombs on a Marine A-4 Skyhawk at Chu Lai. The A-4s could carry up to 3,000 pounds of ordnance.

4Bs from VMFA-531 over North Vietnam to provide antiaircraft suppression fires for a pilot rescue mission. A USAF RF-101 reconnaissance aircraft was down. Arriving at the crash site just north of the DMZ, the Marine pilots joined Air Force F-105 pilots attacking NVA antiaircraft gun positions while the rescue was being completed. This flight was the first occasion of Marine aviators conducting a combat strike in North Vietnam. In the last half of 1965, Marine F-4Bs flew 87 combat air patrols over North Vietnam.

On 6 December, the 1st MAW again expanded its participation in the air war when Marine aircraft struck enemy infiltration and supply routes in Laos. These operations, coordinated by the 2d Air Division, were part of the STEEL TIGER program, started by the Air Force and Navy in the spring of 1965 to reduce the enemy flow of men and material through southern Laos. From 6-31 December, MAG-11 aircraft flew 140 sorties and MAG-12 planes flew 159 sorties over the Laotian panhandle.[12]

As Marine fixed-wing operations increased, a new problem appeared with the onset of the monsoon season. This was especially true at Chu Lai, where the SATS field had to undergo extensive renovation which reduced the runway there to 4,500 feet for periods of time. Normally, this was enough room for operations when using jet-assisted takeoff and mobile-arresting gear for takeoffs and landings, but the monsoon weather made landing and takeoff conditions at the base marginal. Low ceilings, high winds, and heavy rains from 25-27 November caused

all missions to be cancelled.[13] Fortunately, III MAF was able to use the TPQ-10 radar to guide the Phantoms and Skyhawks to their targets once the planes were airborne in spite of the bad weather. Although the number of missions flown increased in December, over 600 scheduled sorties were cancelled because of poor flying conditions.[14]

There were other frustrations for the Marine pilots beside the monsoon weather. During a one-week period in October, MAG-11 suspended all flights because salt water accidentally mixed with the group's fuel supply, but the largest problem for the Marine aviators was aviation ordnance. No missions were cancelled because of lack of munitions, but the pilots were not always able to use the type of ordnance best suited for a specific target. To preserve scarce munitions, 1st MAW policy stated:

> . . . only ordnance required to destroy the target would be expended, and all remaining ordnance would be returned unless doing so constituted a hazard, as is the case in landing into the arresting gear at Chu Lai with napalm tanks.[15]*

In 1965, there were three occasions of operational aircraft loss, resulting in the death of Marine aviators. Two crashes occurred on the same day, 26 October, when two F-4Bs returning from a combat mission crashed into the side of Monkey Mountain. One of the Phantoms had reported engine trouble before the crash. Both crews of the two aircraft were killed.[16] The third incident occurred on 29 December south of Chu Lai. An A-4 from VMA-211, piloted by 1st Lieutenant Thomas F. Eldridge, was escorting a flight of helicopters attempting to resupply a besieged South Vietnamese district headquarters. As the helicopters approached, the enemy opened fire with three heavy machine guns. The Marine lieutenant

---

* Colonel Gray wrote: "1st MAW policy did state that only ordnance required would be expended and the remainder of the load returned to base. Statistics to bear on this would be impossible to obtain, but from experience if on a mission there was anything to bomb 'at' the ordnance would be expended many times in the interest of practice. I don't think we really brought home nearly as much as we might have wanted people to think." Col Roy C. Gray, Comments on draft MS, dtd 28Sep76 (Vietnam Comment File). The Office of Air Force History in its comments observed: "During 1964-65, MACV rules severely curtailed a pilot's choice of alternative targets; established certain free-drop zones; and required [pilots] to jettison all ordnance in designated jettison areas before landing for safety reasons. . . . " Office of Air Force History, Fact Sheet: Expenditure of Ordnance, Jan 77 (Vietnam Comment File).

USMC Photo A701478
An aerial view of the Chu Lai SATS field showing the A-4s of MAG-12 parked between temporary revetments. The SATS runway was reduced to 4,500 feet for periods of time in November and December.

rolled in on the enemy machine gunners in spite of fast approaching darkness and poor weather. Eldridge succeeded in dropping his napalm, but his aircraft was hit and he was wounded in the leg. The wounded Marine nursed his A-4 toward Chu Lai, but it crashed 13 miles from the field. Eldridge was killed.[17]

A significant contribution of Marine fixed-wing air support during 1965 was the performance of Marine Composite Reconnaissance Squadron 1. This jet aircraft unit performed the missions of electronic and photo reconnaissance and electronic countermeasure operations. Flying the Douglas EF-10B, affectionately called "Willie the Whale," the pilots of the squadron provided electronic countermeasure (ECM) and electronic intelligence (ELINT) support under the code name FOGBOUND for the 2d Air Division's and Navy Task Force 77's (carrier task force) ROLLING THUNDER missions over North Vietnam.*

The primary purpose of these flights was to identify and jam enemy fire control radars. During 1965, the VMCJ-1 "Whales" flew 791 sorties in support of strikes over North Vietnam and Laos.[18] Photo reconnaissance missions were flown in Chance-Vought RF-8As, the photoplane version of the Crusader fighter.** In this role, the pilots of VCMJ-1 supported III MAF, as well as the Navy and Air Force, by supplying aerial photos which pinpointed targets in South Vietnam, Laos, and North Vietnam.***

*The EF-10B was a modified version of the Navy F3D Skynight, a two-engine jet night-fighter aircraft first built in 1956.

**The Crusader was a swept-wing, single-jet fighter, first built in 1958.

***Lieutenant Colonel Otis W. Corman, the squadron commander, later wrote: "During May and June the EF-10B were operated at 300 percent of normal utilization. Due to the limited total of EF-10B resources (both aircraft and spare parts) General McCutcheon directed that the utilization rate be limited to 200 percent or 60 hours per month per plane. To achieve this, a 1st MAW liaison officer was assigned to MACV's electronic warfare coordinating authority and VMCJ-1 was tasked to support Air Force and Navy operations in only high threat areas; i.e. strikes inside the SA-2 missile envelope complex." Col Otis W. Corman, Comments on draft MS, dtd [Nov 75] (Vietnam Comment File).

USMC Photo A421519

An F8E Crusader is shown at the Da Nang Airbase with all the armament it is capable of carrying. In 1965, one Crusader squadron, VMF(AW)-312, operated from Da Nang, while VMF(AW)-212 was stationed on the attack carrier USS Oriskany (CVA 34).

Another fixed-wing component of the 1st Marine Aircraft Wing which performed yeoman service was the Marine Aerial Refueler Transport Squadron 152 (VMGR-152). This squadron, reinforced with aircraft from VMGR-353, was based at the Marine Air Station, Futema, Okinawa, but maintained a detachment, usually four aircraft, at Da Nang. The Lockheed KC-130 Hercules aircraft of the squadron orbited over the South China Sea to provide a ready fuel supply to American aircraft.* The presence of these flying fuel tanks was especially valuable during the monsoon season when pilots had to take into consideration that their home field might be closed because of weather. The KC-130s also were used extensively for resupply within South Vietnam and for shuttling personnel and material between South Vietnam, Japan, and Okinawa. Additionally,

the aircraft furnished an important service to the Marine ground units by providing illumination in numerous flare drop missions.

During 1965, one Marine fixed-wing squadron, VMF(AW)-212, participated in the Navy's air war over both North and South Vietnam. VMF(AW)-212, as one of the five squadrons of Attack Carrier Wing 16 (CVW-16), flew combat air strikes for seven months from the attack carrier USS *Oriskany* (CVA 34). On 27 January 1965, Lieutenant Colonel Charles H. Ludden led his squadron from the Marine Corps Air Station, Kaneohe Bay, Hawaii to San Diego, California where it embarked on board the *Oriskany*. The squadron, with 12 Ling-Temco-Vought F-8E Crusader jet fighters, boarded the carrier with a complement of 22 officers, of whom 16 were pilots, and 173 enlisted men.

After a two-month training period, *Oriskany* sailed from San Diego on 5 April, arriving off the Vietnamese coast on 8 May. That same day, the pilots of VMF(AW)-212 exchanged their peacetime orange flight suits for green combat clothing and then flew their first combat missions. Their first strikes over South Vietnam ranged from the Mekong Delta to northern II CTZ. Controlled by U. S. Air Force tactical air controllers (airborne), the "Lancers," as 212 was known, struck enemy troops and supply areas with 5-inch Zuni rockets and 20mm

*Colonel John D. Noble, who commanded MAG-12 until 19 September, remarked in his comments that the KC-130s "provided in-flight fueling to MAG-12 A-4s during most, if not all, of June 1965 while the strip was under construction. In order to carry the optimum ordnance loads from the short operating length of the strip and not disrupt the Seabees' efforts down field at every launch, all A-4 takeoffs were made with light fuel loads. One or more KC-130s would orbit over the field to top off the A-4s with fuel to give them the range and/or endurance needed for their missions." Col John D. Noble, Comments on draft MS, dtd 1Nov76 (Vietnam Comment File).

cannon fire; the F-8s were not equipped to carry bombs.

Two days later, *Oriskany* sailed northward to a position 70 miles off Da Nang known as YANKEE STATION. That day, the 212 pilots flew their first suppression escort for U.S. Navy A-4s of CVW-16 attacking targets south of Hanoi. By 11 June, the F-8Es had been modified. After that date VMF(AW)-212 was capable of carrying MK82 (570 pound), MK83 (983 pound), MK84 (1,970 pound), and MK79 (napalm) bombs. Interestingly, some of the pilots had never trained for dropping bombs with the F-8s and consequently their first bomb drops were made in combat.

The *Oriskany* rotated between YANKEE and DIXIE STATION, established 16 May 100 miles southeast of Cam Ranh Bay, with brief visits to the Philippines for the next seven months. During that

USMC Photo A42282

A helicopter from HMM-361 lands troops from the 2d Battalion, 3d Marines under flare light in Operation MIDNIGHT. This was the first night helicopter assault for the Marine air/ground team in Vietnam.

time, Ludden's squadron was credited with flying 3,018 combat hours and 1,588 combat sorties; 1,058 hours and 595 missions were flown over South Vietnam. Crusaders of the unit were battle damaged on 26 separate occasions; on 5 November one F-8E was lost to enemy ground fire.

When the squadron struck the Hai Duong rail and highway bridge on 5 November 30 miles east of Hanoi, enemy antiaircraft fire hit Captain Harlan P. Chapman's plane. Forced to eject, Chapman parachuted safely but was captured immediately. Chapman was awarded the Distinguished Flying Cross for the mission and was promoted to lieutenant colonel while a prisoner-of-war. He was repatriated to the United States by the North Vietnamese on 12 February 1973. Captain Chapman commented that the CVW-16 commander, Commander James B. Stockdale, USN, had been shot down in September 1965 and that "Lieutenant Colonel Ludden as the senior squadron commander took command of CVW-16 for about two months, making him one of the few Marines to command a CVW."[19]

In November, *Oriskany* completed its WestPac deployment and sailed for the United States. Fifteen days later on 10 December, Ludden led his Crusaders back to MCAS, Kaneohe Bay, while the rest of the squadron unloaded at Pearl Harbor. VMF(AW)-212 transferred to the control of the 1st Marine Brigade from CVW-16.

Helicopter Operations

A Marine helicopter squadron had been operating in Vietnam since 1962. The Marine UH-34s furnished the South Vietnamese with mobility and logistical support. To the individual Marine infantryman in 1965, the helicopter was the vehicle which carried him into battle, provided him with rations, ammunition, and even close air support, and carried him out of battle, dead or alive.

During the July-December period, Marine aviators and ground commanders experimented with new helicopter tactics. One of the more innovative of these experiments occurred on the night of 12 August 1965. Lieutenant Colonel Lloyd F. Childers' HMM-361 and Lieutenant Colonel Clement's 2d Battalion, 3d Marines tried their experiment in an area 10 miles northwest of Da Nang known as Elephant Valley, a narrow river plain between some of the steepest mountains in I CTZ.

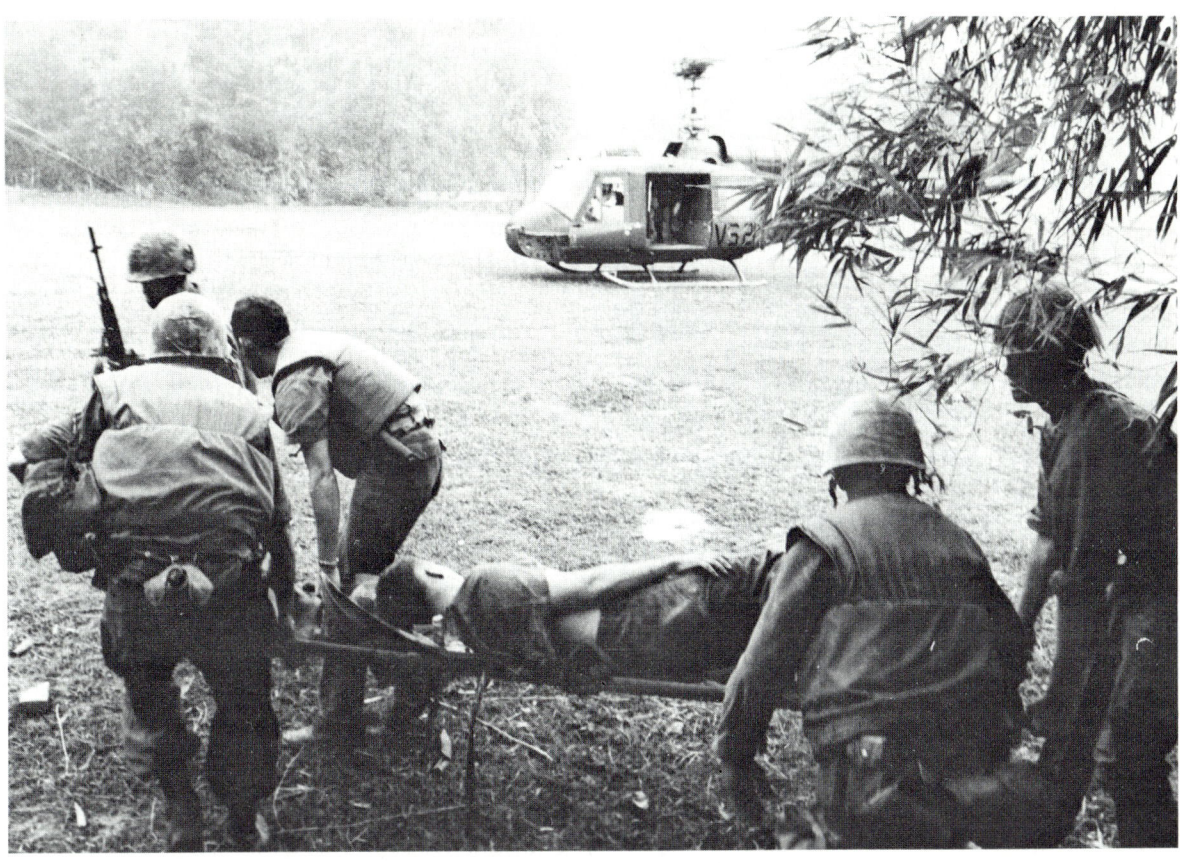

Marines carry a wounded Marine to an evacuation helicopter. A Navy Corpsman (at left without helmet) helps to lift the stretcher.

One week before the operation, appropriately labeled Operation MIDNIGHT, Major Marc A. Moore, Clement's S-3, approached Childers about the feasibility of conducting a night heliborne operation in the valley. The battalion had received information that approximately 50 VC entered the villages in the valley after dark and left the next morning before dawn. The squadron commander studied the problem and decided it was possible for his helicopters to carry out the mission, under favorable weather and moonlight conditions.

The battalion and squadron staffs then worked out the details. They planned for artillery preparation of the landing zone, after which the helicopters would land the troops under the light of flares dropped by Air Force C-123 Providers. A Navy gunfire ship, lying offshore, was to fire star shells to provide wind drift data for the Air Force flare drop. By 12 August, preparations were complete and Lieutenant Colonel

Childers told his pilots at the preflight briefing: "You have the dubious distinction of being the first men to fly a nightime combat helicopter strike."[20]*

To ensure surprise, the nights before the actual landing Marine artillery and the Navy gunfire ship fired missions in the same general area and at the same hour as the proposed landing. The night of 12 August, the artillery slightly increased the intensity of its fire for the landing zone preparation and the

---

* This was an overstatement. HMM-362, under Lieutenant Colonel Archie J. Clapp, had helilifted ARVN forces in a night assault on the Plain of Reeds in the Mekong Delta in 1962. See Whitlow, *U. S. Marines in Vietnam, 1954-64*, Chapter 5. MajGen William R. Quinn observed that HMR-161 "made the first tactical airlift at night in Korea." MajGen William R. Quinn, Comments on draft MS, dtd 30Sep76 (Vietnam Comment File). Night helicopter medical evacuation flights by VMO-6 were almost routine in the last year of the Korean War, one reason the squadron was awarded a Presidential Unit Citation.

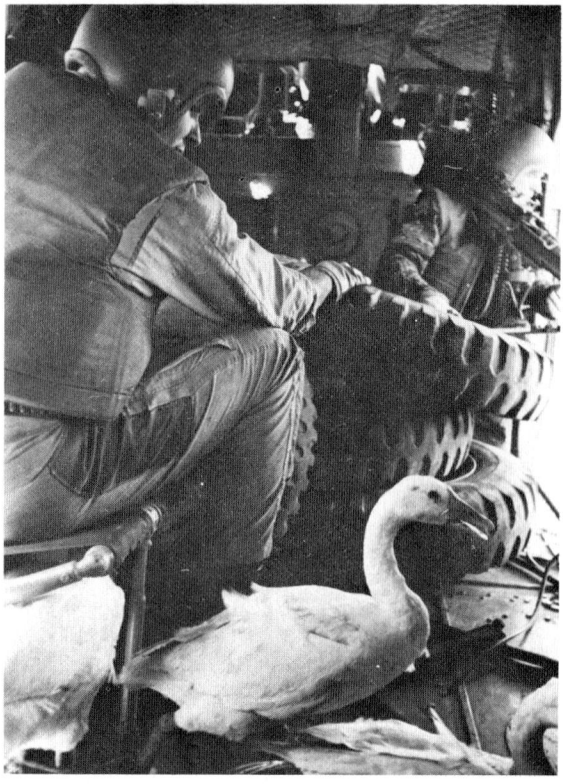

USMC Photo A422610

Marine helicopters carry diverse cargoes while resupplying ARVN outposts. Livestock such as geese, ducks, and chickens were often "passengers."

Navy ship fired star shells. Escorted by four UH-1E gunships from VMO-2, Lieutenant Colonel Childers led his flight of 20 UH-34Ds, 14 from his squadron and 6 from HMM-261, to the objective area. As the helicopters flew through a pass in a ridgeline west of the landing zone, the artillery shifted its fires to the north and east and flare planes began dropping their loads. The UH-34s landed safely and disembarked Company H and a platoon from Company F without incident. Four waves of helicopters landed within 28 minutes and the Marine infantry moved to encircle the Viet Cong. Most of the enemy managed to elude the Marines; Clement's troops killed two VC and detained 30 suspects. Despite the small returns in terms of enemy casualties, the Marines did prove the practicality of night helicopter assaults. Colonel Leslie E. Brown, the operations officer of the wing, concluded: "We've still got to study night lifts, but

now we have a springboard to concentrate on the full potential of night assaults."[21]*

In October, helicopters from Colonel Johnson's MAG-36 and ground troops from Lieutenant Colonel Bodley's 3d Battalion, 7th Marines furnished another example of tactical experimentation during Operation HERCULES. Twenty-six UH-34Ds carried 697 troops of the battalion into the action after Marine fixed-wing aircraft had prepared the landing zones. Four of the troop-laden helicopters did not land, they orbited the objective for two hours, providing a mobile ready reserve force for instant support, if and when necessary.[22]**

During the same period, on 24 October, Lieutenant Colonel Lloyd J. Childers' HMM-361 brought out two Marine reconnaissance companies from the rugged country west of Da Nang, known as

---

*Major Marc A. Moore, the operations officer of the 2d Battalion, remarked that, "The VC were surprised, but many had time to go underground before a detailed search could be made at daylight. Results would have been more complete if the assault units had been permitted to maintain their cordon and conduct a detailed 48-hour search; the only method to obtain extensive results in a VC controlled village. Instead the assault force was ordered to sweep the valley to the west soon after daylight, enabling those VC driven underground to slip into the mountains to the north and south." According to Moore, the detainees reported that "villagers and VC alike were not aware of the landing" until after the helicopters began lifting off after the troops had disembarked. BGen Marc A. Moore, Comments on draft MS, n.d. [Nov] 76 (Vietnam Comment File).

** This is the first time these tactics had been employed by the Marine air-ground team, but Marine helicopters carried ARVN EAGLE and TIGER FLIGHTS as early as 1962. EAGLE FLIGHTS of Marine UH-34Ds loaded with ARVN soldiers orbited the ground operational area as a ready reaction force, should contact be made with the enemy. TIGER FLIGHTS differed in that the ARVN reaction force was not airborne, but was positioned at a designated pickup zone, ready for immediate airlift, should the tactical situations so dictate. At Da Nang in January 1966, the 9th Marines and MAG-16 devised a tactical arrangement termed SPARROW HAWK for which each battalion of the regiment maintained a squad-sized force at a special landing zone as a reaction force. When the decision to commit this force was made, UH-34Ds and UH-1E gunships on strip alert at Marble Mountain Air Facility flew to the LZ, picked up the squad, and transported it to the area of contact. Employment of SPARROW HAWK differed from the TIGER FLIGHTS as the Marines used the squads as separate maneuver elements and not as reinforcements. Whitlow, *U.S. Marines in Vietnam*, Chapter 5, and CO, 9th Marines ltr to CMC, dtd 4Jul66, Subj: Updating of "A Brief History of the 9th Marines."

"Happy Valley" in what Colonel O'Connor, the MAG-16 commander called, "one of the most death-defying feats I've ever seen in aviation." According to O'Connor, who was Childers' co-pilot for the mission, the 3d Reconnaissance Battalion had completed its operation and wanted to be picked up on a ridge, south of Happy Valley:

> The ridge was pretty well covered with timber and foliage. The ground troops had picked out a landing zone that was relatively unobstructed. However the zone had a 45 degree slope and could handle only one aircraft at a time. We approached in flights of three, and two aircraft went in to pick up the troops. Approaching the zone, pilots went in under overhanging trees and hovered on the slope while troops clambored aboard. We took a maximum of five or six each trip, depending on the weight of the troops and the age of the helicopter engine. The whole force of two companies was extracted one helicopter load at a time, as each aircraft penetrated to the slope, and then sneaked out to the valley through overhanging foliage.[23]*

Marine helicopter support was not limited to Marine operations. Both MAGs ferried South Vietnamese troops into battle and resupplied both ARVN and US Special Forces outposts in the I Corps Tactical Zone. MAG-16's record of air operations for September 1965 provides a sample of the support furnished to both Marines and allied forces: its helicopters flew 15,245 sorties, carried 23,991 passengers, hauled 2,504,663 pounds of cargo, and evacuated 410 wounded troops.[24]

At Qui Nhon, the Marine helicopter detachment, later replaced by a complete Marine helicopter squadron, flew in support of both South Vietnamese units and U.S. Army troops, as well as the 2d Battalion, 7th Marines. In one operation, GIBRALTAR, seven of the aircraft from the HMM-161 detachment helped helilift the 1st Brigade, 101st Airborne Division into a suspected enemy base area near An Khe on 19 September. First Lieutenant Gary W. Parker, a member of HMM-161, recalled that the first lift went without incident:

> And I remembered thinking to myself that this looked like another cake walk; however, on the second wave we started receiving automatic weapons fire which was extremely accurate and soon took its toll on all the helicopters, both Army and Marine Corps. In a very short time the air was full of chatter from the pilots reporting hits upon their aircraft and the locations of the enemy gun emplacements. . . . it became quite obvious

USMC Photo A186125

A Marine CH-37 heavy helicopter lifts a damaged UH-34 helicopter from a combat zone. Ground crewmen dismantled the damaged aircraft so it could be carried back to Da Nang.

that we had landed in the middle of a fairly large and well armed enemy force; more firepower was needed . . . .[25]

All seven of the Marine aircraft sustained battle damage. One aircraft was downed, but its crew was rescued by another helicopter. The downed craft was recovered the following day. The Marines counted 57 bullet holes in the seven UH-34s and Parker later wrote: "We all felt that we had been very lucky that day."[26]**

The intensity of helicopter operations naturally caused maintenance problems. By August the UH-34s had exceeded planned flying hours and had to be overhauled four to six months earlier than they would have been under normal operating conditions.

---

*See Chapter 11 for an account of the reconnaissance operation.

**During Operation GIBRALTAR, the 101st Brigade aborted the helilift after two companies of one battalion had been helilifted into the objective area. Another force of U. S. troops and ARVN rangers was helilifted into another landing zone 1,500 meters to the east and linked up with the two stranded companies the next day. The allies killed 226 VC and captured nine while sustaining losses of 13 dead and 44 wounded. *MACV Comd Hist, 1965*, p. 167.

A HAWK missile is seen lifting off during a firing exercise near Chu Lai. During the exercise, the LAAM bat-
talions fired at propeller-driven drones, jet drones, and targets towed by F-8 aircraft.

The arrival of MAG-36 in September helped to relieve the burden, but the helicopters in both groups still remained extremely active. The UH-34, in service since 1957, could carry no more than five to eight Marines in the heat, humidity, and high altitudes of much of I Corps. Moreover, the 34s had a cargo capacity of only 1,500 to 2,000 pounds, but these medium helicopters succeeded in getting the job done. A III MAF press release furnished a vivid description of the accomplishments of the UH-34:

> These Marine copters have been overloaded and flown. They've been punctured more than arms in a sickbay, and flown. They've coughed, sputtered, and smoked, and still they've flown. They've landed in water, on mountainsides, through elephant grass, in ditches, on beaches, and in hedgerows . . . and have taken off again after debarking assault troops or picking up wounded .[27]

Air Defense Responsibilities

Even though it was not likely that the North Vietnamese would launch an airstrike against South Vietnam, the possibility could not be ignored.* An enemy air attack could have caused tremendous damage, especially at the large facilities at Da Nang and Chu Lai. To meet the threat of any enemy air

---

*The Office of Air Force History observed that as of March 1965, the North Vietnamese Air Force had 35 MIG-15s and 17s. By May, the North Vietnamese had a total of 63 MIG-15s and -17s. All of these aircraft were based at Phu Yen airfield near Hanoi. In May, the first three IL-28 Beagle bombers arrived at Phu Yen and by early June totaled eight. These totals remained the same for the rest of 1965. Office of Air Force History, Fact Sheet: North Vietnamese Air Force in 1965, dtd Jan 77 (Vietnam Comment File).

action, four Marine F-4Bs were on alert around the clock, and two Marine light antiaircraft missile battalions, the 1st and 2d, armed with HAWK surface-to-air missiles, were deployed at Da Nang and Chu Lai respectively.

The Commander in Chief, Pacific Air Force (CinCPacAF) was responsible for all air defense in mainland Southeast Asia. He exercised this responsibility through General Moore, Commanding General, 2d Air Division, who was the Mainland Southeast Asia Air Defense Regional Commander. General Walt, the Naval Component Commander Vietnam, acknowledged this Air Force responsibility in the joint memorandum of agreement signed by his deputy, General McCutcheon, and Moore in August.

The air threat from the north never materialized and the LAAM battalions were not called upon to fire their missiles in anger, yet, Colonel George G. Long remembered:

> My main concern as executive officer and [then] commanding officer of the 1st LAAM Battalion . . . was that we would not be granted firing permission early enough on an initial raid to provide the air defense needed. Often there were occasions . . . when unidentified radar tracks were observed at various altitudes inbound to the Da Nang complex from North Vietnamese airspace and after repeated failures at identification they would arrive at the airfield. . . . In every case the CRC [the Air Force Control and Reporting Center] on Monkey Mountain suspected they were friendly and "hold fire" conditions were maintained up to their actual arrival over the field. The LAAM Battalion early warning radars would, as a matter of normal course, acquire these tracks and perform lock-on with the illumination radars. Many of these flights were tracked with the illuminators out to 110 kilometers and at altitudes below 5,000 feet.[28]

During 1965, the two LAAM battalions conducted numerous training exercises and, during the first week of December, both battalions held their first firing exercise on an island north of the Ky Ha Peninsula. The exercise was extremely realistic using a combination of targets: propeller-driven drones, jet drones, and targets towed by F-8 aircraft. Colonel Edward F. Penico, who then commanded the 2d LAAM Battalion, recalled:

> This shoot was the only time that a target towed by piloted aircraft was fired at by a HAWK battery. The computer simulations said it could not be done. The skipper of the target squadron was confident enough that he flew the plane himself . . . .[29]

Although the firing batteries performed well, 11 of the first 18 missiles failed to function for one reason or another. They were old HAWKS, and doubts lingered about the reliability of the missile stocks.[30]*

---

*Colonel Long remarked that the problems with the "shoot . . . are attributable to the lot of the missiles used and should not be considered as an air deficiency." Col George G. Long, Comments on draft MS, dtd 8Nov76 (Vietnam Comment File).

CHAPTER 11

Fire Support and Reconnaissance

Artillery Support

Marine artillery units arrived in Vietnam piecemeal. By mid-July, Colonel William P. Pala had established the 12th Marines headquarters, the artillery regiment of the 3d Marine Division, at Da Nang.* His 1st and 2d Battalions were at Da Nang, but under the operational control of the infantry regiments they supported, the 3d and 9th Marines, respectively. The 2d Battalion, 12th Marines had two 105mm batteries at Da Nang, D and E, while its third battery, F, remained on Okinawa. Two of the 1st Battalion's 105mm batteries, A and B, were at Da Nang and its Battery C was attached to the 3d Battalion, 12th Marines at Chu Lai.

At Phu Bai, the headquarters of the 4th Battalion, 12th Marines, which also arrived in July, took control of the artillery units there. These were one of its 155mm howitzer batteries, Battery M; a 105mm battery, Battery I, 3d Battalion, 12th Marines; and the mortar battery from the 2d Battalion, 12th

Marines. On 16 September, Battery M received six of the newer M-109 155mm self-propelled howitzers and its older M-114A towed pieces were then distributed throughout the artillery battalion. Headquarters Battery and Batteries I and M each manned two of the towed 155s. Lieutenant Colonel Sumner A. Vale later remarked:

> . . . seldom if ever has an infantry battalion commander had so much artillery support under his control as did Taylor, I, and then Hanifin . . . . We had the 105 battery within the BLT organization, [the equivalent of] *two* batteries of 155 howitzers, one towed and one self-propelled, and a battery of howtars . . . . These 24 artillery pieces compensated, in part, that 3/4 had only 3 rifle companies, one being stationed in the Da Nang area.[1]

The reinforced 3d Battalion, 12th Marines, under the operational control of the 4th Marines, provided the artillery support for the Chu Lai TAOR. It included three 105mm batteries, C, G, and H, its 107mm mortar battery, the 1st Platoon, 1st 8-inch Howitzer Battery (SP), and Battery K from the 4th Battalion, 12th Marines equipped with 155mm howitzers.

The 12th Marines headquarters assumed direct control of the two general support batteries at Da Nang. These units were Battery L of 155mm howitzers from the 4th Battalion, 12th Marines and two platoons of the Force Troops 1st 8-inch Howitzer Battery (SP).

As the buildup continued, General Walt made further changes in his artillery dispositions. Battery F, 2d Battalion, 12th Marines, arriving from Okinawa, joined its parent battalion at Da Nang. In August, the 3d Battalion, 11th Marines and the Force Troops 3d 155mm Gun Battery (SP) arrived, reinforcing the artillery at Chu Lai. General Karch, the assistant division commander and Chu Lai coordinator, placed all of the Chu Lai artillery in a battalion group commanded by Lieutenant Colonel

---

*A Marine division had a variety of available artillery support. Its artillery regiment consisted of three direct support and one general support battalions. The three direct support battalions, the 1st, 2d, and 3d, contained three batteries, each with six M101A1 105mm towed howitzers (range 11,300 meters), and one battery of six 107mm howtars (range 5,600 meters), a 4.2-inch mortar tube mounted on the frame of the old 75mm pack howitzer. The 4th Battalion, the general support battalion, had three batteries, each equipped with six 155mm howitzers (range 14,600 meters). In 1965, M-109 self-propelled 155mm howitzers were being phased in to replace the older M114A towed howitzers. The 4th Battalion, 12th Marines deployed to Vietnam with two batteries equipped with self-propelled howitzers and one towed battery. In Vietnam, the Marines found they had a use for both weapons. The heavy, tracked M109SP was largely road bound, while the lighter towed howitzer could be moved either by truck or by helicopter.

Leslie L. Page, the commander of the 3d Battalion, 12th Marines and senior artillery officer at the base. The 3d Battalion, 11th Marines provided direct support for the 7th Marines with two 105mm batteries, G and I, and 155mm howitzer Battery M, 4th Battalion, 11th Marines. Lieutenant Colonel Page attached the 3d 155mm Gun Battery to his 3d Battalion, which provided direct support for the 4th Marines and general support for the entire TAOR. At Da Nang, General Walt returned operational control of the 1st and 2d Battalions to the 12th Marines on 1 September. The command structure of the artillery units remained unchanged through the end of the year, but batteries continued to be attached and detached.[2]

Coordination of artillery fire, particularly in the densely populated Da Nang TAOR, was a constant source of concern to the artillery commanders and their staffs. Lieutenant Colonel Jack K. Knocke, whose 2d Battalion, 12th Marines supported the 9th Marines, reported in July that ''clearance to fire became a critical factor in the timely delivery of fires.'' Artillerymen had to obtain clearances to fire from the Marine fire support coordination centers* (FSCC) at battalion, regimental, and division level and the South Vietnamese district headquarters as well.[3]

The reduced responsiveness of Marine artillery was a prime topic of discussion in September. The 3d Marine division FSCC, the responsibility of Colonel James M. Callender's 12th Marines,** reported that working relations with the South Vietnamese southern sector were extremely cumbersome. The Marines remarked that slow processing of fire clearance requests by the South Vietnamese resulted in excessive loss of time, except in the case of emergency requests. The ARVN had no centralized coordination center and only one or two senior officers possessed the authority to grant clearance for the Americans to shoot. To improve the situation,

USMC Photo A184062

Marines from the 2d Battalion, 12th Marines clean their 105mm howitzer in newly established positions at the Da Nang Airbase in March. The Marines have emplaced the camouflaged netting under standing operating procedures, not because of a North Vietnamese air threat.

General Walt ordered his staff to establish more positive fire support liaison with the ARVN.[4]

During the next few months, cooperation between the 3d Division FSCC and the South Vietnamese military authorities in southern Quang Nam Province gradually improved. In October, the South Vietnamese granted the Marines additional free fire zones in both the northern and southern portions of the Da Nang TAOR.*** Although South Vietnamese clearance still remained slow in the southern sector, the American advisors at Hoi An, in cooperation with the 3d Marine Division FSCC, exerted pressure to improve the situation. By November the division fire support center reported that communications with South Vietnamese officials had improved to the extent that in addition to supporting Marine units, division artillery frequently delivered fire in support of ARVN forces in the southern sector. The expansion of the 9th Marines TAOR in November caused a few problems. Some PF and ARVN units were operating in a portion of the new sector, but these difficulties were easily resolved.[5]

---

*A FSCC is a single location in which are centralized communication facilities and personnel to effect the coordination of all types of fire support.

**Colonel Callender became 12th Marines commander on 30 July. Shortly after his arrival, Colonel Pala was sent to Qui Nhon as the senior Marine officer in the area to coordinate activities with the U.S. Army command there. Lieutenant Colonel Walter E. Stuenkel was acting commander of the regiment from 15-30 July. See Col William P. Pala, Comments on draft MS, dtd 25Oct76 (Vietnam Comment File).

***In free fire zones, all targets were considered to be hostile, so Marine batteries did not have to obtain South Vietnamese clearance before firing.

Coordination with the South Vietnamese was not the only concern of the Marine artillerymen. They also had to worry about low-flying aircraft due to the proximity of major airbases. The intensity of both air operations and artillery fire in the air space above the TAOR presented problems which demanded solution.

The doctrine limiting helicopters to designated routes proved to be too restrictive for both artillery supporting fires and helicopter operations because of the ever increasing volume of helicopter traffic in the TAORs. To alleviate the situation, the wing and the 12th Marines worked out a more flexible policy. The new system provided the pilots with the location of which areas were "hot" and which were "safe." It enabled the aviators to plan their flights accordingly. If the pilot had to fly into a "hot" area, he would receive additional information which enabled him to avoid impact areas and firing positions. The plan operated as follows:

> The pilot reports in to the Direct Air Support Center upon becoming airborne, the DASC gives the pilot the firing and gun positions which are "hot," with times of firing, if applicable. The pilot can then proceed throughout the remaining (safe) portions of the TAOR without restrictions. If the pilot is required to proceed through a "hot" area, the DASC will provide him with fixes to allow the helicopter to proceed within "hot" areas with maximum safety.[6]

This method of coordinating air and artillery fire allowed the Marines to employ artillery more extensively. Artillery missions fired in September show the degree of Marine artillerymen's support of III MAF infantry operations:

Observed combat missions 650
Unobserved call fires 439

Marine gunners from the 12th Marines fire off a round from a 4.2-inch mortar. The Marine Corps in 1965 was replacing its howtars (a mortar tube mounted on a 75mm howitzer frame) with the 4.2-inch mortars in the artillery mortar batteries.

Harassment and interdiction missions 6,448
Registrations 125
Destruction missions 4
The artillery expended over 35,800 rounds of ammunition to complete these missions.[7]

By December, the 12th Marines was firing over 45,000 rounds a month; 6,000 were fired in support of Task Force DELTA in Operation HARVEST MOON.[8] The 12th Marines achieved this fire support increase in spite of an ammunition shortage. During December, the regiment found it necessary to restrict 155mm howitzer firing to targets of opportunity.[9] No infantry unit was refused support because of the lack of ammunition, but the artillerymen were not always able to use the caliber, type of shell, or fuse best suited for a specific target. These restrictions were temporary; the supply situation would improve during the next few months.

Naval Gunfire

Complementing Marine shore-based artillery, naval gunfire support provided another important weapon to General Walt's forces. The Marines expressed their appreciation of naval gunfire in the following terms:

> The current deployment of Marine Corps forces is based upon the sea, with the overwhelming majority within range of naval gunfire support. Naval gunfire is one of the means whereby the material superiority of the United States can be brought to bear against Communist manpower.[10]

The first agreement to employ U.S. naval gunfire against targets in South Vietnam was made in April 1965. On the 17th, the South Vietnamese informed Ambassador Taylor that they agreed in principle with the United States that naval gunfire should be used to support anti-sea infiltration efforts and ground operations of both South Vietnamese and American forces. At that time, Admiral Sharp ordered ComUSMACV and CinCPacFlt to submit plans for the employment of this supporting arm in Vietnam.[11]

In May, representatives from MACV, CinCPacFlt, Seventh Fleet, FMFPac, and III MAF met in Saigon to develop procedures for the conduct of naval gunfire. During the meetings, held on 3-5 May, the conferees ironed out differences of opinion and forwarded a concept of operations to Admiral Sharp for his approval. CinCPac approved the procedures and ordered them to be implemented. On 16 May, the USS *Henry W. Tucker* (DD 875) fired

USMC Photo A185706

Colonel James M. Callender, Commanding Officer, 12th Marines (left), Major General Walt, Commanding General, III MAF (center), and Major General William J. Van Ryzin, Assistant Chief of Staff, G-4, Headquarters Marine Corps (right), pose with the 99,999th and 100,000th artillery rounds to be fired by the 12th Marines in Vietnam. After the picture was taken the two general officers pulled the lanyard on the 105mm howitzers that fired these rounds.

the first U.S. naval gunfire missions at targets in II Corps.[12]

Under the terms of the agreement reached at the May conference, Rear Admiral Raymond F. Dubois, Commander of Navy Task Group 70.8, the Seventh Fleet cruiser and destroyer group, furnished the gunfire ships, but retained operational control of them. Rear Admiral Norvell G. Ward, who headed the Naval Advisory Group, MACV, was designated Commander Coastal Surveillance Force (CTF 115) and, in this capacity, assigned gunfire missions and provided coordination with land forces.[13]

Until the autumn of 1965, all naval gunfire missions had to be adjusted by either ground or air observers, and could be undertaken only on order of CTF 115, in cooperation with South Vietnamese officials. In November, General Westmoreland amended this policy to allow unobserved fire against unpopulated target areas which had been declared hostile by the South Vietnamese. On 22 December Admiral Sharp lifted the restrictions even further when he authorized the commanding officers of naval gunfire ships to initiate unobserved fires in emergency situations when friendly forces were

A Marine-Navy ANGLICO team plots firing targets for the USS Canberra (CAG 2) lying offshore. The UHF radio and antenna that can be seen in the middle of the picture permits the team to talk with both aircraft overhead and ships offshore.

under fire and "when gunfire support could be effected with positive assurance that the friendly forces and/or non-combatants would not be harmed."[14]

Control of naval gunfire did not pose a problem for III MAF. Each of General Walt's direct support artillery battalions had naval gunfire liaison and naval gunfire spotter teams within its organization to be attached to infantry units as required. In addition, the Marine tactical air observers and reconnaissance personnel had been schooled in the methods for control of naval gunfire support.

To provide control and direction of naval gun support for other American and allied units, a detachment of the 1st Air and Naval Gunfire Liaison Company (ANGLICO), a FMFPac Force Troops unit was ordered to Vietnam.* Led by Lieutenant Colonel George H. Albers, the detachment arrived

---

*The Air and Naval Gunfire Liaison Company is a Marine unit specifically designed to support U. S. Army or allied units. It provides the control and liaison agencies associated with the ground elements of a landing force to control and employ naval gunfire and Navy and Marine close air support in the amphibious assault, or other operations when such support is required. In addition to Marines, ten Navy line officers and four enlisted men are assigned to the company.

in Saigon on 21 May. Officially designated Subunit 1, 1st ANGLICO, the unit consisted of 11 officers and 103 enlisted men organized into two shore fire spotting teams and four shore fire control parties. The subunit provided a gunfire liaison team for each corps tactical operations center (TOC). These teams provided the personnel and communications necessary to permit the U.S. senior advisor in each corps area to control naval gunfire through the South Vietnamese TOCs.[15]

In I Corps, the U.S. Air Force was reluctant to allow the use of naval gunfire near Da Nang Airbase for fear of interfering with U. S. air operations. On 8 June, the U.S. Air Force base commander at Da Nang agreed to permit Navy ships to fire at targets beyond a 10-mile radius from the base. The first naval gunfire mission in support of the Marines was not fired until July because of the limited availability of Navy gunfire ships.[16]

On 9 July, General Krulak recommended to General Walt that the Marines make every effort to increase their use of naval gunfire support. On the 18th the III MAF commander ordered all of his subordinate units to take full advantage of naval gunfire ships. In July, four ships, two cruisers and two destroyers, fired 934 rounds in support of Marine

155mm howitzers of the 11th Marines in position to support infantry from forward firing positions during Operation HARVEST MOON. Ammunition and supplies have been brought in by truck from Chu Lai and Da Nang.

operations. During August, navy gunships fired 5,096 rounds for the Marines, including 1,061 rounds in support of Operation STARLITE during which naval gunfire played a major supporting role. The number of missions declined during the remainder of the year; only 2,873 rounds were fired during this period. Nevertheless, two Navy ships remained on station, assigned to I Corps, one that could be deployed anywhere off the coast and the other in Da Nang harbor for harbor defense, but available in a naval gunfire support role during daylight.[17]

In 1965, 72 ships of the U. S. Seventh Fleet provided naval gunfire support for U.S. and allied forces. The Marine-Navy ANGLICO teams of Subunit 1 controlled the firing of nearly 70,000 rounds at 2,411 targets.* In at least one instance, during the

successful November defense of the Thach Tru outpost 20 miles south of Quang Ngai City by the 37th Ranger Battalion, naval gunfire from the U.S. destroyers *O'Brien* (DD 725) and *Bache* (DD 470) was the decisive factor. *O'Brien* fired 1,392 5-inch rounds in 26 hours. The destroyers' fire broke the back of the enemy attack. General Walt witnessed the naval bombardment:

> From a helicopter at about a half mile distance. The destroyer shells stopped the attacking force within fifty yards of the outpost. It was a total and effective surprise to the enemy forces. It nearly annihilated the assault forces of the *18th NVA Regt*.[18]

Other Ground Combat Support

In addition to air, artillery, and naval gunfire, Marine infantry units received vital combat support from the 3d Marine Division amphibian tractor companies and tank companies. The experience of the 3d Tank Battalion was typical of how these organizations functioned in Vietnam. The 3d Tank Battalion Headquarters, Lieutenant Colonel States Rights Jones, Jr., and Company B arrived at Da Nang on 8 July. The battalion's other two gun companies were already in Vietnam, attached to the infantry units. On 24 July, the battalion was assigned a general support mission, but retained operational control only of its Headquarters and Service Company. At Da Nang, Company A was in direct support of the 3d Marines, while Company B was in direct support of the 9th Marines. Company C was

---

*Major Richard E. Romine, who assumed command of Subunit 1 on 25 August 1965, remarked that most of these missions were controlled from the rear seat of L-19 observation aircraft provided by senior U. S. advisors to the corps areas. The subunit operated under MACV control and received administrative support from the Naval Advisory Group in Saigon. Romine commented that much of his time was spent coordinating ''at the four Corps headquarters and the spot team sites. This meant that I traveled frequently to Can Tho, Vung Tau, Bien Hoa, Pleiku, Quang Tri, Qui Nhon and Da Nang from my office in Saigon.'' LtCol Richard E. Romine, Comments on draft MS, dtd 25Oct76 (Vietnam Comment File). Romine had relieved Lieutenant George M. Wasco, USN, who had relieved Lieutenant Colonel Albers on 28 July as Officer-in-Charge, Sub-unit 1.

attached to the 4th Marines at Chu Lai, with one platoon attached to the 3d Battalion, 4th Marines at Phu Bai. In August, Company B, 1st Tank Battalion arrived at Chu Lai with the 7th Marines and remained in support of that regiment. Four months later Company A, 1st Tank Battalion landed with the 2d Battalion, 1st Marines at Phu Bai.

Lieutenant Colonel Milton L. Raphael, who relieved Lieutenant Colonel Jones on 31 August, explained the complicated command and control problems of the tank battalion:

> The battalion commander maintains administrative control of the reinforced battalion and exercises logistic control and/or supervision of all units regardless of location or support status. Tactical control of the gun companies is for the most part in the hands of the supported infantry commander.[19]

Raphael related that he, his staff, and company commanders attempted to influence the tactical employment of their tanks by keeping abreast of friendly and enemy situations in all enclaves and then advising the infantry unit commanders on the employment of tanks to enhance the accomplishment of their missions. The battalion commander exercised control, in that:

> The four gun companies committed outside of the battalion command post maintain daily contact with the

USMC Photo A185834

In a change of command ceremony on 31 August, Lieutenant Colonel Milton L. Raphael (left) accepts the colors of the 3d Tank Battalion from Lieutenant Colonel States R. Jones. Lieutenant Colonel Jones brought the battalion headquarters into Vietnam the previous month.

battalion. . . . The two companies in the Chu Lai enclave submit a consolidated weekly report of all phases of their operations . . . all company commanders come to the battalion command post to attend the monthly battalion command and staff meeting.[20]

By December, the III MAF tank force consisted of 65 M-48 tanks and 12 flame tanks deployed at the three Marine enclaves.* In addition to the tanks, there were 65 ONTOS** from both the 1st and 3d Anti-Tank Battalions and 157 amphibian tractors (LVTP-5)*** from the 1st and 3d Amphibian Tractor Battalions attached to Marine infantry units.

Marine Reconnaissance

All Marine units were exposed to severe doctrinal tests in 1965; for the "Recon" Marines the year was one of change and adjustment. The two committed reconnaissance units, the 3d Reconnaissance Battalion, an integral 3d Marine Division battalion, and the 1st Force Reconnaissance Company, a Force Troops unit, both experienced great difficulty in responding to demands imposed by the three growing TAORs at Da Nang, Chu Lai, and Hue/Phu Bai. The two ground reconnaissance units were different in many respects, which caused many re-evaluations, as well as revelations, during the opening months of Marine ground action in Vietnam.

Reconnaissance missions were clearly defined by tables of organization. A division reconnaissance battalion, in this case the 3d, was charged with the primary mission of conducting "reconnaissance in support of a Marine Division and its subordinate elements." A force level company, on the other

---

* The M-48 was armed with a 90mm gun and two machine guns. The flame tank was identical to the M-48, with the exception that the gun tube which housed the flame thrower was shorter and slightly larger in diameter than the 90mm gun tube.
** The ONTOS was a full-tracked, lightly armored, mobile carrier mounting six 106mm recoilless rifles, four .50 caliber spotting rifles, and one .30 caliber machine gun.
*** The Landing Vehicle, Tracked, Personnel (LVTP-5) was an armored amphibian assault, personnel, and cargo carrier. The LVTP-5 was armed with two .30 caliber machine guns. Modifications of the LVTP-5 used in Vietnam included the LVTR, which could be used to retrieve and repair other LVTs, and the LVTE which could be employed to breach minefields and clear obstacles during amphibious operations and river crossings. In addition, the 1st Amphibian Tractor Battalion at Da Nang included a Provisional Armored Amphibian Platoon of six LVTHs. This vehicle was armed with a turret-mounted 105mm howitzer and one .50 caliber and one .30 caliber machine gun.

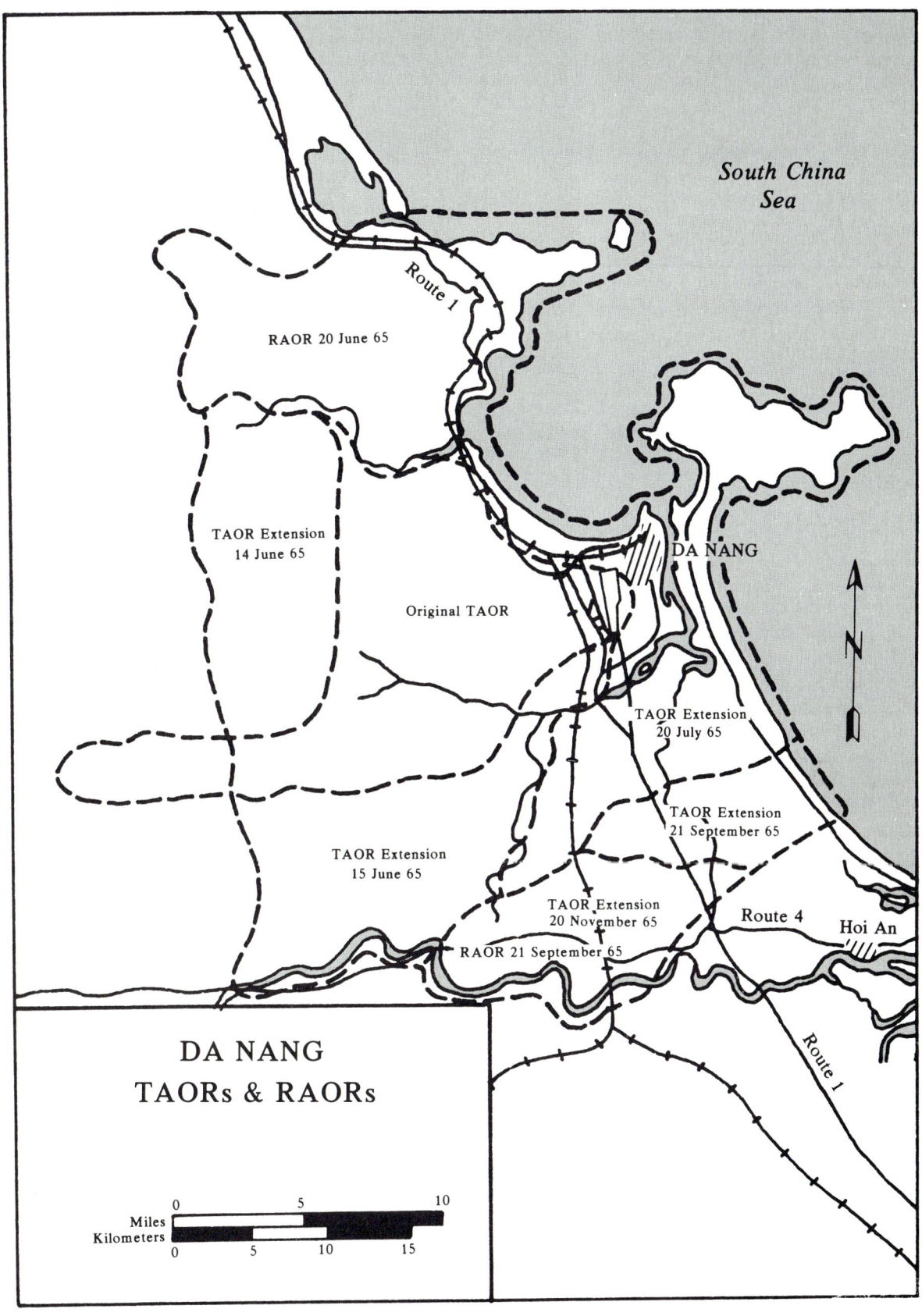

South China Sea

Route 1

RAOR 20 June 65

TAOR Extension
14 June 65

Original TAOR

DA NANG

TAOR Extension
20 July 65

TAOR Extension
21 September 65

TAOR Extension
15 June 65

TAOR Extension
20 November 65

Route 4

Hoi An

RAOR 21 September 65

Route 1

DA NANG
TAORs & RAORs

Miles
Kilometers

0   5   10

0   5   10   15

hand, was to "conduct pre-assault and distant post-assault reconnaissance in support of a landing force."[21]

1st Force Reconnaissance Company, The Early Days

Early beach reconnaissance efforts of Captain David Whittingham's Subunit 1, 1st Force Reconnaissance Company were textbook examples of proper employment of the company. On 23-27 February, Subunit 1, in conjunction with Underwater Demolition Team 12, operating from the USS *Cook* (APD 130), accomplished the reconnaissance of RED Beaches 1 and 2 at Da Nang. As a result, RED Beach 2 was selected as the landing beach for BLT 3/9, the first element of the 9th MEB to land in Vietnam.

The period 15-20 March was devoted to the reconnaissance of the beaches and terrain near Phu Bai. Subunit 1's reports resulted in 3d MEB's decision to send its first BLT to Phu Bai by way of the river approach to Hue and then overland to Phu Bai. The proposed landing beaches were backed by impassable lagoons which made exit almost impossible. For Subunit 1, this was its first real test. The VC were active in the area, but the mission was accomplished without loss and with excellent results.

Eight days later, Subunit 1 undertook the reconnaissance of the beach which was to be the site of the 3d MEB landing, Chu Lai. Its reconnaissance was finished on 30 March, again with excellent results.

On 20 April, 18 days before the Chu Lai landing, the force reconnaissance Marines started a survey of a beach south of the Tra Bong River 10 kilometers southeast of the proposed 3d MEB landing beach. On the 22d the reconnaissance party encountered light resistance. That was not the case the next day. Five Marines on the beach were caught in the crossfire of 25 VC. Corporal Lowell H. Merrell was wounded twice and two sailors in the beach party's LCVP also were hit; all three subsequently died. The 1st Force Reconnaissance Company had lost its first Marine to VC fire. In memory, the new force reconnaissance camp would be named Camp Merrell.

In May, Subunit 1 teams were sent to Special Forces camps to serve as patrol leaders for CIDG patrols. Other teams were assigned to reconnaissance-in-force patrols composed of U.S.- and Australian-led Nungs* which operated from Da Nang. A third mission was to provide quick response patrols to act as security for downed Marine helicopters. Initially, all force reconnaissance reports and debriefings were coordinated by the III MAF G-2, Lieutenant Colonel Robert E. Gruenler.

On 10 July, another platoon reinforced Subunit 1, and during July and August the two platoon subunit operated from the 4th Marines' Chu Lai base. Another force platoon was conducting beach surveys for the Commander, Task Force 76; still another platoon was assigned to the SLF; while the rest of the company was still at Camp Pendleton.

On 11 August, Major Malcolm C. Gaffen, the company commander, arrived and relieved Captain Whittingham as subunit commander. During Operation STARLITE, in August, Subunit 1 was attached to the 2d Battalion, 4th Marines, and the 3d Platoon, attached to the SLF, landed with BLT 3/7. At the conclusion of STARLITE, Subunit 1 returned to Da Nang.

The company headquarters and a fourth platoon arrived on 24 October while the subunit was participating in Operation RED SNAPPER with the 2d Battalion, 3d Marines north of Da Nang. At the conclusion of RED SNAPPER, the four platoons were reunited at their Camp Merrell base on China Beach south of Da Nang. The China Beach site had been selected because of its ready access to the ocean for amphibious training and because it provided enough room for parachute requalification.

The arrival at Camp Merrell of two-thirds of the company and the fact that the 5th and 6th Platoons had moved west to Okinawa suggested that soon the company would be operating as an independent force unit carrying out the "distant port-assault reconnaissance" specified in the table of organization.

During the summer and fall, company units had experienced a variety of operational difficulties. Communications problems were rampant. The force

---

*Nungs are ethnic Chinese, residents of Kwangsi Province, but an appreciable number inhabited northern North Vietnam. They are noted for their martial skills. As such, many served, willingly, under the French, and, for this reason, emigrated to South Vietnam in 1954. At one time after the formation of the Republic, the South Vietnamese Army included a division of Nungs, but it was broken up because of its potential threat to the incumbent government. Nungs, hired on as mercenaries, eventually came under the domain of U.S. Special Forces and other agencies involved in unconventional warfare.

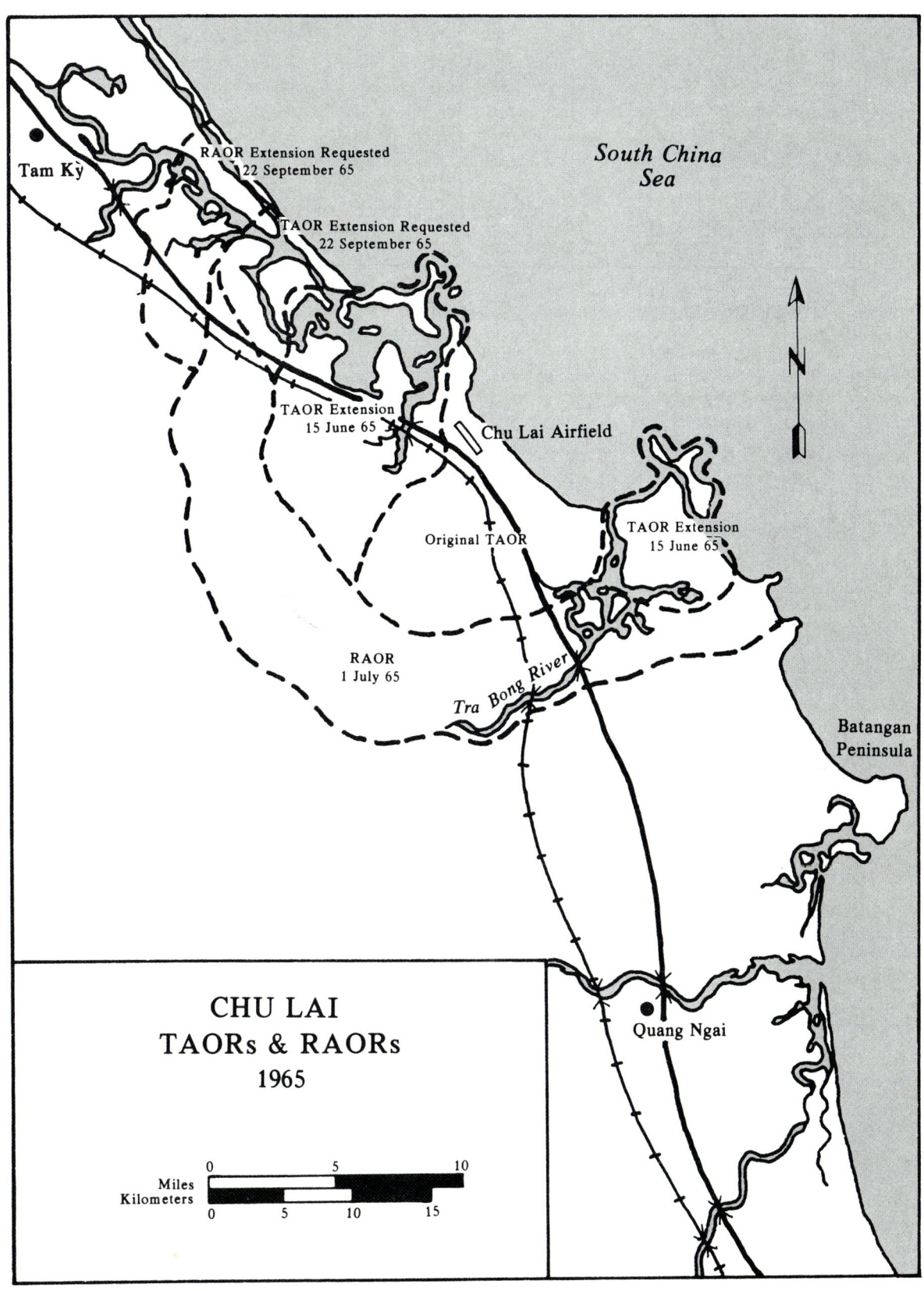

Tam Kỳ

RAOR Extension Requested
22 September 65

TAOR Extension Requested
22 September 65

South China
Sea

N

TAOR Extension
15 June 65

Chu Lai Airfield

Original TAOR

TAOR Extension
15 June 65

RAOR
1 July 65

Tra Bong River

Batangan
Peninsula

CHU LAI
TAORs & RAORs
1965

Miles
Kilometers

Quang Ngai

0   5   10
0   5   10   15

USMC Photo A184814

Marines from Company C, 3d Reconnaissance Battalion cross the Nong River near Phu Bai in a rubber raft. The reconnaissance company, attached to the 3d Battalion, 4th Marines, is supporting a battalion search and clear operation.

platoon with BLT 2/1 during DAGGER THRUST II in September had to be extracted because radio contact could not be established. Another unit was landed from a Coast Guard patrol boat on the relatively secure coast near Hai Van Pass north of Da Nang to test communications and control, and this operation, too, was a ''bust.'' The company's vehicles were ''down;'' supply problems were legion; and the partially developed MAF staff was not designed to deal with such difficulties.[22]

General Walt's solution was to transfer Subunit 1 to the operational control of the 3d Marine Division, which in turn transferred the unit to ''opcon'' 3d Reconnaissance Battalion. The transfer was effective 30 October; two days later Subunit 1, 1st Force Reconnaissance Company became 1st Force Reconnaissance Company (-) with a strength of nine officers and 103 enlisted men.[23]

In effect, the force company became a sixth, albeit smaller, company of the reinforced 3d Reconnaissance Battalion. Although the ''in country'' elements of ''1st Force'' were assembled at last, the assimilation by ''division recon'' was not an entirely satisfactory solution; some knotty problems arose.

3d Reconnaissance Battalion, Opening Moves

When the 9th MEB landed at Da Nang on 8 March, a platoon from Company A, 3d Reconnaissance Battalion attached to BLT 3/9, became the first division reconnaissance element to be ''resident'' in Vietnam. Other platoons arrived as attachments to BLTs, a platoon from Company B with BLT 3/4, a platoon from Company D with BLT 1/3, and a second Company D platoon with BLT 2/3. Platoon attachments lasted until 13 April, at which time the four ''in country'' reconnaissance platoons were regrouped as a new Company D, 3d Reconnaissance Battalion. Captain Patrick G. Collins' Company D operated as the brigade reconnaissance company of the 9th MEB until 7 May, when Lieutenant Colonel Don H. ''Doc'' Blanchard, his battalion staff, and the rest of the battalion landed at Chu Lai with the 3d MAB. ''Doc'' Blanchard did not stay at Chu Lai very long; on the 12th, he, his staff, battalion headquarters, and Companies A and C moved to Da Nang where they were reunited with Company D. Company B remained at Chu Lai. In the process, Companies A and B were brought up to strength by integrating the Company D platoons which had arrived with the battalion at Chu Lai; there were no longer two Company D elements. Company C was detached from Da Nang to the 3d Battalion, 4th Marines at Hue/Phu Bai on 26 May.

On 13 September, Company C moved again, returning to Da Nang, leaving its 3d Platoon at Hue/Phu Bai still attached to the 3d Battalion, 4th Marines. Battalion integrity was improved somewhat on 19 September by a directive from General Walt which stated that the reconnaissance battalion should be used in general support of the 3d Marine Division.[24] Although this measure simplified command and control, the division was still operating from three separate enclaves, and three separate reconnaissance elements were required. On the 19th, reinforcement of division reconnaissance was accomplished by attaching Company C, 1st Reconnaissance Battalion, which had arrived in August as an attachment to the 7th Marines.

The new battalion commander since 1 September, Lieutenant Colonel Roy R. Van Cleve, ordered some adjustments on 20 September in order to comply with III MAF's general support order. The new dispositions were: Headquarters, Companies A, C(-), and D at Da Nang; one Company C platoon at Hue/Phu Bai; and newly designated Reconnaissance Group ALPHA, composed of Company B and attached Company C, 1st Reconnaissance Battalion, at Chu Lai.[25]

During this entire period, the reconnaissance

battalion was faced with the question of "reconnaissance of what." The Hue/Phu Bai, Da Nang, and Chu Lai enclaves were essentially defensive positions. By virtue of III MAF's mission, all reconnaissance efforts were defensive patrols, but the restrictions imposed by the TAORs limited the patrols to "their own front yard," and there were many people in the "yard."[26]

Geography solved part of the problem. The physical characteristics of the Hue/Phu Bai lodgment provided the Marines with excellent observation. This had resulted in the reduction of the reconnaissance force there to only one platoon in September.

At the other two enclaves, RAORs (reconnaissance areas of operation) evolved slowly. On 19 June, at the recommendation of Lieutenant Colonel Blanchard, General Walt had approved the formation of a RAOR that extended from 4 to 10 kilometers forward of the Da Nang defensive positions.[27] At Chu Lai, the RAORs were as required by the two regiments there, the 4th and 7th Marines. Even with the formation of Reconnaissance Group ALPHA in September, the two Chu Lai-based reconnaissance companies continued to function as direct support companies for the respective regiments.

Another limiting factor which influenced the range and duration of reconnaissance patrols was the radio equipment then in use. The PRC-47 radio was too big and too heavy for small teams, but it did have sufficient range. The smaller, lighter PRC-10 did not have the range for deep patrols. Both sets used up batteries at a high rate, and battery consumption was accelerated by the climate which reduced battery life by more than half. Of all the patrol equipment, only water had a higher priority than batteries, and both were heavy. Patrols were caught up in the simple equation which restricted patrol duration to the number of batteries that could be carried, which, in turn, was reduced still further by the amount of other equipment and supplies which had to be carried.

Radio relay stations helped to solve the radio range problem to some degree, but the arrival, in November, of the PRC-25 radio with its long-life BA 386 battery finally enabled reconnaissance Marines to carry out deeper, long duration patrols. Although communications were vastly improved, reconnaissance units were continually faced with the grim reality of heavier loads for longer patrols.

The size of reconnaissance patrols, especially in

USMC Photo A185990

LtCol Roy R. Van Cleve, commander of the 3d Reconnaissance Battalion, holds up a Viet Cong flag captured in Operation TRAILBLAZER. The operation took place in a VC-dominated area, 16 miles southwest of Da Nang, nicknamed "Happy Valley."

the Da Nang TAOR, became a matter of great concern. Although the Marines were operating from fixed bases in relatively secure areas, patrols had to be large enough to fight their way out of any entrapment and deal with the possibility of ambush. Sergeant Richard A. Van Deusen of Company D, 3d Reconnaissance Battalion recalled this uneasy situation:

> It's very hard in an alien country to hide yourself—I mean, you're going along, and people are all over the place, and they know you're out there, so this right away compromises any chance of "recon." It all depends on the area you're in. Now if you're in the mountains, you can live there for days before they ever realize you're up there. Sometime they never know you're up there. But if you're south—and each treeline has a village on it—the only good chance you have is moving at night.[28]

By mid-1965, both force and division reconnaissance formations began experiencing utilization problems which ranged from assignments in total disregard of existing doctrine to assignment that had nothing to do with reconnaissance.

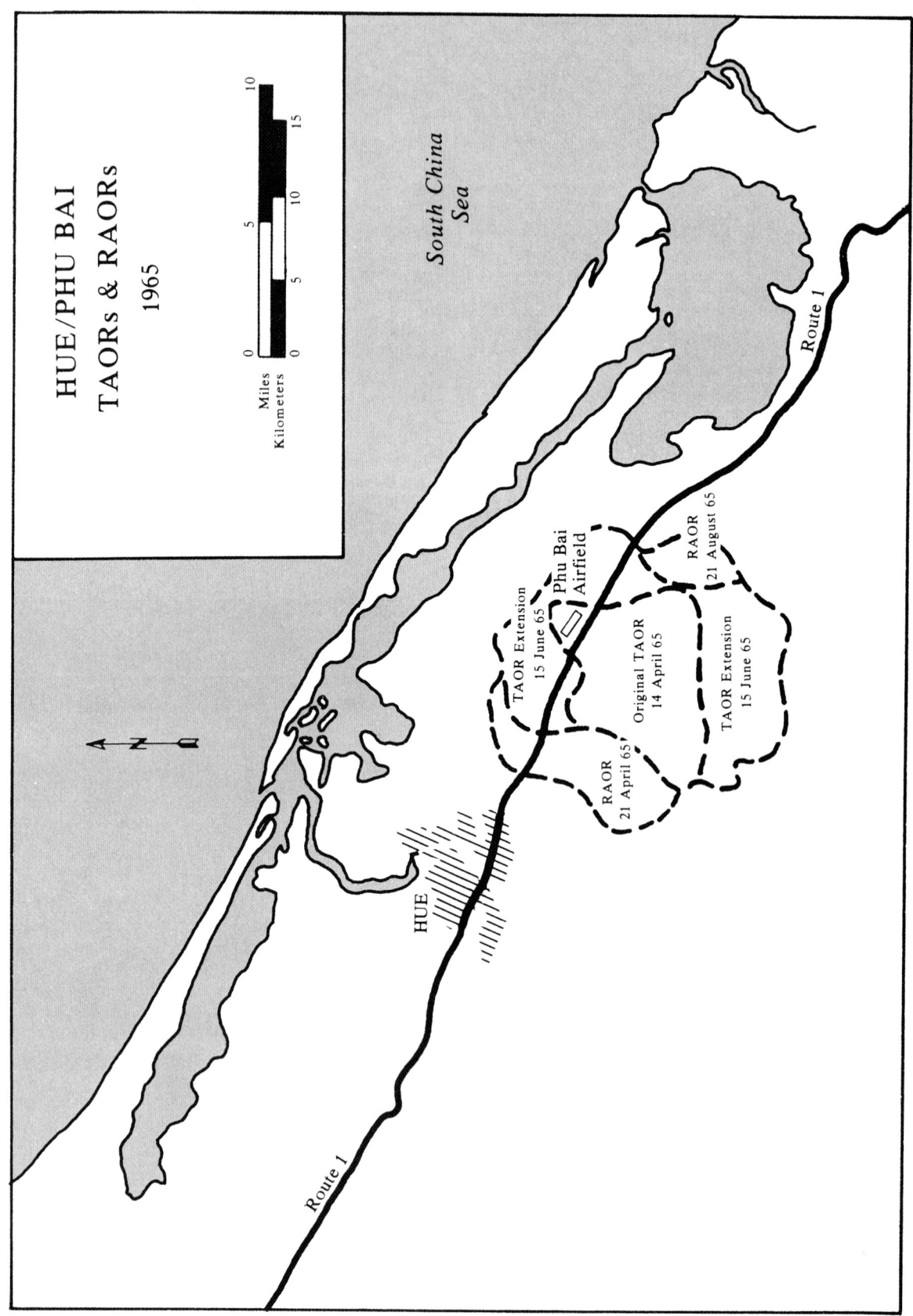

HUE/PHU BAI
TAORs & RAORs
1965

Miles

Kilometers

South China
Sea

Route 1

TAOR Extension
15 June 65

Phu Bai
Airfield

RAOR
21 August 65

RAOR
21 April 65

Original TAOR
14 April 65

TAOR Extension
15 June 65

HUE

Route 1

Reflecting on this situation, the 3d Reconnaissance Battalion commander, Lieutenant Colonel Van Cleve, recalled:

> They were being used for any mission that might come up. If you didn't have somebody else to do it, why, give it to recon. They ended up on some raider-type missions; they ended up as CP security frequently on operations. As a result of this, General Walt decided that the reconnaissance effort should be controlled at the reconnaissance battalion level, and that any request for reconnaissance type missions would come through the Division staff, the Division reconnaissance officer, G-3/G-2, advising, ''Yes, this is a reconnaissance type mission,'' or ''No, this is not a reconnaissance type mission.'' Division would task reconnaissance battalion to provide to whatever organization was asking for the necessary forces. People were realizing there was a lot of talent in the Recon Battalion that was not being used for strictly recon purposes, and the Divisions and MAF were losing a lot of potentially valuable information. [29]

Were reconnaissance Marines ''fighters'' or ''finders''? When the first revision of the provisional M-Series table of organization was published on 20 February 1958, it stated that ''The [Division] Reconnaissance Battalion may be employed as a unit to screen the advance of the Division or execute counter reconnaissance missions.'' These were clearly defined fighting missions. The publication of the approved M-1428 (Division Reconnaissance Battalion) Table of Organization, 5 March 1961, reversed this concept stating ''The Reconnaissance Battalion . . . will be employed to gain intelligence,'' and ''It is not equipped for decisive or sustained combat . . . . It is not capable of screening or counterreconnaissance missions,'' but, the concept went on to explain, commanders supported by division reconnaissance could, in the event the reconnaissance element was in danger of being ''overwhelmed,'' ''reinforce the reconnaissance force, directing that force to destroy the enemy.'' [30]

Revision 1 of 23 September 1963, still in effect in 1965, carried the transition a step further by deleting the ''destroy the enemy'' option, and reiterated the ''not equipped for decisive or sustained combat'' restriction, but some damage had been done. Misinterpretation of mission and the natural aggressiveness engendered by the demanding physical conditioning program required by reconnaissance units produced a strange analgam of ''fighting'' and ''finding'' reconnaissance Marines. [31]

Many senior Marines had been members of special units during World War II, notably the raider and parachute battalions, and all Marines were familiar with their legendary exploits. Of the senior commanders in Vietnam in 1965, four were raider battalion veterans: Major General Walt and three of his regimental commanders, Colonels Wheeler, Dupras, and Peatross. There was bound to be some ''raider'' thinking, but the Commanding General, FMFPac, Lieutenant General Krulak, resolutely insisted that ''Combat assault operations, including amphibious raids, are missions to be conducted by rifle companies, rather than reconnaissance units.'' [32] Nevertheless, during the summer and fall of 1964, Company C, 3d Reconnaissance Battalion had actually trained as the battalion's ''raid'' company. [33] The die was cast.

By 12 March 1965, Company D, 3d Reconnaissance Battalion had been reconstituted in Vietnam. It was the 9th MEB's reconnaissance company, and, as such, in April it claimed more VC ''kills'' than all of the ''in country'' infantry units, even through patrolling beyond the Da Nang and Chu Lai TAORS was not authorized until 20 April. The company commander, Captain Patrick G. Collins, recalled: ''. . . surveillance and observation

USMC Photo A185989

Marines from the 3d Reconnaissance Battalion prepare to make camp during Operation TRAILBLAZER in an enemy base area. The VC had used the hut in the background for food storage, class rooms, living area, and as a medical aid station.

The 3d Reconnaissance Battalion honor guard stands in front of the monument dedicating its base camp to First Lieutenant Frank S. Reasoner, former Company A commander who was killed on 12 July 1965. Lieutenant Reasoner was posthumously awarded the Medal of Honor for his actions during that engagement.

missions quite frequently turned into contact with the Viet Cong and having some quite spirited actions . . . . '' More specifically, Colonel Frank E. Garretson, the 9th Marines Commander, would tell Captain Collins: ''You find [them]; we'll bail you out.''[34]

As a result, early reconnaissance patrols were large, usually between 12 and 22 Marines; a number were even larger company-strength patrols. Large patrols did not guarantee absolute safety. On 12 July, an 18-man patrol from Company A operating near Dai Loc 18 kilometers southwest of Da Nang tangled with a VC company. One officer was killed and three men were wounded.

The dead officer, First Lieutenant Frank S. Reasoner, was posthumously awarded the Medal of Honor for his actions on 12 July, the first Marine action in Vietnam to merit the nation's highest honor. The 3d Reconnaissance Battalion's camp at Da Nang was named Camp Reasoner, but the lieutenant's heroic death did little to solve the patrol security dilemma. This enigma was only solved later when the TAORS were enlarged to include the rugged, sparsely inhabited terrain to the west, and when reconnaissance efforts were concentrated on the business of finding the enemy.

The III MAF commander, General Walt, realized that reconnaissance units, properly utilized, were well equipped to locate an enemy who had already established a reputation for blending into the surroundings, a phantom army which was seldom seen armed and concentrated. Even when VC concentrations were sighted, they were usually on the move, and presented fleeting targets at best. Regular Marine ground formations were too clumsy for this mission; the VC they found generally wanted to be found. General Walt decided that since reconnaissance patrols could find the VC, then the patrols should be provided with a means to destroy the enemy. Accordingly, he allowed patrols to call in air and artillery strikes. Slow clearance procedures hindered this application in the Da Nang TAOR, but the system proved to be successful at Chu Lai. The concept was refined, and in 1966 it was adopted as a standard tactic, then known as STINGRAY.[35]

Any doubts about the mission of reconnaissance Marines were resolved by General Walt's September directive which restored the division reconnaissance battalion to its general support role. Lieutenant Colonel Van Cleve's appreciation of his mission essentially put an end to the "raider" days, although some experimentation still persisted.

On 18 October, two 3d Reconnaissance Battalion companies hiked into "Happy Valley" for Operation TRAILBLAZER. Their mission was to determine the size of enemy concentrations in the hills west of the Da Nang TAOR. For six days, 18-24 October, the reconnaissance force prowled the hills. Two VC were killed, but five separate enemy base areas were discovered and a vast amount of trail network information was accumulated. TRAILBLAZER was the last of the reconnaissance-in-force operations conducted by the 3d Reconnaissance Battalion. A new trend was in motion. By December, the battalion was concentrating on patrolling, sending out more, smaller patrols; a company-size patrol was the exception.

Force and Division Reconnaissance Merged

The force reconnaissance Marines viewed their attachment to division "recon" with trepidation, and the first weeks of the new arrangement were not without some trying moments. During November, 1st Force Reconniassance Company executed division reconnaissance-type patrols in the Da Nang area, but the III MAF planners had not forgotten the force company's capabilities. As a result, on 27 November the 2d Platoon was returned to III MAF

operational control and sent to Special Forces Camp A-106 at Ba To, 42 kilometers south-southwest of Quang Ngai. On 7 December, III MAF reassigned another force platoon, the 3d, to Camp A-107, Tra Bong, 27 kilometers southwest of Chu Lai, on the upper reaches of the Tra Bong River. Their mission, code named BIRDWATCHER, was ". . . to test the feasibility of *deep* patrols."[36] At last force "recon" was going deep, but the 2d Platoon at Ba To was in for a tough school session.

At 0530, 15 December three reconnaissance teams (20 Marines and CIDG troops), plus a 61-man base defense reaction force, moved out "to determine location, identity, strength, movement, and armament of VC/PAVN units." More than 70 Communists were sighted during the next two days, but the U.S./Vietnamese reconnaissance force had made a serious mistake. The patrol base had not been moved for two nights. The only redeeming feature of this situation was that the base was on a hill, the best defensive terrain in the area.

By 1730 16 December all teams had returned to the patrol base, but the planned move back to Ba To was cancelled when dense fog settled over the camp. The force of 81 Marine, Special Forces, CIDG, and Nung troops was stuck in the same camp site for the third consecutive night.

At 1900 the Viet Cong began walking mortar rounds across the patrol base. The Vietnamese lieutenant in charge of the patrol was mortally wounded and a U.S. Special Forces sergeant was hit. Enemy automatic weapons swept the hill position as the mortar bombardment continued. Then the assault started. Between 150 to 200 Viet Cong attacked. Confusion swept through the mixed force of defenders; they broke up into small groups. The Marines, now led by Gunnery Sergeant Maurice J. Jacques, withdrew into a small perimeter, but of the 13 Marines assigned to the patrol five were already missing. In the perimeter, a Marine was hit, their corpsman was seriously wounded, and a second Marine was killed. Jacques' Marines moved off the hill into the darkness. They hid in a clump of banana trees, formed a defensive perimeter, and waited for the dawn, hoping that aerial observers would spot them in the morning. Of the 13 Marines, 4 were still missing and one was known to be dead.

Dawn came, but the fog persisted. There was no possibility of being seen from the air. The Marines tried to regain the trail back to Ba To, but enemy troops firing at what were probably other stragglers drove them back into the bush. After moving about four kilometers they found thicker cover and started moving up a ridgeline; they knew the trail to Ba To was on top of the ridge. At this time they were joined by two CIDG survivors, but the two Vietnamese almost were killed in the process. A Vietnamese with the Marines saved them by causing the Marines to hold fire as they came out of the bushes.

The Marines reached the Ba To trail, but again they were faced with a tough decision. It is a bad practice to use trails in enemy territory, but the Marines had to get away quickly and fog still blanketed the area. Fortunately the wind picked up, and it was so loud that it covered any noise the patrol made, so Jacques decided to "head for home." Putting the two Vietnamese stragglers out as the point on the trail, the Marines moved out. They reached Ba To without incident.

An hour after Gunnery Sergeant Jacques' party arrived at the base, another Marine survivor, wounded Lance Corporal Donald M. Woo, was brought in. Determined to survive, Lance Corporal Woo had been captured and escaped twice, and, in turn, captured two NVA soldiers and forced them, at knife point, to carry him to Ba To.

On 21 December the two missing Marines were found, dead. A patrol found 14 bodies: three Marines, the Special Forces sergeant, the Viet-namese lieutenant patrol leader, and nine CIDG troops.

As a result of the Ba To experience, and some other misadventures, a long standing force reconnaissance operational procedure was suspended. Previous training practices had dictated that when a force reconnaissance patrol was discovered it was to split up, each member evading on his own. After Ba To, force patrols went in together, stayed together, and came out together.

The 2d and 3d Platoons were returned to 3d Reconnaissance Battalion control on 24 December. On the 28th, Captain William C. Shaver relieved now Lieutenant Colonel Gaffen who was transferred upon his promotion.

As the year ended, both force and division reconnaissance units could state that their respective situations were much improved. Although "force" was not pleased with the prospect of remaining under the paternal hand of the 3d Reconnaissance Battalion, the force company was, at last, able to conduct deep missions, and the company's supply situation was vastly improved. Division reconnaissance was still spread between three enclaves, but it also had room to maneuver; the threat of compromise was vastly diminished. Coordination, cooperation, and understanding of reconnaissance capabilities and limitations were improving. "Recon" had a clear view of the future.

CHAPTER 12

Logistics and Construction

The Logistic Situation—III MAF Naval Responsibilities—RED BALL and CRITIPAC—
The Force Logistic Support Group—Engineering and Construction

The Logistic Situation

When the decision was made in early 1965 to commit major U.S. combat forces in South Vietnam, MACV was prepared to support only the 20,000 U.S. troops already there. General Westmoreland, therefore, requested the commitment of Marines to the I Corps area since the Marine units were the only readily available forces prepared to support themselves over the beaches in an area of few ports and airfields.[1] According to one source:

> The Marine Corps equipment posture was at its highest peacetime level of readiness since the Korean War. Modern equipment and ammunition with adequate backup stocks were available to equip and support units required for mobilization, and to improve the combat capability of the Fleet Marine Forces.[2]

This report overstated the case of Marine logistic preparedness. Logistics for the Marines in Vietnam soon became a major problem, despite the fact that for the first time a combat force had been deployed with a computerized supply system. The computerization broke down "right off the bat . . . when the stock cards began swelling due to the high humidity and the cards wouldn't fit in the machine." Record keeping had to be accomplished manually for an extended period, slowing down the entire operation.[3]

A malfunctioning requisition system compounded supply difficulties. In contrast to the practice in World War II and Korea, the Marine Corps in Vietnam used a "pull" system of resupply rather than forced feeding. Units made requisitions based on predicted usage, but the predictions, even with the incorporation of a "Combat Active Factor," underestimated the unique demands of the Vietnam situation. Colonel Mauro J. Padalino, the III MAF Force Logistic Support Group (FLSG) commander, later explained:

> Those calculations never envisioned either the harsh environment (degraded roads, Chu Lai, etc.) nor the

garrison, war-time 24-hour around-the-clock type operations the Corps experienced. In a free-type battlefield situation where there is constant forward movement with minimal pauses for consolidation, there is less wear and tear on equipment and supplies by comparison, to the in-place situation.[4]

Padalino pointed out that the dirt roads were initially trafficable, but in time "they were reduced to deep powder or mud" resulting in an "astronomical rise in demand for repair parts." The FLSG commander concluded "the garrison environment imposed a much broader base of demand on the supply system—requisitions for salt and pepper shakers competed with requisitions for combat essentials."[5]

Many commodities such as fork lifts, barbed wire, and field fortifications were in short supply. One of the most acute shortages was radio batteries, which, since there was no refrigeration, "instead of lasting 25 hours . . . pooped out in four hours."[6] For a short period in May, III MAF found it necessary to limit patrol activity because of the lack of batteries for PRC-10 radios. The logistic situation saw some improvement on 5 June, when the Defense Department finally permitted General Greene to release emergency FMFPac mount-out supplies for shipment to Vietnam.

The impact of the release of the mount-out supplies was still modest. One Marine commander later remarked that this action "was akin [to applying] . . . a bandaid to a massive wound."[7] By the end of June, the Marine Corps pipeline, designed to support a peacetime consumption rate, was beginning to show the strain. Colonel Nickerson, the III MAF G-4 at the time, commented: " . . . there was no magic solution for the deluge of problems except hard, intelligent work—the use of imagination, ingenuity, and common sense was ever important."[8] Nickerson would assign a particular problem to a member of his

Navy Photo K31362
Merchant ships in Da Nang Harbor wait their turn to unload their cargo. At the end of December 1965, 12 ships were in the harbor waiting to be unloaded.

staff and that officer would then become the "duty expert" and action officer for that matter. Colonel Harold A. Hayes, who became the III MAF G-4 on 26 August, recalled the early morning briefings that he held for General Walt and the rest of the III MAF staff where he had to report on the "low, low supply levels at different times in aviation gas, artillery ammunition, and even rations."[9]

One particularly serious shortage during 1965 was that of aviation ordnance. The data used to forecast aviation ammunition needs in early 1965 failed to reflect the actual combat needs or delivery capabilities of the aircraft deployed to Vietnam.[10] Thus, from the very beginning, the F-4B pilots, and later the A-4 pilots, had to conserve ammunition and to make value judgments on the necessity for firing at assigned targets. No targets were left unhit, but the Marines had to employ their resources sparingly and, on at least one occasion, the 1st Marine Aircraft Wing ordered F-4B squadrons not to expend rockets unless they were being used to support Marines.[11] According to Colonel Robert F. Conley, who commanded MAG-11 from July to November 1965: "Without the Navy's strong support in this field, we would not have been able to function."[12] The aviation ammunition situation, like the rest of the logistic problems that the Marines faced, could not be corrected until a productive pipeline was

established and adequate port and storage facilities were built.*

III MAF Naval Responsibilities

In his role as Naval Component Commander (NCC),** the III MAF commander was in the U.S. Pacific Fleet chain of command rather than that of MACV. In this capacity he was responsible for base construction in I Corps and the operation of all ports, beaches, and depots from Quang Ngai to the DMZ. Colonel Nickerson, in his 16 May concept of logistic support for III MAF, projected a Naval Support Activity under the NCC that would carry out the above assignments, as well as provide common item support for all U.S. forces in I Corps, but the Navy did not have the available manpower for the activation of such a unit. In a message to Admiral

---

*Colonel Thomas J. O'Connor, 1st MAW chief of staff until August 1965, observed: "We discovered that we had dipped deeply into the national war reserve ammunition supplies in the United States. That's what happens when you initiate a war, but try to conduct business as usual in the United States as if no war were going on." Col Thomas J. O'Connor, Comments on draft MS, dtd 27Nov76 (Vietnam Comment File).

**As NCC, General Walt did not control all U.S. Naval Forces in South Vietnam. The Naval Advisory Group and CTF 115 remained separate entities.

Navy Photo K31382

Stacks of cargo crowd the unloading pier at Da Nang. The overcrowded and undermanned Naval Support Activity at Da Nang was unloading 2,505 measured tons a day by the end of 1965.

Sharp on 28 May, Admiral David L. McDonald, the Chief of Naval Operations, pointed out that a Naval Support Activity could not be formed without the mobilization of certain units of the reserve. McDonald stated that he was asking for more personnel, "but in the meantime, the task will have to be accomplished within our existing resources." On 5 June, nevertheless, Admiral Roy L. Johnson, CinCPacFlt, ordered the NCC to take over common item support in I Corps, stating that he and General Krulak, Commanding General, FMFPac, would provide additional personnel and equipment.[13]

In an evaluation of the NCC responsibility for running the ports and providing logistic support in I Corps, Colonel Nickerson observed on 15 June that "Port operations continue to be conducted by CG III MAF under the cognizance of the NCC staff" and that III MAF would have to continue using it own personnel and equipment for this task until the establishment of a Naval Support Activity.

Nickerson concluded that until the matter of the Naval Support Activity was "resolved, Commander Seventh Fleet and the NCC must work together to get the job done."[14]

With the complex problems confronting them, the Marines and the Navy attempted to organize their available resources to best carry out the mission of operating port terminals, unloading and moving cargo, and all the other tasks associated with an advance naval base. On 10 July, General Walt formally activated a Provisional Naval Component Support Activity and assigned Colonel Robert W. Boyd as its commander. In effect, Boyd, who had already been acting in this capacity, was the Da Nang port director. On 17 July, the Secretary of the Navy authorized the establishment of a Naval Support Activity, Da Nang and four days later Admiral Johnson promulgated the mission and tasks for the new organization. The Naval Support Activity was to be under the command of Commander, Service

Force, U.S. Pacific Fleet, but under the operational control of the NCC. It was not until 15 October, however, that the Naval Support Activity was officially activated and began relieving Marine amphibious forces of this basic Navy mission. Finally, on 24 December, General Walt deactivated the Provisional Naval Component Support Activity and established a permanent Naval Component Command staff, observing that there had been no formal staff distinction between his responsibilities as Commanding General, III MAF and NCC and that "the steady increasing magnitude of the staff requirements" required the separation of the staff functions of the two commands. Colonel Boyd then became Deputy Chief of Staff, Naval Component Command and reported directly to General Walt. At the same time, Marine and Navy senior commanders began discussing whether the entire Naval Component Command responsibility should be assumed by a separate Navy command, rather than remaining under III MAF.[15]

The importance of the Naval Support Activity to III MAF was obvious in that all resupply was provided by either sea or air. In July 1965, slippage in air and sea schedule deliveries caused III MAF to reduce its stock level of individual combat rations from a 30-day to a 15-day supply level.[16] The situation gradually improved as additional personnel and equipment arrived to reinforce the Naval Support Activity. From an average daily discharge of only slightly over 1,000 measured tons at the port of Da Nang prior to September, the rate increased to a figure of 2,505 measured tons by the end of the year.[17] There were still problems because of inadequate unloading facilities at the port. At the end of November, 17 ships were in Da Nang harbor unloading or waiting to be unloaded. This figure was reduced to 12 by the end of December, but seven of these ships had been in port longer than two weeks, and four had been in port over a month.[18]

At Chu Lai, heavy seas caused by the monsoon season brought about further complications. In October, huge swells damaged the causeway causing the seaward portion to start to sink. This expeditionary dock was inoperative for an extended period since it was not considered practical to restore it until the worst of the monsoon was over. In spite of this frustration, 19 LSTs were unloaded at Chu Lai during October.[19]

A much more critical handicap was a leak which developed in the fuel line of the amphibious assault fuel system (AAFS) at Chu Lai during October. Two amphibious assault fuel systems, one at Da Nang and the other at Chu Lai, were established after the 5 August VC attack on the Esso POL depot at Lien Chieu which destroyed most of the commerical fuel storage in I Corps.* Each of these two systems was capable of holding 300,000 gallons of various types of fuel, resupplied directly from tankers off the coast or in the harbor. When the leak developed in the fuel line at Chu Lai, heavy seas prevented divers from making repairs until December. During the interim, the NSA devised a temporary expedient by installing a buoyant system of 5,000 feet of flexible hose from the AAFS supported by empty 55-gallon drums. Chu Lai depended upon this source for fuel until the bottom-laid line was repaired.[20] In December, aviation fuel for MAG-12 at Chu Lai again became critically short for a two-day period because of a break in the offshore lines.[21]**

RED BALL and CRITIPAC

With the rapid influx of the remainder of the 3d Marine Division, new elements of the 1st Marine Aircraft Wing, and the introduction of units of the 1st Marine Division into the already overcrowded facilities at Da Nang and Chu Lai, logistic problems could be expected. These were reflected in shortages of equipment, fuel, ammunition, and supplies. As already stated, one of the main problems was slow unloading of ships at the undeveloped ports in South Vietnam. Colonel Harold A. Hayes, the III MAF G-4 during the second half of 1965, observed:

> The "humor" of having to dump truck loads of canned soft drinks to get in the cargo holds for much needed artillery ammunition (the soft drinks were deck loaded in . . . boxes which disintegrated in the rains); the arrival of soap for the Vietnamese—partially used bars from hotels the Wives' Clubs gathered—which truly lathered on decks, in trucks, and in storage (what a mess); the horror of unloading ammunition in Da Nang Harbor and having

---

*Lien Chieu is inside the Da Nang Harbor on the south shore of Hai Van Peninsula. At the time of the attack, the area was outside of the Marines' Da Nang TAOR and was guarded by two understrength Regional Force companies. Two JP-4 storage tanks were destroyed and three others damaged resulting in the loss of 1,650,000 gallons of aviation fuel.

**The wing's chronology goes on to state: "In order to conserve fuel available at this airfield and continue to meet operational commitments, A-4 aircraft were launched with light fuel loads, then refueled from KC-130F tankers before and after conducting missions." 1st MAW ComdC, Dec65.

to stack and temporarily store [it] at dock side in the city. One VC could have erased a huge hunk of Da Nang had he gotten in! [22]

In I Corps, all shipping was offloaded at Da Nang and then some cargo had to be reloaded on LSTs to support the base at Chu Lai. This created fluctuations in the volume of supplies reaching committed units. The heavy wear and tear on equipment caused by the heat, humidity, and monsoons created additional frustrations.

Solutions had to found. In August, a logistics assistance team from FMFPac arrived at Da Nang to study the situation there. By the 24th, the team had completed its report and made its recommendations.[23] General Krulak's headquarters instituted two new programs based on the team's findings, the RED BALL and the CRITIPAC systems.

The first of these, the RED BALL Program, which went into effect on 22 September, sought to identify and solve critical supply shortages throughout the Western Pacific. When an important item of supply or equipment was found to be in short supply it was given a RED BALL designation. This meant that as soon as an item was designated RED BALL, all FMFPac supply echelons were alerted and the status of these items was closely monitored by individual action officers at each intermediary headquarters. It was their responsibility to see that the RED BALL item was shipped to Vietnam in the most expeditious manner possible, including specially arranged air shipment.[24] For an item to be placed on RED BALL, it had to be combat essential and meet specifications determined by FMFPac, which were refined periodically in the light of experience. For example, the 3d Marine Division reported in December:

> During the month . . . the number of RED BALL items increased to such a number that it became necessary to refine the criteria for placing an item on RED BALL. It must be a repair part for equipment, the loss of which would put the unit in . . . Combat Readiness Category 3 or 4. At this time, the number of line items on RED BALL is 80.[25]*

The second supply innovation, the CRITIPAC Program, was established by FMFPac in November. Under this concept, the Marine Corps Supply Center at Barstow, California automatically furnished, without request, each major Marine unit in Viet-

nam, usually battalion or squadron size, one shipment of critical supplies which were normally required on a routine basis. As a result of the first shipment which arrived in November, the 3d Marine Division indicated that 51 combat essential items were removed from deadline. General Walt recommended that some modifications be made in future shipments to include some items which were essential and to delete others which were not.[26] Both new additions to the Marine Corps Supply system, the RED BALL and the CRITIPAC, helped to alleviate the III MAF logistic situation.**

The Force Logistic Support Group

The Force Logistic Support Group under Colonel Padalino had grown from 700 personnel who deployed with the 9th MEB to nearly 3,000 officers and men by the end of the year.*** Under the overall control of the FLSG at Da Nang, two force logistic support units (FLSU) had been established at Chu Lai and Phu Bai. Built on the nucleus of the 3d Service Battalion, the FLSG was reinforced by personnel from the 3d Force Service Regiment on Okinawa and from the 1st Force Service Regiment at Camp Pendleton, California. The FLSG at Da Nang centrally controlled all furnished material, assisted by two data processing platoons. Supplies were provided either from one of the three stock points in I Corps, or the requisition was transmitted electronically to the 3d Force Service Regiment on Okinawa. The FLSG was also responsible for first to third echelon

---

*Category 3 indicated that a unit was marginally capable for combat while Category 4 shows that a unit is unprepared for combat.

**The extent of this relief is a matter of some conjecture. According to FMFPac, the RED BALL and CRITIPAC Programs resulted in a decrease in percentage of deadlined equipment from 15 percent in the fall to 12.5 percent by the end of 1965. *FMFPac, Marine Forces in Vietnam, Mar65-Sep67*, v.I, p. 8-14. MACV on the other hand reported: "Year end deadline rate for III MAF was: overall, 14 percent; electronic, 11 percent; engineer, 32 percent; motor transport 11 percent; and ordnance, 5 percent." *MACV, Comd Hist, 1965*, p. 116. In any event there was no doubt that the supply situation was better than in October 1965, when III MAF reported: "Shortage of spare parts affected readiness to the extent that the operation readiness of several units decreased to the marginally combat ready category." III MAF ComdC, Oct65, p. 7.

***Colonel Robert J. Oddy commanded the Force Logistic Support Group from 6-29 May 1965. Colonel Oddy also continued to command the 3d Service Battalion which left a rear echelon behind on Okinawa. Col Robert J. Oddy, Comments on draft MS, dtd 25Oct76 (Vietnam Comment File).

maintenance; fourth echelon maintenance was performed on Okinawa by the 3d Force Service Regiment.*

Some measure of the size of FLSG operations is indicated in the following excerpts from its December report:

   a. Data Processing key punched 66,100 cards, and processed 8,777,700 transactions . . .
   b. Clothing in the amount of $98,063 was provided . . .
   c. Shipping and Receiving processed 3,688 short tons, 360,900 cubic feet of outgoing material and 2,014 short tons, 225,271 cubic feet of incoming material . . .
   d. 6,469 maintenance work orders were received and 6,250 work orders were completed during the period.[27]

The FLSG organization had grown to such an extent that in September 1965, General Krulak stated that he had decided to transform the FLSG into a Force Logistic Command (FLC), but this did not happen until 1966.[28]

Engineering and Construction

A significant construction and engineering effort took place at all three Marine enclaves during 1965. Civilian firms and Seabee units worked on port development, airfield construction, and base development. Marine engineering units not only assisted in these projects when required, but also continued to furnish combat support to III MAF. Colonel William M. Graham, Jr., the III MAF engineering officer, observed: "For my money, Vietnam in 1965 was an engineers' war and not many other units could satisfactorily fulfill their mission without engineer support."[29]

The 3d Engineer Battalion, like the rest of the 3d Marine Division support units, deployed to Vietnam as attachments to other units. In May, Major Bernard A. Kaasmann established a forward battalion headquarters at Da Nang. Under his control at Da Nang were Companies A from the 3d and C from the 7th Engineer Battalions. Company B, 3d Engineer Battalion was at Chu Lai with one platoon at Phu Bai.

USMC Photo A184410

Marine engineers from Company C, 7th Engineer Battalion wield a pick and shovel in building a new road up Hill 327 in March 1965. This was one of the first tasks completed by the engineers.

To build the Chu Lai SATS field, the engineers had to send almost all of their earthmoving equipment from Da Nang to Chu Lai. Roads at Da Nang began to deteriorate rapidly and manual labor replaced mechanization. Lieutenant Colonel Nicholas J. Dennis, who had assumed command of the 3d Engineer Battalion on Okinawa in early May and later in the month arrived in Vietnam, recalled that he questioned the necessity for the transfer of equipment between the two enclaves, but that Colonel Graham "easily convinced me that the *transfer* was ordered."[30]

Even after the Chu Lai airfield was completed, the tasks facing the engineers were enormous. Major Kaasmann later commented:

   To maintain the staggering miles of road network and make repairs on existing and destroyed bridges with

---

*At that time, all depot or 5th echelon maintenance was performed in the U.S. According to FMFPac, "as the effects of climate and sustained usage amplified maintenance requirements and as forces-in-country steadily grew, this concept became too costly . . . ." For example by the end of 1965, 5,500 items had been evacuated from RVN for repair. To alleviate this situation, some fourth echelon maintenance was moved to South Vietnam in 1966. FMFPac, *Marine Forces in Vietnam, Mar65-Sep67*, v. I, p. 8-14.

Marine engineers construct the 3d Marine Division command post bunker. When completed it was estimated that the massive timber and concrete complex would be capable of supporting the weight of three battleships.

construction material available required a great deal of ingenuity and improvisation. . . . Heavy engineer earth-moving equipment and dump trucks were operated from dawn until dusk, seven days a week. Mechanics worked during hours of darkness performing required preventative maintenance and making repairs so equipment and vehicles were ready to roll at first light.[31]

Lieutenant Colonel Dennis, after touring all three enclaves, officially assumed command of the 3d Engineer's forward headquarters at Da Nang on 29 May. He suggested an extensive road improvement program to General Walt, which included building bridges and laying culverts throughout the TAORs to prepare for the forthcoming monsoon season. Dennis also recommended the deployment of the remaining battalion units from Okinawa, Company C, Headquarters and Service Company, and Support Company. By 8 July, the entire 3d Engineer Battalion was in Vietnam.[32]

One of the major engineering accomplishments during this period was the installation of the LAAM battery on Monkey Mountain. According to Colonel O'Connor:

The engineering unit had to move southward along the Monkey Mountain ridge from the Air Force control position through dense jungle. The distance was about three miles to the highest point on the ridge. They constructed a shelf road suitable for military vehicles along the contours of several steep slopes. Upon arrival at the selected peak, they shaved off the top of it to make a flat area for emplacement of a section of a battery. The job took about three weeks and required explosives, bulldozers, and graders to establish cuts and culverts along the way.[33]

About the same time, Dennis' battalion completed construction support for the 3d Medical Battalion, which included "air-conditioned operating rooms, strongbacked, screened ward tents, air-conditioned recovery room tents." According to Dennis:

I vividly recall General Walt visiting 'Charlie Med' and directing immediate construction of the above listed

A Marine stands guard on a newly built 195-foot span near Marble Mountain. The engineers erected the bridge in three days.

facilities. We completed this project . . . [with the cooperation] of many other units . . . including special air shipment from Okinawa of the refrigeration units and lumber.[34]

Following the 1 July attack on the Da Nang Airfield and the enlargement of the TAOR, General Walt ordered the movement of the 3d Marine Division command posts away from the airfield and the construction of bunkers along the main line of resistance (MLR) in the new areas. According to Dennis, General Walt personally informed him of his construction requirements for the 3d Marine Division CP complex. It was located north of Hill 327 and:

> . . . evolved into a monster [bunker] in excess of 300 feet long and 40 to 50 feet deep. It was designed to absorb, without damage, a hit by a 120mm mortar. The columns (12''x12'' timbers) were on 10' centers and in most cases anchored to a 4' cube of concrete . . . The columns supported 12''x12'' caps and roof members consisting of a layer of 8''x8'' timbers, three laminations of 3''x12'' with three feet of earth and six inches of crushed rock as a burster layer. It was air conditioned, lighted and included some private toilet facilities.[35]

Dennis assembled a force of 60 troops for the construction of troop quarters, the division CP, and

the MLR bunker program which was to consist of 1,098 units. At the same time, other engineering requirements ranged from clearing new areas and building new roads to taking down strong-backed tents, moving them, and then putting them up again. The battalion also kept the roads open, built new bridges, and repaired those that were down.[36]

On 24 August, the 7th Engineer Battalion, under Lieutenant Colonel Ermine L. Meeker, joined the 3d Engineers in Vietnam. The 7th Engineers, a Force Troops unit, had a greater heavy construction capability. According to Lieutenant Colonel Dennis, "The 7th Engineers were most welcome. The engineer support tasks were just too massive and overwhelming for a combat engineer unit."[37]

The 7th Engineers, unlike the 3d, operated directly under III MAF rather than the division.* During its first month in Vietnam, the battalion built

---

*Company C of the 7th Engineers remained under the operational control of the 3d Engineer Battalion. Company C of the 1st Engineer Battalion arrived with the 7th Marines at Chu Lai. Both engineer companies at Chu Lai were under the administrative control of the 3d Engineer Battalion.

USMC Photo A186354

A member of the 3d Engineer Battalion use a mine detector to sweep a road as South Vietnamese civilians driving oxen veer off to the right. As evidenced by the heavy tire tracks, the road is in great use and an obvious place for the VC to plant their mines.

a large ferry boat to carry supplies between the Da Nang Airbase and Tiensha Peninsula and erected two bridges spanning rivers south of Da Nang. Monsoon weather had caused extensive flooding of many of the main supply routes and storage dumps in the area and better drainage facilities were required. By the end of the month, the battalion could list 16 major projects that it had undertaken in support of the MAF, division, and wing. These ranged from extensive road building to the erection of 33 warehouses for the FLSG.[38]

During the last quarter of 1965, despite shortages of material and repair parts,* problems with

---

* Colonel Dennis observed that material requirements ''far outstripped our sources of supply, even though we had requisitioned all materials via special channels.'' The battalion obtained some of its material from cantonment program supplies controlled by the Seabees, some through Marine Corps channels, and some through local purchase. Colonel Dennis remembered: ''I kept one SNCO in Da Nang searching for material and a representative in Saigon performing the same task. Without them we would not have accomplished the task. There was a continuous material shortage.'' Col Nicholas J. Dennis, Comments on draft MS, dtd 3Nov76 (Vietnam Comment File).

equipment, and washouts and flooding caused by the monsoon, the 3d Engineers was able to provide effective combat and combat service support to the 3d Division. The engineers furnished mine detection and demolition teams in support of infantry operations and made daily sweeps of the main supply routes for mines and booby traps. Lieutenant Colonel Dennis established a mine warfare course, one week for engineer personnel and one day for other troops, at the 3d Engineers' base area. All 3d Marine Division replacements were required to go through the program.

South of Da Nang, the battalion removed 16 kilometers of unused railroad rails and converted the railroad bed into a road to become part of the division's main supply route. By December, Companies A and C were primarily committed to road and bridge construction in the Da Nang TAORs of the 3d and 9th Marines, while Company C, 7th Engineer Battalion was involved in cutting timbers to be used for bunkers along the division's main defensive lines.[39]

The construction requirements at both Da Nang and Chu Lai were too extensive for Marine Corps engineering units to undertake by themselves. A civilian construction firm worked on the expansion of the main airfield at Da Nang, while the 30th Naval Construction Regiment, Captain Harold F. Liberty, USN, with four Seabee battalions built helicopter facilities at Marble Mountain and Ky Ha. The Marble Mountain facility construction was approved by CinCPac in July and by 25 August MAG-16 was operating from the base. The Seabees also built a 400-bed hospital just west of the Marble Mountain Air Facility, but construction there was temporarily disrupted by the VC attack on 28 October. At Chu Lai, Seabees, assisted by Major Kennedy's Marine Air Base Squadron 36 and Marine engineers, built a second helicopter air facility on the Ky Ha Peninsula. Colonel Johnson's MAG-36 flew its first missions from the new facility on 12 September.[40]

The experience of the Seabees, who were supported by Lieutenant Colonel Wilson's MABS-12 and Marine engineering units at the Chu Lai SATS field, was typical of the frustration that the contruction units faced in South Vietnam. On 3 July, the Seabees finished the last portion of the 8,000-foot runway, but only a few weeks later the northern half of the runway had to be closed because of soil erosion under the matting. No sooner had this project been completed than the Marines discovered that heavy rains and sand erosion had caused the foundation of the southern half of the runway to crumble. The matting became wavy and disjointed, unsafe for jet operations.[41] On 25 September, the Marines closed the southern portion of the runway and the Seabees applied a soft cement base mixed with sand under the AM-2 matting to try to attain stabilization.[42] This work was completed on 10 November, but by that time the northern foundation was eroding again. The Seabees made nightly repairs, but by the end of year it was apparent that the northern half would have to be lifted once more and restabilized with the same cement-sand mixture used on the southern portion. This time the sand was packed without using any other material, and then a light layer of asphalt was applied over the sand. Before replacing the aluminum matting, a thin plastic membrane was installed to keep rain from settling in the soil and undermining the runway.[43] These efforts proved successful, and the ''tinfoil strip'', as the runway became nicknamed, was still in use five years after it had been built. Not even the SATS planners at Quantico in 1955 had envisioned that a SATS field could be constructed in such soil conditions and then used in all types of weather for such an extended period.[44]

General Walt expressed his appreciation of the engineering effort in the following terms:

> Never have the Marine Engineers and the Navy CB's been faced with more urgent and difficult problems, and never have they responded more positively and effectively than in the Vietnam I Corps area during 1965-66. Their support was magnificent and of the highest professional order. They worked as an integrated team with always the ''can do'' attitude.[45]

The entire Marine logistics and support effort was perhaps summed up best by General McCutcheon's description of the SATS field: ''It worked, but it took some doing.''[46]

PART V
OTHER MARINE ACTIVITIES

CHAPTER 13

The SLF of the Seventh Fleet

Disbandment of the SLF—A New Mission—The Reestablishment of the SLF—Command and Control Changes—The First DAGGER THRUST Raids—Further Changes in the SLF—The Saigon Conference— The Second Series of DAGGER THRUST Raids—The SLF at the End of the Year

---

Disbandment of the SLF

The landing of the 9th MEB and the deployment of reinforcing Marine units to Vietnam during the spring of 1965 seriously depleted the Marine forces with the Seventh Fleet. Lieutenant Colonel Edmund G. Derning's BLT 2/9 which had become the Seventh Fleet Special Landing Force (SLF) battalion in late February, was tasked as the floating reserve for the Da Nang landing of 8 March. Derning's attached shore party and the landing craft from the attack transport USS *Bexar* (APA 237) and the landing ship dock USS *Thomaston* (LSD 28) assisted in landing the brigade's supplies and men. In addition, the pilots of Lieutenant Colonel Joseph Koler, Jr.'s HMM-365, the SLF helicopter squadron on board the amphibious assault ship USS *Princeton* (LPH 5), flew their aircraft from the ship to the Da Nang Airbase. There the 23 UH-34s were turned over to HMM-162 whose personnel arrived by KC-130 from Okinawa. After Koler's pilots returned to the *Princeton*, the ship sailed for Okinawa to take on replacement aircraft. The other ships of the amphibious ready group (ARG) carrying the SLF, *Thomaston* and *Bexar*, recovered their landing craft and reembarked the BLT's shore party on 12 March and steamed northward to rendezvous with the *Princeton*.

After a seven-day port call at Hong Kong, the force returned to Subic Bay for refurbishing of equipment and for training. In mid-April, the SLF was once more off the coast of Vietnam, covering the landings of BLTs 2/3 and 3/4. The group then sailed for Okinawa where both HMM-263 and BLT 2/9 disembarked. At this point, the Seventh Fleet and FMFPac dissolved the SLF, because its amphibious shipping was required for the landing of the 3d Marine Amphibious Brigade at Chu Lai.

The senior Marine and Navy Pacific commanders recognized that the disbandment of the SLF was a temporary measure. During a visit to Vietnam and Okinawa in May, Lieutenant General Krulak, the FMFPac commander, met with Vice Admiral Paul P. Blackburn, Commander Seventh Fleet; the two agreed that the SLF should be reconstituted when additional amphibious shipping became available. Krulak suggested that this should take place when the first elements of the 7th Marines arrived on Okinawa from California.[1]

A New Mission

Throughout the spring, American commanders in the Pacific discussed the possibility of employing the Seventh Fleet's SLF in a series of amphibious raids on VC/NVA infiltration and marshalling points along the coast of South Vietnam. On 14 March, representatives from MACV and the Pacific Fleet reached an agreement in Saigon for a naval coastal surveillance campaign, Operation MARKET TIME. The agreement contained provisions for carrying out amphibious raids using South Vietnamese Marines, U.S. Marine battalions, or combined South Vietnamese and U.S. Marine forces. The MACV and CinCPacFleet staffs were to evaluate available intelligence and agree on suitable target areas for these raids. The first targets were to be in unpopulated areas, which would allow the amphibious forces relative freedom of action. After the two commands had agreed on suitable target areas, the CinCPacFleet staff was to prepare a concept of operations from which the amphibious commander was to make his detailed plans. Completed plans were then to be submitted to ComUSMACV for his concurrence and for South Vietnamese clearance for the raids.[2]

Both General Westmoreland and Admiral Johnson ratified the results of the Saigon conference. In their transmittal of the agreement to Admiral

Sharp, CinCPac, on 14 May for approval, Westmoreland and Johnson observed that the planning guide for the raids "insofar as possible will be *Doctrine for Amphibious Operations* (FM 31-ll/NWP 22 (A))." The two commanders noted that although the South Vietnamese Armed Forces were to request such raids, "in fact ComUSMACV will stimulate RVNAF requests for operations desired by the U.S."[3]

Although General Westmoreland was enthusiastic about the prospects of amphibious raids, he wanted them to be conducted solely by South Vietnamese forces.[4] It soon became obvious that the South Vietnamese Armed Forces were so overextended that they could not carry out these operations alone. On 9 June, General Westmoreland informed Admiral Sharp that U.S. amphibious operations would be welcome and inquired about the status of the 14 March agreement. The CinCPac commander replied that the agreement was still under review, but that U.S. raids could be conducted.[5] By mid-June, General Krulak radioed General Walt:

> We should get the SLF reconstituted as soon as possible, because it is plain that CinCPac and MACV are getting serious about amphibious raids as a part of MARKET TIME. I am asking CinCPacFleet to press 7th Fleet to get the SLF shipping to Okinawa in advance of the currently 1 July date.[6]

The Reestablishment of the SLF

On 19 June, FMFPac reactivated the Marine special landing force for planning purposes. It was to consist of Lieutenant Colonel Charles H. Bodley's BLT 3/7, which had arrived on Okinawa from Camp Pendleton, and Lieutenant Colonel Norman G. Ewers' HMM-163, which had arrived on Okinawa from Da Nang. Since Ewers was the senior of the two, he became the SLF commander as well as retaining command of his squadron. On 24 June, the two units embarked in the ships of Task Group 76.5, the Seventh Fleet designation for its amphibious ready group. Commanded by Captain David A. Scott, USN, the task group was composed of the USS *Iwo Jima* (LPH 2), USS *Point Defiance* (LSD 31), and the USS *Talladega* (APA 208). The force sailed from Buckner Bay, Okinawa on 26 June for South Vietnam.

Because of increased enemy activity in II Corps during May and June and the fear of a general Communist offensive there, the first mission of the SLF was the protection of the U.S. Army's large logistic facilities at Qui Nhon. General Westmoreland had requested the deployment of a Marine battalion to Qui Nhon until U.S. infantry forces arrived. On 1 July, Bodley's BLT 3/7 made an administrative landing at Qui Nhon. The battalion remained ashore for six days until relieved by Lieutenant Colonel Leon N. Utter's BLT 2/7. Reembarked, the SLF remained offshore. Ewers' squadron, flying from the *Iwo Jima*, provided helicopter support for Utter's battalion at Qui Nhon. On 20 July, HMM-163 was relieved of this support mission when a 10-plane detachment from HMM-161 arrived at Qui Nhon from Da Nang. The ARG/SLF reverted to its role as the Pacific Fleet's ready reserve and sailed for Subic Bay.

Command and Control Changes

At the time Seventh Fleet and FMFPac reconstituted the SLF, some changes were made in the administrative chain of command of the fleet's amphibious forces. With the deployment of the 3d Marine Division and skeleton III MAF headquarters from Okinawa to Vietnam, General Collins relinquished the designation Commanding General, FMF, Seventh Fleet (CG TF 79). This role was assumed by Brigadier General Melvin D. Henderson, the assistant 3d Marine Division commander, commanding the division's forces remaining on Okinawa.

Admiral Blackburn wanted Henderson's assignment as CG TF 79 to be made a primary duty; General Krulak demurred. He explained that the position had always been an additional duty task, "discharged by the senior officer of those FMFPac Forces assigned to the operational control of Com7thFlt." According to Krulak, that senior officer's primary mission was to the "total command responsibilities related to his force." Specifically referring to General Henderson, Krulak continued:

> The obligation implicit in his duties, pivoting as they will upon readying forces for service in Vietnam and supervision of 3d MarDiv (Rear) administrative and logistic matters related to support of our forces engaged in the conflict, mitigate against changing the basic procedure followed in the past. However, am confident that Henderson will be able to fulfill the TF 79 responsibilities to your satisfaction following the past system, and I will ensure that he is provided with proper staff support to do the job.[7]

Krulak ended his message to Blackburn mentioning

Ships of the Seventh Fleet Amphibious Ready Group (from left to right) the attack transport USS Bexar *(APA 237), the amphibious assault ship USS* Princeton *(LPH 5), the dock landing ship USS* Thomaston *(LSD 28), and destroyer escort USS* Joseph E. Connelly *(DE 450) in formation in the South China Sea with BLT 2/9 and HMM-365 embarked, in March 1965. Helicopters of HMM-365 fly above the ships while the* Princeton's *crew spell out the groups' designations, TG 76.5 and 79.5, on the flight deck.*

that he had discussed the situation with Admiral Johnson and that the latter concurred.

Admiral Blackburn acknowledged that Henderson's primary assignment was as 3d Marine Division assistant division commander, but he still had certain reservations. The Seventh Fleet commander told Krulak that although they both understood the command relationships between CGFMFSeventhFlt, CGFMFPac, and ComSeventhFlt, other might not. To avoid any misunderstanding, Blackburn suggested:

> It must be understood by all concerned that CG-FMFSeventhFlt as CTF 79 will be immediately responsible to ComSeventhFlt for planning and operations and, in that context, his primary duty is a CGFMFSeventhFlt rather than as Assistant Commander, 3d Marine Division.[8]

At this point, General Krulak replied that he did not believe any further discussion of the topic would prove fruitful. He told Blackburn:

> As you say, you and I understand the matter. There are only two other key personages involved, Walt and Henderson. I have ensured that they are both familiar with . . . your order. There is no reason that I can see to fear that Henderson will not carry out his instructions as stated in your Op Order. Those instructions are clear, and certainly they are binding.[9]

With this reply, General Krulak believed that he had "put the whole affair on ice."[10]

Admiral Blackburn, nevertheless, elected, with the concurrence of General Krulak, to activate a second Marine FMF command within the Seventh Fleet. On 28 June, he ordered the establishment of a Ready Afloat Force within the fleet, which included a Ready Afloat Marine Amphibious Brigade (RAMAB) headquarters. This headquarters, which at this juncture consisted of Marine Colonel Horace E. Knapp, Jr. and a small staff, was assigned the Navy designation TF 78. Admiral Blackburn transferred control of the SLF from TF 79 to TF 78, thus resulting in a change of designation for the SLF from TG 79.5 to TG 78.5.

The Marines were not wholly satisfied with the new command arrangements. There were, in effect, two parallel Marine commands within the Seventh Fleet, which blurred command responsibility. General Henderson, as CTF 79 and CGFMFSeventh Fleet, lost direct administrative control of the SLF, but retained responsibility for the amphibious readiness of the Marine forces on Okinawa. Colonel Knapp, as Commander TF 78, reported operationally to Rear Admiral Don W. Wulzen, TF 76 commander, but administratively to FMFPac. Lieutenant Colonel Ewers as SLF commander retained operational control of both BLT 3/7 and his own helicopter squadron. While afloat, Ewers reported operationally to the ARG commander and administratively to Task Force 78.

Several of the senior Marine commanders believed that the ensuing dilution of Marine authority within the fleet could allow the SLF to be used for non-amphibious purposes, to the detriment of its mission. A case in point took place on 22 July. After the SLF had been released from its reserve role at Qui Nhon, the Navy diverted the ships of the ARG to assist in a salvage mission off Pratas Reef, 200 miles southeast of Hong Kong, where the destroyer USS *Frank Knox* (DD 742) had run aground. Two of the three ARG ships, the *Talladega* and the *Iwo Jima*, remained at the salvage site until 31 July. After a short port visit to Hong Kong, both ships arrived back at Subic Bay on 12 August. In the meantime, a third ARG ship, the LSD *Point Defiance,* had unloaded some of its equipment at Subic Bay to make more deckroom and then returned to the salvage operation where it remained until 19 August. On that date, all three ships were ordered to sail directly to Vietnam so that the SLF could participate in Operation STARLITE. According to the SLF commander, splitting the amphibious ready group resulted in leaving behind some of the amphibious equipment unloaded by the *Port Defiance* at Subic and the incremental arrival of BLT 3/7 in the battle area.[11]

After Operation STARLITE, General Henderson, as TF 79 commander and senior Marine officer in the Seventh Fleet, expressed his concern to General Krulak about the involuntary diversion of the SLF from training and refitting to salvage operations:

> It appears that both the battalion commander and the SLF commander were concerned about the degradation of physical fitness of Marine personnel caused by confinement aboard ship. . . . The SLF commander although concerned, felt that higher authority was directing these movements with full appreciation of effect on integrity and readiness of SLF and refrained from objecting or coming up on the air to set forth his concern.[12]

General Henderson suggested that new liaison arrangements had to be made with both the SLF and the Seventh Fleet so there would not be a reoccurrence of similar incidents.

Since General Henderson, as 3d Marine Division assistant division commander, was about to depart for Da Nang, the responsibility for establishing the new relationships devolved upon his successor as CGFMFSeventhFlt, Major General Lewis J. "Jeff" Fields, the commanding general of the 1st Marine Division. General Fields had assumed command of the 1st Division on 11 August, just before its deployment to the Western Pacific. Accompanied by a small command group, the new division commander left California four days later for Okinawa, stopping en route at FMFPac headquarters in Honolulu. On 24 August, he opened the command post of the 1st Marine Division (Fwd) on Okinawa and at the same time assumed his new command responsibilities in the Seventh Fleet as CG TF 79.

General Fields had his own doubts about command relationships within the Seventh Fleet. He believed that the organization of the SLF at the time "was still a reflection of our peacetime activities in the Western Pacific," and "to think that whoever was senior of the two commanders, helicopter squadron or infantry battalion, would command the SLF as well as his own unit was ridiculous . . . ." According to Fields, he decided, after much discussion with his staff, that the next SLF would be provided with an expanded headquarters to command both the helicopter squadron and infantry battalion, "leaving their commanders to carry out the duties for which they had been intended and assigned." By furnishing such a command, Fields thought that he "would have a commander of the force who could properly assist, and respond to the Navy commander's operations and plans."[13]

On 11 September, he incorporated these views in a message to Admiral Blackburn. Fields proposed making the RAMAB/TF 78 commander and his staff the headquarters of the SLF. The Marine general further suggested that, "in order to provide for clearer lines of communication and to accurately portray actual relationships, I shall redesignate TG 78.5 as TG 79.5." He then declared, "my larger TF 79 staff will conduct all required joint planning functions with CTF 76 as well as providing you with advice concerning landing force matters." In effect, Fields was recommending the abolishment of the RAMAB command except as a paper designator until that time an actual MAB was activated.[14]

Admiral Blackburn did not concur with the proposed alterations and stated that he would "make all decisions concerning the organization of the Seventh Fleet."[15] According to General Krulak, the Seventh Fleet Commander misunderstood General Fields' intentions and believed that the latter had overreached himself. Krulak explained:

> While not Blackburn's idea, the TF 78 and TG 78.5 organization made its advent under his regime, and I'm sure he views its existence with a certain amount of personal pride. Furthermore it has been my experience that whereas the Navy has sometimes abused the SLF they, at the same time, have been sensitive and jealous of the slightest interference with it.[16]

General Krulak advised General Fields "to pick up the pieces and try to make something of it." The FMFPac commander observed that he was not interested in "either challenging or assuaging Blackbun, but rather in making things better for our forces afloat." Krulak stated that the SLF had been maltreated and that this concerned him. In his view, the problem stemmed, in part, from the disparity in rank between the Navy and Marine commanders of the amphibious forces "and lack of an appropriate air/ground (SLF) headquarters." Krulak recommended that Fields remind the Seventh Fleet commander that the latter's responsibility did not include the internal organization of the Marine Corps forces, "specifically the assignment of a Marine colonel as SLF commander is outside the authority of the operational commander."[17]

General Fields, in his reply to Admiral Blackburn, remarked that he had no intention of usurping any of the prerogatives of the Seventh Fleet commander, but stood his ground on the reorganization of the SLF command. He insisted that as the officer responsible for organizing, equipping, training, and providing forces for the SLF, he was in the best position "to determine who should be placed in direct command of these forces."[18]

At this point, the entire question of the organization and control of the SLF was held in abeyance. General Fields stated that for the time being he would hold off the transfer of the commander of the RAMAB to the SLF. On the other hand, Admiral Blackburn, who wanted two SLFs in the Seventh Fleet, which would justify an amphibious brigade headquarters, was denied this request by CinCPacFlt. Admiral Johnson informed Blackburn that with the continuing commitment to Vietnam there were neither enough Marine troops or

helicopters in the Western Pacific to form a second SLF.[19]

In the meantime, some changes had occurred in the unit composition of the SLF. After STARLITE and a short refurbishing visit to Subic Bay, BLT 3/7 was unloaded at Chu Lai and was attached to III MAF in early September. The ARG sailed for Okinawa where it embarked Lieutenant Colonel Robert T. Hanifin's BLT 2/1, the new SLF battalion. HMM-163 was retained as the SLF helicopter squadron and Lieutenant Colonel Ewers still kept his "two hats" as commander of the SLF and the squadron. The ARG/SLF returned to Vietnamese waters on 10 September as the covering force for the landing of the U. S. Army's 1st Cavalry Division (Airmobile) at Qui Nhon.

The First DAGGER THRUST Raids

While off Qui Nhon, the SLF prepared to carry out the first of the long delayed series of amphibious raids in support of the MARKET TIME anti-infiltration operations. Since June, CinCPac, CinCPacFlt, Seventh Fleet Amphibious Forces, and MACV had worked out the details of the raids, to be known as DAGGER THRUST. In late July, Admiral Sharp approved the outline plans for three DAGGER THRUST raids, as well as the implementation of the 14 March MACV-CinCPacFlt anti-infiltration agreement. In accordance with this agreement, the raids were to be quick thrusts by the SLF into suspected enemy concentration points followed by immediate retraction of the landing force. Established amphibious doctrine dictated that the Navy amphibious commander would retain control of the Marine forces ashore since no permanent beachhead was to be established. Admiral Blackburn designated Rear Admiral Don W. Wulzen, CTF 76, as the amphibious task force commander for the DAGGER THRUST mission. By mid-September, Wulzen had completed his detailed landing plans and, on 21 September, General Westmoreland obtained South Vietnamese clearance for the first raids.

This series of DAGGER THRUST operations was to consist of three raids in rapid succession on widely dispersed coastal objective areas. After carrying out the first raid on the Vung Mu Peninsula, 20 miles south of Qui Nhon, the SLF was to strike a second target 50 miles to the south in the Ben Goi area, 27

Marines from BLT 2/1 return to their quarters on board the Iwo Jima *(LPH 2) after debarking from HMM-163's helicopters. They have just completed DAGGER THRUST I, the first of a series of amphibious raids against suspected enemy concentration points, which took place in September 1965 on the Vung Mu Peninsula, 20 miles south of Qui Nhon.*

miles north of Nha Trang. The third obective was Tam Quan, 30 miles south of Quang Ngai City. All three DAGGER THRUST raids were to take place in as brief a period as circumstances permitted.

On 22 September, the command ship USS *Estes* (AGC 12), Admiral Wulzen's flagship, and the high speed transport USS *Diachenko* (APD 123) rendezvoused with the ships of the ARG off Qui Nhon. Colonel Edwin G. Winstead, who had relieved Colonel Knapp as commander of the RAMAB/TF-78 after STARLITE, had joined Admiral Wulzen on board the USS *Estes* and was the designated commander of the landing force, the Marine counterpart to the amphibious task force commander. The task force then proceeded to Chu Lai where the SLF carried out a dress rehearsal for DAGGER THRUST on the 23d. After reembarkation, the task force was joined by two destroyers, the USS *Mason* (DD 852)

and the USS *Small* (DD 838), and steamed for Vung Mu, the first target.

All three DAGGER THRUST raids were disappointing. During DAGGER THRUST I, the SLF landed over the beach and by helicopter on the morning of 25 September. After searching the peninsula and finding no sign of the enemy battalion that was supposed to be there, the Marines reembarked and sailed for Ben Goi Bay. During DAGGER THRUST II, Lieutenant Colonel Hanifin's BLT did not even land. Three Marine reconnaissance teams from a force reconnaissance detachment, embarked on board the *Iwo Jima*, transferred to the *Diachenko*, and then, accompanied by South Vietnamese UDT personnel, went ashore in small boats on the evening of 27 September. One team lost radio contact, but the helicopters of HMM-163 found it.[20] Since none of the teams had reported

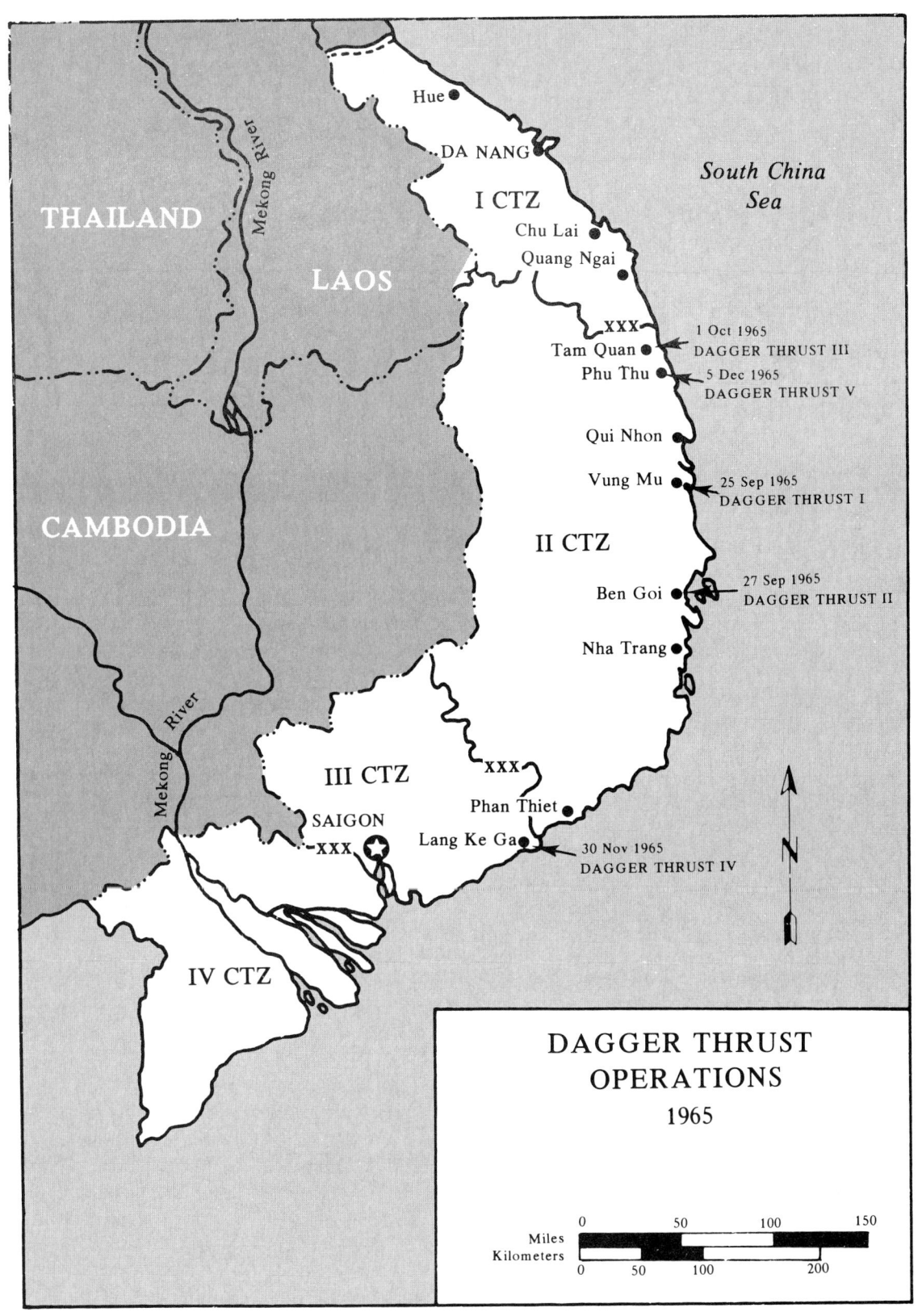

THAILAND

LAOS

CAMBODIA

Mekong River

Mekong River

Hue ●

DA NANG ●

I CTZ

South China
Sea

Chu Lai ●
Quang Ngai ●

XXX
Tam Quan ●   1 Oct 1965
                          DAGGER THRUST III
Phu Thu ●   5 Dec 1965
                          DAGGER THRUST V

Qui Nhon ●

Vung Mu ●   25 Sep 1965
                          DAGGER THRUST I

II CTZ

Ben Goi ●   27 Sep 1965
                          DAGGER THRUST II

Nha Trang ●

III CTZ   XXX

SAIGON ★   Phan Thiet ●
XXX   Lang Ke Ga ●   30 Nov 1965
                                 DAGGER THRUST IV

N

IV CTZ

DAGGER THRUST
OPERATIONS
1965

	Miles	Kilometers
0	50	100	150
0	50	100	200

Marines from BLT 2/1 land near Tam Quan, 30 miles south of Quang Ngai City, during DAGGER THRUST III. The battalion encountered a small VC guerrilla force during the operation.

any enemy and the Marines had lost the element of surprise, Admiral Wulzen decided to cancel the landing. The battalion came ashore at Tam Quan on 1 October for DAGGER THRUST III and met some resistance from local guerrillas. The next day Lieutenant Colonel Hanifin received orders ''to break contact and withdraw.''[21] As the Pacific Command's contingency force, Admiral Sharp had ordered the SLF to be reembarked and sail for Indonesian waters where Communist forces had attempted to overthrow the government. The first DAGGER THRUST series was over.

Colonel Ewers observed that although he believed the overall concept was valid, the DAGGER THRUST operations revealed several limitations, especially in planning and command relations. The SLF commander declared that the intelligence was dated and that the SLF/ARG staffs should have been more involved in the planning. He claimed that the detailed scheme of maneuver prepared at the amphibious task force commander's level allowed almost no flexibility on the part of the BLT commander. Ewers concluded:

> In amphibious raiding the initiative is ours and there is no compelling reason to rush from target to target. . .BLT planners were harried by changes and the urgent requirements of naval counterparts.[22]

Ewers' position was supported by other Marine commanders. In a later report, General Krulak also

maintained that the raid concept was sound, declaring that ''raids cause VC in an area to move . . . exhibit a U.S. presence . . . and . . . serve as excellent training for battalions to be committed . . . .'' Like Ewers, the FMFPac commander was of the opinion that ''the full impact of these benefits has not been realized . . . a review of target intelligence and planning procedures would appear prudent.''[23]

Further Changes in the SLF

Several changes occurred in October following the release of the ARG/SLF from the Indonesian alert. Captain Thomas R. Weschler, USN, relieved Captain Scott as the ARG commander. There was also an exchange of amphibious shipping. The new ARG consisted of the USS *Valley Forge* (LPH 8), USS *Montrose* (APA 212), and USS *Monticello* (LSD 35). At the same time, 11 October, Lieutenant Colonel Mervin B. Porter's HMM-261 replaced HMM-163 as the SLF helicopter squadron and Porter also relieved Ewers as the SLF commander.

The relief of units and shipping was relatively routine and had been planned for some time, but Generals Krulak and Fields took this occasion to institute their long-delayed restructuring of the SLF command and staff. On 17 October, General Krulak notified Headquarters Marine Corps that ''due to accelerated tempo . . . increased complexity of command and control, and for continuity,'' General Fields was assigning a Marine colonel ''with an initial staff of 3 officers and 5 enlisted men'' to the SLF.[24] General Fields decided to make his TF 79 chief of staff, Colonel John R. Burnett, the new SLF commander, rather than Colonel Winstead, who remained as TF 78 and RAMAB commander. According to General Fields:

> It was obvious that the commander of the RAMAB was of little consequence to me at the time and particularly to the operations of the SLF. He, naturally, could advise CTF 76, but he could never command the SLF as such. I decided to let him be and designated my Chief of Staff, Colonel Burnett, who had been a naval aviator and was an excellent solid Marine versed in all aspects of operations in the area, as Commander of the SLF.[25]

The SLF kept the 78.5 designator, and thus, on paper, remained subordinate to RAMAB. Nevertheless, Krulak and Fields, without directly challenging Admiral Blackburn, not only strengthened the SLF commander's position vis-a-vis his Navy counterpart, but made the RAMAB headquarters obviously superfluous. Colonel Burnett assumed command of the SLF from Lieutenant Colonel Porter on 18 October. With the SLF reconstituted and restructured, American planners began discussing a second series of DAGGER THRUST raids.

The Saigon Conference

The Marines were not the only ones who were unhappy with the command and control of the SLF and the DAGGER THRUST raids. During a discussion with General Walt in July, General Westmoreland indicated his dissatisfaction with the limited authority he enjoyed over the force.[26] The MACV commander wanted an arrangement in which it would be unnecessary for him to go to the Seventh Fleet when he wanted the SLF. Furthermore, MACV and CinCPacFlt had debated, since the Chu Lai landing in May, what criteria should be used to establish an amphibious objective area (AOA) during an amphibious landing or raid in Vietnam. According to doctrine, the amphibious task force commander controlled all air, land, and sea forces in the geographical area delineated as the AOA during an amphibious operation. In Vietnam, this raised two specific questions which impinged

upon Westmoreland's authority and South Vietnam's sovereignty ''the control of air traffic within the AOA . . . and coordination with friendly ground forces who are conducting operations inland within the perimeter of the AOA.''[27]

After the first DAGGER THRUST raids, on 8 October General Westmoreland proposed a joint MACV-CinCPacFleet conference in Saigon to discuss the raids and to plan future ones. He suggested a 10-point agenda which included critiques of DAGGER THRUST I, II, and III from both Seventh Fleet and MACV perspectives; intelligence for future raids; target acquisitions; and ''resolution of amphibious objective area and restricted air space problems for future raids.''[28] Admiral Johnson' agreed to the conference and added some agenda items of his own. The CinCPacFleet Commander, like General Westmoreland, wanted to resolve the AOA problem and was willing to make some concessions. He directed that Navy and FMFPac representatives to the conference hold to a ''Navy/Marine position which will allow flexibility within the AOA, but will not weaken the doctrine. . . .''[29]

The conference took place on 26-28 October 1965 in Saigon. Captain Weschler, the ARG comander, as the senior officer present, served as chairman. There were representatives from the various MACV component commands, including III MAF and 2d Air Division, as well as the amphibious commands under the jurisdiction of CinCPacFleet. During the two-day meeting, the conferees came to several understandings. They agreed on three specific targets for the next series of DAGGER THRUST raids, but at the same time called for a revision of the criteria for establishing targets. They planned for the new series of raids to take place from 25 November through 7 December and allowed that ''predicated on the early approval and dissemination of revised target list and success of in-country briefings, the requirement for specific raid notification can be reduced'' from 60 to 24 hours. They settled the sensitive issue of command and control of air and ground units in the AOA by simply reducing the AOAs used during the previous DAGGER THRUST raids ''to a 10-mile arc inland and a 25-mile arc seaward unless specific target situation dictates an increase.'' This decision satisfied both sides, for the time being. MACV could work with the restrictions imposed on it by the 10-mile inland arc, while the reduced AOA still permitted the Navy amphibious task force commander to control naval gunfire and other supporting arms including aviation. The amphibious commander was to reserve a 10-nautical-mile-wide air corridor at an altitude of 7,000 to 10,000 feet for civilian aircraft. This compromise was possible without any violation of amphibious doctrine since the chances of any enemy air opposition were nil and because of the limited range of the VC antiaircraft weapons.[30]

The Second Series of DAGGER THRUST Raids

By 10 November both Admiral Johnson and General Westmoreland approved the recommendations of the Saigon conference and the Seventh Fleet amphibious forces began preparing for the next DAGGER THRUSTs. After completion of detailed plans on 26 November, the ARG/SLF, which earlier in the month had been the floating reserve for the BLUE MARLIN operations, sailed for the DAGGER THRUST IV amphibious objective area, Lang Ke Ga, in III Corps. This VC-controlled and suspected infiltration point was on the coast, 90 miles east of Saigon.

For DAGGER THRUST IV, the Marines and Navy had made some more changes in command and control. Although Admiral Wulzen in the USS *Eldorado* (AGC 11) had joined the amphibious task group, Captain Weschler, the ARG commander, retained his position as amphibious task force commander. Colonel Burnett, the SLF commander, was to be the commander of the landing force, unlike the earlier DAGGER THRUST raids when this position was assumed by the TF 78/RAMAB commander. Admiral Blackburn had bowed to the inevitable and, on 24 November, announced his intention to dissolve TF 78. In the interim, he made General Fields commander of both TF 78 and TF 79.[31]

DAGGER THRUST IV followed the same pattern as the earlier DAGGER THRUST raids. On 30 November, the SLF battalion landed as planned at Lang Ke Ga, but, with the exception of scattered tank traps in the beach area and isolated incidents of small arms fire, it encountered no opposition. The next day the battalion reembarked, ending the operation, with no casualties to either side.

The final DAGGER THRUST raid, DAGGER THRUST V began on 5 December near the Phu Thu

Navy Photo 1114070A

Marines of BLT 2/1 run to board HMM-261 helicopters on board the Valley Forge *(LPH 8) during Operation DAGGER THRUST V, in December 1965. The white-capped Navy crewman in the left forefront has just led the Marines to their specific helicopter.*

village complex, 40 miles north of Qui Nhon. This time the battalion was moderately successful, surprising a small VC force. During the two-day operation, the Marines killed 26 enemy and detained 38 suspects. The Marine battalion sustained casualties of three dead and 10 wounded. In retrospect, the DAGGER THRUST raids failed to achieve their overall objective, the quick exploitation of intelligence and resulting contact with large enemy formations. Admiral Johnson, several years later, observed:

> The excessive time involved in planning and coordinating with the MACV levels resulted in completely stale intelligence. Furthermore, by the time MACV had completed his all important coordination and alerting of ARVN forces and Province Chiefs, we had also completely spooked the VC and they had flown the coop.[32]

The SLF at the End of the Year

Following the completion of DAGGER THRUST V, Colonel Burnett attended the final III MAF planning briefing for Operation HARVEST MOON on 8 December. General Walt had requested that the SLF be assigned as the reserve force for the multibattalion U.S. Marine-ARVN operation in the Que Son Valley. The enemy was the old STARLITE foe, the *1st VC Regiment*. Both MACV and CinCPacFlt approved the request, and the SLF helicopter squadron was committed to the operation on 9 December. The infantry battalion landed the next day. When the operation ended on 19 December, the SLF reembarked in its shipping. Hanifin's battalion suffered 12 dead and 52 wounded during the extended operation.

After HARVEST MOON, the SLF underwent further changes in unit composition and designation. On 21 December, Hanifin's battalion was unloaded at the mouth of the Hue River and replaced Lieutenant Colonel Sumner A. Vale's 3d Battalion, 4th Marines at Phu Bai. The latter battalion embarked on the SLF ships for a return voyage to Okinawa as a unit of the FMFPac intratheater transplacement program. At the same time, Vice Admiral John J. Hyland, who had relieved Admiral Blackburn earlier in the month as Seventh Fleet commander, officially dissolved the RAMAB/TF 78 headquarters. The SLF assumed the fleet designation TG 79.5 and reported administratively to General Fields in his capacity as CG TF 79. On 29 December,

BLT 3/4 landed at Okinawa and on New Year's Eve, BLT 2/3, commanded by Lieutenant Colonel William K. Horn, became the new SLF battalion.[33]

During the year, the SLF proved its value as a mobile floating reserve. Although the results of the DAGGER THRUST raids were less than expected, the SLF air and ground units played important roles in both STARLITE and HARVEST MOON. The SLF served as a successful contingency force for the Qui Nhon landing in July, and, later in the year, during the Indonesian crisis. By the end of 1965, the organizational problems with the Navy had been resolved and some of the doctrinal debates with MACV had been temporarily put aside. Nevertheless the questions about the extent of the amphibious objective area and command and control of forces in the AOA would continue to arise periodically for the rest of the war.*

---

* The former Pacific Fleet commander, Admiral Roy L. Johnson, remarked: "Command relationships and who exercised operational control over what, where, and when were controversial in varying degrees from the very beginning of active involvement of U. S. forces in N. and S. Vietnam." In reference to the Seventh Fleet amphibious forces, the former CinCPacFlt stated that the "ARG/SLF was kicked around and whipsawed more than any other operational unit that I can think of." Admiral Johnson declared that much of this "had its genesis in the CTF 79/78 arguments." He did not believe that the establishment of TF 78 (RAMAB) was a good solution, but stated that Admiral Blackburn did not have "very many options open to him." Admiral Johnson faulted the Marines for not being willing to appoint a full time CTF 79 (Commanding General, FMF Seventh Fleet), and this failure, the former Pacific Fleet commander claimed, seriously diluted "the command prerogative of Com7thFlt . . . ." He also observed that "There were others who had designs on control of the SLF, notably MACV, who did not want to be bothered with going through any [other] command if he wanted to use them in some emergency of his determination." Adm Roy L. Johnson, Comments on draft MS, dtd 12Aug77 (Vietnam Comment File). Admiral John J. Hyland, who relieved Admiral Blackburn as Commander Seventh Fleet in November 1965, commented in the same vein as Admiral Johnson: "The potential problem with the SLF had nothing to do with its performance or its excellence or its utilization. The difficulty was principally a political one between Navy and Army doctrine. . . . Specifically with regard to the SLF the Army wanted operational control. I always felt that once they had been given it they never would have released it, and the SLF would simply become another Army unit ashore. We would never be able to get it back aboard ship for use in some other area which might be more important." Adm John J. Hyland, Comments on draft MS, dtd 3Aug77 (Vietnam Comment File).

CHAPTER 14

Advisors and Other Marine Activities

Marine Advisors to the Vietnamese Marine Corps—Marine Advisors to the Rung Sat Special Zone—U.S. Marines of the I Corps Advisory Group—Marines Serving with MACV Headquarters in Saigon—Company L, Marine Support Battalion—Embassy Marines

Marine Advisors to the Vietnamese Marine Corps

The Marine Corps principal advisory effort outside of I Corps was with the Vietnamese Marine Corps. Headquartered in Saigon and under the operational control of the MACV Naval Advisory Group, the Marine Advisory Unit, commanded by Colonel William P. Nesbit, functioned as the advisory liaison link between the South Vietnamese Marines and the American command. At the beginning of 1965, the Marine Advisory Unit had an authorized strength of 19 officers and one enlisted man. The Marine Advisory Unit consisted of the senior Marine advisor, his deputy, 5 major or captain infantry battalion advisors, 1 captain artillery advisor, and 10 lieutenant advisors, 6 of whom served as assistant advisors to the battalions. The remaining four lieutenants served as motor transport, supply, communications, and engineer advisors. One noncommissioned officer served as the unit's administrative assistant.*

At this time the South Vietnamese Marine Corps consisted of a Marine brigade (VNMB) of five infantry battalions supported by its own artillery and amphibious support battalions. The Commandant, Brigadier General Le Nguyen Khang, who had led the Vietnamese Marines since 1960 except for a short three-month period following the Diem coup, was also the Commander of the Capital Military Region, Saigon and the surrounding area, and reported

directly to the Joint General Staff.** The Vietnamese Marine battalions together with the South Vietnamese airborne brigade made up the nation's strategic reserve, and normally operated as "fire brigade" reinforcements wherever needed in Vietnam. One Marine battalion always remained near Saigon, ostensibly to protect the capital. Although Khang was responsible for administrative and logistic support of his units, he had operational control only over those battalions in the Capital Military Region.

The South Vietnamese Marine Corps (VNMC) had suffered its worst defeat of the war on 31 December 1964, when the *9th VC Division* eliminated the 4th Battalion of the VNMC as an effective fighting force near Binh Gia, a Catholic resettlement village 40 miles east of Saigon.*** Major Lane Rogers, advisor to the 3d VNMC Battalion, who had volunteered on 1 January to go to Binh Gia and assist with the evacuation of the dead and wounded, recalled:

> The next three days were spent searching for bodies; we found more than 100 (friendlies) and no VC. . . . The body hunt was a mess. It was stinking hot and you could not get away from the smell. . . . The third day, after finally getting bodybags . . . we bagged up the 4th Battalion bodies.[1]

Rogers remembered that Colonel Nguyen Thanh Yen, the Assistant Commandant of the Vietnamese Marine Corps, was in charge of the body recovery operation and had issued "vats of local saki" to the

---

*MACV strength reports of 31 December 1964 listed the actual strength of the Marine Advisory Unit as 22 officers and seven enlisted. Seven of these Marines were performing temporary duty as on-the-job trainees from the 3d Marine Division. This program ended in April 1965.

**On 5 January, the Vietnamese Marine Corps became a separate service from the Vietnamese Navy, although for a two-week period in April General Khang also served as the Navy CNO when the Joint General Staff ousted the then CNO, Rear Admiral Chung Tan Cang.

***See Whitlow, *U.S. Marines in Vietnam, 1954-64*, for a detailed account of the Binh Gia battle.

USMC Photo A186435

Colonel John A. MacNeil, senior Marine advisor, inspects Vietnamese Marines' M-1 rifles. Material readiness was a matter of primary concern for the Marine Advisory Unit in 1965.

working party, all survivors from the 4th Battalion. The American Marine advisor later remarked:

> We were all sick . . . (and so you can guess what the ''bag detail'' was like). That evening we loaded troops and bodies into about ten 6x6s and drove off to Vung Tau. As we made the turn at Ba Ria onto Route 15 . . . one of the body bags rolled off one of the trucks. The messy recovery action drew a crowd and the wailing started. The word was out that the 4th Battalion was wiped out.[2]

The results of Binh Gia were an ominous portent for 1965. MACV and the South Vietnamese command feared that the Viet Cong Communists might be ready to enter into the final phase of their war to take over the county. At the time, no one knew the exact size of the enemy force that had defeated the government units at Binh Gia. Rumors abounded, including one that the VC had been led by a general riding a white horse. Even discounting such stories, the South Vietnamese Joint General Staff knew the enemy force had been larger than any encountered before, although it was not until later that MACV learned that the Communists had formed the *9th VC Division* from two independent regiments. After clearing the Binh Gia battlefield, the South Vietnamese Joint General Staff ordered a joint airborne and Marine operation to find and destroy the Communist attacking force. In response to the Joint General Staff order, the Vietnamese Marine Brigade launched Operation NGUYEN VAN NHO, named

after the slain commander of the 4th Battalion. General Khang committed all three of his effective infantry battalions (the 5th Battalion was still being formed) to the operation. He maintained one battalion in reserve near the brigade's headquarters at Vung Tau while establishing a two-battalion task force headquarters under Colonel Yen at Ba Ria (Phuoc Le), 14 miles to the north. The two forward battalions then swept a 25-square-mile area extending 10 miles northeast of Ba Ria and including Binh Gia.

The results of the operation, which lasted until 7 February, were disappointing. According to Colonel Nesbit, NGUYEN VAN NHO, under brigade control, revealed the weaknesses of the brigade staff in directing a large force in the field and the ''inadequacy of the brigade TO [Table of Organization] for sustained operations.'' In order to fully man the advisory staff billets for the two headquarters, FMFPac provided eight Marine officers and 11 enlisted men while MACV sent two officers and seven enlisted men. Although this improvised American advisory staff quickly established itself at Vung Tau ''and functioned well,'' Colonel Nesbit described the operation ''as one of cautious defense, and therefore not eminently successful in destroying VC.''[3] Another Marine advisor, Major William G. Leftwich, Jr., called the operation ''lethargic'' and observed that the task force headquarters played a static role while the ''two battalions operated sometimes independently and sometimes in concert.''[4] Even more bluntly, Major Rogers provided the following description of the operation:

> [Colonel] Yen was TF Commander at Ba Ria, while General Khang commanded from Vung Tau. . . . I was (briefly, thank God) TF advisor to Yen at Ba Ria and did nothing there, nor did Yen. . . . We found no VC, no caches, no traces, nothing. Reportedly the VC were long gone. I was told the Airborne [operating north of the Marines] did find some rice. As for the ''VC general,'' the ''VC Division,'' the general's ''white horse,'' we never saw a sign.[5]

Following the end of NGUYEN VAN NHO, the Joint General Staff ordered General Khang to send a VNMC task force to II Corps to bolster the ARVN forces holding Binh Dinh Province. Once more Colonel Yen commanded the task force headquarters, now called Task Force ALPHA. Absorbing some of the lessons learned during the NGUYEN VAN NHO campaign, TF ALPHA consisted of a 72-man headquarters and two infantry battalions, the

1st and 3d, and totaled 1,360 men.* The Marine Advisory Unit also beefed up its advisory effort to the task force by providing a two-man headquarters team headed by Major Leftwich in addition to the four-battalion advisors. Arriving at Bong Son, Yen reported to the Commanding General, 22d ARVN Division.

On 9 March, Task Force ALPHA had its first significant encounter with the enemy. Yen's Marines evaded a planned ambush by the *2d VC Regiment*. The VNMC force had been ordered south from Bong Son that day to provide relief for the besieged district town of Hai An. Before leaving Bong Son, Yen learned from intelligence sources that while one VC battalion had entered the town, another had been positioned along the road to ambush any relief column. The Marine force conducted a 10-mile forced march and struck the flank of the VC ambush.

Major Leftwich played a significant role in the action that followed. Before leaving Bong Son, the Marine advisor arranged for tactical air support and when contact was established with the Viet Cong late that afternoon, he moved forward with the assault elements to control air strikes against the enemy positions. As darkness set in, the outmaneuvered enemy disengaged, leaving behind 63 dead. Thus, the Marines had forced the relief of Hai An. Task Force ALPHA casualties were four killed and 11 wounded, including the two headquarters advisors; Major Leftwich was wounded, and his assistant, First Lieutenant Dempsey H. Williams, was killed.[6]**

One month later, the 2d VNMC Battalion tangled with the *2d VC Regiment*.*** At midnight on 7 April, elements of the *93d, 95th*, and *97th Viet Cong*

Battalions struck the defensive position of the Vietnamese Marines. The battle raged for five hours during which the Vietnamese Leathernecks repulsed 10 consecutive waves of attackers. As daylight neared, the *2d VC Regiment* withdrew leaving behind 59 dead, 10 wounded, and 71 weapons. Intelligence sources later stated that the Viet Cong had carried away another 70 dead and over 200 wounded. Marine losses were remarkably low considering the ferocity of the action. Four Marines had been killed and 22 wounded. For its heroic stand, the 2d VNMC Battalion was later awarded the U.S. Presidential Unit Citation.[7]

Task Force ALPHA, which remained in II Corps for the balance of 1965, fought one other significant engagement with the enemy. On the 5th of August, the Special Forces camp at Duc Co near the Cambodian border was attacked by a VC regiment. Three days later, Task Force ALPHA and an ARVN armored task force, departed Pleiku to relieve the Duc Co garrison. The next day, they came into heavy contact with a NVA battalion dug in astride Route 19. The South Vietnamese attacked and dislodged the enemy, only to have the rear of the column attacked by another reinforced NVA battalion. Battered by air strikes all night long, the enemy unit, later identified as the *32d NVA Regiment*, launched a final attack at dawn and then withdrew from the battlefield. The next day, the South Vietnamese moved into Duc Co and broke the siege. The South Vietnamese infantry, with the support of U.S. and VNAF air strikes, claimed to have killed over 400 of the enemy and captured 71 weapons. VNMC losses were 28 killed, 60 wounded, and 3 missing. Significantly, the 5th VNMC Battalion, which had become operational on 22 May and then replaced the 2d Battalion two weeks later, had acquitted itself well in this its first major combat action. The battle was the first major contact with North Vietnamese forces operating in South Vietnam.[8]

While two VNMC battalions operated continuously with Task Force ALPHA, the other infantry battalions also saw extensive action. Two were assigned as a major reaction force to be used anywhere in South Vietnam while the remaining one was held near Saigon under the control of General Khang in his capacity as Capital Military Region commander.

Several indications of increased combat effectiveness began to appear after mid-year. In

---

*Although the authorized strength of the battalions was 931 men each, in 1965 Marine battalions only reached this strength when they returned to their base camps; a field strength of 600 was not uncommon. Each battalion maintained its own base camp and a handful of troops, including wounded, remained behind as guards and logistic and administrative support.

**For their actions, Major Leftwich was awarded the Navy Cross and Lieutenant Williams posthumously awarded the Silver Star Medal. Major Leftwich returned to his duties as Task Force ALPHA senior advisor on 25 March after 17 days hospitalization.

***The 2d Battalion had replaced the 3d on 9 March. Throughout 1965, the battalions of Task Force ALPHA rotated about every three months between other assignments and II Corps.

Captain William H. Bond, senior Marine advisor to the 4th Vietnamese Marine Battalion, checks machine gun alinement with Captain Do Dinh Vuong, commander of the battalion's 4th Company. Note the Vietnamese Marine Corps insignia on Captain Do's cap.

November 1965, the two-battalion Task Force ALPHA achieved a casualty ratio of five to one in favor of the Marines. On 10 November, the 3d Battalion participated with the 2d Battalion, 7th Marines in an amphibious landing from Seventh Fleet Ships during Operation BLUE MARLIN. South Vietnamese Marine morale was on the rise, as evidenced by a declining desertion rate in the second half of 1965.

Many problems still remained especially in logistics, administration, delegation of authority, unit training, and assumption of responsibility by junior officers and noncommissioned officers. Both Colonel Nesbit and his successor, Colonel John A. MacNeil, who relieved Nesbit in September, continued to work on correcting shortcomings.[9]

The senior Marine advisors, supported by General Westmoreland, objected to a Joint General Staff mid-year plan to form a sixth Marine battalion in the fall

of 1965. Colonel Nesbit pointed out to General Khang that it would be best to wait until July 1966 ''when the present five battalions would be better operationally and some prior planning could be done.''[10] Khang accepted the American advice and postponed the formation of the 6th VNMC Battalion until 1966. The South Vietnamese Marine staff and the Marine Advisory Unit, nevertheless, continued to plan for the expansion of the South Vietnamese Marine Corps.

The Marine Advisory Unit also grew in size, corresponding with the expansion and planned expansion of the Vietnamese Marine Brigade. In May, five more billets were added to the advisory unit. These included: an operations officer/task force advisor (major); an amphibious support advisor (major); an administrative specialist (warrant officer); an administrative clerk (corporal); and a supplyman (staff sergeant). In November, MACV authorized two Marine advisors for the planned 6th Vietnamese Marine battalion and a Navy chief hospital corpsman was added as medical advisor. By the end of 1965, the Marine Advisory Unit had an authorized strength of 24 officers, 1 warrant officer, and 4 enlisted men.*[11]

Marine Advisors to the Rung Sat Special Zone

The Rung Sat Special Zone (RSSZ) was an area of about 400 square miles, 85 percent of which is dense mangrove swamp. Literally translated, Rung Sat means ''assassins' forest'' and was so named because of the bandits and rebels who inhabited its marshlands. It lies along the Long Tao River which connects Saigon with the South China Sea.

On 15 April 1964, responsibility for the Rung Sat was assigned to the Vietnamese Navy (VNN). Lieutenant Commander Nguyen Van Tai, a former VNMC major, was assigned to command the 1,200-man military garrison which consisted of six Regional Force companies, 13 Popular Force platoons, and one river boat company (eight LCVPs).

Since all Rung Sat operations would be amphibious efforts and the VNN had been assigned primary responsibility for the area, the U.S. Naval Advisory Group requested U.S. Marines to advise the Viet-

---

*The MACV history shows the actual strength of the Marine Advisory Unit on 31 December 1965 as 25 officers and five enlisted. *MACV Comd Hist 1965*, p. 90.

namese forces. The advisory staff consisted of a U.S. Marine major as senior military advisor to the Rung Sat Special Zone and a headquarters team of three officers and two enlisted and two subsector teams, each with one officer and three enlisted.[12]

Major Edward J. Bronars, who arrived in Vietnam during the summer of 1964, was the first senior military advisor to the Rung Sat Special Zone. On 30 July 1965, Major Albert C. Smith, Jr., succeeded Bronars as the senior advisor and remained in that position through the end of the year. During this period, the authorized number of U.S. advisors in the Rung Sat was reduced to nine, eight Marines and one Navy corpsman. In addition to the billet of senior advisor, there were two other officer billets, an infantry advisor and an intelligence advisor. The five enlisted billets were operations, intelligence, psychlogical warfare, communication, and Navy hospital corpsman.[13]*

Advisor duties encompassed aiding the Vietnamese in planning and executing small amphibious operations to rid the Rung Sat of the Viet Cong hiding in its swamps. Advisors accompanied the Vietnamese troops on all operations. The Marines also arranged for coordinated aerial observation of the Rung Sat, close air support of operations, and naval gunfire spotters and liaison personnel whenever U.S. warships were available for support. Requests for medical evacuation, flare ship support, photo reconnaissance, and command and control helicopter support were also initiated by the advisory staff.[14]

U.S. Marines of the I Corps Advisory Group

In September 1964, the Marine Corps agreed to furnish 60 Marines to the I Corps Advisory Group to assist the U.S. Army in advising the 1st and 2d ARVN Divisions. These 24 officer and 36 enlisted billets were intermingled with the Army advisory positions of the 1st through 6th ARVN Regiments and the artillery battalions of both divisional and corps artillery.

General Westmoreland proposed to General Greene, the Marine Corps Commandant, during the

USMC Photo A186444

Communications advisor to the Rung Sat Special Zone, Marine Sergeant Raymond S. Komo, stands guard on the banks of the Long Tao River as a Vietnamese Regional Force mortar team sets up. The Long Tao was the northern tributary feeding into the Rung Sat.

latter's visit to Saigon in April 1965, that the Marine Corps should take over the entire advisory responsibility for ICTZ. This proposal would have raised the number of Marine advisors in I Corps to about 800 men.[15] The plan was never implemented, but on 7 August General Walt assumed the role of senior U.S. advisor to I Corps and became responsible for the U.S. military advisory effort in the five northern provinces. The makeup of the I Corps advisory group remained predominately Army.**

---

* The MACV Strength Report 1Jan65, dtd 11Jan65, p. 77, indicates that the advisory staff of the Rung Sat Special Zone on 1 January consisted of 13 Marines, seven permanently assigned to fill nine permanent billets and six assigned under long-term temporary duty (in excess of 120 days).

** The exact number of Marines serving as advisors in I Corps is not known. The authors have not been able to uncover any Joint Table of Distribution for the I Corps Advisory Group that would provide this information. Furthermore, all Marine advisors in 1965 administratively were carried on the roles of Headquarters Battalion, HQMC. The unit diary entries for many of these Marines do not indicate the assignment to a specific unit, but simply state "assigned to advisory duty MACV." MACV strength figures show a total of 98 Marines serving in an advisory capacity on 31 December 1965 throughout Vietnam. (*MACV Comd Hist, 1965*, Table -II-6). A MACV Joint Table of Distribution for the Naval Advisory Group shows 53 Marines authorized to that command including the Marines in the Rung Sat and serving as advisors to the Vietnamese Marine Corps. (USMACV, US Naval Advisory Group, Joint Table of Distribution, dtd 15Nov65 (OAB, NHD). Presumably 45 Marines were serving as advisors in I Corps.

USMC Photo A183650

Major Charles ''Uncle Charles'' K. Whitfield, artillery advisor (on the left of the picture), and his assistants, Captain Richard J. Coogan (extreme right) and Staff Sergeant Ronald M. Blakely (third from right) supervise gun laying. During 1965, the Vietnamese Marine artillery battalion was converting from the 75mm pack howitzer to the 105mm howitzer as pictured.

The Marines in the I Corps Advisory Group were assigned to battalion advisory teams consisting of two officers, a noncommissioned officer, and a radioman. Marine captains occupied positions as senior battalion advisors, while lieutenants became assistant battalion advisors. The Marine infantry and artillery noncommissioned officers served as weapons advisors, and the Marine radiomen manned the advisor communications network.

The role of advisor to the Vietnamese Armed Forces during 1965 was a difficult task, but one with many rewards. Major Letfwich, after serving with the Marine Advisory Unit, provided the following advice to future Marine advisors, and indeed any advisor:

> So much has been written about the advisory business that I felt some sort of mystic aura has grown up around the much overworked subject of ''rapport.'' My modest experience with the Vietnamese, and that of many others,

is that they generally recognize, admire, and respond to the same qualities that we—or any nationality do. There are peculiar customs to be sure, but these are insignificant beside those characteristics that transcend all boundaries of language and nationality. The officer who is knowledgeable in his trade, unafraid of work, well-mannered, and possessed of a sense of humor will succeed here as he does everywhere else. . . . A single American is obviously casting his lot with his counterparts and is generally accepted on this basis, unless he isolates himself by his own misactions.[16]

Marines Serving with MACV Headquarters in Saigon

On 1 January 1965, 25 Marines were serving on the MACV staff in Saigon. The senior Marine was General Westmoreland's J-2, Brigadier General Carl A. Youngdale, who had filled the billet of MACV intelligence officer since January 1964. When

General Youngdale completed his overseas tour on 13 July, he was not replaced by another Marine.*

Early in 1965, a discussion took place between the Department of the Army and ComUSMACV over the replacement of Youngdale. Although the joint staff of MACV was already preponderantly Army, U. S. Army authorities thought that the billet should be assigned to an Army brigadier. General Westmoreland explained:

> Much of the MACV staff consists of a purely Army advisory effort and results in a staff which appears to be heavily weighted with Army personnel. The RVNAF and Joint General Staff organizations are both predominately Army and demand a large Army contingent in the MACV staff.[17]

When the Marine Corps informed General Westmoreland in March that it would not be able to provide an officer of equal rank to replace Youngdale, the matter was settled and the billet was assigned to the Army.

With the rapid influx of American troops into Vietnam, the authorized strength of the MACV staff grew from 1,702 men in January to 2,427 servicemen at the end of 1965. Marine Corps billets on the joint staff correspondingly increased to 131 that year. Because of the time requirements necessary to transfer personnel overseas, only 56 of these positions had been filled by 31 December.

During 1965, 35 Marine officers arrived to fill staff positions. Among these officers were Colonels George L. Hollowell, Chief, Operations Branch, J-3; Webb D. Sawyer, Chief, Plans Branch, J-4; Maxie R. Williams, Chief, US/SEATO Division; and Francis F. Parry, Combat Operations Center.

On 11 November, a MACV steering committee recommended the establishment of a combat operations center within the J-3 Division to provide a centralized MACV agency for the collection and dissemination of information to enhance MACV direction of operations and control of subordinate commands. General Westmoreland approved the recommendation and proposed to Admiral Sharp that the operations center be headed by a Marine Corps

brigadier general. After consulting with General Greene and the other Joint Chiefs, Sharp concurred.[18]

When the Combat Operations Center was activated in mid-November, its first director was a Marine, Colonel Parry. Describing his assignment to the MACV staff, Parry stated when he departed for Vietnam the previous month, he was told that he was to be the plans officer for a joint command. Upon arrival, he discovered that MACV had decided not to activate such a command and he was assigned, instead, to the MACV J-3 Division. Colonel Parry remembered that: ''After several days in J-3 Operations learning the ropes, Bill DePuy [Brigadier General William E. DePuy (USA), the MACV J-3] called me in and told me that General Westmoreland had decided to organize a Combat Operations Center.'' According to Parry, General DePuy told him that the ''Air Force was holding up the assignment of a Marine BG to MACV because they wanted more general officer slots on the staff. Bill asked me to organize the COC and be its director until such time as the Marine BG arrived.''[19] Marine Brigadier General William K. Jones relieved Colonel Parry as director of the Combat Operations Center on 31 December 1965.

Another Marine MACV staff officer, Colonel Webb D. Sawyer, recalled his service as head of MACV J-4 Plans Branch:

> From the time of the landing of the Marine Brigade, throughout the buildup of forces within Vietnam, the logistic planners at MACV never came down from the overhead. It was a never ending cycle of short-fuzed studies, high level conferences in Honolulu, SEATO logistic planning meetings in Bangkok, and consultations with ARVN.[20]

Confronted with this myriad of problems, Sawyer found his job challenging but satisfying. He concluded: ''Anyway, all in all, it was a most exciting and interesting year.''[21]

Company L, Marine Support Battalion

One small and unheralded Marine unit, Company L, Marine Support Battalion, redesignated on 1 January 1965 from Subunit 1, Company C, Marine Support Battalion, provided a vital intelligence function for MACV during 1965. Headquartered at Phu Bai with the Army's 8th Radio Research Unit, the unit consisted of one officer and 31 enlisted cryptologists. The company was augmented by one

---

*According to Colonel Webb D. Sawyer, General Westmoreland appointed him ''Commanding Officer of the Marine Corps Unit, Headquarters, U. S. Military Assistance Command, Vietnam,'' in that he had become the senior Marine on the MACV staff upon the departure of General Youngdale. BGen Webb D. Sawyer, Comments on draft MS, dtd 25Oct76 (Vietnam Comment File).

officer and 10 enlisted men from Naval Communications Station, Philippines. Both contingents formed Detachment ALPHA, NavComSta, Philippines. Captain Donald J. Hatch, the Company L commander, was also the Detachment ALPHA commander. On 21 July, Major William A. Scott, Jr., relieved Captain Hatch. By the end of December, Company L consisted of two officers and 77 enlisted Marine cryptologists. Captain Hatch observed:

> The stationing of this unit in Vietnam was an outgrowth of a detachment from the First Composite Radio Company, FMFPac having been in country on a TAD basis for many months. Company L was the first permanent unit assigned.[22]

Embassy Marines

The Marine Security Guard, led by Staff Sergeant William D. Kerakos, at the American Embassy in Saigon numbered 30 men. The mission of the Marines was to safeguard classified material and to protect U. S. personnel and property. During the year the detachment established two new watches, one at the U. S. Information Service Building and the other at the home of the Deputy Ambassador. An individual guard was on post an average of 49 hours a week.

During periods of political unrest, the guards were kept busy preventing Vietnamese street crowds from entering the Embassy. The physical threat against the building became a reality on the morning of 30 March when a bomb, secreted in a car across the street from the Embassy, exploded. The blast killed 11 persons and wounded 163, and did extensive damage to the building. A secretary to the Deputy Ambassador was the only American fatality, but 52 U. S. citizens were injured. The other dead victims were Vietnamese nationals, four policemen, the civilian driver for the Marine guard, and a Viet Cong terrorist. All of the Marines escaped unscathed. Off duty personnel immediately returned to the Embassy. The building was closed, a security check conducted; by mid-afternoon the Embassy was back to normal routine. This incident, more than any other during 1965, demonstrated to the detachment that it too was in the frontlines.

CHAPTER 15

Conclusion

The 10-month period of March to December 1965 was one of expansion and experimentation for Marine forces in Vietnam. During the year, Marine units from California to Okinawa prepared for deployment to Vietnam. General Karch's 9,000 Marines of the 9th MEB were quickly absorbed by the division-wing force, III MAF. By the end of the year, General Walt had over 42,000 men in ICTZ. Since the landing on 8 March, the Marines had extended their influence from eight square miles around the Da Nang Airfield to three coastal enclaves containing over 804 square miles.

As III MAF's TAORs expanded into the densely populated coastal ricelands, the Marines found the Viet Cong intermingled with the local villagers and turned to a variety of pacification experiments to ferret out the Communists and win back the population. They employed counterguerrilla techniques such as combined action companies and civic action projects such as the GOLDEN FLEECE rice harvesting operations. By the end of 1965, the Marines were still unable to measure many real pacification gains.

General Walt's balanced approach for the elimination of the Communist threat initially stressed the establishment of secure beachheads at Da Nang, Chu Lai, and Phu Bai. During the March-June consolidation phase the Marines lost 34 killed and 157 wounded, while killing 270 Viet Cong. By mid-1965 with this phase completed, III MAF began a two-pronged campaign to destroy main force Communist units, and at the same time root out the Viet Cong infrastructure. Operations STARLITE and HARVEST MOON encountered the Viet Cong in regimental strength. During the last six months of 1965 the Marines suffered 420 killed and 1,936 wounded, while killing 2,295 enemy soldiers and capturing more than 700 weapons.[1]

There could be no doubt that large-scale, conventional operations were to play a much larger role during the coming year. By the end of 1965, General Westmoreland's intelligence staff estimated that eight regular NVA regiments had arrived in South Vietnam. General Walt had received approval of his request for two full divisions and a reinforced aircraft wing. The 1st Marine Division was scheduled for deployment to I CTZ in early 1966, as were more aircraft squadrons.

Despite the emphasis on troop movement, reinforcement, and engagement of the enemy's larger units, the war was far from conventional. General Krulak cautioned:

> The conflict between the North Vietnamese and the hardcore VC on the one hand and the U. S. on the other hand could move to another planet today and we would still not have won the war. On the other hand if the subversion and guerrilla efforts were to disappear, the war would soon collapse as the Viet Cong would be denied food, sanctuary, and intelligence.[2]

As 1965 drew to a close there was some hope for peace. Both the allies and the Viet Cong agreed to short truces over the Christmas and New Year holidays and President Johnson opened his "peace offensive." He ordered the bombing of North Vietnam suspended for an extended period and dispatched American envoys to visit world capitals in an effort to initiate peace negotiations with the other side. Everyone involved in the war in Vietnam talked of peace, but there was no peace. The prediction of a Vietnamese soothsayer would come true; 1966 would be a year of a "lot of fighting and killing."[3]

Notes

PART I
ESTABLISHING THE ENCLAVES

Introduction

1. MilHistBr, Office of the Secretary, General Staff, Hq, USMACV, Comd Hist, 1964, dtd 15Oct65 p. 102.
2. Adm Ulysses S. G. Sharp, USN, CinCPac, and Gen William C. Westmoreland, ComUSMACV, *Report on the War in Vietnam* (As of 30 June 1968) (Washington: GPO, 1968), p. 95, hereafter Sharp and Westmoreland, *Report on the War*. For a more detailed account see Capt Robert H. Whitlow, USMCR, *U. S. Marines in Vietnam: The Advisory and Combat Assistance Era, 1954-1964* (Washington: Hist&MusDiv, HQMC, 1977), Chap. 10, hereafter Whitlow, *U. S. Marines in Vietnam, 1954-64.*

Chapter 1

The Call for Marines

Unless otherwise noted the material in this chapter is derived from: MilHistBr, Office of the Secretary, General Staff, Hq, USMACV, Comd Hist, 1965, dtd 20Apr66, hereafter *MACV Comd Hist, 1965*; 9th MEB ComdD Mar65; MAG-16 ComdD 16Jan-Mar65, dtd 8Apr65; HQMC Msg File; CNO, Flag Plot Msg File, Jan-Mar65 (OAB, NHD), hereafter *Flag Plot File*; BGen Frederick J. Karch, intvw by Oral HistU, Hist Div, HQMC, dtd 15Jan72 (Oral Hist Coll, Hist&MusDiv, HQMC), hereafter *Karch Intvw;* Vietnam Comment File; Department of Defense, *United States-Vietnam Relations, 1945-1967*, 12 bks (Washington: GPO, 1971), hereafter *Pentagon Papers* with appropriate section title and book, and section, volume or tab, and page number; LtCol John J. Cahill and Jack Shulimson, "History of U. S. Marine Corps Operations in Vietnam, Jan-Jun 65," MS (Hist&Mus Div, HQMC), hereafter Cahill and Shulimson, "USMC Ops RVN, Jan-Jun 65"; Jack Shulimson, "U. S. Marines in Vietnam, Introduction," MS, pt 1 of LtCol Ralph F. Moody, *et. al.*, "Marines in Vietnam, 1954-May 1968," MS, 8 pts (Hist&MusDiv, HQMC), hereafter, Shulimson, "U. S. Marines in Vietnam, pt 1."

Alert and Realert

1. BGen Frederick J. Karch, Presentation to the Command and Staff College, MCS, Quantico, dtd 27May65 (Oral Hist Coll, Hist&Mus Div, HQMC), hereafter *Karch Presentation.*

2. See MCCC, Items of Significant Interest for 20 and 31Jan65.

Air Retaliation and the Arrival of the HAWKS

3. *Washington Post and Times Herald*, 8Feb65, p. 1.
4. LtCol Bertram E. Cook, Comments on draft MS, dtd 25Oct76 (Vietnam Comment File), hereafter *Cook Comments*. See also Col George G. Long, Comments on draft MS, dtd 8Nov76 (Vietnam Comment File), hereafter *Long Comments*.
5. *Cook Comments*.
6. *Ibid*.
7. *Long comments*. See also Capt Ronald G. Richardson, intvw by MCS Quantico, dtd 8Feb66 (No. 50, Oral Hist Coll, Hist&MusDiv, HQMC).
8. *Long Comments*. See also MajGen Andrew W. O'Donnell and staff, Comments on draft MS, dtd 29Oct76 (Vietnam Comment File), hereafter *O'Donnell and staff Comments*.
9. "The Rolling Thunder Program Begins," *Pentagon Papers*, bk 4, sec. IV-C-3, pp. xii-xiv, and pp. 27-47. See also JCS Historical Section, Joint Secretariat, Comments on draft MS, dtd 10Nov76 (Vietnam Comment File), hereafter *JCS History Comments*.

Land the Marines

10. Quoted in "The Rolling Thunder Program Begins," *Pentagon Papers*, bk 4, sec. IV-C-3, p. 31. See also *JCS History Comments*.
11. ComUSMACV msg to JCS, dtd 9Feb65 (*Flag Plot File*).
12. JCS Memorandum (JCSM) 100-65, dtd 11Feb65 as cited in "Marine Units Go To Da Nang," *Pentagon Papers*, bk 4, sec. IV-C-4, p. ix. See also "The Rolling Thunder Program Begins," *Ibid.*, bk 4, sec. IV-C-3, pp. 31-47 and *JCS History Comments*.
13. General William C. Westmoreland, *A Soldier Reports* (New York, New York: Doubleday & Co., 1976), p. 123, hereafter Westmoreland, *A Soldier Reports*; *MACV Comd Hist, 1965*, p. 30.
14. Quoted in "Marine Units Go to Da Nang," *Pentagon Papers*, bk 4, sec. IV-c-4, pp. 2-5.
15. *Karch Intvw*.
16. *MACV Comd Hist, 1965*, p. 31.
17. DOD Tlgram 6166, dtd 2Mar65 as cited in "Marine Units Go to Da Nang," *Pentagon Papers*, bk 4, sec. IV-C-4, p. 6.
18. CinCPac msg to JCS, dtd 3Mar65, as cited in *Ibid.*, pp. 7-8.

The Landing

19. Maj Ruel T. Scyphers, Comments on draft MS, dtd 18Oct76 (Vietnam Comment File).
20. 3/9 ComdD, Mar65, pt II, p. 5.
21. *Karch Intvw.*
22. 3/9 ComdD, Mar 65, pt III.
23. MajGen Keith B. McCutcheon, Comments on Cahill and Shulimson draft MS, ''USMC Ops RVN, Jan-Jun65,'' dtd 24Apr68 (Vietnam Comment File).
24. LtCol Herbert J. Bain, Comments on draft MS, dtd 30Oct76 (Vietnam Comment File), hereafter *Bain Comments.*
25. CTF 76 Sit Rep No. 18, dtd 9Mar65 (*Flag Plot File*).
26. *Bain Comments.*

Chapter 2

The 9th MEB in Vietnam

Unless otherwise noted the material in this chapter is derived from: *MACV Comd Hist, 1965*; 9th MEB ComdDs, Mar-Apr65; HQMC Msg File; *Flag Plot File*; Vietnam Comment File; *Karch Intvw*; *Karch Presentation*; *Pentagon Papers*; Cahill and Shulimson, ''USMC Ops RVN, Jan-Jun65''; Shulimson, ''U. S. Marines in Vietnam, pt 1''; Jack Shulimson ''U. S. Marines in Vietnam, May-December 1965,'' MS, pt 2 of LtCol Ralph F. Moody *et. al.*, ''Marines in Vietnam 1954-May1968,'' hereafter Shulimson, ''Marines in Vietnam, pt 2''; BGen Edwin H. Simmons, ''Marine Corps Operations in Vietnam, 1965-66,'' *Naval Review, 1968* (Annapolis: U. S. Naval Institute, 1968), pp. 2-35, hereafter Simmons, ''Marine Corps Ops, 1965-66.''

The First Weeks

Additional sources for this section are: BLSG ComdDs, Mar-Apr65; MAG-16 ComdDs, Mar-Apr65.
1. JCS msg to CinCPac, dtd 6Mar65 as cited in ''Marine Combat Units Go to Da Nang,'' *Pentagon Papers*, bk 4, sec. IV-C-4, p. 1. Westmoreland quoted in FMFPac, ''Operations of the III Marine Amphibious Force, Vietnam, March-September 1965,'' n.d., hereafter FMFPac, *III MAF Ops, Mar-Sep65.*
2. BGen Frederick J. Karch ltr to Col Clifford B. Drake, dtd 26Mar65, covering ltr to *Karch Presentation.*
3. Colonel Robert J. Oddy, Comments on draft MS, dtd 25Oct76 (Vietnam Comment File).
4. *Karch Presentation.*
5. LtCol George H. Smith, intvw by MCSC Albany, dtd 21Apr66 (No. 111, Oral Hist Coll, Hist&MusDiv, HQMC).
6. Maj Pat Morgan, Comments on draft MS, dtd 28Oct76 (Vietnam Comment File).
7. BGen Webb D. Sawyer, Comments on draft MS, dtd 25Oct76 (Vietnam Comment File).
8. *Karch Presentation.*
9. Col Norman G. Ewers, Comments on draft MS, dtd 7Oct76 (Vietnam Comment File). See also *O'Donnell and staff Comments.*
10. Col Thomas J. O'Connor, Comments on draft MS, dtd 27Nov76 (Vietnam Comment File), hereafter *O'Connor Comments.*
11. 3/9 ComdD, Mar65.
12. FMFPac, *III MAF Ops, Mar-Sep65*, p. 21.
13. *Karch Presentation.*

Estimate of the Situation

Additional sources for this secton are: Dept of the Army, SE Asia Msg File (CMH, DA), hereafter *CMH Msg File* and Westmoreland, *A Soldier Reports.*
14. ComUSMACV msg to CinCPac, dtd 27Mar65 (CMH Msg File). See also Westmoreland, *A Soldier Reports*, pp. 126-29.
15. See ''Phase I in the Buildup of U. S. Forces, the Debate,'' *Pentagon Papers*, bk 4, sec. IV-C-5, pp 56-59 for copies of these earlier recommendations.
16. ComUSMACV msg to CinCPac, dtd 27Mar65 (*CMH Msg File*). This message provides a resume of the 26 March MACV ''Estimate of the Situation.'' See also Westmoreland, *A Soldier Reports*, p. 125.
17. LtGen Victor H. Krulak, Comments on Shulimson draft MS. ''U. S. Marines in Vietnam, pt 1,'' dtd 11Aug69 (Vietnam Comment File), hereafter *Krulak Comments*, 69.
18. NSAM-328, dtd 6Apr65 as reprinted in ''Phase I in the Buildup of U. S. Forces, the Debate,'' *Pentagon Papers*, bk 4, sec. IV-C-5, pp. 124-26. See also Westmoreland, *A Soldier Reports*, pp. 130-31.

More Marines Arrive

Additional sources for this section are: FMFPac ComdC, Mar-Dec65; FMFPac Deployment SitReps, 1965; 3d MEB Sit Reps, 5-12Apr65; 3d Marines ComdD, Apr65; MAG-16 ComdD, Apr65.
19. Col Rex C. Denny, Comments on draft MS, dtd 10Nov76 (Vietnam Comment File), hereafter *Denny Comments.*
20. CGFMFPac msg to CMC, dtd 31Mar65 in FMFPac Deployment SitReps 1965.
21. CGFMFPac msg to CMC, dtd 1Apr65 in *Ibid*; Col Richard A. Savage, Comments on draft MS, dtd 2Nov76 (Vietnam Comment File).
22. *Denny Comments.*
23. ComUSMACV msg to CG9thMEB, dtd 12Apr65 (HQMC Msg File).
24. CG1st MAW msg to CO, VMFA-531, dtd 12Apr65 (*Ibid*).
25. Col Rex C. Denny, Comments on Cahill and Shulimson draft MS, ''USMC Ops RVN, Jan-Jun65,'' dtd 16Apr68 (Vietnam Comment File).
26. Col Otis W. Corman, Comments on draft MS, n.d. [Nov 76] (Vietnam Comment File).
27. *Karch Presentation.*

An Expanded Mission

28. *MACV Comd Hist, 1965, p. 40.*
29. LtGen Victor H. Krulak, Comments on draft MS, dtd 2Aug77 (Vietnam Comment File), hereafter *Krulak Comments*, 77.

30. 3d Marines ComdD, Apr 65.

31. Capt Gaetano F. Squillace, intvw by MCS, Quantico, dtd 11 Jan 66 (No. 27, Oral Hist Coll, Hist&MusDiv, HQMC).

32. *Karch Presentation*.

33. *The Washington Post and Times Herald*, 2 May 65, p. 3.

Chu Lai

Additional sources for this section are: 3d MAB ComdD, Apr-May 65; 3d MEB SitReps, 26 Apr-12 May 65.

34. "Phase I in the Buildup of U. S. Forces, the Debate," *Pentagon Papers*, bk 4, sec. IV-C-5, p. 21. See also Westmoreland, *A Soldier Reports*, p. 132.

35. Telephone conversation between FMFPacCC and MCCC, dtd 28 Nov 67 as cited in Cahill and Shulimson, "USMC Ops RVN, Jan-Jun 65," p. 200.

36. *Krulak Comments, 77*.

37. *Denny Comments*.

38. LtCol Charles L. Goode, Comments on draft MS, dtd 7 Oct 76 (Vietnam Comment File), hereafter *Goode Comments*.

39. *O'Connor Comments*.

40. Col Norman R. Nickerson, Comments on draft MS, dtd 28 Oct 76 and 9 Aug 77 (Vietnam Comment File), hereafter *Nickerson Comments*.

41. Col Hardy Hay, Comments on Cahill and Shulimson draft MS, "USMC Ops RVN, Jan-Jun 65," dtd 5 May 68 (Vietnam Comment File). Hay in this letter provides a detailed account of the Saigon meeting.

42. Col Hardy Hay, Comments on draft MS, dtd 22 Oct 76 (Vietnam Comment File).

43. *O'Connor Comments*.

44. Col Edward Cook, Comments on draft MS, dtd 14 Oct 76 (Vietnam Comment File).

45. CGFMFPac, Trip Summary, Visit to WestPac, 14-21 May 1965, n.d., p. A-8.

46. Col William M. Graham, Comments on draft MS, dtd 18 Nov 76 (Vietnam Comment File).

Chapter 3

Formation and Development of III MAF

Unless otherwise noted the material in this chapter is derived from: *MACV Comd Hist, 1965*; FMFPac, *III MAF Ops, Mar-Sep 65*; III MAF ComdD, May 65; III MAF ComdC, Jun 65; 3d MarDiv (Fwd) ComdD, May 65; 3d MarDiv ComdC, Jun 65; 1st MAW (Adv) ComdD, May 65; 1st MAW (Adv) ComdC, Jun 65; HQMC Msg File; Vietnam Comment File; Cahill and Shulimson, "USMC Ops RVN, Jan-Jun 65"; Shulimson, "Marines in Vietnam, pt 1"; Shulimson, "Marines in Vietnam, pt 2"; *Pentagon Papers*; Simmons, "*Marine Corps Ops, 1965-66*."

The Birth of III MAF

1. Quoted in CinCPacFlt msg to CGIIIMEF, dtd 7 May 65 (HQMC Msg File).

2. Col Victor J. Croizat, Comments on Shulimson draft MS, "Marines in Vietnam, pt 1," dtd 12 Aug 69 (Vietnam

Comment File); Simmons, "Marine Corps Ops, 1965-66," p. 10; Gen Wallace M. Greene, Jr., Comments on draft MS, dtd 1 Aug 77 (Vietnam Comment File).

3. ComUSMACV ltr to CGIIIMEF, dtd 5 May 65, Subj: Letter of Instruction, encl 11, III MAF ComdC, May 65.

4. ComUSMACV msg to CinCPac, dtd 8 May 65 (HQMC Msg File).

5. *Ibid*.

The Le My Experiment

Additional sources for this section are: III MAF, Civic Action Report, 8 Mar-15 Jul 65, dtd 18 Jul 65, hereafter *III MAF Civic Action Report*; 3d Marines ComdD, May 65; 2/3 ComdD, May 65; LtCol David A. Clement, intvw by MCB, Camp Lejeune, dtd 6 Aug 66 (No. 189, Oral Hist Coll, Hist&MusDiv, HQMC), hereafter *Clement Intvw*; LtCol David A. Clement, "Le My: A Study in Counter-Insurgency," *Marine Corps Gazette*, v. 95, no. 11 (Nov 67), pp. 18-24, hereafter Clement, "Le My."

6. Statement of Capt Nguyen Hoa, dtd 16 Jun 65, Effect of Marine Corps Operations in Le My Area, encl 5, *III MAF Civic Action Report*.

7. *Clement Intvw*.

8. BGen Marc A. Moore, Comments on draft MS, n.d. [Nov 76] (Vietnam Comment File), hereafter *Moore Comments*.

9. Capt Lionel V. Silva, intvw by MSC, Quantico, dtd 2 Feb 66 (No. 37, Oral Hist Coll, Hist&MusDiv, HQMC).

10. *Moore Comments*.

11. Col David A. Clement, Comments on draft MS, dtd 5 Oct 76 (Vietnam Comment File), hereafter *Clement Comments*.

12. 3d Mar Div (Adv) ComdD, May 65.

13. CGFMFPac, Trip Summary, Visit to WestPac, 14-21 May 1965, n.d., hereafter *CGFMFPac May Trip Summary*.

Building the Chu Lai Airfield

Additional sources for this section are: MABS-12 ComdC, May 65; MAG-12 ComdC, Jun 65; LtGen Keith B. McCutcheon, "Marine Aviation in Vietnam, 1962-70," *Naval Review 1971* (Annapolis: U. S. Naval Institute, 1971), pp. 122-55, hereafter McCutcheon, "Marine Aviation"; LtCol Charles L. Goode, Chu Lai Report, encl 2, *Goode Comments*, hereafter *Chu Lai Report, Goode Comments*.

14. *Chu Lai Report, Goode Comments*.

15. *Ibid*.

16. *Ibid*.

17. *Nickerson Comments*.

18. *Chu Lai Report, Goode Comments*.

19. *Ibid*.

20. *Ibid*.

21. *Ibid*.

22. Col John D. Noble, Comments on draft MS, dtd 1 Nov 76 (Vietnam Comment File).

23. MajGen Keith B. McCutcheon, Comments on Cahill and Shulimson draft MS, "USMC Ops RVN, Jan-Jun 65," dtd 24 Apr 68 (Vietnam Comment File).

24. LtCol Robert W. Baker, Comments on draft MS, dtd 28Oct76 (Vietnam Comment File).

25. Col Hardy Hay, Comments on draft MS, dtd 22Oct76 (Vietnam Comment File), hereafter *Hay Comments*.

III MAF in Transition

Additional sources for this section are: FLSG ComdD, May 65; FLSG ComdC, Jun65.

26. Gen Lewis W. Walt, Comments on draft MS, dtd 10Aug77 (Vietnam Comment File), hereafter *Walt Comments*.

27. Maj Ruel T. Scyphers, Comments on draft MS, dtd 18Oct76 (Vietnam Comment File).

28. *CGFMFPac May Trip Summary*.

29. *Hay Comments*.

30. *Nickerson Comments*

31. *Ibid*.

32. See *MACV Comd Hist, 1965*, pp. 106-07; LtGen Joseph M. Heiser, Jr., USA, *Vietnam Studies: Logistic Support* (Washington D. C.: Dept of the Army, 1974), pp. 9-11; VAdm Edwin B. Hooper, USN, *Mobility, Support, Endurance* (Washington: NHD, 1972), p. 72, hereafter Hooper, *Mobility, Support, Endurance*.

33. *Nickerson Comments*.

34. AC/S G-4 III MAF memo to CGIIIMAF, dtd 16May65, Subj: Concept of Logistic Support, encl 14, III MAF ComdC, May 1965.

35. *Hay Comments*.

The Seeds of Pacification

Additional sources for this section are: *III MAF Civic Action Report*; Clement, "Le My"; Capt Russel H. Stolfi, USMCR, *U. S. Marine Corps Civic Action Efforts in Vietnam March 1965-March 1966* (Washington: Hist Br, G-3 Div, HQMC, 1968), hereafter Stolfi, *USMC Civic Action, 65-66*.

36. Quoted in Capt William D. Parker, USMCR, *U. S. Marine Civil Affairs in I Corps, Republic of Vietnam, April 1966-April 1967* (Washington: Hist Div, HQMC, 1970), p. 2.

37. Gen Wallace M. Greene, Jr., intvw by Hist Div, HQMC, dtd 19 May73 (Oral Hist Coll, Hist&Mus Div, HQMC).

38. III MAF Force Order 1750.1, dtd 7 Jun 65, encl 7, *III MAF Civic Action Report*.

39. *Clement Comments*.

40. *Ibid*.

41. *Ibid*.

June Operations in the Three Enclaves

Additional ources for this section are: 3d Marines ComdC, Jun 65; 4th Marines ComdC, Jun 65; 3/4 ComdC, Jun65.

42. 3d MarDiv ComdC, Jun65.

43. *Ibid*.

44. Col Joseph R. Fisher, Comments on Cahill and Shulimson draft MS, "USMC Ops RVN, Jan-Jun65," dtd 14May68 (Vietnam Comment File).

45. LtCol Harold D. Fredericks, Comments on draft MS, dtd 24Nov76 (Vietnam Comment File).

46. *CGFMFPac May Trip Summary*.

47. Unsigned and undated document entitled "Zone A, Hue/Phu Bai," encl 8, 3d Marines ComdC, Jun65.

Chapter 4

Reinforcement and Expansion

Unless otherwise noted the material in this chapter is derived from: *MACV Comd Hist, 1965*; FMFPac, *III MAF Ops, Mar-Sep65*; III MAF ComdCs, Jul-Aug65; 3d MarDiv ComdCs, Jul-Aug65; 1st MAW (Adv) ComdC, Jul-Aug65; HQMC Msg File; Vietnam Comment File; Shulimson, "Marines in Vietnam, pt 2"; Jack Shulimson "U. S. Marine Corps Operations in the Republic of Vietnam, Jul-Dec65," MS (Hist&Mus Div, HQMC), hereafter Shulimson, "USMC Ops RVN, Jul-Dec65"; *Pentagon Papers*; Westmoreland, *A Soldier Reports;* Gen Lewis W. Walt, *Strange War, Strange Strategy, A General's Report on Vietnam* (New York: Funk&Wagnalls, 1970), hereafter Walt, *Strange War, Strange Strategy;* Simmons, "Marine Corps Ops, 1965-66"; Chester L. Cooper, Judith E. Corson, Laurence J. Legere, David E. Lockwood, and Donald M. Weller, *The American Experience with Pacification in Vietnam*, 3 vols. (Washington: Institute for Defense Analysis, Mar 1972), hereafter Cooper *et. al., The American Experience with Pacification*.

The Need for Further Reinforcements

1. *MACV Comd Hist, 1965*, pp. 140-41; Cooper *et. al., The American Experience with Pacification*, v. 3, pp. 206-217. The quotes are from Technique of Pacification Operations, Anx E, *Chien Thang* Plan, dtd 22Feb64, as cited in Cooper *et. al., The American Experience with Pacification*, v. 3, p. 207.

2. *MACV Comd Hist, 1965*, p. 141; Cooper, *et. al., American Experience with Pacification*, v. 3, p. 228.

3. Cooper, *et. al., The American Experience with Pacification*, v. 1, p. 4.

4. Quoted in Simmons, "Marine Corps Ops, 1965-66," p. 15.

5. Quoted in "Phase I in the Buildup of U. S. Forces, the Debate," *Pentagon Papers*, bk 4, sec. IV-C-5, p. 90; *MACV Comd Hist, 1965*, pp. 35, 40-41; Westmoreland, *A Soldier Reports*, pp. 139-40.

6. JCS msg 2400, dtd 22Jun65 as cited in "Phase I in the Buildup of U. S. Forces, the Debate," *Pentagon Papers*, bk 4, sec. IV-C-5, p. 28. See also pp. 25-28, 90-91, 94, and 104; *MACV Comd Hist, 1965*, pp. 35, 40-41.

7. Westmoreland, *A Soldier Reports*, 139-40. See also *MACV Comd Hist, 1965*, p. 41.

8. Westmoreland, *A Soldier Reports*, p. 140.

9. Quoted in "Phase I in the Buildup of U. S. Forces, the Debate," *Pentagon Papers*, bk 4, sec. IV-C-5, p. 104.

10. CMH, Comments on draft MS, dtd 15Nov76 (Vietnam Comment File).

11. ComUSMACV memo to CMC, dtd 28Apr65, Subj: Deployment of an Airmobile Division to the High Plateau. See also ComUSMACV msg to CinCPac, dtd 13Jun65 as reprinted

in ''Phase I in the Buildup of U. S. Forces, the Debate,'' *Pentagon Papers*, bk 4, sec. IV-C-5, p. 101.

12. Adm Ulysses S. G. Sharp, Comments on draft MS, dtd 8Aug77 (Vietnam Comment File). See also ''Phase I in the Buildup of U. S. Forces, the Debate,'' bk 4, sec. IV-C-5, pp. 26-7; Westmoreland, *A Soldier Reports*, p. 144.

The Establishment of the Qui Nhon Enclave

13. Col Charles H. Bodley, Comments on draft MS, dtd 27Oct76 (Vietnam Comment File).

14. *Ibid*.

15. MACV msg to CinCPac, dtd 2Jul65 (HQMC Msg File).

16. III MAF Op 304-65, dtd 4Jul65, encl 8, III MAF ComdC, Jul65.

The Attack on the Airfield

Additional sources for this section are: 3d Marines ComdC, Jul65; 1/9 ComdC, Jul65; 1/3 ComdC, Jul65; 2/3 ComdC, Jul 65; *Karch Intvw*.

17. III MAF Intelligence Rept to ComUSMACV, dtd 3Jul65, Subj: Interrogation of NVA POW.

18. Col Verle E. Ludwig, Comments on draft MS, dtd 8Oct76 (Vietnam Comment File), hereafter *Ludwig Comments*.

19. Entry for 1Jul65, 3d MarDiv G-3 Jnl, 3d MarDiv ComdC, Jul65.

20. *Walt Comments*.

21. *Ibid*.

22. Resume of Activities, Movements and Results, pt II, 3d MarDiv ComdC, Jul 65.

23. *Ludwig Comments*.

24. *Hay Comments*.

25. *Krulak Comments, 77*.

Expansion to the South

Additional sources for this section are: HQMC, Cam Ne Report, Aug-Sep65; 3d Marines ComdCs, Jul-Aug65; 9th Marines ComdCs, Jul-Aug65; 1/9 ComdCs, Jul-Aug65; 2/9 ComdCs, Jul-Aug65; 1/9 AAR 1-65, dtd Aug65; LtCol William H. Clark, intvw by MCB, CamPen, circa Feb66 (No. 63, Oral Hist Coll, Hist&Mus Div, HQMC).

26. *Walt Comments*.

27. *Krulak Comments, 77; Walt Comments*.

28. BGen Nguyen Chanh Thi ltr to CGIIIMAF, dtd 20Jul65, Subj: TAOR of III MAF, encl 3, III MAF ComdC, Jul65.

29. *Ibid*.

30. LtCol William H. Clark memo, dtd 17July65, Subj: Provisional Base Defense Battalion, encl 7, LtCol William H. Clark, Comments on draft MS, dtd 17Nov76 (Vietnam Comment File), hereafter *Clark Comments*.

31. *Clark Comments*.

32. CO 2/9 memo to CO 9th Marines, dtd 9Aug65, Subj: Debriefing Rept, 2/9 ComdC, Aug65.

33. Maj John A. Buck, Comments on draft MS, dtd 9Nov76 (Vietnam Comment File).

34. Statements of LtCol V. E. Ludwig and Capt H. B. West in HQMC, Cam Ne Report, Aug-Sep65.

35. LtCol V. E. Ludwig Statement in *Ibid*.

36. CMC (AH-wwg) memo to Asst SecDef (PA), dtd 9Aug65, Subj: Mr. Morley Safer report of Marine attack on the village of Cam Ne, and Summary of CBS-TV newsbroadcast, evening, 5Aug65 in *Ibid*. For the *Gazette* editorial quote, see ''The War in Vietnam: Cam Ne (4),'' *Marine Corps Gazette*, v. 49, no. 10 (Oct 1965), pp. 28-30, p. 30.

37. Quoted in CGFMFPac msg to CMC, dtd 7Aug65 in HQMC, Cam Ne Rept, Aug-Sep65.

Further Reinforcements

38. *MACV Comd Hist, 1965*, pp. 40-42. See also ''Phase I in the Buildup of U. S. Forces, the Debate,'' *Pentagon Papers*, bk 4, sec. IV-C-5, pp. 25-31.

PART II
THE BIG BATTLES

Chapter 5

Operation STARLITE: The First Big Battle

Unless otherwise noted the material in this chapter is derived from *MACV Comd Hist, 1965*; HqFMFPac, ''U. S. Marine Corps Forces in Vietnam, March 1965-September 1967,'' n.d., 2 vols., hereafter FMFPac, *Marine Forces in Vietnam, Mar65-Sep67*; FMFPac, *III MAF Ops, Mar-Sep65*; III MAF ComdCs, Jul-Aug65; 3d MarDiv ComdC, Aug65; 1st MAW (Adv) ComdC, Jul-Aug65; 7th Marines ComdC, Aug65; HQMC Msg File; Vietnam Comment File; Shulimson, ''Marines in Vietnam, pt 2''; Shulimson, ''USMC Ops RVN, Jul-Dec65;'' Simmons, ''Marine Corps Ops, 1965-66''; BGen Oscar F. Peatross, ''Application of Doctrine: Victory at Van Tuong Village,'' *Naval Review 1967* (Annapolis: U. S. Naval Institute, 1967), pp. 2-13, hereafter Peatross, ''Victory at Van Tuong''; Col Oscar F. Peatross, intvw by HistDiv, HQMC, dtd 15Jul66 (No. 157, Oral Hist Coll, Hist&Mus Div, HQMC), hereafter *Peatross Intvw, 1966*.

Intelligence and Planning

1. Simmons, ''Marines Corps Ops, 1965-66,'' p. 18.

2. MajGen Leo J. Dulacki, Comments on Shulimson draft MS, ''USMC Ops RVN, Jul-Dec65,'' dtd 14May71 (Vietnam Comment File), hereafter *Dulacki Comments, 71*; LtGen Leo J. Dulacki, Comments on draft MS, n.d. [Jul 77] (Vietnam Comment File).

3. Col James F. McClanahan, Comments on draft MS, dtd 18Oct76 (Vietnam Comment File). See also 4th Marines ComdC, Aug65.

4. *Dulacki Comments, 71*.

5. MajGen Oscar F. Peatross, intvw by Hist&MusDiv, HQMC, dtd 12Apr73 (Oral Hist Coll, Hist&MusDiv, HQMC); *Walt Comments*.

6. MajGen Oscar F. Peatross, Comments on Shulimson draft MS, "USMC Ops RVN, Jul-Dec65," dtd 7Jun71 (Vietnam Comment File), hereater *Peatross Comments, 71*.

7. *Peatross Intvw, 1966*.

The Battle

Additional sources for this section are: MAG-16 ComdC, Aug65; MAG-11 ComdC, Aug65; MAG-12 ComdC, Aug65; CTF 79.5 ComdC, 19Jun-10Oct65, dtd 27Oct65; 2/4 ComdC, Aug65; 3/3 ComdC, Aug65; 3/7 ComdC, Jun-Sep65; 1st Lt Richard M. Purnell, intvw by MCB CamPen, dtd 23Feb66 (Oral Hist Coll, Hist&MusDiv, HQMC); Gy Sgt Jack Marino, Jr, intvw by MCB Camp Lejeune, dtd 25Nov66 (No. 246, Oral Hist Coll, Hist&MusDiv, HQMC); "Statement of Major Andrew G. Comer, U. S. Marine Corps, concerning personal observations, impressions and participation in combat operations while serving as Executive Officer of 3d Battalion, 3d Marines during Operation STARLITE, 16August-20August 1965, in the Republic of South Vietnam," n.d., encl to Maj Andrew G. Comer, Comments on draft MS, dtd 17 Nov 76 (Vietnam Comment File), hereafter *Comer Statement*.

8. Maj Howard B. Henry, intvw by MCAS El Toro, *circa* Aug66 (No. 188, Oral Hist Coll, Hist&MusDiv, HQMC).

9. Maj Andrew G. Comer, Comments on draft MS, dtd 17Nov76 (Vietnam Comment File).

10. *Comer Statement*

11. *Ibid*.

12. *Ibid*.

13. *Ibid*.

14. *Ibid*.

15. Entry for 18Aug65, 7th Marines S-3 Jn1, 7th Marines ComdC, Aug65.

The Aftermath

Additional sources for this section are: 3/12 ComdC, Aug65; 1/7 ComdC, Aug65; 3/7 ComdC Jun-Sep65.

16. MajGen Oscar F. Peatross, Comments on draft MS, dtd 26Oct76 (Vietnam Comment File), hereafter *Peatross Comments, 76*.

17. LtGen Leslie E. Brown, transcrpt of intvw by Hist&MusDiv, HQMC, dtd 14Aug75 (Oral Hist Coll, Hist&MusDiv, HQMC), p. 11.

18. *Walt Comments*.

19. Col Floyd J. Johnson, Jr., Comments on draft MS, dtd 29Nov76 (Vietnam Comment File).

20. *Peatross Comments*, 71.

21. 1/7 AAR, dtd 22Aug65, 7th Marines ComdC, Aug65, p. 3.

22. *Krulak Comments*, 77.

23. Col Don P. Wyckoff, Comments on draft MS, dtd 16Oct76 (Vietnam Comment File).

24. *Walt Comments*.

Chapter 6

The Enemy Refuses to Give Battle: September-November Operations

Unless otherwise noted the material in this chapter is derived from: *MACV Comd Hist, 1965*; FMFPac, *Marine Forces in Vietnam*, Mar65-Sep67; FMFPac, *III MAF Ops, Mar-Sep65*; HqFMFPac, Operations of U. S. Marine Forces Vietnam, monthly reports, Sep-Nov65, hereafter FMFPac, *III MAF Ops*, with appropriate month; III MAF ComdCs, Sep-Nov65; 3d MarDiv ComdCs, Sep-Nov65; 1st MAW ComdCs, Sep-Nov65; TG79.5 ComdCs, Sep-Nov65; HQMC Msg File; Vietnam Comment File; Shulimson, "Marines in Vietnam, pt 2"; Shulimson, "USMC Ops RVN, Jul-Dec65''; Walt, *Strange War, Strange Strategy;* Simmons, "Marine Corps Ops, 1965-66."

Operation PIRANHA

Additional sources for this section are: 7th Marines ComdC, Sep65; RLT-7 AAR 2-65, Operation PIRANHA, dtd 25Sep65, hereafter *PIRANHA AAR;* MAG-12 ComdC, Sep65; MAG-11 ComdC, Sep65; MAG-16 ComdC, Sep65; 1/7 ComdC, Sep65; 3/7 ComdC, Sep65; 3/3 ComdC, Sep65.

1. BLT 1/7 OpO 123-65, dtd 4Sep65 in *PIRANHA AAR*.

2. *PIRANHA AAR*.

Much Ado About CS, Operation STOMP

Additional sources for this section are: 2/7 ComdC, Sep65; Col Leon N. Utter, Comments on Shulimson draft MS, "U.S. Marines in Vietnam, pt 2," dtd 19Jun70 (Vietnam Comment File), hereafter *Utter Comments*; Maj Alvin Doublet, intvw by MCB, CamPen, dtd 14Jun66 (No. 137, Oral Hist Coll, Hist&MusDiv, HQMC), hereafter *Doublet Intvw*.

3. Quoted in Lester A. Sobel, Editor-in-Chief, *Facts on File Year-book 1965*, v. XXV (New York: Facts on File, Inc., 1966), p. 322.

4. *Utter Comments*.

5. LtCol Raymond W. Wilson, Comments on draft MS, dtd 25Oct76 (Vietnam Comment File).

6. *New York Times*, 11Sep65, p. 11.

7. *Utter Comments*.

October-November Operations

Additional sources for this section are: MAG-16 ComdCs, Oct-Nov65; MAG-36 ComdCs, Oct-Nov65; 7th Marines ComdC, Nov65; 2/3 ComdC, Oct65; 3/4 ComdC, Oct65; 2/4 ComdC, Oct65; 1/7 ComdC, Nov65; 2/7 ComdC, Nov65; 3/3 ComdC, Nov65.

Chapter 7

The 1st VC Again: Operation HARVEST MOON

Unless otherwise noted the material in this chapter is derived from *MACV Comd Hist, 1965;* FMFPac, *Marine Forces In Vietnam, Mar65-Sep67;* FMFPac, *III MAF Ops,* Nov-Dec65; III MAF ComdCs, Nov-Dec65; 1st MAW ComdCs, Nov-Dec65; 3d MarDiv ComdCs, Nov-Dec65; TG 79.5 ComdC, Dec65; TF DELTA, AAR, Operation HARVEST MOON, dtd 28Dec65, hereafter *TF DELTA AAR Opn HARVEST MOON;* MAG-12 ComdCs, Nov-Dec65; 12th Marines ComdC, Dec65; 3/3 ComdC, Dec65; 2/7 ComdC, Dec65; HQMC Msg File; Vietnam Comment File; Shulimson, ''Marines in Vietnam, pt 2''; Shulimson, ''USMC Ops RVN, Jul-Dec65''; Walt, *Strange War, Strange Strategy;* Simmons, ''Marine Corps Ops, 1965-66.''

The Abandoment of Hiep Duc

1. *O'Connor Comments.*
2. *Ibid.*
3. *Ibid.* See also MAG-16 ComdC, Nov 65, p. 5.
4. Simmons, ''Marine Corps Ops, 1965-66,'' p. 22.
5. *Ibid.*
6. ComUSMACV ltr to CGIIIMAF, dtd 22Nov65, Subj: Letter of Instruction, encl 2, III MAF ComdC, Nov 65.
7. CGFMFPac msg to CGIIIMAF, dtd 22Nov65 (HQMC Msg File).

Activation of Task Force DELTA and Planning the Operation

8. Simmons, ''Marine Corps Ops, 1965-66,'' p. 26.

The VC Strike and the Marines are Committed

9. *Washington Post and Times Herald,* 9Dec65, p. 3.
10. Capt Edward J. Lloyd, intvw by MCRD, San Diego, dtd 26Oct67 (No. 1640, Oral Hist Coll, Hist&MusDiv, HQMC).
11. Col Michael R. Yunck, Comments on draft MS, dtd 22Oct76 (Vietnam Comment File). See also *TF DELTA AAR, Opn HARVEST MOON.*

The Search of the Phouc Ha Valley

12. Hist Div, HQMC, Memo for the Record, dtd 8Jun71, Subj: Phone Con with MajGen Jonas M. Platt (Ret) (Vietnam Comment File), hereafter *Platt Phone Con, Jun 71.*
13. Hist Div, HQMC, Memo for the Record, dtd 28Jan70, Subj: Interview with MajGen Jonas M. Platt (Vietnam Comment File), hereafter *Platt Interview, Jan 70.*

The Fight at Ky Phu

Additional source for this section is LtCol Leon N. Utter, ''Solid Contact for 2/7,'' *Marine Corps Gazette,* v. 50, no. 4 (Apr66), pp. 25-30.

14. Maj Nicholas H. Grosz, Comments on draft MS, n.d. [Dec 76] (Vietnam Comment File).
15. Capt Nicholas H. Grosz, intvw by MCRD, Parris Island, S.C., dtd Aug66 (No. 195, Oral Hist Coll, Hist&MusDiv, HQMC).

The Wrap-Up

16. Col Nicholas J. Dennis, Comments on draft MS, dtd 3Nov76, (Vietnam Comment File), hereafter *Dennis Comments, 76.*
17. MAG-12 AAR, Operation HARVEST MOON, dtd 25Dec65, App 1, MAG-12 ComdC, Dec65.
18. CGFMFPac, Trip Summary, Visit to WestPac, 3-11 Dec65, dtd 14Dec65, pp. 4-5.

PART III
THE CONTINUING WAR

Chapter 8

Defending and Expanding the Base Areas

Unless otherwise noted the material in this chapter is derived from: *MACV Comd Hist, 1965;* FMFPac, *Marine Forces in Vietnam, Mar65-Sep67;* FMFPac, *III MAF Ops, Mar-Sep65;* FMFPac, *III MAF Ops,* Oct-Dec 65; III MAF ComdCs, Aug-Dec65; 3d MarDiv ComdCs, Aug-Dec65; 1st MAW ComdCs, Aug-Dec65; MAG-11 ComdCs Aug-Dec65; MAG-12 ComdCs Aug-Dec65; MAG-16 ComdCs Aug-Dec65; MAG-36 ComdCs, Sep-Dec65; 3d Marines ComdCs, Aug-Dec65; 4th Marines ComdCs, Aug-Dec65; 7th Marines ComdCs, Aug-Dec65; 9th Marines ComdCs, Aug-Dec65; 3/4 ComdCs, Aug-Dec65; HQMC Msg File; Vietnam Comment File; Shulimson, ''Marines in Vietnam, pt 2''; Shulimson, ''USMC Ops RVN, Jul-Dec65''; Westmoreland, *A Soldier Reports;* Walt, *Strange War, Strange Strategy;* Simmons, ''Marine Corps Ops 1965-66.''

The Evolution of a Strategy

1. Quoted in Westmoreland, *A Soldier Reports,* pp. 142-45. See also Sharp and Westmoreland, *Report on the War,* p. 100.
2. ComUSMACV ltr to CG III MAF, dtd 21Nov65, Subj: Letter of Instruction, encl 2, III MAF ComdC, Nov65.
3. BGen Frederick J. Karch, Comments on draft MS, dtd 11Jan77 (Vietnam Comment File); HistDiv, Memo for the Record, dtd 9Mar72, Subj: Conference with BGen Simmons, (Ret), Director of Marine Corps History and Museums (Vietnam Comment File).
4. ComUSMACV ltr to CGField Force, Vietnam, dtd 10Dec65, Subj: Tactical Employment of U.S. Forces and Defensive Action (Folder No. VA (1) Guidance from MACV), MACV Historical Records, 1966, NFRC, Washington, (Accession No. 69A702) and Westmoreland, *A Soldier Reports,* pp. 165-66.

5. Copy of LtGen Victor H. Krulak personal ltr to Hon Robert S. McNamara, Secretary of Defense, dtd 11Nov65 (LtGen Victor H. Krulak Personal Papers Collection (PC 486) Hist&MusDiv, HQMC).

Further Deployments and Realinements

Additional material for this section is derived from: HQMC, General Officer Symposium Book, dtd 15Jul66, hereafter *1966 General Officer Symposium Book*.

6. *MACV Comd Hist*, 1965, p. 26.

7. "The Chief of Staff's Overview," Sec. IIB, *1966 General Officer Symposium Book*, p. 3.

Refinement of Command Relations

Additional source for this section is Col Don P. Wyckoff, intvw by HQMC, dtd 5Jun67 (No. 762 Oral Hist Coll, Hist&MusDiv, HQMC), hereafter *Wyckoff Intvw*.

8. CGIIIMAF msg dtd 12Aug65, encl 3, III MAF ComdC, Aug65.

9. I Corps Senior Advisor, I Corps Advisory Group ltr to ComUSMACV, dtd 27Jul65, Subj: I Corps Advisory Group Responsibilities, encl 2, App 1, III MAF ComdC, Aug65.

10. See CGIIIMAF msg to CGFMFPac, dtd 30Oct65 (HQMC Msg File) and *MACV Comd Hist, 1965*, pp. 97-98.

11. *Wyckoff Intvw*.

12. FMFPac, *III MAF Ops, Mar-Sep65*, p. 14.

Expanding the TAORs

13. CGIIIMAF ltr to CGICorps, dtd 13Sep65, Subj: Expansion of Currently Assigned TAOR at Da Nang, encl 1, III MAF ComdC, Sep65.

14. BGen Nguyen Chanh Thi, CGICorps, ltr to CGIIIMAF, encl 2, III MAF ComdC, Sep65.

15. Col Sumner A. Vale, Comments on draft MS, Shulimson, "USMC Ops RVN, Jul-Dec65," dtd 4Jun71 (Vietnam Comment File).

Attacks on the Airfields and Hill 22

Additional material for this section is derived from: CGIIIMAF ltr to CGFMFPac, n.d., Subj: Report of Viet Cong Attack of Marble Mountain Air Facility and Chu Lai Airfield of 28Oct65, encl 6, III MAF ComdC, Oct65, hereafter *Viet Cong Attack Report;* 1/1 ComdC, Oct65; *Brown Intvw; Karch Intvw*.

16. *Brown Intvw*, p. 19.

17. *Karch Intvw*.

18. *O'Connor Comments*.

19. *Ibid.*, and *Viet Cong Attack Report*.

20. *Viet Cong Attack Report*.

21. 3d MarDiv ComdC, Oct65, p. 7.

22. CO 9th Marines ltr to CG3dMarDiv, dtd 30Oct65, Subj: Special Report of Squad-sized Ambush Conducted on 27Oct65, encl 4, 9th Marines ComdC, Oct65.

23. *Ibid.*

24. *Viet Cong Attack Report*, p. 9.

25. 1/1 AAR No. 3, dtd 31Oct65, encl 15, 1/1 ComdC, Oct 65.

26. Hist&MusDiv, Memo for the Record, dtd 14 Oct 76, Subj: Oral Comments of MajGen Harold A. Hatch on draft MS (Vietnam Comment File).

27. Telephone con between Capt Robert H. Whitlow and GySgt Russel L. Kess, dtd 10Jul73.

28. CGFMFPac msg to CMC, dtd 30Oct65 (HQMC Msg File).

29. 3d Marines ComdC, Oct 65, p. 21.

30. 1/1 ComdC, Nov65, p. 6.

31. CGFMFPac msg to CMC, dtd 28Oct65 (HQMC Msg File).

Base Defense

Additional material for this section is derived from: BGen Edwin H. Simmons, Comments on draft MS, Shulimson, "Marines in Vietnam, pt 2," dtd 2Jan70 (Vietnam Comment File), hereafter *Simmons Comments, Jan 70*.

32. Col George W. Carrington, Comments on draft MS, dtd 24Nov76 (Vietnam Comment File), hereafter *Carrington Comments*.

33. Briefing for MajGen Larsen, CGUSATFA and MajGen Kinnard, CG1stAirCavDiv, dtd 15Sep65, encl to *Simmons Comments, Jan 70*.

34. III MAF G-3 Section, Agenda Subject, Base Defense Command, dtd 4Oct65, encl, *Simmons Comments, Jan70*.

35. *Carrington Comments*.

36. *Dennis Comments*, 76.

37. 3/9 OpO 321A-65, dtd 14Sep65, encl 3, 3/9 ComdC, Sep65.

38. 3d MarDiv OpO 327-65, dtd 15Aug65, encl 1, 3d MarDiv ComdC, Aug65.

39. III MAF G-3 Section, Agenda Subject, War Dog Requirements, dtd 4Jan66, encl 10, III MAF ComdC, Jan66.

40. *Carrington Comments*.

41. LtCol Harold A. Hatch, intvw by MCB, CamPen, dtd 6Jul66 (No. 156, Oral Hist Coll, Hist&MusDiv, HQMC), hereafter *Hatch Intvw*.

Extended Patrolling

Additional material for this section is derived from 1/7 ComdC, Dec65; 1/9 ComdC, Dec65; LtGen Lewis W. Walt, intvw by III MAF, dtd 30Jan67 (No. 337, Oral Hist Coll, Hist&MusDiv, HQMC), hereafter *Walt Intvw; Hatch Intvw*; LtCol James P. Kelly, intvw by MCS, Quantico, dtd 18Oct66 (No. 229, Oral Hist Coll, Hist&MusDiv, HQMC), hereafter *Kelly Intvw*.

42. *Walt Intvw*.

43. 3d MarDiv ComdCs, Oct and Dec65.

44. *Hatch Intvw*.

45. *Kelly Intvw*.

46. MCCC, Items of Significant Interest, dtd 5Dec65.

47. *Kelly Intvw*.

48. CO 1/9 ltr to CO 9th Marines, dtd 30Dec65, Subj: Special Report of Company B patrol of 27Dec65, encl 5, 1/9 ComdC, Dec65.

Chapter 9
Pacification

Unless otherwise noted the material in this chapter is derived from: *MACV Comd Hist, 1965*; FMFPac, *Marine Forces in Vietnam, Mar65-Sep67*; FMFPac, *III MAF Ops, Mar-Sep65*; FMPac, *III MAF Ops*, Oct-Dec65; III MAF ComdCs, Jul-Dec65; 3d MarDiv ComdCs, Jul-Dec65; HQMC Msg File; Vietnam Comment File; Shulimson, ''Marines in Vietnam, pt 2''; Shulimson, ''USMC Ops RVN, Jul-Dec65;'' MajGen Donald M. Weller, USMC (Ret), Unprocessed Working Papers on Pacification, hereafter *Weller Working Papers*; Walt, *Strange War, Strange Strategy*; Stolfi, *Civic Action*; Simmons, ''Marine Corps Ops, Vietnam 1965-66''; Cooper *et. al., The American Experience with Pacification*.

The Combined Action Program

Additional sources for this section are: FMFPac, ''The Marine Combined Action Program, Vietnam, Aug65-Jan67,'' n.d., hereafter FMFPac, *Combined Action Program*; 3d Marines ComdCs, Jul-Dec65; 4th Marines ComdCs, Jul-Dec65; 7th Marines ComdCs, Aug-Dec65; 9th Marines ComdCs, Jul-Dec65; 3/4 ComdCs, Jul-Dec65; 1st Lt Paul R. Ek, intvw by MCB, CamPen, dtd 10Feb66 (No. 46, Oral Hist Coll, Hist&MusDiv, HQMC), hereafter *Ek Intvw, Feb66*; Hist Div, HQMC, Memo for the Record, dtd 10Nov72, Subj: Interview with Capt Paul R. Ek, (Vietnam Comment File), hereafter *Ek MR, 10Nov72*; Capt John J. Mullen, Jr. USMC, Student Staff Study, AWS, Quantico, Va, ''Modification to the III MAF Combined Action Program in the Republic of Vietnam,'' dtd 19Dec68, hereafter *Mullen Study*.

1. Walt, *Strange War, Strange Strategy*, p. 29.
2. U. S. Marine Corps, *Small Wars Manual* (Washington: GPO, 1940), p. I-32.
3. Walt, *Strange War, Strange Strategy*, p. 81.
4. Copy of LtGen Wallace M. Greene, Jr., personal ltr to MajGen Richard G. Weede, USMC, C/S USMACV, dtd 27Feb63 (General Wallace M. Greene, Jr. Personal Papers Collection (PC 511) Hist&MusDiv, HQMC).
5. *Ek Intvw, Feb66*.
6. *Ek MR, 10Nov72*.
7. Stolfi, *Civic Action*, p. 1.
8. LtCol Sumner A. Vale, intvw by MCRD, Parris Island, SC, dtd 14Feb67 (No. 372, Oral Hist Coll, Hist&MusDiv, HQMC).
9. 3d Marines ComdC, Dec65, p. 3.
10. Walt, *Strange War, Strange Strategy*, pp. 105-106.
11. III MAF OpO 305-66, Short Title: Phong Bu, dtd 24Nov65 (III MAF Plans/Orders 1965).
12. These letters are reproduced in FMFPac, *Combined Action Program*, pp. 32-33. See also III MAF G-3 Section, Agenda Subj: RF/PF Status and Improvement, dtd 5Jan66, encl 6, III MAF ComdC, Jan66.

Protection of the Harvest: GOLDEN FLEECE

Additional sources for this section are: 9th Marines ComdCs, Sep-Oct65; 1/9 ComdC, Sep65; 1/1 ComdC, Oct65;

2/3 ComdC, Sep65; 2/4 ComdC, Oct65; LtCol Verle E. Ludwig, intvw by HQMC, dtd 23Jan67 (No. 294, Oral Hist Coll, Hist&MusDiv, HQMC), hereafter *Ludwig Intvw*; Clement, ''Le My''; LtCol Verle E. Ludwig, ''Bus to Tra Khe,'' *Marine Corps Gazette*, v. 50, no. 10 (Oct66), pp. 32-36.

13. *Ludwig Intvw*.
14. 9th Marines ComdC, Sep65, p. 1.
15. *Ludwig Intvw*; 9th Marines FragO 36-65, dtd 9Sep65, encl 2, 9th Marines ComdC, Sep65; *Walt Comments*.
16. *Ludwig Intvw*.
17. Col David A. Clement, Comments on draft MS, Shulimson, ''Marines in Vietnam, pt. 2,'' dtd 12Mar70 (Vietnam Comment File).
18. III MAF ComdC, Oct65.
19. III MAF Staff Study, dtd 26Nov65, Subj: Study to determine data on the USMC assisted Summer/Fall 1965 Rice Harvest, encl 7, III MAF ComdC, Nov65.

Cordon and Search: The Seeds of COUNTY FAIR and Population Control

Additional sources for this section are: 9th Marines ComdC, Aug-Dec65; 3d Marines ComdCs, Aug-Dec65; *Simmons Comments, Jan70*.

20. Col Sumner A. Vale, Comments on draft MS, Shulimson, ''USMC Ops RVN, Jul-Dec65,'' dtd 4Jun71 (Vietnam Comment File).
21. *Simmons Comments, Jan70*.
22. *Ludwig Intvw*.
23. LtCol Charles Ward, Comments on draft MS, dtd 27Oct76 (Vietnam Comment File).

Civic Action

Additional source for this section is the I Corps Joint Coordinating Council Minutes, v. I, Sep65-Dec66, hereafter *ICJCC Minutes*, with specific date.

24. Walt, *Strange War, Strange Strategy*, ch. 7.
25. See *ICJCC Minutes*, dtd 6Sep65.
26. *ICJCC Minutes*, dtd 4Oct65.
27. Mr. Marcus J. Gordon, Comments on draft MS, Shulimson, ''Marines in Vietnam, pt 2,'' dtd 10Feb70 (Vietnam Comment File).
28. 3d MarDiv ComdC, Oct65, p. 25.
29. Stolfi, *Civic Action*, p. 53 and footnote 28, p. 90.

The Ngu Hanh Son Campaign and the Frustrations of Pacification

Additional sources for this section are: Reports on Quang Nam Pacification Program, Nov65-Feb66 in *Weller Working Papers*.

30. *MACV Comd Hist, 1965*, p. 233; Cooper *et. al., The American Experience with Pacification*, v. 3, pp. 233-34.
31. I Corps Advisory Group, Fact Sheet on Quang Nam Special Sector, dtd 8Nov65, encl 10, III MAF ComdC, Oct65.

32. CGFMFPac msg to CMC, dtd 18Sep65 (HQMC Msg File).

33. CG 3dMarDiv ltr to COs 3d, 9th, 4th, and 7th Marines, dtd 26Oct65, Subj: Protection of RVN Officials, encl 58, 3d Marines ComdC, Oct65.

34. 1/3 ComdC, Dec65.

35. 3/7 ComdC, Dec65, p. 2.

PART IV
SUPPORTING THE TROOPS

Chapter 10

Marine Aviation in Vietnam

Unless otherwise noted the material in this chapter is derived from: *MACV Comd Hist, 1965*; FMFPac, *Marine Forces in Vietnam, Mar65-Sep67*; FMFPac, *III MAF Ops, Mar-Sep65*; FMFPac, *III MAF Ops*, Oct-Dec65; FMFPac ComdC, Mar-Dec65; III MAF ComdCs, May-Dec65; 1st MAW ComdCs, May-Dec65; HQMC Msg File; *Flag Plot File*; Vietnam Comment File; Shulimson, ''U.S. Marines in Vietnam, pt 1''; Shulimson, ''Marines in Vietnam, pt. 2''; LtCol Ralph F. Moody, Maj Thomas E. Donnelly, and Captain Moyers S. Shore, ''Backing up The Troops,'' MS, pt 8 of LtCol Ralph F. Moody *et. al.*, ''Marines in Vietnam, 1954-May68,'' hereafter, Moody *et. al.*, ''Backing up the Troops, pt 8''; Cahill and Shulimson, ''USMC Ops RVN, Jan-Jun65''; Shulimson, ''USMC Ops RVN, Jul-Dec65''; Simmons, ''Marine Corps Ops, 1965-66''; LtGen Keith B. McCutcheon, ''Marine Aviation in Vietnam, 1962-1970,'' *Naval Review 1971* (Annapolis: U. S. Naval Institute, 1971), pp. 122-55, hereafter McCutcheon, ''Marine Aviation.''

Deployments

Additional sources for this section are: 1st MAW (Rear) ComdCs, Jul-Dec65; MAG-11 ComdCs, Jul-Dec65; MAG-12 ComdCs, May-Dec65; MAG-16 ComdCs, Mar-Sep65; MAG-36 ComdCs, Sep-Dec65.

1. Col Robert J. Lynch, Jr., Comments on draft MS, dtd 2Sep76 (Vietnam Comment File).

2. Col Richard A. Savage, Comments on draft MS, dtd 2Nov76 (Vietnam Comment File).

Control of Marine Aviation

3. Lynn Montross, Maj Hubard D. Kuokka, and Maj Norman W. Hicks, *The East Central Front—U.S. Marine Operations in Korea, 1950-1953*, v. IV, (Washington: HistBr, G-3 Div, HQMC, 1962), pp. 15-18.

4. CinCPac msg to ComUSMACV, dtd 29Mar65 (*Flag Plot File*).

5. CinCPac msg to ComUSMACV, dtd 24Apr65 (*Flag Plot File*).

6. HqUSMACV Directive 95-4, dtd 13Jul65, encl 10, Tab F, G-3 Div, HQMC, Staff Visit West Pac, Nov-Dec65.

7. 1st MAW ComdC, Jul-Aug 65, pt III, sec. 2, Air Defense, and App 9, Memorandum of Agreement between CG 2d Air Div and CG 1st MAW, n.d.

Fixed-Wing Operations

Additional sources for this section are: MAG-11 ComdCs Jul-Dec65; MAG-12 ComdCs, Jul-Dec65; VMF-212 (AW) ComdC, 1965, dtd 10Dec65.

8. FMFPac, *Marine Forces in Vietnam, Mar65-Sep67*, v.I, pp. 6-5—6-6.

9. 1st MAW ComdC, Dec65, p. 3-5.

10. 1st MAW ComdC, Jul-Aug65, p. 4.

11. Col Norman G. Ewers, Comments on draft MS, dtd 7Oct76 (Vietnam Comment File).

12. 1st MAW ComdC, Dec65; MAG-11 ComdC, Dec65; and MAG-12 ComdC, Dec65. See also FMFPac, *Marine Forces in Vietnam, Mar65-Sep67*, v. II, pp. 32-37.

13. 1st MAW ComdC, Nov65, p. 2-4.

14. 1st MAW ComdC, Dec65, p. 2-2.

15. 1st MAW ComdC, Jul-Aug65, p. 2-3.

16. MAG-11 ComdC, Oct65, encl 4, p. 13.

17. MAG-12 ComdC, Dec65, p. 1.

18. FMFPac, *Marine Forces in Vietnam, Mar65-Sep67*, v. II, p. 36.

19. LtCol Harlan P. Chapman, Comments on draft MS, dtd 29Oct76 (Vietnam Comment File).

Helicopter Operations

Additional sources for this section are: MAG-16 ComdCs, Mar-Dec65 and MAG-36 ComdCs, Jul-Dec65.

20. III MAF Press Release 428-65, dtd 15Aug65, encl 5, MAG-16 ComdC, Jul-Aug65.

21. *Ibid.*, and BGen Marc A. Moore, Comments on draft MS, n.d. [Nov76] (Vietnam Comment File).

22. 3d MarDiv ComdC, Oct65, p. 15.

23. *O'Connor Comments*.

24. MAG-16 ComdC, Sep65, p. 14.

25. Maj Gary W. Parker, Comments on draft MS, dtd 15Oct76 (Vietnam Comment File).

26. *Ibid.*

27. III MAF Press Release 612-65, dtd 16Sep65, encl 1, MAG-16 ComdC, Sep65.

Air Defense Responsibilities

Additional sources for this section are: 1st LAAM Bn ComdCs, Feb-Dec65 and 2d LAAM Bn ComdCs, Sep-Dec65.

28. Col George G. Long, Comments on draft MS, dtd 8Nov76 (Vietnam Comment File).

29. Col Edward F. Penico, Comments on draft MS, dtd 13Dec76.

30. CGFMFPac, Trip Summary, Visit to WestPac, 3-11Dec65, dtd 14Dec65, p. 14.

Chapter 11

Fire Support and Reconnaissance

Unless otherwise noted the material in this chapter is derived from: *MACV Comd Hist*, 1965; FMFPac, *Marine Forces in Vietnam, Mar65-Sep67*; FMFPac, *III MAF Ops, Mar-Sep65*; FMFPac, *III MAF Ops*, Oct-Dec65; III MAF ComdCs, May-Dec65; 3d MarDiv ComdCs, May-Dec65; HQMC Msg File; Vietnam Comment File; Shulimson, "U.S. Marines in Vietnam, pt 1"; Shulimson, "Marines in Vietnam, pt 2"; Moody *et. al.,* "Backing Up The Troops, pt 8"; Cahill and Shulimson "USMC OPs RVN, Jan-Jun65"; Shulimson, "USMC Ops RVN, Jul-Dec65"; Simmons, "Marine Corps Ops, 1965-66."

Artillery Support

Additional sources for this section are: 12th Marines ComdCs, Jul-Dec65; 1/12 ComdCs Mar-Dec65; 2/12 ComdCs, Jul-Dec65; 3/12 ComdCs, Jun-Dec65; 4/12 ComdCs, Jul-Dec65; 3/11 ComdCs, Aug-Dec65.

1. Col Sumner A. Vale, Comments on draft MS, dtd 12Aug77 (Vietnam Comment File); 4/12 Comd C, Sep65.

2. See for the command changes, 3d MarDiv OpO 327-65, dtd 15Aug65 and 3d MarDiv OpO 329-65, Aug65, encls 1 and 3, 3d MarDiv ComdC, Aug65. See also 12th Marines ComdCs, Aug and Sep65, and 3/12 ComdC, Aug65.

3. 2/12 ComdC, Jul65, p. 3.

4. 3d MarDiv ComdC, Sep65, p. 17.

5. FSCC portions of 3d MarDiv ComdCs, Oct-Dec65.

6. 1st MAW ComdC, Jul-Aug65, pt III, sec. 13, pp. 3-4.

7. 12th Marines ComdC, Sep65, p. 5.

8. *Ibid.*, Dec65, p. 5, and Prov Arty Bn AAR, encl 1, TF DELTA AAR, Opn HARVEST MOON, p. 6.

9. 3/12 ComdC, Dec65.

Naval Gunfire

An additional source for this section is: Naval Gunfire Requirements, CMC File 32, (General Wallace M. Greene, Jr. Personal Papers Collection (PC 511) Hist&MusDiv, HQMC), hereafter *Naval Gunfire File (Greene Papers)*.

10. HQMC, AO3H, Talking Paper, dtd 20Jun65, Subj: Naval Gunfire Support, Tab U, *Naval Gunfire File (Greene Papers)*.

11. *MACV Comd Hist, 1965*, p. 176.

12. *Ibid.*, p. 178, and Naval History Division, "History of U.S. Naval Operations in the Vietnam Conflict, 1965-67," MS, Feb71, v. III, pt 2, p. 478 hereafter NHD, "History of U.S. Naval Opns, 1965-67."

13. *MACV Comd Hist* 1965, p. 176.

14. *Ibid.*, p. 178.

15. *Ibid.*, pp. 178-9.

16. HqIIIMAF, G-3 Sec, Memo for the AC/S, G-3, dtd 16Sep65, Subj: Naval Gunfire Activities, encl 1, III MAF ComdC, Aug65.

17. *Ibid.*, and HqIIIMAF, G-3 Sec, Agenda Subject: Naval Gunfire Support, dtd 4Jan66, encl, III MAF ComdC, Jan 66.

18. NHD, "History of U.S. Naval Opns, 1965-67," p. 487; Simmons, "Marine Corps Ops, 1965-66," p. 22; 1st ANGLICO ComdC, Jul-Dec65; *Walt Comments*.

Other Ground Combat Support

Additional sources for this section are 3d Tank Bn ComdCs, Jul-Dec65; 3d Anti-Tank Bn ComdCs, Jul-Dec65; 1st AmTrac Bn, ComdCs, Jul-Dec65.

19. 3d TankBn ComdC, Nov 65.

20. *Ibid.*

Marine Reconnaissance

Additional sources for this section are 1st Force Recon Co ComdCs, Sep-Dec65; 3d Recon Bn ComdCs, May-Dec65; *Simmons Comments, Jan70*; LtCol Roy R. Van Cleve, intvw by MCB, CamPen, dtd 17Jun66 (No. 144, Oral Hist Coll, Hist&MusDiv, HQMC), hereafter *Van Cleve Intvw*; Capt James L. Compton, intvw by MCB, Quantico, dtd 30Jun67 (No. 339, Oral Hist Coll, Hist&MusDiv, HQMC), hereafter *Compton Intvw*; GySgt Gus A. Koch, intvw by MCB, Camp Lejeune, dtd 21Apr67 (No. 643, Oral Hist Coll, Hist&MusDiv, HQMC), hereafter *Koch Intvw*; LCdr Ray W. Stubbe, USN, "Paddles, Parachutes, and Patrols," MS (Hist&MusDiv, HQMC), hereafter Stubbe, "Paddles, Parachutes, and Patrols."

21. HQMC, Revision 1, Table of Organization M-1428, Reconnaissance Battalion, Marine Division, Fleet Marine Force, dtd 23Sep63, hereafter *Rev 1, TO M-1428*; HQMC Table of Organization M-4623, Force Reconnaissance Company, Fleet Marine Force, dtd 23Sep63.

1st Force Reconnaissance Company: The Early Days

An additional source for this section is: Capt David Whittingham, intvw by Hq FMFLant, dtd 15Feb66 (No. 81, Oral Hist Coll, Hist&MusDiv, HQMC).

22. BGen Edwin H. Simmons, intvw by Hist&MusDiv, dtd 26Aug77 (Oral Hist Coll, Hist&MusDiv, HQMC).

23. 1st Force Recon Co ComdC, Oct65.

3d Reconnaissance Battalion, Opening Moves

An additional source for this section is: LtCol Russell B. Tiffany, intvw by Hist&MusDiv, dtd Sep77 (Oral Hist Coll, Hist&MusDiv, HQMC), hereafter *Tiffany Intvw*.

24. CG 3dMarDiv msg to 3dMarDiv, dtd 19Sep65, encl 3, 3d Recon Bn ComdC, Sep65; *Van Cleve Intvw*.

25. 3d Recon Bn ComdC, Sep65.

26. *Tiffany Intvw*.

27. 3d Recon Bn ComdC, Jun65.

28. Quoted in Stubbe, "Paddles, Parachutes, and Patrols," p. 553.

29. *Van Cleve Intvw*.

30. HQMC, Provisional Table of Organization M-1428, Reconnaissance Battalion, Marine Division, Fleet Marine Force, dtd 20Feb58; HQMC, Table of Organization M-1428, Reconnaissance Battalion, Marine Division, Fleet Marine Force, dtd 8Mar61.

31. *Rev 1, TO M-1428*.

32. Quoted in Stubbe, ''Paddles, Parachutes and Patrols,'' p. 491.

33. *Ibid.*, p. 448.

34. *Ibid.*, p. 490.

35. Capt Francis J. West Jr., USMCR, ''Stingray 70,'' *United States Naval Institute Proceedings*, v. 95, no. 11 (Nov69), pp. 26-37.

Force and Division Reconnaissance Merged

36. BGen Edwin H. Simmons, Comments on draft MS, dtd 29Sep76 (Vietnam Comment File).

Chapter 12

Logistics and Construction

Unless otherwise noted the material in this chapter is derived from: *MACV Comd Hist, 1965*; FMFPac, *Marine Forces in Vietnam, Mar65-Sep67*; FMFPac, *III MAF Ops, Mar-Sep65*; FMFPac, *III MAF Ops*, Oct-Dec65; FMFPac ComdC, Mar-Dec65; III MAF ComdCs, May-Dec65; 3d MarDiv ComdCs, May-Dec65; 1st MAW ComdCs, May-Dec65; FLSG ComdCs, May-Dec65; HQMC Msg File; Vietnam Comment File; Shulimson, ''U.S. Marines in Vietnam, pt 1''; Shulimson, ''U.S. Marines in Vietnam, pt 2''; Moody *et. al.*, ''Backing Up The Troops, pt 8''; Cahill and Shulimson, ''USMC Ops RVN, Jan-Jun65''; Shulimson, ''USMC Ops RVN, Jul-Dec65''; Sharp and Westmoreland, *Report on the War*; Hooper, *Mobility, Support, and Endurance*; Simmons, ''Marine Corps Ops, 1965-66.''

The Logistic Situation

1. Sharp and Westmoreland, *Report on the War*, p. 100.

2. HQMC, Staff Study, dtd 6Jun69, Subj: Logistic Posture at the Start of the Vietnam Buildup.

3. *Nickerson Comments.*

4. BGen Mauro J. Padalino, Comments on draft MS, dtd 23Oct76 (Vietnam Comment File).

5. *Ibid.*

6. *Nickerson Comments.*

7. *Dennis Comments, 76.*

8. *Nickerson Comments.*

9. Col Harold A. Hayes, Comments on draft MS, dtd 29Oct76 (Vietnam Comment File).

10. CGFMFPac msg to CinCPacFlt, dtd 14May65 (HQMC Msg File).

11. Cahill and Shulimson, ''USMC Opns RVN, Jan-Jun65,'' p. 189.

12. BGen Robert F. Conley, Comments on draft MS, dtd 28Oct76 (Vietnam Comment File).

III MAF Naval Responsibilities

13. AC/S G-4 III MAF memo to CGIIIMAF, dtd 16May65, Subj: Concept of Logistic Support, encl 14, III MAF ComdC, May 1965; CNO msg to CinCPac, dtd 28May65 (*Flag Plot File*); AC/S G-4 III MAF Position Paper, dtd 15Jun65, Subj: Operation of Ports, Beaches, and Depots from Chu Lai to DMZ, encl, III MAF ComdC, Jun65, hereafter *III MAF G-4 Position Paper, Jun 65*; Hooper, *Mobility, Support, and Endurance*, pp. 70-71.

14. *III MAF G-4 Position Paper, Jun65.*

15. III MAF ComdCs, Jul-Dec65; Force/Naval Component Command Order 5400.1, dtd 24Dec65, encl 4, III MAF ComdC, Dec65; Hooper, *Mobility, Support, and Endurance*, pp. 37-38, 78.

16. III MAF ComdC, Jul65, p. 5.

17. FMFPac, *Marine Forces in Vietnam, Mar65-Sep67*, v. I, p. 8-27.

18. FMFPac, *III MAF Ops*, Dec65, p. 3.

19. III MAF ComdC, Oct65, p. 8.

20. *Ibid.*, p. 7 and FMFPac, *III MAF Ops*, Dec65, pp. 43-44.

21. 1st MAW ComdC, Dec65, p. 2-4.

RED BALL and CRITIPAC

22. Col Harold A. Hayes, Jr., Comments on draft MS, dtd 29Oct76 (Vietnam Comment File).

23. III MAF ComdC, Aug65, p. 7.

24. FMFPac, *Marine Forces in Vietnam, Mar65-Sep67*, v. I, p. 8-9.

25. 3d MarDiv ComdC, Dec65, p. 14.

26. *Ibid.*, p. 15, and FMFPac, *III MAF Ops*, Dec65.

The Force Logistic Support Group

27. FLSG ComdC, Dec65, p. 2.

28. FMFPac ComdC, Mar-Dec65, p. 16.

Engineering and Construction

Additional sources for this section are: 3d Engr Bn ComdCs, Jul-Dec65; 7th Engr Bn ComdCs, Aug-Dec65.

29. Col William M. Graham, Comments on draft MS, dtd 8Nov76 (Vietnam Comment File).

30. Col Nicholas J. Dennis, Comments on draft MS, dtd 18Aug77 (Vietnam Comment File).

31. LtCol Bernard A. Kaasmann, Comments on Cahill and Shulimson draft MS, ''USMC Opns RVN, Jan-Jun65,'' dtd 24Apr68 (Vietnam Comment File).

32. ''Background of Deployment to the Republic of Vietnam,'' n.d., encl 2, *Dennis Comments, 76*, hereafter *Background of Deployment.*

33. *O'Connor Comments.*

34. *Dennis Comments, 76.*

35. *Ibid.*, and *Background of Deployment.*

36. *Dennis Comments 76.*

37. *Ibid.*

38. 7th Engr Bn ComdCs, Sep65 p. 5 and Nov65, p. 3.

39. MACV-4PR Memo for the Record, dtd 23Sep65, Subj: Establishing of Committee to Survey 16 Kms of Railroad Prior to Acquiring for Use by Marine Corps, encl, BGen Webb D. Sawyer, Comments on draft MS, dtd 3Nov76 (Vietnam Comment File); *Dennis Comments, 76*; 3d Engr Bn ComdC, Dec65.

40. MAG-36 ComdC, Sep65, p. 2.

41. 1st MAW ComdC, Sep65, p. 2-4.
42. *Ibid.*, p. 3-10.
43. McCutcheon, ''Marine Aviation,'' pp. 129-30.
44. *Ibid.*, p. 130.
45. *Walt Comments.*
46. MajGen Keith B. McCutcheon, Comments on Cahill and Shulimson draft MS, ''USMC Opns RVN, Jan-Jun65,'' dtd 24Apr68 (Vietnam Comment File).

PART V
OTHER MARINE ACTIVITIES

Chapter 13

The SLF of the Seventh Fleet

Unless otherwise noted the material in this chapter is derived from: *MACV Comd Hist, 1965;* FMFPac, *III MAF Ops Mar-Sep65;* FMFPac, *III MAF Ops*, Oct-Dec65; FMFPac, ComdC, Mar-Dec65; ComPhibFor, U. S. Seventh Flt, ''History of Amphibious Opns in South Vietnam, Mar65-Dec66,'' n.d.; SLF (TG 78.5) ComdC, 19Jun-10Oct65; SLF (TG 78.5/79.5) ComdC, 11Oct-31Dec65; HQMC Msg File; Shulimson, ''U.S. Marines in Vietnam, pt 1''; Shulimson, ''Marines in Vietnam, pt 2''; Cahill and Shulimson, ''USMC Ops RVN, Jan-Jun65''; Shulimson, ''USMC Opns RVN, Jul-Dec65''; LtCol Ralph F. Moody and Benis M. Frank, ''SLF Operations in Vietnam,'' MS (Hist&MusDiv, HQMC).

Disbandment of the SLF

Additional sources for this section are: BLT 2/9 ComdD, 23Dec64-7Mar65; BLT 2/9 ComdD, Mar-Apr65.
1. CGFMFPac, Trip Summary, Visit to West Pac, 14-21 May 1965, n.d., p. 17.

A New Mission

An additional source for this section is CinCPacFlt/ComUSMACV Agreement of 14Mar65, Subj: Anti-Sea Infiltration Operations, encl 2, FMFPac, Provisions of Close Air Support for Seventh Fleet Operations, Operation DECKHOUSE III in Support of ComUSMACV in RVN, dtd 19Aug66, hereafter *CinCPacFlt/ComUSMACV Mar Agreement.*
2. Amphibious Opns on RVN Coastline and Adjacent Islands, Anx B, *CinCPacFlt/ComUSMACV Mar Agreement.*
3. MACV-J3 ltr to CinCPac, dtd [14May65], Subj: Transmittal of Agreement (*CinCPacFlt/ComUSMACV Mar Agreement*).
4. CGFMFPac, Trip Summary, Visit to West Pac, 14-21 May 1965, n.d., p. 13.
5. CinCPac msg to PacFlt, dtd 27Jun65 (GP-5 DAGGER THRUST, *Flag Plot File*).
6. CGFMFPac msg to CGIIIMAF, dtd 12Jun65 (HQMC Msg File).

The Reestablishment of the SLF

The general source for this section is SLF (TG 78.5) ComdC, 19Jun-10Oct65.

Command and Control Changes

7. As quoted in CGFMFPac msg to AdminO 3d MarDiv, dtd 13Jun65 (HQMC Msg File).
8. *Ibid.*
9. *Ibid.*
10. *Ibid.*
11. SLF (TG 78.5) ComdC, 19Jun-10Oct65, p. 5.
12. CTF 79 msg to CGFMFPac, dtd 23Aug65 (HQMC Msg File).
13. LtGen Lewis J. Fields, Comments on draft MS, dtd 21Oct76 (Vietnam Comment File), hereafter *Field Comments.*
14. CTF 79 msg to ComSeventhFlt, dtd 11Sep65 (HQMC Msg File).
15. Quoted in CGFMFPac msg to CTF 79, dtd 15Sep65.
16. *Ibid.*
17. *Ibid.*
18. Quoted in CTF 79 msg to CGFMFPac, dtd 14Sep65 (HQMC Msg File).
19. MCCC, Items of Significant Interest, dtd 14Sep65.

The First DAGGER THRUST Raids

20. *O'Donnell and Staff Comments.*
21. Col Robert T. Hanifin, Comments on Shulimson draft MS, ''USMC Ops RVN, Jul-Dec65,'' dtd 1Jun71 (Vietnam Comment File).
22. CTF 78.5, Post Opns Report for DAGGER THRUST Targets 2, 4, and 11, dtd 5Oct65, encl 9, SLF (TG 78.5) ComdC, 19Jun-10Oct65.
23. FMFPac, *III MAF Ops*, Nov65, p. 7.

Further Changes in the SLF

24. FMFPac msg to CMC, Sit Rep No. 201, dtd 17Oct65 (HQMC Msg File).
25. *Field Comments.*

The Saigon Conference

26. As quoted in CGFMFPac msg to CMC, dtd 29Jul65 (HQMC Msg File).
27. CinCPacFlt msg to CGFMFPac and ComPhibPac, dtd 20Oct65 (CinCPacFlt Briefer's File, OAB, NHD).
28. ComUSMACV msg to CinCPacFlt, dtd 8Oct65 in *Ibid.*
29. CinCPacFlt msg, 20Oct65, *op.cit.*
30. CTF 115 msg to CinCPacFlt, dtd 28Oct65 (CinCPacFlt Briefer's File OAB,NHD).

The Second Series of DAGGER THRUST Raids

31. ComSeventhFlt msg to CTF 79, dtd 24Nov65 (GP-5 DAGGER THRUST, *Flag Plot File*).
32. Adm Roy L. Johnson, Comments on draft MS, dtd 12Aug77 (Vietnam Comment File).

The SLF at the End of the Year

33. FMFPac ComdC, Mar-Dec65.

Chapter 14

Advisors and Other Marine Activities in Vietnam

Unless otherwise noted the material in this chapter is derived from: *MACV Comd Hist 1965*; Unit Diaries of Casual Company (RUC 54013) and Company B (RUC 54026) HqBn, HQMC; Vietnam Comment File; Shulimson, ''U.S. Marines in Vietnam, pt 1''; Cahill and Shulimson, ''USMC Opns RVN, Jan-Jun65''; Shulimson, ''USMC Opns RVN, Jul-Dec65.''

Marine Advisors to the Vietnamese Marine Corps

Additional sources for this section are: MAU, NavAdvGp, MACV, After Tour Reports, hereafter *ATR* with individual name and report date; MAU, After Action Reports (AARs); SMA, MAU, Monthly Evaluation Reports, Jan-Dec65; NavGp, MACV, Monthly Fact Sheets, Jan-Dec65; SMA, NavGp, MACV ltr to CMC, dtd 13Jul66, Subj: Organization, Employment, and Support of the Vietnamese Marine Corps; SMA, MACV, ltr to CMC, dtd 22Mar73, Subj: Vietnamese Marine Corps/Marine Advisory Unit Historical Summary, 1954-73.

1. LtCol Lane Rogers, Comments on draft MS, n.d. [Jan77] (Vietnam Comment File), hereafter *Rogers Comments*.
2. *Ibid.*
3. Col William P. Nesbit, *ATR*, dtd 1Sep65, hereafter *Nesbit ATR*.
4. Maj William G. Leftwich, *ATR*, dtd 10Jan66, hereafter *Leftwich ATR*.
5. *Rogers Comments*.
6. SMA, TF ALFA AAR, 9-13Mar65, dtd 7Jun65.
7. SMA, TF ALFA AAR, 1-26Apr65, dtd 8Jun65.
8. *Leftwich ATR* and Maj William G. Leftwich, ''Decision at Duc Co,'' *Marine Corps Gazette*, v. 51, no. 2 (Feb66), pp. 34-38.
9. SMA, MAU, Monthly Evaluation Reports, Jan-Dec65.
10. *Nesbit ATR*.
11. USMACV, U.S. Naval Advisory Group, Joint Table of Distribution, dtd 15Nov65 (OAB, NHD), hereafter *MACV JTD, Nov 65*.

Marine Advisors of the Rung Sat Special Zone

Additional material for this section is derived from: Naval Advisory Group, MACV, Monthly Fact Sheets No. 17, Jan-Dec65, Subj: Rung Sat Special Zone, hereafter, *NavGp, RSSZ*;

LtCol Albert C. Smith, Jr., ''Rung Sat Special Zone,'' *U.S. Naval Institute Proceedings*, v. 94, no. 4 (Apr 1968), pp. 117-18.

12. *NavGp, RSSZ*, May65, dtd 7May65.
13. *MACV JTD, Nov65*.
14. *NavGp, RSSZ*.

U.S. Marines of the I Corps Advisory Group

15. CMC/CGFMFPac Conference at HqFMFPac, dtd 28Apr65 (No. 6298, Oral Hist Coll, Hist&MusDiv, HQMC); CGFMFPac msg to CG 3d MarDiv, dtd 13Apr65 (HQMC Msg File).
16. *Leftwich ATR*.

Marines Serving with MACV Headquarters Saigon

17. *MACV Comd Hist, 1965*, pp. 93-94.
18. *Ibid.*, p. 94.
19. Col Francis F. Parry, Comments on draft MS, dtd 18Oct76 (Vietnam Comment File).
20. BGen Webb D. Sawyer, Comments on draft MS, dtd 25Oct76 (Vietnam Comment File).
21. *Ibid.*

Company L, Marine Support Battalion

The material for this section is derived from: Unit Diaries of Company L, Marine Support Battalion (RUC 54101) 1-4Jan65, (RUC 54043) 5Jan-31Dec65; MACV Strength Report, 1Jan65, dtd 11Jan65.

22. LtCol Donald J. Hatch, Comments on draft MS, dtd 22Oct76 (Vietnam Comment File).

Embassy Marines

The material for this section is derived from Marine Security Guard, American Embassy, Saigon, RVN, Quarterly and Special Incident Reports, 1965.

Chapter 15

Conclusion

1. FMFPac, *Marine Forces in Vietnam, Mar65-Sep67*, v. 1, p. 9-14, and v. 2, pp. 86-98.
2. LtGen Victor H. Krulak, MajGen Keith B. McCutcheon, and MajGen Lewis W. Walt, intvw by MCDEC, dtd Dec65 (No. 6001, Oral Hist Coll, Hist&Mus Div, HQMC).
3. Quoted in Simmons, ''Marine Corps Ops, 1965-66,'' p. 27.

Appendix A
Marine Task Organizations and Command List January—December 1965

Marine Unit Vietnam (CTU 79.3.5)
1 Jan-9 Mar

Commanding Officer
Col John H. King, Jr. .1 Jan-9 Mar
Sub-Unit 2, MABS-16
LtCol Thomas E. Vernon . . . . .1 Jan-9 Mar
HMM-365
LtCol Joseph Koler, Jr. . . . . .1 Jan-18 Feb
HMM-163
LtCol Norman G. Ewers . . . . .18 Feb-9 Mar
1st LAAM Battalion
LtCol Bertram E. Cook, Jr. . . . . .8 Feb-9 Mar
Co L, 3/9
Capt John J. Sheridan . . . . .1 Jan-23 Jan
Co D, 1/3
Capt Terry Turner .23 Jan-9 Mar
Co C, 7th Engineer Battalion
Maj William G. Bates . . . . .14 Feb-9 Mar

9th Marine Exeditionary Brigade
8 Mar-6 May

9th MEB Headquarters
Commanding General
BGen Frederick J. Karch . . . . .8 Mar-6 May
Deputy Commander
Col Donald H. Stapp . . . . .8 Mar-3 Apr
Col Clifford F. Quilici . . . . .4 Apr-6 May
Chief of Staff
Col Lowell D. Grow . . . . .8 Mar-3 Apr
Col Donald H. Stapp . . . . .4 Apr-6 May
G-1
Maj Ruel T. Scyphers . . . . .8 Mar-13 Mar
Maj Samuel E. Englehart . . . . .14 Mar-6 May
G-2
Maj Edmund J. Regan, Jr. . . . . .8 Mar-6 May
G-3
LtCol Joseph E. Muir . . . . .8 Mar-6 May
G-4
LtCol Joseph G. Cervell . . . . .8 Mar-16 Apr
LtCol Joseph S. Heitzler . . . . .17 Apr-6 May

MAG-16
Col John H. King, Jr. . . . . .9 Mar-6 May

H&MS-16
Maj John J. McMasters . . . . .14 Mar-6 May
HMM-163
LtCol Norman G. Ewers . . . . .9 Mar-6 May
HMM-162
LtCol Oliver W. Curtis . . . . .9 Mar-6 May
VMFA-531
LtCol William C. McGraw, Jr. . . . . .10 Apr-6 May
VMCJ-1
LtCol Otis W. Corman . . . . .16 Apr-6 May
VMO-2
LtCol George F. Bauman . . . . .3 May-6 May

Sub-Unit 2, MABS-16

LtCol Thomas E. Vernon . . . . .9 Mar-6 May
MASS-2
LtCol Paul L. Hitchcock . . . . .16 Apr-6 May
1st LAAM Battalion
LtCol Bertram E. Cook, Jr. . . . . .9 Mar-6 May

3d Marines
Col Edwin B. Wheeler . . . . .12 Apr-6 May
1/3
LtCol Herbert J. Bain . . . . .8 Mar-27 Apr
LtCol William H. Lanagan, Jr. . . . . .28 Apr-6 May
2/3
LtCol David A. Clement . . . . .10 Apr-6 May
3/9
LtCol Charles E. McPartlin, Jr. . . . . .8 Mar-6 May
3/4
LtCol Donald R. Jones . . . . .14 Apr-27 Apr
LtCol William W. Taylor . . . . .28 Apr-6 May

Brigade Logistic Support Group
LtCol George H. Smith . . . . .12 Mar-6 May

Brigade Artillery Group
Captain Myron J. Kandra . . . . .11 Mar-11 Apr
Maj Gilbert W. Ferguson . . . . .12 Apr-6 May
1/12
Maj Gilbert W. Ferguson . . . . .12 Apr-6 May

Brigade Engineer Group
Maj William G. Bates . . . . .12 Mar-6 May

227

III Marine Amphibious Force *
6May-31Dec

*III Marine Expeditionary Force redesignated to III Marine Amphibious Force on 7 May.

III MAF Headquarters
Commanding General
MajGen William R. Collins 6May-4Jun
MajGen Lewis W. Walt .4Jun-31Dec

Deputy Commanding General
BGen Marion E. Carl .12May-24May
BGen Keith B. McCutcheon 6Jun-31Dec

Chief of Staff
Col Regan Fuller 6May-11Sep
Col George C. Axtell, Jr. 12Sep-31Dec

Deputy Chief of Staff
Col Olin W. Jones, Jr. .15Jun-18Aug
Col Howard E. Wertman 19Aug-31Dec

G-1
Col Frederick C. Dodson 6May-24May
LtCol Donald T. Doxey 25May-7Aug
Col Don W. Galbreaith .8Aug-31Dec

G-2
Col Horace E. Knapp, Jr. 6May-10May
LtCol Edward Cook 11May-30Jun
Maj Robert E. Gruenler .1Jul-9Jul
LtCol Dale N. Davis 10Jul-26Jul
Col Leo J. Dulacki 27Jul-31Dec

G-3
Col Hardy Hay 6May-9Jul
LtCol Rex C. Denny, Jr. 10Jul-14Jul
Col Edwin H. Simmons 15Jul-31Dec

G-4
Col Norman R. Nickerson 12May-27Jul
LtCol Joseph S. Heitzler 28Jul-25Aug
Col Harold A. Hayes, Jr. 26Aug-31Dec

G-5 *
Col Elmer G. Glidden, Jr. 23Aug-28Oct
Maj Charles J. Keever .29Oct-31Dec

*On 29 October, the G-5 changed from Plans Officer to Civil Affairs/Psychological Warfare Officer and a new billet, G-6 Plans officer, was established.

G-6
Col Elmer G. Glidden, Jr. 29Oct-31Dec

3d Marine Division *
6May-31Dec

*Until the arrival of the 9th Marines on 6 July, the 3d Marine Division had two command echelons, the 3d Marine Division (Forward) at Da Nang and the 3d Marine Division (Rear) on Okinawa.

3d Marine Division Headquarters
Commanding General
MajGen William R. Collins 6May-3Jun
MajGen Lewis W. Walt .4Jun-31Dec

Assistant Division Commander, Da Nang
BGen Frederick J. Karch 18Jun-3Aug
BGen Melvin D. Henderson 4Aug-10Dec
BGen Lowell E. English 22Dec-31Dec

Assistant Division Commander, Chu Lai
BGen Frederick J. Karch 5Aug-8Nov
BGen Jonas M. Platt 9Nov-31Dec

Chief of Staff
Col Clifford F. Quilici 6May-14May
Col Andrew I. Lyman 15May-13Aug
Col Donald W. Sherman 14Aug-31Dec

G-1
Col Edward H. Greason .6May-27Jun
Col Robert M. Port 28Jun-31Dec

G-2
Maj Charles T. Williamson 6May-24Aug
LtCol Richard J. Schriver 25Aug-31Dec

G-3
Col Royal E. North 12May-12Aug
Col Don P. Wyckoff 13Aug-31Dec

G-4
LtCol John D. Ross 12May-30Jun
Col Frank R. Wilkinson, Jr. 1Jul-31Dec

G-5 *
Maj John Colia 15Dec-31Dec
*The division established the billet of Civil Affairs Psychological Warfare Officer on 15 December.

Headquarters Battalion
Maj Charles W. Abbott .6May-18Jul
Maj John E. Watson, Jr. 19Jul-31Dec

3d Marines
Col Edwin B. Wheeler 6May-15Aug
Col Norman R. Nickerson 16Aug-22Nov
Col Thell H. Fisher 23Nov-31Dec

4th Marines
Col Edward P. Dupras, Jr. 7May-24Jul
Col James F. McClanahan 25Jul-31Dec

7th Marines
Col Oscar F. Peatross 15Aug-31Dec

9th Marines
Col Frank E. Garretson .6Jul-11Aug
Col John E. Gorman 12Aug-31Dec

12th Marines
Col William P. Pala 8Jul-14Jul
LtCol Walter E. Stuenkel 15Jul-30Jul
Col James M. Callender 31Jul-31Dec

1/1
LtCol Donald V. McCloskey 28Aug-27Sep
LtCol Harold A. Hatch .28Sep-31Dec

2/1 *
LtCol Robert T. Hanifin, Jr. 23Dec-31Dec
*Part of the SLF 5Sep-22Dec.

1/3 *
LtCol William H. Lanagan, Jr. 6May-1Sep
LtCol Robert R. Dickey III 19Nov-31Dec
*1/1 relieved 1/3 on 31Aug ending the intertheater battalion transplacement system. 1/1 did not redesignate to 1/3.

2/3 *
LtCol David A. Clement 6May-10Nov
LtCol William K. Horn .11Nov-19Nov
*2/3 departed Vietnam for Okinawa as the first battalion involved in the newly instituted intra-theater battalion rotation program. The newly formed 1/3 replaced 2/3 at Da Nang.

3/3

LtCol William D. Hall 12May-30Jun
LtCol Joseph E. Muir .1Jul-10Sep
Maj Andrew G. Comer 11Sep-14Sep
LtCol Willim H. Lanagan, Jr. 15Sep-29Nov
LtCol Joshua W. Dorsey III 30Nov-31Dec

1/4

LtCol Harold D. Fredericks 7May-30May
LtCol Robert J. Perrich .31May-31Dec

2/4

LtCol Joseph R. Fisher 7May-14Oct
LtCol Rodolfo L. Trevino 15Oct-31Dec

3/4 *

LtCol William W. Taylor .6May-30Sep
LtCol Sumner A. Vale .1Oct-22Dec
*2/1 relieved 3/4 at Phu Bai on 22Dec and the latter unit
sailed for Okinawa under the intra-theater battalion rotation
system.

1/7

LtCol James P. Kelly 15Aug-31Dec

2/7 *

LtCol Leon N. Utter 7Jul-31Dec
*Located at Qui Nhon 7Jul-4Nov. During the period 7Jul-
4Aug, III MAF had operational control of 2/7. After that
period, the U. S. Army's Task Force Alpha, which became I
Field Force, Vietnam in November, had the operational control
of the unit.

3/7 *

LtCol Charles H. Bodley 3Sep-31Dec
*Part of the SLF Jun-Sep.

1/9

LtCol Verle E. Ludwig 16Jun-31Dec

2/9

LtCol George R. Scharnberg 6Jul-31Aug
LtCol William F. Donahue, Jr. 1Sep-31Dec

3/9 *

LtCol Charles E. McPartlin, Jr. 6May-17Jun
LtCol Robert J. Tunnell, Jr. 14Aug-30Sep
LtCol William W. Taylor 1Oct-31Dec
*3/9 departed Vietnam on 17Jun under the battalion intra-
theater transplacement system. The newly formed 3/9
returned to Vietnam on 14Aug.

3/11

LtCol William H. Peck 16Aug-29Dec
LtCol Paul B. Watson, Jr. 30Dec-31Dec

1/12

Maj Gilbert W. Ferguson 6May-8Jul
LtCol Warren E. McCain 9Jul-31Dec

2/12

LtCol Jack K. Knocke .7Jul-1Sep
LtCol Eugene O. Speckart 2Sep-31Dec

3/12

Maj Jesse L. Gibney, Jr. 7May-9Jul
LtCol Leslie L. Page 10Jul-31Dec

4/12

LtCol Edwin M. Rudzis 8Jul-31Dec

1st Amphibian Tractor Battalion

LtCol Jack Glenn 21Jul-30Jul
LtCol William D. Pomeroy 31Jul-31Dec

3d Anti-Tank Battalion

Maj Edward E. Brooks . . . . .9Jul-15 Jul
LtCol Bruce A. Heflin 16Jul-31Dec

3d Engineer Battalion

Maj Bernard A. Kaasman 20May-28May
LtCol Nicholas J. Dennis 29May-31Dec

3d Medical Battalion

LCdr John W. Davis, USN 9Jun-20Jul
Cdr Almon C. Wilson, USN 21Jul-31Dec

3d Motor Transport Battalion

LtCol Arthur C. Beverly 16Jun-26Jun
Capt William D. McGuire 27Jun-3Jul
Col Edward Cook 4Jul-11Aug
Maj Freddie J. Baker 12Aug-31Dec

3d Reconnaissance Battalion

LtCol Don H. Blanchard 7May-30Aug
LtCol Roy R. Van Cleve 31Aug-31Dec

3d Shore Party Battalion

Maj John M. Dean .1Nov-31Dec

3d Tank Battalion

LtCol States R. Jones, Jr. 8Jul-30Aug
LtCol Milton L. Raphael 31Aug-31Dec

5th Communication Battalion

LtCol Hercules R. Kelly, Jr. 12Nov-31Dec

7th Engineer Battalion

LtCol Ermine L. Meeker 24Aug-31Dec

9th Motor Transport Battalion

Maj Joseph F. Jones .1Nov-31Dec

1st Marine Aircraft Wing *
11May-31Dec

*Designated 1st MAW (Advance) 11May-31August.

1st MAW Headquarters
Commanding General

MajGen Paul J. Fontana 11May-23May
BGen Keith B. McCutcheon 24May-31Dec

Assistant Wing Commander

BGen Marion E. Carl 1Sep-31Dec

Chief of Staff

Col Thomas J. O'Connor 11May-4Aug
Col Thomas G. Bronleewe, Jr. 5Aug-31Dec

G-1

Col Jack W. Morrison 11May-21May
LtCol Wilbur D. Wilcox 22May-26May
Maj Roger D. Swanson 27May-14Aug
Col Wilbur D. Wilcox 15Aug-31Dec

G-2

Col Lowell D. Grow .11May-11Jun
LtCol Jack W. Dindinger 12Jun-16Jul
LtCol Billy H. Barber 17Jul-31Dec

G-3

Col Douglas A. Bangert 11May-21May
LtCol Robert L. Lamar 22May-1Jul
Col Leslie E. Brown .2Jul-17Sep
Col Michael R. Yunck 18Sep-9Dec
Col Roy C. Gray, Jr. .10Dec-31Dec

G-4

Col Martin B. Roush .11May-17Jun
Col Robert J. Lynch, Jr. 18Jun-31Dec

G-5 *

Col Fred J. Frazer 22Sep-31Dec
*Plans officer for Base Development and Military Construction.

MWHG-1

Col Albert L. Jones.........................29Jun-14Jul
LtCol Bertram E. Cook, Jr. 15Jul-1Aug
Col Edward I. Lupton 2Aug-31Dec

MAG-11

Col Robert F. Conley 7Jul-2Nov
Col Emmett O. Anglin, Jr. 3Nov-31Dec

MAG-12

Col John D. Noble 16May-18Sep
Col Leslie E. Brown 19Sep-31Dec

MAG-16

Col John H. King, Jr. 6May-6Aug
Col Thomas J. O'Connor 7Aug-31Dec

MAG-36

Col William G. Johnson 1Sep-31Dec

H&HS-1

Maj Robert A. Walker 11May-26Jul
Maj Chester A. Liddle, Jr. 27Jul-31Dec

H&MS-11

LtCol Alfred F. McCaleb, Jr. 7Jul-5Aug
Capt Albert K. Charlton 6Aug-10Aug
LtCol William H. Bortz, Jr. 11Aug-31Dec

H&MS-12

LtCol John W. Kirkland 25May-26Dec
Maj William E. Garman 27Dec-31Dec

H&MS-16

Maj John J. McMasters.....................6May-9Sep
LtCol Jerome L. Goebel 10Sep-31Dec

H&MS-36

LtCol Thomas G. Mooney 1Sep-31Dec

MABS-11

LtCol Eddie E. Pearcy 7Jul-9Dec
Maj Douglas A. McCaughey, Jr. 10Dec-31Dec

MABS-12

LtCol Alexander Wilson 7May-24Sep
LtCol John W. Parchen......................25Sep-31Dec

MABS-16

LtCol Thomas E. Vernon 6May-31Dec

MABS-36

Maj Jack A. Kennedy 1Sep-31Dec

MASS-2

LtCol Paul L. Hitchcock 6May-26May
LtCol Edward I. Lupton 27May-1Aug
LtCol Ralph L. Cunningham, Jr. 2Aug-31Dec

HMM-161

LtCol Gene W. Morrison....................7May-18Sep
LtCol Rex C. Denny, Jr. 19Sep-31Dec

HMM-162 *

LtCol Oliver W. Curtis 6May-15May
*Relieved by HMM-365. Unit then returned to Okinawa for rotation to ConUS.

HMM-163 *

LtCol Norman G. Ewers 6May-21Jun
*Relieved by HMM-261; assigned as SLF squadron 27Jun-10Oct when it was relieved by HMM-261.

HMM-261 *

LtCol Mervin B. Porter......................22Jun-10Oct
*SLF squadron 10Oct-31Dec.

HMM-263

LtCol Truman Clark 12Oct-31Dec

HMM-361

LtCol Lloyd F. Childers 1Aug-31Dec

HMM-362

LtCol James Aldworth 2Sep-31Dec

HMM-363 *

Maj Willis D. Kellogg 1-2Sep
LtCol George D. New 3Sep-31Dec
*Located at Qui Nhon 1Sep-31Dec; under operational control of CG, Task Force Alpha (USA).

HMM-364

LtCol William R. Lucas 4Sep-31Dec

HMM-365 *

LtCol Joseph Koler, Jr.......................15May-30Jul
*HMM-365 relieved by HMM-361.

VMA-211

LtCol William E. Garman 11Oct-31Dec

VMA-214

LtCol Keith O'Keefe........................21Jun-31Dec

VMA-223 *

LtCol Alexander Wilson 15Dec-31Dec
*VMA-311 relieved by VMA-223 under intra-theater rotation program.

VMA-224 *

LtCol Thomas E. Mulvihill 4Oct-31Dec
*VMA-224 replaced VMA-225 under intra-theater rotation program.

VMA-225

LtCol Robert W. Baker 1Jun-30Sep

VMA-311

LtCol Bernard J. Stender 1Jun-24Nov
LtCol Jack W. Harris........................25Nov-14Dec

VMCJ-1

LtCol Otis W. Corman 6May-3Nov
LtCol Francis C. Opeka 4Nov-31Dec

VMFA-115

LtCol Clyde R. Jarrett 15Oct-31Dec

VMFA-323

LtCol Andrew W. O'Donnell 1Dec-31Dec

VMFA-513 *

LtCol Walter C. Stewart, Jr. 15Jun-14OCt
*VMFA-513 replaced by VMFA-115 under intra-theater rotation program.

VMFA-531

LtCol William C. McGraw, Jr.................6May-15Jun

VMFA-542

LtCol Richard A. Savage 10Jul-3Dec

VMF(AW)-312

LtCol Richard B. Newport....................19Dec-31Dec

VMO-2

LtCol George F. Bauman 3May-31Dec

VMO-6

LtCol Robert J. Zitnik......................1Sep-31Dec

1st LAAM Battalion
LtCol Bertram E. Cook, Jr. 6May-14Jul
Maj George G. Long 15Jul-14Nov
LtCol Clyde L. Eyer 15Nov-31Dec

2d LAAM Battalion
LtCol Edward F. Penico 10Sep-31Dec

Force Logistic Support Group
Col Robert J. Oddy 6May-24May
Col Mauro J. Padalino 25May-31Dec

Force Engineer Group *
Maj William G. Bates 6May-12May
Maj Bernard A. Kaasmann 13May-20May
*Force Engineer Group was dissolved on 20 May.

Naval Construction Regiment-30
Capt Harold F. Liberty, USN 19May-31Dec

Naval Construction Battalion-4*
Cdr Worthen A. Walls, USN 15Dec-31Dec
*NMCB-4 replaced NMCB-10 at Chu Lai, the latter unit
rotating to ConUS.

Naval Constuction Battalion-5
Cdr William F. Russel, USN 26May-31Dec

Naval Construction Battalion-8
Cdr Pharo A. Phelps, USN 26Sep-31Dec

Naval Construction Battalion-9
Cdr Richard E. Anderson, USN 27Jun-31Dec

Naval Constuction Battalion-10
Cdr John M. Bannister, USN 7May-15Dec

Appendix B

Glossary of Terms and Abbreviations

A-1E—Douglas Skyraider, a propeller-driven, single-engine, attack aircraft also known as the AD-5

A-4—Douglas Skyhawk, a single-seat, light-attack jet bomber in service on board carriers of the U.S. Navy and with land-based Marine attack squadrons.

AAR—After Action Report

AdminO—Administrative Officer

Adv—Advanced

AGC—Amphibious Command Ship

AKA—Attack Cargo Ship

ANGLICO—Air&Naval Gunfire Liaison Company

AOA—Amphibious Objective Area

APA—Attack Transport Ship

APD—High Speed Transport Ship

ARG—Amphibious Ready Group

ARVN—Army of the Republic of Vietnam

ASP—Ammunition Storage Point

ASRT—Air Support Radar Team

ArtyGru—Artillery Group

BGen—Brigadier General

BDA—Bomb Damage Assessment

BLSG—Brigade Logistic Support Group

BLT—Battalion Landing Team

Bn—Battalion

C-117D—Douglas Skytrain, a twin-engine, transport aircraft which became operational in the Marine Corps in 1943

C-130—Lockheed Hercules, a four-engine, turboprop transport aircraft

Capt—Captain

CAS—Close Air Support

CG—Commanding General

CH-37—Sikorsky twin-engine, assault, heavy transport helicopter which carried three crew members and 36 passengers

Chron—Chronology

ChronHist—Chronological History

CinCPac—Commander in Chief Pacific

CinCPacFlt—Commander in Chief Pacific Fleet

Class (I-V)—Categories of military supplies, e.g., Class I Rations; Class III - POL; Class V - Ammunitions

CMC—Commandant of the Marine Corps

CNO—Chief of Naval Operations

CO—Commanding Officer

Col—Colonel

Com—Commander

ComUSMACV—Commander, U.S. Military Assistance Command, Vietnam

ComdC—Command Chronology

ComdD—Command Diary

Composite Marine Aircraft Group—An aircraft group consisting of both helicopters and fixed-wing aircraft squadrons

CP—Command Post

CPX—Command Post Exercise

CTZ—Corps Tactical Zone

DASC—Direct Air Support Center—A subordinate operational component of the Marine air control system designed for control and direction of close air support and other direct air support operations

DD—Destroyer

DFC—Distinguished Flying Cross

DIA—Defense Intelligence Agency

Dtd—Dated

DRV—Democratic Republic of Vietnam

DMZ—Demilitarized Zone separating North and South Vietnam

ECM—Electronic Counter Measures

ELINT—Electronic Intelligence

Engr—Engineer

F-4B—McDonnell Phantom II, a twin-engined, two-seat, long-range, all-weather jet interceptor and attack bomber

F-4C—U.S. Air Force version of the above

FLSG—Force Logistic Support Group

FLSU—Force Logistic Support Unit

FMFPac—Fleet Marine Force Pacific

Free Strike Area—A zone in which air strikes could be directed without prior RVN clearance

FSR—Force Service Regiment

Fwd—Forward

G—Refers to staff positions on a general staff, e.g., G-1 would refer to the staff member responsible for personnel; G-2 Intelligence; G-3 Operations; G-4 Logistics; etc.

GCI—Ground-Controlled Intercept

Gen—General

GVN—Government of Vietnam

H-Hour—In connection with planned operations, it is the specific hour the operation begins

HAWK—A mobile, surface-to-air, guided missile designed to defend against enemy aircraft flying at low altitudes and short-range rocket missiles

HistBr, G-3 Div, HQMC—Historical Branch, G-3 Division, Headquarters, U.S. Marine Corps

HistMusDiv, HQMC—History and Museums Division, HQMC. Replaced HistBr, G-3 Div, HQMC

HistOff—Historical Office

HMM—Marine Medium Helicopter Squadron

J-—The designations for members of a joint staff which includes members of several services comprising the command, e.g., J-1 would refer to the staff member responsible for personnel; J-2 Intelligence; J-3 Operations; J-4 Logistics; etc.

JCS—Joint Chiefs of Staff

JGS—Joint General Staff (Vietnamese)

JTD—Joint Table of Distribution

KC-130—The in-flight refueling tanker configuration of the C-130 Lockheed Hercules.

L-Hour—In planned helicopter operations, it is the specific hour the helicopters land in the landing zone

LCM—Landing Craft, Mechanized

LCVP—Landing Craft, Vehicle and Personnel

LogSptGru—Logistic Support Group

LPD—Amphibious Transport Dock

LPH—Amphibious Assault Ship

LSD—Dock Landing Ship

LST—Tank Landing Ship

LSU—Logistic Support Unit

Lt—Lieutenant

LtCol—Lieutenant Colonel

LtGen—Lieutenant General

Ltr—Letter

LVTP—Landing Vehicle Tracked, Personnel

MAAG—Military Assistance Advisory Group

MAB—Marine Amphibious Brigade

MABS—Marine Air Base Squadron

MAC—Marine Amphibious Corps

MACS—Marine Air Control Squadron

MACV—Military Assistance Command Vietnam

MAF—Marine Amphibious Force

MAG—Marine Aircraft Group

Main Force—Refers to organized Viet Cong battalions and regiments as opposed to local VC guerrilla groups

Maj—Major

MajGen—Major General

MarDiv—Marine Division

_Marines—Designates a Marine regiment, e.g., 3d Marines

MASS—Marine Air Support Squadron

MATCU—Marine Air Traffic Control Unit

MAW—Marine Aircraft Wing

MCAF—Marine Corps Air Facility

MCAS—Marine Corps Air Station

MCCC—Marine Corps Command Center

MEB—Marine Expeditionary Brigade

MEBLEX—MEB Landing Exercise

MedCap—Medical Civilian Assistance Program

MEF—Marine Expeditionary Force

MilHistBr—Military History Branch

Mogas—Motor gas

MS—Manuscript

Msgs—Messages

MUV—Marine Unit, Vietnam

MWHQ—Marine Wing Headquarters

NAG—Naval Advisory Group

NAS—Naval Air Station

NIS—National Intelligence Survey

NLF—National Liberation Front

NMCB—Naval Mobile Construction Battalion

NMCC—National Military Command Center

NWC—National War College

O-1B—Cessna, single-engine, observation plane, also known as the OE-1

OAB. NHD—Operational Archives Branch, Naval History Division

OpOrder—Operation Order

OPlan—Operation Plan

OpSum—Operation Summary

OSJS(MACV)—Office of the Secretariat, Joint Staff (Military Assistance Command, Vietnam)

PAR—Progressive Aircraft Rework

PAT—Political Action Team, the forerunner of the Revolutionary Development Teams. Vietnamese political cadre who were assigned missions of pacification and represented the government of Vietnam in the hamlets of Vietnam

PF—Popular Force; Vietnamese militia who were usually employed in the defense of their own communities

POL—Petroleum, Oil, and Lubricants

Regt—Regiment

RF—Regional Force; Vietnamese militia who were employed in a specific province

RF-8A—The reconnaissance version of the F-8 Chance Vought Crusader fighter

RLT—Regimental Landing Team

RRU—Radio Research Unit

ROLLING THUNDER—Code name for U.S. air operations over North Vietnam

RVN—Republic of Vietnam

RVNAF—Republic of Vietnam Armed Forces

S—Refers to staff positions on regimental and battalion levels. S-1 would refer to the staff member responsible for personnel; S-2 Intelligence; S-3 Operations; S-4 Logistics, etc.

SAM—Surface-to-Air Missile

SAR—Search and Rescue

SAR/Maint Team—Search, rescue, and maintenance team

SEAsia—Southeast Asia

Seatail—Follow-on shipping

SEATO—Southeast Asia Treaty Organization

SecState—Secretary of State
SHUFLY—The designation for the Marine Aviation Task Unit in RVN until January 1965 when it was redesignated Marine Unit, Vietnam (MUV)
SitRep—Situation Report
SLF—Special Landing Force
Song—Vietnamese word for river
Sortie—An operational flight by one aircraft
Sqdron—Squadron

TAC(A)—Tactical Air Coordinator (Airborne)
TAOR—Tactical Area of Responsibility
TE—Task Element
TF—Task Force
TG—Task Group

USMAAG—U.S. Military Assistance Advisory Group
USMACV—U.S. Military Assistance Command, Vietnam

VC—Viet Cong
VCC—Viet Cong Captured
VCS—Viet Cong Suspect (captured)
VMFA—Marine Fighter Attack Squadron
VNAF—Vietnamese Air Force
VNMB—Vietnamese Marine Brigade
VNMC—Vietnamese Marine Corps
VMA—Marine Attack Squadron
VMGR—Marine Aerial Refueling Squadron
VMO—Marine Observation Squadron

Appendix C

Chronology of Significant Events

1 Jan—TE 79.3.3.6 at Da Nang was designated Marine Unit, Vietnam (MUV), TU 79.3.5, by direction of CG FMFPac. The organization and its operations remained essentially as before.

7 Feb—Communist guerrillas attacked a United States compound at Pleiku, and U.S. aircraft retaliated by striking targets in North Vietnam, initiating a new phase of the war. U.S. forces in South Vietnam totaled 23,000. U.S. dependents were ordered evacuated from RVN.

8 Feb—Battery A, 1st LAAM Battalion arrived at Da Nang via C-130; it was operational the next day.

10 Feb—The Viet Cong blew up a U.S. military billet at the coastal city of Qui Nhon killing 23 soldiers.

13 Feb—More elements of the 1st LAAM Battalion (-), commanded by Lieutenant Colonel Bertram E. Cook, Jr., arrived at Da Nang by sea and air. Two full batteries and supporting elements were 100 percent operational five days later.

17 Feb—Company C of the USMC 7th Engineer Battalion began arriving at Da Nang by LST. HMM-163, commanded by Lieutenant Colonel Norman G. Ewers, relieved Lieutenant Colonel Joseph Koler, Jr.'s HMM-365 as the operating squadron of TU 79.3.5.

28 Feb—USMC tactical unit strength in RVN was 1,248, broken down as follows:

HMM-163	230
Sub-Unit 1	203
Security Company (D/1/3)	260
Total MUV	693
1st LAAM Bn (-)	405
CO C, 7th Engr Bn	150
Total, New Elements	555
Total, USMC (Tactical)	1,248

These figures do not include USMC advisors, Embassy Marines, MACV staff personnel, and various other categories of Marines assigned outside the Da Nang area.

8 Mar—The 9th Marine Expeditionary Brigade (MEB) commanded by Brigadier General Frederick J. Karch, landed at Da Nang. The MEB included two Marine Battalion Landing Teams (BLTs) — 3/9 (Lieutenant Colonel Charles E. McPartlin, Jr.) which landed over Red Beach 2, and 1/3 (Lieutenant Colonel Herbert J. Bain) which arrived by air from Okinawa. The 9th MEB mission was to defend the Da Nang Airbase. This was the first U.S. ground combat unit to land in RVN.

9 Mar—The MUV (TU 79.3.5) was placed under operational control of the 9th MEB and designated MAG-16, commanded by Colonel John H. King, Jr. HMM-163 remained in direct support of ARVN I Corps; other elements of the expanding MAG (Sub-Unit 2, MABS-16) were in direct support of the 9th MEB. The 1st LAAM Battalion was placed under operational control of MAG-16 with a mission to defend Da Nang Airbase from air attack.

9 Mar—Lieutenant Colonel Oliver W. Curtiss' HMM-162 arrived at Da Nang.

14 Mar—Sub-Unit 2 was redesignated MABS-16; H&MS-16 was activated at Da Nang under the operational control of MAG-16 (-).

23 Mar—Current composition of 9th MEB is as follows:

9th MEB	4,612
HqCo	145
BLT 1/3	1,124
BLT 3/9	1,115
Brigade Logistic Support Group	583
Brigade Engineer Group	224
Brigade Artillery Group	235
MAG-16(-)	
H&MS-16(-)	88
MABS-16(-)	208
HMM-162	233
HMM-163	246
1st LAAM	411

2 Apr—The United States announced the intention of sending several thousand more troops to Vietnam.

10 Apr—Lieutenant Colonel David A. Clement's BLT 2/3 landed at Da Nang. Task Force Alpha of the BLT was helilifted to the Phu Bai airstrip, 45 miles north of Da Nang near Hue, to assume the defense of that area. Lieutenant Colonel William C. McGraw, Jr.'s F-4B squadron, VMFA-531, arrived at Da Nang.

12 Apr—The RLT-3 commander, Colonel Edwin B. Wheeler, and his headquarters arrived; he assumed command of all BLTs ashore.

13 Apr—An HMM-162 detachment of 10 UH-34D helicopters was established at Phu Bai. VMFA-531 flew its first combat mission in RVN.

14 Apr—Lieutenant Colonel Donald R. Jones' BLT 3/4 arrived in Vietnam and moved to Phu Bai where it relieved Task Force Alpha.

16 Apr—MASS-2 (Lieutenant Colonel Paul L. Hitchcock) arrived Da Nang and established the DASC west of the runway. Lieutenant Colonel Otis W. Corman's VMCJ-1 arrived at Da Nang, coming under operational control of MAG-16 but remaining under administrative control of MAG-12, which was still located at Iwakuni, Japan.

19 Apr—RLT-3 reorganized as 3d Marines (Rein); a larger Tactical Area of Responsibility (TAOR) was established at Da Nang and a TAOR was established at Phu Bai for 3/4.

20 Apr—ComUSMACV authorized a change in General Karch's mission for ground forces to include (1) aggressive combat patrolling within TAORs and (2) preparation for conducting offensive operations as a mobile reaction force. High-level Honolulu conference recommended to President Johnson the deployment of III MEF to Da Nang and the landing of a MEB at Chu Lai.

20 Apr—The landing of additional Marine Corps units at Da Nang resulted in the following organization:

9 MEB

HqCo	240
3d Marines (-)(Rein)	3751
HqCo	(286)
1stBn, 3d Marines	(1099)
2dBn, 3d Marines	(1267)
3dBn, 9th Marines	(1099)
Brigade Artillery Group	548
HqBtry (-), 12th Marines	(26)
Btry A, 1stBn, 12th Marines	(120)
Btry B, 1stBn, 12th Marines	(119)
Btry F, 2dBn, 12th Marines	(120)
Btry L, 4thBn, 12th Marines	(112)
1st 8''HowBtry	(51)
Brigade Engineer Group	299
Brigade Logistics Support Group	656
MAG-16	1613
H&MS-16 (-)	(111)
MABS-16 (-)	(232)
VMFA-531 (-)	(300)
HMM-162	(126)
HMM-163	(233)
1stLAAM Bn	(413)
MASS-2	(100)
VMCJ-1	(98)
BLT 3/4 & DetHMM 162	1500
Total 9th MEB	8607

All units were located at Da Nang, except for BLT 3/4 and a detachment of 10 UH-34 helicopters from HMM-162, located at Phu Bai.

21 Apr—VMCJ-1 flew its first electronic countermeasures (ECM) missions from Da Nang Airfield and MASS-2 became fully operational.

22 Apr—The first real Marine ground action with the Viet Cong occurred--a reconnaissance company on patrol was fired on by an estimated 10 to 150 Viet Cong; VMFA-531 provided air support; one enemy was killed, one Marine was slightly wounded.

28 Apr—Companies E and F of the 2d Battalion, 3d Marines participated in the first coordinated ground operation with ARVN forces in RVN.

3 May—The advance party of the III MEF, including its commander, Major General William R. Collins, arrived at Da Nang.

5 May—ComUSMACV promulgated a Letter of Instruction giving the mission of III MEF: ''In general render combat support to RVNAF (Republic of Vietnam Armed Forces).

In coordination with CG, I Corps, participate in or provide for the defense of Hue-Phu Bai, Da Nang, and Chu Lai airfields and ancillary facilities. Maintain the capability to conduct, on order, deep patrolling and offensive operations and reserve reaction operations in coordination with CG, I Corps. Be prepared to execute U. S. contingency plans as directed by ComUSMACV.''

6 May—The III MEF headquarters was established at Da Nang Airbase, commanded by Major General Collins, who was also designated the Naval Component Commander (NCC) for ComUSMACV. The 9th MEB was deactivated as an operating unit and the 3d Marine Division (Forward), also commanded by Major General Collins, was established and assumed command of its assigned units in RVN. With the Chu Lai landings on 7 May, seven of the 3d Division infantry battalions were committed in RVN, supported by most of the 12th Marines and substantial portions of all other elements of the division.

7 May—III MEF was redesignated III MAF. 3d MAB, commanded by Brigadier General Marion E. Carl, consisting of RLT-4 (Colonel Edward P. Dupras, Jr.), the advance elements of MAG-12 (Colonel John D. Noble), and Naval Mobile Construction Battalion 10 (Commander John M. Bannister, USN) landed at Chu Lai with the mission of occupying the terrain necessary to construct an expeditionary airfield there. The 173d Airborne Brigade, the U.S. Army's first ground combat unit, arrived in RVN on this date.

10 May—The first radar-controlled bomb drops in combat were made by VMFA-531, controlled by MASS-2; 24 MK-81 (260 pound) bombs were expended in ''Happy Valley'' and the target was reported completely covered.

11 May—2d Battalion, 3d Marines cleared the village of Le My, liberating it from over two years of Viet Cong control. The village became a model of the Marine Corps civic action program. The 1st MAW (Adv), commanded by Major General Paul J. Fontana, was established at Da Nang.

12 May—Lieutenant Colonel William D. Hall's BLT 3/3 landed at Chu Lai. Brigadier General Carl was designated III MAF deputy commander. RLT-4 was redesignated 4th Marines as the Chu Lai amphibious operation terminated.

15 May—HMM-365, commanded by Lieutenant Colonel Joseph Koler, Jr., relieved Lieutenant Colonel Curtiss' HMM-162 at Da Nang.

24 May—Brigadier General Keith B. McCutcheon arrived and relieved Major General Fontana as CG 1st MAW (Adv).

31 May—USMC strengths by area:

Da Nang	9,224
Chu Lai	6,599
Hue-Phu Bai	1,614
TAD in-country	121
Total	17,558

1 Jun—Eight A-4 Skyhawk jet attack aircraft from VMA-225 (Lieutenant Colonel Robert W. Baker) and VMA-311 (Lieutenant Colonel Bernard J. Stender) landed at the Chu Lai expeditionary airfield. The first aircraft, piloted by Colonel Noble, the MAG-12 commander, touched down at 0801 to signify the opening of the airfield. (Construction

had started after the 3d MEB landed on 7 May, 24 days earlier). Only 3,600 feet of the runway was complete on 1 June—therefore, the A-4s used jet-assisted takeoff (JATO) for launching and mobile arresting gear (MOREST) for landing. Four Skyhawks led by Lieutenant Colonel Robert W. Baker, VMA-225, launched the first Chu Lai-based strike at 1329, flying sorties seven miles southwest of the Chu Lai TAOR in support of ARVN forces.

4 Jun—Major General Lewis W. Walt assumed command of III MAF and the 3d MarDiv (Fwd) at 0900, relieving Major General Collins in a formal indoor ceremony.

5 Jun—Brigadier General Keith B. McCutcheon relieved Major General Fontana as CG 1st MAW at Iwakuni, Japan. He returned to Da Nang on 7 June.

13 Jun—ComUSMACV directed III MAF to prepare an emergency contingency plan for the movement of two infantry battalions to Pleiku in II Corps area. The plan was completed and forwarded to ComUSMACV on 14 June.

15 Jun—At Da Nang VMFA-513, commanded by Lieutenant Colonel Walter C. Stewart, Jr., relieved VMFA-531, which chopped to 1st MAW (Rear) marking the first in-country relief of a USMC jet squadron.

17 Jun—Lieutenant Colonel Verle E. Ludwig's 1st Battalion, 9th Marines relieved the 3d Battalion, 9th Marines at Da Nang and assumed the responsibility formerly held by 3/9 in the defense of the airbase; 3/9 was the first Marine battalion to be rotated from RVN.

18 Jun—Brigadier General Karch returned to Da Nang and assumed duties as Assistant Division Commander (ADC), 3d MarDiv (Fwd).

19 Jun—Approximately 350 inhabitants of Pho Nam Thuong and Nam Yen villages moved into the Le My area.

21 Jun—Lieutenant Colonel Mervin B. Porter's HMM-261 relieved Lieutenant Colonel Ewer's HMM-163 at Da Nang; HMM-163 became the SLF helicopter squadron.

27 Jun—Lieutenant Colonel Clement's 2d Battalion, 3d Marines received 12,000 pounds of clothing and food for distribution to the refugees at Le My. Three days later the 4th Marines at Chu Lai distributed over 800 pounds of clothing to local residents who had been relocated to clear real estate for the airfield.

30 Jun—III MAF strength in RVN not including Seabees was as follows:

Da Nang	9,618
Chu Lai	6,771
Phu Bai	1,652
Other	115
Total	18,156

Total arrived by area during June:

Da Nang	1,496
Chu Lai	2,002
Phu Bai	204
Total	3,702

1 Jul—Viet Cong forces conducted a mortar/infantry attack on the Da Nang Airbase under cover of darkness, providing cover for demolition teams that broached the tactical wire surrounding the field and severely damaged six USAF aircraft. The one Viet Cong captured in the attack reported that he was from the *3d Battalion, 18th Regiment, 325th People's Army of Vietnam (PAVN) Division* and that the attack force trained and rehearsed for 30 days before

executing its mission. The SLF, composed of the 3d Battalion, 7th Marines (Lieutenant Colonel Charles H. Bodley) and HMM-163 (Lieutenant Colonel Norman G. Ewers), landed at Qui Nhon to protect an enclave at the seaward end of Route 19, the main highway from Pleiku.

3 Jul—The Chu Lai SATS runway (8,000 feet) and taxiway were completed.

6 Jul—RLT-9 (Colonel Frank E. Garretson) with BLT 2/9 (Lieutenant Colonel George R. Scharnberg) landed at Da Nang.

8 Jul—Lieutenant Colonel Leon N. Utter's BLT 2/7 relieved the SLF battalion, Bodley's BLT 3/7, which then re-embarked in ARG shipping.

10 Jul—Lieutenant Colonel Richard A. Savage's F-4B squadron, VMFA-542, arrived at Da Nang and commenced operations.

14 Jul—MAG-11 (Colonel Robert F. Conley) assumed operational control of VMFA-542 and VMFA-513 at Da Nang.

21 Jul—Written confirmation was received for expansion of the Da Nang TAOR and for the establishment of a recon-naissance zone for the Chu Lai TAOR.

29 Jul—Official sources announced plans to increase the U.S. active duty military force by about 300,000 men. The 1st Brigade, 101st Airborne Division arrived in RVN on this date.

31 Jul—III MAF strengths in RVN not including Seabees were as follows:

Da Nang	15,204
Chu Lai	6,949
Phu Bai	2,052
Qui Nhon	1,644
Other	115
Total	25,964

Total arrived by area during July:

Da Nang	5,743
Chu Lai	395
Phu Bai	178
Qui Nhon	1,651
Total	7,967

2 Aug—Operation BLAST OUT, a coordinated USMC/ARVN operation involving 1/3 and elements of the 4th ARVN Regiment, was conducted 10 miles southwest of Da Nang.

3 Aug—Company D, 1/9 conducted a one day operation in the vicinity of Cam Ne, south of Da Nang. A CBS television crew, accompanying the company, filmed a Marine setting fire to a Vietnamese hut. This film, which was shown on the evening news, led to a debate in the press about U.S. tactics in Vietnamese villages.

5 Aug—The Viet Cong attacked the Esso POL storage terminal at Lien Chieu, destroying two JP-4 storage tanks and inflicting extensive damage on three more. Operational control of 2/7 (at Qui Nhon in the II Corps area) passed to U.S. Army Task Force ALFA, the Army field command in RVN.

7 Aug—The CG III MAF was designated as the Senior Adviser (SA) for I Corps and assumed operational control of the I Corps Advisory Group.

11 Aug—The first tactical delivery of the cluster bomb unit (CBU) by USMC aircraft took place. The addition of this

weapon to the aviation ordnance arsenal broadened the air support capabilities of the 1st MAW.

12 Aug—The first all-Marine night helicopter assault took place starting at 2400.

14 Aug—The Navy announced four-month involuntary extensions of duty for Navy and Marine Corps enlisted personnel. Coordinating headquarters were established at Chu Lai under the 3d MarDiv ADC, Brigadier General Karch.

15 Aug—The Headquarters of the 7th RLT and 1/7 came ashore at Chu Lai. Colonel Oscar F. Peatross commanded the regiment. At Da Nang, elements of 3/9 came ashore making it the first battalion to be re-introduced into RVN (See 8 March and 17 June 1965 entries).

16 Aug—3/9 relieved 1/9 as the Base Defense Battalion at Da Nang.

17 Aug—2/4 and 3/3 were assigned to the 7th Marines for Operation STARLITE.

18-24 Aug—Operation STARLITE. Three Marine battalions—1/7, 2/4, and 3/3—attached to the 7th Marines, and supported by air, artillery, and naval gunfire, conducted an amphibious-heliborne search and destroy operation in the Van Tuong village complex south of Chu Lai. The purpose of the attack was to eliminate an enemy force—the *1st VC Regiment,* reportedly 2,000 strong—which had built up for an attack on Chu Lai. Strong resistance was encountered, requiring the support of BLT 3/7 from the SLF. The USMC units advanced through the objective area in two days, and then were joined for mopping up operations by Vietnamese forces. Casualties were as follows:

	KIA	DOW	WIA
USMC	45	6	203
VC	614	9	

The Viet Cong dead were confirmed by body count. It was estimated that the actual enemy KIA total ran much higher because of the large number of caves and tunnels that were sealed or destroyed. (On 9 September an agent source reported that the VC had suffered 1,430 KIA, in Operation STARLITE).

26 Aug—In response to a CG III MAF request made in June, 11 sentry dogs and handlers arrived as the initial element of the 1st Provisional Dog Platoon, which was planned to consist ultimately of two squads, a sentry dog squad and a patrol dog squad.

28 Aug—1/1 arrived at Da Nang to relieve 1/3.

31 Aug—President Johnson called for "a new and mighty people-to-people program to bring American aid to victims of the war in RVN." The total III MAF strength in RVN not including Seabees was broken down as follows:

Da Nang 18,063
Chu Lai 10,277
Phu Bai 2,114
Qui Nhon 1,616
Other 92
Total 32,162
Total arrived by area during August:
Da Nang 4,725
Chu Lai 2,684
Total arrived 7,409

Total departed by area during August:
Da Nang . . . . .1,029 (1/3 departed)
Phu Bai 68
Qui Nhon 35
Total departed 1,132
Net Gain, August 6,277

1 Sep—1/3 departed RVN for Okinawa, where it was relieved by BLT 3/5, and then returned to CONUS. A total of 10,919 personnel of FMFPac remained in Okinawa and Japan.

7-10 Sep—Operation PIRANHA. Following the decisive Marine Corps victory over the *1st Viet Cong Regiment* in Operation STARLITE (18-24 August), intelligence information disclosed that other VC forces were building up on the Batangan Peninsula, still farther south of Chu Lai. Operation PIRANHA, another regimental-level amphibious-heliborne attack, was executed to clear the area. It exacted at least 163 Viet Cong killed and served notice once again upon the VC of the hazards of concentrating their forces. Subsequently they reverted to small unit operations in I Corps area.

11 Sep—BLT 2/1, which arrived on Okinawa 27 August from CONUS and subsequently embarked as the SLF, assumed a position within six-hours reaction time of Qui Nhon, prepared to land and provide security, if required, for debarkation of the Army's 1st Cavalry Division (Airmobile).

18 Sep—The first elements of the Army's 1st Cavalry (Airmobile) Division landed at Qui Nhon.

23 Sep—The Defense Department said that General Westmoreland had the authority to permit use of tear gas.

28 Sep—The total III MAF strength in RVN not including Seabees by area was as follows:
Da Nang 18,641
Chu Lai 13,601
Phu Bai 2,172
Qui Nhon 1,773
Total 36,187
Total arrived by area during September:
Da Nang 3,222
Chu Lai 3,384
Qui Nhon 327
Total 6,933
Total departed by area during September
Phu Bai 26
Net Change 6,907

14 Oct—The CG, I Corps approved extension of the Chu Lai TAOR. A USMC sniper team was formed in the Hue-Phu Bai TAOR. The team used Winchester Model 70 rifles with 8-Unertl telescopic sights and killed two Viet Cong at a range of more than 700 yards in the first exercise of the new tactic. Later, M-1D rifles with telescopic sights were utilized.

18 Oct—Operation TRAIL BLAZER, a six-day deep patrol and series of ambushes by the 3d Reconnaissance Battalion, began from a patrol base about 15 miles southwest of Da Nang. The purpose of the operation was to determine the extent of VC concentration in the main valleys leading from the mountains into the Da Nang TAOR and to determine the probability of enemy attack from that area.

Two VC were killed in the operation, and five enemy complexes of training camps, workshops, and bivouac areas were destroyed. Accumulated intelligence was used in developing an aerial target list. Two companies from 3/3 launched Operation TRIPLE PLAY, a two-day search and destroy effort conducted 12 miles north of Chu Lai. The results: 16 VC KIA, 6 VCC, and 18 VCS, with only two Marines wounded.

26 Oct—Operation DRUM HEAD, a coordinated two-day sweep effort involving 3/7 and an ARVN platoon, began southwest of Chu Lai. Results: one VC killed and 26 suspects captured; one USMC killed and two wounded.

27 Oct—Operation GOLDEN FLEECE (begun 8 Sep 65) was terminated. This operation by the 9th Marines was an effort to deny as much rice as possible to the VC during the Summer/Fall 1965 rice harvest. USMC units provided protection for Vietnamese farmers in their fields while the rice crop was harvested. It is estimated that 512,400 lbs. of threshed rice were denied the VC as a result.

28 Oct—On the night of 28 October, Viet Cong suicide squads launched simultaneous and coordinated attacks on Marine installations at Marble Mountain near Da Nang and at Chu Lai. Even though most of the attackers were killed, the few who got through used satchel charges to blow up 19 helicopters and damage the hospital at Marble Mountain, while at Chu Lai they destroyed two fixed-wing attack aircraft. Ground actions during the night indicated that other planned attacks were thwarted by Marine patrols.

3 Nov—BLACK FERRET, a three-day combined USMC/ ARVN search and destroy operation of regimental scope, began in an area 10 miles south of the Chu Lai airstrip, on the north side of the Song Tra Bong. Participating were: two companies from 1/7; two companies from 3/7; 3/11; two platoons from the 1st Reconnaissance Battalion; and two battalions from the 4th Regiment of the 2d ARVN Division. VC forces avoided contact, limiting their resistance to sporadic small arms fire and booby traps. In one instance, a booby-trapped 81mm mortar round wounded six Marines and killed Miss Dickie Chapelle, the war correspondent, who was accompanying USMC units on the maneuver. Numerous fortifications and tunnels were destroyed by attacking forces, and Marine strike aircraft wiped out a number of boats and structures along the Song Tra Bong. Results: 2 VC killed, 20 captured (5 WIA), and 64 suspects apprehended. Eight Marines and one Navy corpsman were wounded. Helicopters returned the Marines to Chu Lai upon conclusion of the operation on 5 November.

7 Nov—BLT 2/7 was withdrawn from Qui Nhon (see 10-12 November entry below); HMM-161 remained at Qui Nhon in support of II Corps forces.

10-12 Nov—Operation BLUE MARLIN, a combined USMC/VNMC operation between Chu Lai and Tam Ky, 20 miles to the north, took place. On 7 November, BLT 2/7 was lifted in amphibious shipping from its former TAOR at Qui Nhon to Chu Lai, where it was joined by the 600-man 3d Battalion, Vietnamese Marine Corps. The two units conducted a combined amphibious assault on 10 November across beaches just north of Tam Ky. Four

companies of BLT 2/7 in one LVT wave and two LCM waves landed unopposed, followed by the remainder of the BLT and the 3d Battalion, VNMC, in on-call boat serials and helicopters. Surf at the beach was very high, and the anchor chains of the APA *Paul Revere* and the LST *Windham County* parted. After sweeping inland to Route 1, the landing force pivoted southward astride the highway and executed a search and destroy operation to the Chu Lai TAOR. Resistance was light, and casualties were few. A Vietnamese civilian reported that the VC had withdrawn from the objective area two days previously. At the conclusion of the operation, the RVN Marines were returned by helicopter to their base area south of Quang Ngai. 2/7 rejoined its parent regiment at Chu Lai, replacing 3/3, which embarked for Phase II of BLUE MARLIN (see 16-18 November entry) and subsequent operations at Da Nang.

16-18 Nov—BLUE MARLIN (Phase II), similar in scope and concept to Phase I (10-12 November), was conducted. At Chu Lai, 3/3 embarked in the same amphibious shipping used in Phase I and landed on 16 November over beaches south of Hoi An, about 22 miles south of Da Nang. The landing was accomplished smoothly, with one wave of LVTs and two of LCMs, followed by artillery and Ontos in on-call serials. Ashore, the landing force was joined by two RVN Ranger battalions and two RVN special companies in a coordinated search and destroy operation north to the Song Cua Dai. Activity was characterized by scattered but sharp contacts as the VC again avoided confrontation with the landing force. Fortifications, tunnels, and man-traps were destroyed in quantity. Combined results were: 25 VC killed, 15 captured, 79 suspects apprehended, and 9 weapons seized. Two ARVN soldiers were KIA, one ARVN was wounded, and three USMC were wounded. At the conclusion of the operation, 3/3 was lifted to the Da Nang area by amphibious shipping and helicopter.

17-18 Nov—Marine air elements from III MAF were instrumental in preventing a Viet Cong victory at Hiep Duc, about 25 miles west of Tam Ky. On the 17th, 30 UH-34D helicopters, supported by fixed-wing attack aircraft, lifted 788 ARVN troops to the relief of an invested ARVN garrison at Hiep Duc. In this initial lift, 20 of the 30 transport helicopters were hit by ground fire as they approached the landing zone. Despite marginal flying weather, accompanying attack aircraft and armed helicopters dropped some 14 tons of high explosive bombs and fired 512 rockets, as well as 1,532 rounds of 20mm cannon projectiles, into VC positions near the landing areas. VC losses during the period were a comfirmed 38 KIA, with many more probables. The following day, 22 UH-34Ds lifted 463 more ARVN troops to Hiep Duc, making the total lift for two days 1,251. The helilifted troops were successful in defeating the assault on Hiep Duc, but were unable to clear the VC from the critical areas to the northwest. At the request of CG I Corps, 3/7 was alerted to reinforce the ARVN units. Extremely bad weather prevented the helilift of 3/7 into Hiep Duc. While awaiting improved weather, the battalion was diverted to assist an ARVN Ranger battalion under siege at Thach Tru, south of Quang Ngai (see 22-24 November entry).

22-24 Nov—On the late afternoon of 22 November, at the request of CG, I Corps, 3/7 began reinforcing an ARVN Ranger battalion which had come under attack by an estimated VC regiment about 20 miles south of Quang Ngai. At the same time, the Seventh Fleet SLF moved to a position off Quang Ngai, ready to land on two hours notice. Before the Marines arrived, 71 ARVN had been killed, 74 wounded, and 2 were missing. VC losses were 175 KIA by U.S. body count and 225 by ARVN estimate, not including those killed by air or naval gunfire beyond the immediate battle area. Three VC were captured, in addition to 5 recoilless rifles, 9 machine guns, 2 submachine guns, and 114 rifles. Six enemy 60mm mortars were destroyed. An undetermined number of enemy dead were credited to Marine strike aircraft, which flew 39 sorties in marginal weather against the initial assaults. When the Marines landed, they secured the landing zones, occupied night defensive positions, and early the next morning cleared the critical terrain, capturing 17 Viet Cong, killing 3, and seizing 2 rifles and 5 carbines. On the morning of the 24th the situation was stabilized and 3/7 returned to Chu Lai by helicopter. Marine losses in the encounter were two killed and one wounded.

23 Nov—By this date there were approximately 20 scout/sniper teams of four men each positioned throughout the III MAF area. On 23 November a team at Phu Bai killed two VC and wounded one at a range of 1,000 meters.

30 Nov-1 Dec—Operation DAGGER THRUST IV. On 30 November the SLF (BLT 2/1 and HMM-261) executed an amphibious raid at Lang Ke Ga, on the coast 17 miles southwest of Phan Thiet and about 70 miles east of Saigon. Immediately prior to the landing, leaflets were dropped along the routes of advance, giving brief warning to the villagers. Contact was negligible.

Nov III MAF summary:

Patrols 3,488
Ambushes 2,576
Sniper posts 175
Total offensive ground operations 6,242
Enemy contacts 226
Enemy KIA 126
Enemy WIA 33
Enemy captured 22
Fixed-wing strike sorties 2,551
Helicopter sorties 23,629
Rainfall . . . . more than 30 inches
Most rain in one day . . . . 7.8 inches

30 Nov— The III MAF strength in RVN not including Seabees and Naval Support Activity was as follows:

Da Nang 21,948
Chu Lai 14,452
Phu Bai 2,328
Qui Nhon 254
Other 89
Total 39,071

Personnel strengths fluctuated by area during November due to reassignment between enclaves, replacement, attrition, and movement of battalions. Net strength change for November 422

8-20 Dec—Operation HARVEST MOON was conducted approximately 25 miles northwest of Chu Lai. Units involved were Task Force DELTA, 2/7, 3/3, 2/1 (from SLF), and 3 ARVN battalions. These units were supported by USMC aircraft and artillery and by four B-52 strikes.

	KIA	WIA	MIA	
USMC	51	256	1	

	KIA	VCC	VCS	RALLIERS
VC	407	33	231	3

22 Dec—The U.S. military command in Vietnam ordered a 30-hour Christmas cease-fire. A military spokesman said that similar instructions had been issued by South Vietnamese Government military leaders. No action would be taken by allied or RVNAF forces except in self-defense.

31 Dec—USMACV released the following figures to news media in Saigon:

U.S. Military Strength in RVN 1Jan65 23,000
U.S. Military Strength in RVN 31Dec65 181,000
RVNAF Total Strength 1Jan65 559,500
RVNAF Total Strength 31Dec65 679,000
Enemy Military Strength in RVN 1Jan65 103,000
Enemy Military Strength in RVN 31Dec65 230,000
U.S. losses during the year 1,300
RVNAF losses during the year 11,000
Enemy losses during the year(KIA) 34,000
Enemy losses during the year(captured) 6,000
III MAF total arrived during December:
   Da Nang 188
   Chu Lai 138
   Phu Bai 81
   Total 407
III MAF total departed during December
   Chu Lai 452
   Qui Nhon 25
   Total 477
Net Change . . . . -70

31 Dec—III MAF strength in RVN not including Seabees and Naval Support Activity was as follows:

Da Nang 22,464
Chu Lai 13,995
Phu Bai 2,354
Qui Nhon 226
1st Anglico 53
Total 39,092

31 Dec—III MAF ground operations for the week ending 31 December were as follows:

Patrols 1,169
Ambushes 633
Platoon Operations 40
Company Operations 6
Battalion Operations 3
VC KIA 81
VC Captured 6

31 Dec—Results of III MAF Operations since 8 March 1965:

	KIA and DOW	WIA	MIA
USMC	342	2,047	18

	KIA	WIA	POW	VCS
VC	2,627	314	535	2,827

31 Dec—A total of 14,528 FMFPac personnel remained in Okinawa and Japan.

Appendix D

Medal of Honor Citations, 1965

The President of the United States in the name of The Congress takes pride in presenting the MEDAL OF HONOR posthumously to

FIRST LIEUTENANT FRANK S. REASONER
UNITED STATES MARINE CORPS

for service as set forth in the following

CITATION:

For conspicuous gallantry and intrepidity at the risk of his life above and beyond the call of duty while serving as Commanding Officer, Company A, 3d Reconnaissance Battalion, 3d Marine Division in action against hostile Viet Cong forces near Da Nang, Vietnam on 12 July 1965. The reconnaissance patrol led by Lieutenant Reasoner had deeply penetrated heavily controlled enemy territory when it came under extremely heavy fire from an estimated 50 to 100 Viet Cong insurgents. Accompanying the advance party and the point that consisted of five men, he immediately deployed his men for an assault after the Viet Cong had opened fire from numerous concealed positions. The slashing fury of the Viet Cong machine gun and automatic weapons fire made it impossible for the main body to move forward. Repeatedly exposing himself to the devastating attack he skillfully provided covering fire, killing at least two Viet Cong and effectively silencing an automatic weapons position in a valiant attempt to effect evacuation of a wounded man. As casualties began to mount his radio operator was wounded and Lieutenant Reasoner immediately moved to his side and tended his wounds. When the radio operator was hit a second time while attempting to reach a covered position, Lieutenant Reasoner, courageously running to his aid through the grazing machine gun fire, fell mortally wounded. His indomitable fighting spirit, valiant leadership and unflinching devotion to duty provided the inspiration that was to enable the patrol to complete its mission without further casualties. In the face of almost certain death he gallantly gave his life in the service of his country. His action upheld the highest traditions of the Marine Corps and the United States Naval Service.

The President of the United States in the name of The Congress takes pleasure in presenting the MEDAL OF HONOR to

CORPORAL ROBERT E. O'MALLEY
UNITED STATES MARINE CORPS

for service as set forth in the following

CITATION:

For conspicuous gallantry and intrepidity in action against the communist (Viet Cong) forces at the risk of his own life above and beyond the call of duty while serving as Squad Leader in Company "I", Third Battalion, Third Marines, Third Marine Division (Reinforced), near An Cu'ong 2, South Vietnam, on 18 August 1965. While leading his squad in the assault against a strongly entrenched enemy force, his unit came under intense small arms fire. With complete disregard for his personal safety, Corporal O'Malley raced across an open rice paddy to a trench line where the enemy forces were located. Jumping into the trench, he attacked the Viet Cong with his rifle and grenades, and singly killed eight of the enemy. He then led his squad to the assistance of an adjacent Marine unit which was suffering heavy casualties. Continuing to press forward, he reloaded his weapon and fired with telling effect into the enemy emplacement. He personally assisted in the evacuation of several wounded Marines, and again regrouping the remnants of his squad, he returned to the point of the heaviest fighting. Ordered to an evacuation point by an officer, Corporal O'Malley gathered his besieged and badly wounded squad and boldly led them under fire to a helicopter for withdrawal. Although three times wounded in this encounter, and facing imminent death from a fanatic and determined enemy, he steadfastly refused evacuation and continued to cover his squad's boarding of the helicopters while, from an exposed position, he delivered fire against the enemy until his wounded men were evacuated. Only then, with his last mission accomplished, did he permit himself to be removed from the battlefield. By his valor, leadership, and courageous efforts in behalf of his comrades, he served as an inspiration to all who observed him, and reflected the highest credit upon the Marine Corps and the United States Naval Service.

The President of the United States in the name of The Congress takes pride in presenting the MEDAL OF HONOR posthumously to

LANCE CORPORAL JOE C. PAUL
UNITED STATES MARINE CORPS

for service as set forth in the following

Citation:

For conspicuous gallantry and intrepidity at the risk of his life above and beyond the call of duty as a Fire Team Leader with Company H, Second Battalion, Fourth Marines, during Operation STARLITE near Chu Lai in the Republic of Vietnam on 18 August 1965. In violent battle, Corporal Paul's platoon sustained five casualties as it was temporarily pinned down by devastating mortar, recoilless rifle, automatic weapons, and rifle fire delivered by insurgent communist (Viet Cong) forces in well-trenched positions. The wounded Marines were unable to move from their perilously exposed positions forward of the remainder of their platoon, and were suddenly subjected to a barrage of white phosphorous rifle grenades. Corporal Paul, fully aware that his tactics would almost certainly result in serious injury or death to himself, chose to disregard his own safety and boldly dashed across the fire-swept rice paddies, placed himself between his wounded comrades and the enemy, and delivered effective suppressive fire with his automatic weapon in order to divert the attack long enough to allow the casualties to be evacuated. Although critically wounded during the course of the battle, he resolutely remained in his exposed position and continued to fire his rifle until he collapsed and was evacuated. By his fortitude and gallant spirit of self-sacrifice in the face of almost certain death, he saved the lives of several of his fellow Marines. His heroic action served to inspire all who observed him and reflect the highest credit upon himself, the Marine Corps and the United States Naval Service. He gallantly gave his life in the cause of freedom.

The President of the United States takes pleasure in presenting the MEDAL OF HONOR to

FIRST LIEUTENANT HARVEY C. BARNUM, JR.
UNITED STATES MARINE CORPS

for service as set forth in the following

CITATION:

For conspicuous gallantry and intrepidity at the risk of his life above and beyond the call of duty as Forward Observer for Artillery, while attached to Company H, Second Battalion, Ninth Marines, Third Marine Division (Reinforced), in action against communist forces at Ky Phu in Quang Tin Province, Republic of Vietnam, on 18 December 1965. When the company was suddenly pinned down by a hail of extremely accurate enemy fire and was quickly separated from the remainder of the battalion by over five hundred meters of open and fire-swept ground, and casualties mounted rapidly, Lieutenant Barnum quickly made a hazardous reconnaissance of the area seeking targets for his artillery. Finding the rifle company commander mortally wounded and radio operator killed, he, with complete disregard for his own safety, gave aid to the dying commander, then removed the radio from the dead operator and strapped it to himself. He immediately assumed command of the rifle company, and moving at once into the midst of the heavy fire, rallying and giving encouragement to all units, reorganized them to replace the loss of key personnel and led their attack on enemy positions from which deadly fire continued to come. His sound and swift decisions and his obvious calm served to stabilize the badly decimated units and his gallant example as he stood exposed repeatedly to point out targets served as an inspiration to all. Provided with two armed helicopters, he moved fearlessly through enemy fire to control the air attack against the firmly entrenched enemy while skillfully directing one platoon in a successful counter-attack on the key enemy positions. Having thus cleared a small area, he requested and directed the landing of two transport helicopters for the evacuation of the dead and wounded. He then assisted in the mopping up and final seizure of the battalion's objective. His gallant initiative and heroic conduct reflected great credit upon himself and were in keeping with the highest traditions of the Marine Corps and the United States Naval Service.

Appendix E
List of Reviewers

USMC General Officers

Gen Wallace M. Greene, Jr. (Ret.)
Gen Lewis W. Walt (Ret.)
LtGen Leslie E. Brown
LtGen Leo J. Dulacki (Ret.)
LtGen Lewis J. Fields (Ret.)
LtGen Victor H. Krulak (Ret.)
MajGen Marion E. Carl (Ret.)
MajGen Paul J. Fontana (Ret.)
MajGen Harold A. Hatch
MajGen Joseph Koler, Jr.
MajGen Andrew W. O'Donnell
MajGen Oscar F. Peatross (Ret.)
MajGen Jonas M. Platt (Ret.)
MajGen William R. Quinn (Ret.)
MajGen Donald M. Weller (Ret.)
MajGen Carl A. Youngdale (Ret.)
BGen Robert F. Conley (Ret.)
BGen Frederick J. Karch (Ret.)
BGen Marc A. Moore
BGen Mauro J. Padalino (Ret.)
BGen Webb D. Sawyer (Ret.)
BGen Edwin H. Simmons (Ret.)

USMC Colonels

Col Emmett O. Anglin, Jr. (Ret.)
Col Charles H. Bodley (Ret.)
Col Robert W. Boyd (Ret.)
Col George W. Carrington, Jr. (Ret.)
Col Edward Cook (Ret.)
Col Otis W. Corman (Ret.)
Col Nicholas J. Dennis (Ret.)
Col Rex C. Denny, Jr. (Ret.)
Col Alvin J. Doublet
Col Joshua W. Dorsey III
Col Edward P. Dupras, Jr. (Ret.)
Col Norman G. Ewers (Ret.)
Col Joseph R. Fisher (Ret.)
Col Don W. Galbreaith (Ret.)
Col Jesse L. Gibney, Jr.
Col John E. Gorman (Ret.)

Col William M. Graham, Jr. (Ret.)
Col Roy C. Gray, Jr. (Ret.)
Col Edward H. Greason (Ret.)
Col John E. Greenwood
Col Hardy Hay (Ret.)
Col Harold A. Hayes, Jr. (Ret.)
Col George L. Hollowell (Ret.)
Col Floyd J. Johnson, Jr.
Col Charles J. Keever
Col James P. Kelly (Ret.)
Col Horace E. Knapp, Jr. (Ret.)
Col Jack K. Knocke (Ret.)
Col Robert L. La Mar (Ret.)
Col George G. Long (Ret.)
Col Verle E. Ludwig (Ret.)
Col Andrew I. Lyman (Ret.)
Col Robert J. Lynch, Jr. (Ret.)
Col James F. McClanahan (Ret.)
Col William P. Nesbit (Ret.)
Col Norman R. Nickerson (Ret.)
Col John D. Noble (Ret.)
Col Royal E. North (Ret.)
Col Thomas J. O'Connor (Ret.)
Col Robert J. Oddy (Ret.)
Col Keith O'Keefe (Ret.)
Col Leslie L. Page (Ret.)
Col William P. Pala (Ret.)
Col Francis F. Parry (Ret.)
Col Edward F. Penico (Ret.)
Col Robert M. Port (Ret.)
Col Mervin B. Porter (Ret.)
Col Richard A. Savage (Ret.)
Col Richard J. Schriver (Ret.)
Col Donald W. Sherman (Ret.)
Col Donald H. Stapp (Ret.)
Col William W. Taylor (Ret.)
Col Rodolfo L. Trevino (Ret.)
Col Leon N. Utter (Ret.)
Col Sumner A. Vale (Ret.)
Col Roy R. Van Cleve (Ret.)
Col Maxie R. Williams (Ret.)
Col Don P. Wyckoff (Ret.)
Col Michael R. Yunck (Ret.)

USMC Lieutenant Colonels

LtCol Herbert J. Bain (Ret.)
LtCol Robert W. Baker (Ret.)
LtCol Billy H. Barber (Ret.)
LtCol Harlan P. Chapman (Ret.)
LtCol Lloyd F. Childers (Ret.)
LtCol William H. Clark (Ret.)
LtCol Bertram E. Cook, Jr. (Ret.)
LtCol Samuel E. Englehart (Ret.)
LtCol Harold D. Fredericks (Ret.)
LtCol Charles L. Goode (Ret.)
LtCol Donald J. Hatch
LtCol Lane Rogers
LtCol Richard E. Romine (Ret.)
LtCol Walter E. Stuenkel (Ret.)
LtCol Ralph E. Sullivan (Ret.)
LtCol Russell B. Tiffany
LtCol Charles Ward
LtCol Raymond W. Wilson (Ret.)

USMC Majors

Maj John A. Buck (Ret.)
Maj Andrew G. Comer (Ret.)
Maj Paul R. Ek
Maj Nicholas H. Grosz, Jr.
Maj Pat Morgan (Ret.)
Maj John J. Mullen, Jr.
Maj Gary W. Parker
Maj Ruel T. Scyphers (Ret.)

Others

Historical Division, Joint Secretariat, Joint Chiefs of Staff
Center of Military History, Department of the Army
Office of Air Force History, Department of the Air Force
Naval History Division, Department of the Navy
Gen William E. DePuy, USA (Ret.)
Adm John J. Hyland, USN (Ret.)
Adm Roy L. Johnson, USN (Ret.)
Adm Ulysses S.G. Sharp, USN (Ret.)
Gen William C. Westmoreland, USA (Ret.)
VAdm Edwin B. Hooper, USN (Ret.)
RAdm Don W. Wulzen, USN (Ret.)
Mr. Peter Braestrup

Appendix F

Task Organization:
III MAF and Naval Component Command
as of 31 Dec 1965

	USMC		USN		
	Off	Enl	Off	Enl	TOTAL
I. Naval Component Command (I CTZ)	9	19	224	4789	5041
A. *Headquarters* (DA NANG)	6	18	1		25
1. Det, Sub Unit 2, H&SCo HqBn	5	7	1		13
2. Det, 5th Comm Bn		10			10
3. Det, H&HS-1, MWHG, FMAW	1	1			2
B. *30th NCR*	3	1	78	2023	2105
1. Hq, 30th NCR (DA NANG)	3	1	6	25	35
2. MCB-4 (CHU LAI)			18	498	516
3. MCB-5 (DA NANG)			17	552	569
4. MCB-8 (DA NANG)			21	397	418
5. MCB-8 (PHU BAI)			1	49	50
6. MCB-9 (DA NANG)			15	502	517
C. *Nav Supt Act*			145	2766	2911
1. DA NANG (PCS)			101	2281	2382
2. DA NANG (TDY)			15	291	306
3. Station Hospital (DA NANG)			29	184	213
4. CHU LAI Detachment				10	10
II. III Marine Amphibious Force	2429	35869	194	1497	39989
A. *HQ III MAF (DA NANG)*	97	723	5	11	836
1. Staff	75	120	5	2	202
2. 5th CommBn(-)	18	584		9	611
3. Prov Dog Plt	1	11			12
4. 7th CI Tm (CHU LAI)	3	8			11
B. *Base Defense Bn* (DA NANG)	32	955	3	51	1041
1. 3d Bn 9th Marines	32	955	3	51	1041
C. *7th Engr Bn* (-) *(Rein)* (DA NANG)	35	998	1	16	1050
1. 7th Engr Bn (- Co C)	29	855	1	16	901
2. 1st Bridge Co (-)	6	143			149
D. *9th MT Bn* (-) *(Rein)* (DA NANG)	18	397	1	9	425
E. *Sub Unit -1, 1st ANGLICO*	5	42	6		53
1. SAIGON	1	14	1		16
2. BIEN HOA		5	1		6
3. BERIA	1	3			4
4. DA NANG		4	1		5
5. QUANG NGAI	1	3			4
6. QUI NHON	1	2			3
7. PLEIKU		4	1		5
8. NHA TRANG		2	1		3
9. CAN THO	1	5	1		7
F. *Det J, 1st Radio Bn FMF*	2	65			67
1. HQ & TM 1 (DA NANG)	1	35			36

	USMC		USN		
	Off	Enl	Off	Enl	TOTAL
2. Team 2 (CHU LAI)	1	26			27
3. Team 3 (PHU BAI)		4			4
G. *3d Marine Division* (-) (*Rein*), FMF	1056	21162	106	1045	23369
1. *HqBn* (-) (DA NANG)	155	1508	13	27	1703
a. HqCo	119	690	13	27	849
b. Comm Co (-)	11	356			367
c. Service Co	15	318			333
d. MP Co (-)	5	111			116
e. 3d CIT	4	16			20
f. Det, 1st ITT	1	17			18
2. *3d Marines* (-) (*Rein*) (DA NANG-PHU BAI)	168	3830	10	174	4182
a. *HqCo* (*Rein*) (DA NANG)	17	219	1	5	242
(1) Det, HqBn, 3d MarDiv		3			3
b. *1stBn, 1st Marines* (DA NANG)	37	983	3	57	1080
c. *1stBn, 3d Marines* (DA NANG)	39	1023	3	53	1118
d. *2dBn, 1st Marines* (*Rein*) (PHU BAI)	75	1602	3	59	1739
(1) 2dBn, 1st Marines	40	999	3	50	1092
(2) Det, HqBn, 3d MarDiv	1	6			7
(3) 1st Plt (Rein), Co A, 1st ATBn (5 M50A1 Ontos)	1	19			20
(4) 1st Plt (Rein), Co A, 1st EngrBn	1	44			45
(5) 1st Plt(Rein), Co A, 1st TkBn (5 M48A3 Tanks)	1	27			28
(6) 1st Plt (Rein), Co A, 1st Recon Bn	1	23			24
(7) 4thBn, 12th Marines (-) (Rein) (PHU BAI)	30	484		9	523
(a) HqBtry (-) (Rein) (CMR Team)	14	161		3	178
(b) Btry M, 4thBn (SP) (6-155How)	4	120		2	126
(c) Btry B, 1stBn, 11thMar, (6-105How)	8	124		2	134
(d) 107mm Mortar Btry, 1stBn, 11th Marines (6 Mortars)	4	79		2	85
3. *ADC Command Group* (CHU LAI)	7	26			33
4. *4th Marines* (-) (*Rein*) (CHU LAI)	107	2654	6	128	2895
a. *HqCo*	24	268	2	2	296
(1) Det, HqBn, 3d MarDiv	3	16			19
b. *1stBn, 4th Marines*	35	968	2	58	1063
c. *2Bn, 4th Marines*	34	969	2	58	1063
d. *CoB* (-) (Rein), 3d ATBn	2	67		2	71
(1) Co B (-)	1	40			41
(2) Det, H & S Co, 3d AT Bn	1	27		2	30
e. *CoB* (-) (*Rein*), 3dEngrBn	3	119		2	124
(1) Co B(-)	3	75			78
(2) Det Support Co		44		2	46
f. *CoA* (-) (*Rein*), 1st AmTracBn, FMF (34 LVTP-5, 1 LVTC, 1 LVTR-1, 2 LVTE)	5	168		4	177
g. *Co C*(-) *3d TkBn, FMF* (12 M48A3 Tanks)	4	95		2	101
(1) Co C(-)	4	85			89
(2) Det, H&SCo (3 M67A2 Flame Tanks)		10		2	12
5. *Artillery Bn Group* (CHU LAI)	76	1273	6	24	1379
a. *3dBn* (-), *11th Marines*	36	593	2	11	642
(1) Hq Btry	11	150	2	3	166
(2) Btry G (6-105 How)	7	118		2	127
(3) Btry H (6-105 How)	8	120		2	130
(4) Btry I (6-105 How)	7	125		2	134
(5) 107mm Mortar Btry (6 Mortars)	3	80		2	85

	USMC		USN		
	Off	Enl	Off	Enl	TOTAL
b. *3dBn* (-) (Rein), *12th Marines*	40	680	4	13	737
(1) HqBtry (Rein)	14	164	4	11	193
(a) HqBtry	14	150	4	11	179
(b) Det, CMR HqBtry, 12th Marines		14			14
(2) Btry G (6-105How)	8	114			122
(3) Btry H (6-105How)	7	113			120
(4) Btry M, 4thBn, 11thMar (6-155How)	5	131		2	138
(5) 3d 155 Gun Btry (SP) (-) FMF (4-155Guns)	4	113			117
(6) 1st Plt, 1st 8'' HowBtry(SP) (2-8'' How)	2	45			47
6. 7th Marines (Rein) (CHU LAI)	147	3576	11	183	3917
a. *HqCo* (-) (Rein)	21	281	2	3	307
(1) HqCo (-)	17	224	2	3	246
(2) Det, HqBn, 3dMarDiv	4	57			61
b. *1st Bn, 7th Marines*	39	979	3	62	1083
c. *2d Bn, 7th Marines*	38	914	3	55	1010
d. *3d Bn, 7th Marines*	37	942	3	57	1039
e. Co C (Rein), *1st AT Bn* (15 M50A1 Ontos)	3	85		2	90
(1) Co C	2	59			61
(2) HqCo (-)	1	26		2	29
f. Co C (Rein), *1st EngrBn*	4	157		1	162
g. Co A (Rein), *3d AmTracBn*	5	218		3	226
7. 9th Marines (DA NANG)	115	3090	10	168	3383
a. *HqCo*	15	193	2	3	213
b. *1st Bn, 9th Marines*	35	969	3	56	1063
c. *2d Bn, 9th Marines*	36	958	2	54	1050
d. *3d Bn, 3d Marines*	29	970	3	55	1057
8. 12th Marines (-) (Rein) (DA NANG)	111	1705	8	36	1860
a. *HqBtry* (-) (2-CMRS)	22	209	3	4	238
b. *1st 8''How Btry* (SP) (-) (Rein) (4-8'' How)	7	161		3	171
c. *3d Plt, 3d 155 Gun Btry* (SP), FMF (2-155Guns)	1	35		1	37
d. *1st Bn, (-) 12th Marines*	43	701	2	14	760
(1) HqBtry	14	163	2	4	183
(2) Btry A (6-105How)	7	115		2	124
(3) Btry A, 1st Bn, 11thMar (6-105How)	8	124		2	134
(4) 107mm Mortar Btry (6 Mortars)	3	75		2	80
(5) Btry C, 1st Bn, 12thMar (6-105How)	8	110		2	120
(6) Btry K, 4thBn, 12thMar (6-155 (SP))	3	114		2	119
e. *2dBn* (-), *12th Marines*	38	599	3	14	654
(1) HqBtry	14	153	3	5	175
(2) Btry D (6-105How)	7	114		2	123
(3) Btry E (6-105How)	7	109		1	117
(4) Btry F (6-105How)	7	106		3	116
(5) Btry L, 4thBn, 12thMar (6-155 (SP))	3	117		3	123
9. *3d AT Bn* (-) (Rein) (DA NANG)	15	305		10	330
a. H&SCo	9	147		7	163
b. Co A (-) (Rein) (10 M50A1 Ontos)	3	63		1	67
c. Co C (Rein) (20 M50A1 Ontos)	3	95		2	100
10. *3d EngrBn* (-) (Rein) (DA NANG)	28	686	1	13	728
a. H&SCo	10	117	1	13	141
b. Support Co	4	268			272
c. Co A (-)	5	74			79
d. Co C	6	147			153
e. Co C, 7th EngrBn	3	80			83
11. *3d MedBn* (-) (DA NANG)	3	101	27	153	284
a. H&SCo	3	101	8	45	157
b. Co C			18	102	120
c. Co D			1	6	7

	USMC		USN		
	Off	Enl	Off	Enl	TOTAL
12. *3d ReconBn* (DA NANG)	21	302	1	17	341
a. H&SCo	9	99	1	6	115
b. Co A	4	66		4	74
c. Co C	4	68		3	75
d. Co D	4	69		4	77
13. *Recon Group* Alpha (CHU LAI)	8	132		5	145
a. Co B (-) (Rein), 3d ReconBn	4	63		2	69
(1) H&SCo					
(2) 1st Plt					
(3) 2d Plt					
b. Co C (Rein), 1st ReconBn	4	69		3	76
14. *1st Force ReconCo* (DA NANG)	9	128		5	142
15. *3d MT Bn* (-) (DA NANG)	10	154		8	172
a. H&SCo	7	84		8	99
b. Co A (-) (15 M-35, 2 1/2-ton trucks)	2	39			41
c. 2dPlt, CoB (15 M-35, 2 1/2 ton trucks)	1	31			32
16. *1stAmTracBn* (-) (Rein), *FMF* (DA NANG)	26	639	2	13	680
a. H&SCo (12 LVTP-5, 3 LVTC-1, 1 LVTR-1)	17	319	2	11	349
b. 1st Prov Armored Amphib Plt (6 LVTH-6)	2	74		2	78
c. Co B (Rein) (54 LVTP-5, 4 LVTC-1, 1 LVTR-1)	7	246			253
17. *3d TkBn* (-) (Rein) (DA NANG)	23	489	1	11	524
a. H&SCo (-) (2 M48A3 Tks)	15	267	1	7	290
b. Co A(-) (Rein) (12 M48A3 Tks and 3 M67A2 Flame Tks)	3	89		2	94
c. Co B(Rein) (17 M48A3 Tks and 3 M67A2 Flame Tks)	5	110		2	117
d. 1st Plt, Co C (5 M48A3 Tks)		23			23
18. *3d Shore Party Bn* (-) (DA NANG)	22	438	1	25	486
a. H&SCo	12	184	1	10	207
b. Co A	3	86		5	94
c. Co B	4	82		5	91
d. Co C	3	86		5	94
19. *Co C, 1st Shore Party Bn* (CHU LAI)	5	126	1	10	142
20. *3d Dental Co* (DA NANG)			8	35	43
H. *First Marine Aircraft Wing*	1086	8332	40	147	9605
1. *MWHG-1*	267	2159	12	50	2488
a. H&HS-1 (DA NANG)	141	803	10	28	982
b. MASS-2	19	119			138
(1) Det A (CHU LAI)	4	18			22
(2) Det B (DA NANG)	4	19			23
(3) Det C (CHU LAI)	3	13			16
(4) DASC (DA NANG)	7	19			26
c. MACS-7	23	221		2	246
(1) Det A (PHU BAI)	3	17			20
d. 1st LAAM Bn (DA NANG)	31	481	1	10	523
e. 2d LAAM Bn (CHU LAI)	32	449	1	10	492
2. *MAG-11* (DA NANG)	178	1817	5	21	2021
a. H&MS-11	34	416			450
b. MABS-11	13	490	3	16	522
c. VMFA-115	41	274	1	2	318
d. VMFA-323	43	278	1	2	324
e. VMCJ-1	29	222			251
f. VMF (AW)-312	18	137		1	156
3. *MAG-12* (CHU LAI)	166	1654	6	26	1852
a. H&MS-12	41	364			405
b. MABS-12	19	519	3	22	563
c. VMA-211	29	179		2	210
d. VMA-214	24	176	1		201

	USMC Off	USMC Enl	USN Off	USN Enl	TOTAL
e. VMA-223	27	178	1	2	208
f. VMA-224	22	176	1		199
g. MATCU-67	4	62			66
4. *MAG-16*	240	1407	9	21	1677
a. H&MS-16 (DA NANG)	31	281			312
b. MABS-16 (DA NANG)	13	341	5	6	365
c. Det MABS (PHU BAI)		12			12
d. Det MABS (QUANG NGAI)		2			2
e. DET MABS (QUANG TRI)		2			2
f. SU 1, MABS-16 (DA NANG)	10	61		1	72
g. HMM-161 (PHU BAI)	50	178	1	3	232
h. HMM-263 (DA NANG)	46	175	1	3	225
i. HMM-361 (DA NANG)	51	158	1	3	213
j. VMO-2 (DA NANG)	33	136	1	5	175
k. MATCU-68 (DA NANG)	6	61			67
5. *MAG-36*	235	1295	8	29	1567
a. H&MS-36 (CHU LAI)	34	315			349
b. MABS-36 (CHU LAI)	14	342	4	26	386
c. HMM-362 (CHU LAI)	53	160	1		214
d. HMM-363 (QUI NHON)	54	176	2	3	235
e. HMM-364 (CHU LAI)	54	152	1		207
f. VMO-6 (CHU LAI)	26	150			176
I. *Force Logistics Support Group*	98	3195	32	218	3543
1. *Force Logistics Support Group* (DANANG)	52	1649	4	31	1736
a. H&SCo (-) (Rein) 3d SvcBn	22	373	3	15	413
b. Supply Co (-) (Rein) 3d SvcBn	22	750	1	16	789
c. Maint Co (-) (Rein) 3d SvcBn	6	399			405
d. Truck Co (-) (Rein) 3d SvcBn	2	127			129
2. *Force Logistic Support Unit-1* (CHU LAI)	38	1308	19	130	1495
a. *FLSU Headquarters*	24	871		8	903
(1) H&SCo (Provisional)	11	197		8	216
(2) Supply Co (Provisional)	7	326			333
(3) Maint Co (Provisional)	6	348			354
b. *Shore Party Group (Provisional)*	4	136	1	10	151
(1) Co C, 1st SPBn	4	136	1	10	151
c. *MT Group (Provisional)*	10	268		4	282
(1) Co A(-), 7th MTBn	3	84		2	89
(2) 2dPlt, Co C, 9th MTBn	1	27			28
(3) Co C(-) 1st MTBn	3	81		1	85
(4) Co C, 3d MTBn	3	76		1	80
d. *Co B, 3d MedBn (Rein)*		33	18	108	159
3. *Force Logistic Support Unit-2* (PHU BAI)	8	238	9	57	312
a. *FLSU Headquarters*	6	190		4	200
(1) H&SCo (Provisional)	3	40		4	47
(2) Supply Plt		62			62
(3) Maint Plt	3	88			91
b. *Co B, 3d MTBn* (-)	2	37			39
c. *Co A, 3d MedBn*		11	9	53	73

INDEX

☆ U.S. Government Printing Office 1978 M-O M-275-257